Love Known

Richard Strier

Love Known

Theology and Experience in
George Herbert's Poetry

The University of Chicago Press

Chicago and London

Publication of this work was supported in part by a contribution
from the Hyder E. Rollins Fund.

The University of Chicago Press, Chicago 60637
The University of Chicago Press, Ltd., London

Library of Congress Cataloging in Publication Data

Strier, Richard.
  Love known.

  Bibliography: p.
  Includes index.
  1. Herbert, George, 1593–1633—Criticism and interpre-
tation.   2. Christian poetry, English—History and
criticism.   3. Theology, Protestant, in literature.
4. Justification—History of doctrines.   5. Protestantism
and literature.   I. Title.
PR3508.S75   1983   821'.3   83-6798
ISBN 0-226-77716-2 (cloth)
ISBN 0-226-77717-0 (paper)

To the memory of my parents,
Florence and Charles

Contents

Acknowledgments ix

Introduction xi

1. Dust and Sin: The Denial of Merit 1

2. The Attack on Reason 29

3. Interlude: Theology or Philosophy? 61

4. *Vindiciae Gratiae:* The Rejection of Bargaining 84

5. The New Life: Conversion 114

6. The Heart Alone: Inwardness and Individualism 143

7. The Heart's Privileges: Emotion 174

8. The Limits of Experience 218

Afterword 253

Bibliography 255

Index of Herbert Poems 271

General Index 273

Acknowledgments

Many people have contributed to the making of this book. My longest and greatest debt is to Herschel Baker, whose unwavering belief in this project and its author's ability to carry it through helped me to persevere in it. Without his extraordinary personal and scholarly generosity, I am not sure that this book would exist.

I have been fortunate in my colleagues as well as in my mentor. The remarkable group of Renaissance scholars in the English Department at the University of Chicago, John M. Wallace, Janel M. Mueller, Michael Murrin, and David Bevington, provided me with a wonderful mixture of encouragement, challenge, and scrupulous criticism. Winthrop P. Wetherbee took time out of a very busy schedule to read and comment on the manuscript of this book, and William R. Veeder worked through the manuscript with patient and loving ferocity. Whatever mistakes and infelicities remain are entirely a testimony to my own unteachability.

I am grateful to the Dean of the Humanities Division at Chicago, Karl J. Weintraub, and to the two chairmen under whom I have worked, Stuart M. Tave and James E. Miller, Jr., for providing me with much-needed leave time for writing. All my colleagues in the English Department at Chicago have helped make the Department a supportive and stimulating community. The graduate students in English 390, Metaphysical Poetry, at Chicago from 1973 to 1979 contributed to this book through their intelligent and probing reception of my ideas. I especially profited from the written work and conversation of the late Mark Gromer. Dorothy Pesch typed and retyped the manuscript with her characteristic precision and good humor.

Outside of Chicago, I am grateful for the support and encouragement shown to me by a number of scholars of English Renaissance literature, particularly Paul Alpers, Stanley Fish, and Barbara K. Lewalski. I am indebted to John S. Coolidge and John R. Knott for extremely helpful comments.

Two of my graduate students at Brandeis University in 1982/83, Joan Rutter and Claudia Yukman, prepared the Bibliography.

Kathryn Hellerstein helped with proofreading and much else.

Introduction

This book argues for the centrality of a single doctrine to George Herbert's poetry and theology: the doctrine of justification by faith. Since this doctrine was the central tenet of the Protestant Reformation, much of the effort of the book is to demonstrate that these two centers coincide. My aim in doing this is not merely to locate Herbert correctly in the spectrum of Protestant or Christian doctrine. Ultimately, my commitment is to the illumination of the poetry. Many of Herbert's best lyrics can be read "as poems" per se, but when read in this way, apart from specific theological content, many details remain puzzling or blurred and, most of all, the poems lose their point and force. A purely "internal" reading of the poems can show *that* they have certain shapes or emphases but cannot show *why*. The poems can be explicated without truly being rendered intelligible. The largest claim I wish to make is that the context into which I am placing the poems brings them into focus in a remarkable way: puzzling or unnoticed details emerge into clarity and distinction; some neglected poems emerge into prominence; and the familiar poems take on new clarity of argument. All the poems gain cogency and point.

The convincingness of the historical theses of this book must rest on my success in rendering the poems intelligible. The readings provide the primary (though not exclusive) evidence for the theses, while the theses guide the readings. Whether this circle is a virtuous or a vicious one will depend on the persuasiveness of the readings and on the "naturalness" of my groupings of the poems. I do not mean to suggest that my groupings and rubrics are the only possible or productive ones, but only that they are plausible and, as Herbert said in his poem about such "constellations" in scripture, "more then fancy."[1] If my readings or groupings seem forced, then either my historical theses are false or the demonstration of their truth through their practical fruitfulness must await a more skillful expositor. My readings, moreover, intend to be complete, not in the sense of definitive but in the sense of dealing with whole poems in a relatively systematic way.[2] I have tried to avoid selective quotation, and I have based my claims about the theological meaning and point of poems on readings of whole poems and of poems as wholes. Only a special theory leads one to hold that poems do not or cannot make assertions or express positions, and yet it is true that what poems assert or express is often to be found in their details and design as well as in their outright assertions and that sometimes such assertions are strongly qualified by their context. My aim is to reveal the immanent (and actual) intentions of Herbert's lyrics, not to construct a system on the basis of bits and pieces of them. Again the historical will depend upon the literary.

In arguing for the centrality of a single doctrine to Herbert's poetry, I might seem to be attempting to turn one of the great technical foxes of English poetry into a monomaniacal hedgehog. My reply to this can only be the hedgehog's traditional line of defense—that his one trick is "a good one."[3] Justification by faith alone is an extraordinarily rich and powerful theological doctrine, one that means to transform the religious consciousness. Fully accepted, it cannot exist in isolation or as one among many others.[4] It demands a central and commanding role; all other doctrines and positions must derive their energy from it. I believe that Herbert recognized this and that part of his genius was to have grasped this doctrine and many of its implications very profoundly. I believe that Yeats was right in placing Herbert with Luther and Calvin and in describing him as "stirred to an imaginative intensity" by, as Yeats put it, "some form of propaganda."[5] Our sense of Herbert's technical virtuosity can only be increased by the recognition of an underlying thematic core. In terms of technique, he remains as much the fox, the virtuoso, or the Schubert as ever.[6]

---

1. "The H. Scriptures" (II), line 10, in *The Williams Manuscript of George Herbert's Poems*, intro. Amy M. Charles (Delmar, N.Y., 1972), p. 38ʳ.

2. On this sense of completeness in readings, see Stanley Cavell, *Pursuits of Happiness: The Hollywood Comedy of Remarriage* (Cambridge, Mass., 1981), p. 278.

3. For "The fox has many tricks, the hedgehog only one—one good one," see Archilochus of Paros in *Greek Lyrics*, trans. Richard Lattimore, 2d ed. (Chicago, 1960), p. 4 (no. 17).

4. Compare A. G. Dickens, *The English Reformation* (New York, 1964), pp. 59–60.

5. W. B. Yeats, *A Vision* (1938; New York, 1961), pp. 172–76 (Phase 25).

6. For Herbert as the Schubert of English poetry, see Frank Kermode's review of Helen Vendler's *The Poetry of George Herbert* (Cambridge, Mass., 1975) in the *New York Times Book Review* (6 July 1975), p. 13.

To say that Herbert grasped the power and regulatory role of the doctrine of justification by faith is to explain the role of Luther in my study. It has been argued that no aspect of Luther's thought is fully understood until it has been seen as a "simple corollary" of the doctrine of justification.[7] Luther himself insisted that the doctrine "cannot be beaten into our ears enough or too much."[8] My major claim is that Herbert also felt this way and that he understood and experienced the doctrine of justification by faith in much the way Luther did. I want to be clear from the outset about the relation I am positing between Herbert and Luther. I am not claiming that Herbert was a Lutheran. I am not even claiming that he was directly influenced by Luther. Possibly he was—some of Luther's works, especially the important commentary on Galatians that so affected Bunyan, were available in English, and Herbert could easily have read Luther in Latin—but direct influence cannot be documented.[9] Indirect influence, however, was almost inevitable. *Anyone* who emphasizes justification by faith with theological clarity and lyrical intensity will sound like Luther. Moreover, Luther's influence in England, through his prominence in Foxe's *Acts and Monuments* and the influence of Tyndale's Lutheran New Testament on all later English Protestant bibles, has been characterized as "not to be measured by the phrases of catechisms or articles or liturgies or hymns" but rather by "attitudes and aspirations." William Clebsch, from whom I have been quoting, has argued that Englishmen of the sixteenth and seventeenth century "viewed, in a certain profound sense, the real Luther," whose message meant more than the details of officially "Lutheran" doctrine.[10]

My book does not attempt to survey the whole of Herbert's theology or to treat all the theological topics addressed in the poetry. My focus, as I have said, is on the expression and implications of a single doctrine. This focus produces the connection between Herbert and Luther. In some respects, Herbert is quite unlike Luther. Most importantly, he does not share Luther's rejection of asceticism, affirmation of ordinary life, and defense of the body and the physical. Nor does Her-

---

7. See Einar Billing, *Our Calling*, trans. Conrad Bergendoff (Philadelphia, 1964), p. 4; and B. A. Gerrish, *Grace and Reason: A Study in the Theology of Luther* (Oxford, 1962), p. 8, n. 2, and pp. 57–58.

8. See p. 70 below.

9. On the availability of Luther's work in England, see Gordon Rupp, *The Righteousness of God: Luther Studies* (London, 1953), chap. 2; idem, *Studies in the Making of the English Protestant Tradition* (Cambridge, 1947), chaps. 3 and 8; and William A. Clebsch, "The Elizabethans on Luther," in *Interpreters of Luther: Essays in Honor of William Pauck*, ed. Jaroslav Pelikan (Philadelphia, 1968), pp. 97–120. Sargent Bush, Jr., and Carl J. Rasmussen tell me that in their survey of the Emmanuel College Library, 1584–1637, they found a surprisingly large number of Luther's biblical commentaries in Latin. For Bunyan, see p. 115 below.

10. Clebsch, "The Elizabethans on Luther," pp. 116–17.

bert share the Eucharistic theology in which Luther articulated his defense of the physical.[11] Herbert's Eucharistic theology (like that of Cranmer and the English Renaissance Church as a whole) is closer to Calvin's than to Luther's, and Herbert is at times strongly drawn in a world-and-flesh–rejecting direction.[12] In his attitude toward the central doctrine of the Reformation, however, Herbert's position *is* Luther's—that is the sum and substance of my argument. Their positions are the same at the center, not the periphery, and not all Herbert's positions are as tightly bound to this center as Luther's are. Many of them are so bound, however, and my study will try to demonstrate that the great majority of Herbert's finest lyrics express and flow from this center.

Although Luther is, for the reasons I have given, prominent in my study, he is by no means the only theologian or divine I have drawn upon in glossing and interpreting Herbert's poetry. I have used Calvin freely, not for those points wherein he differed from Luther but for cogent and apt formulations of the views they shared. Calvin himself asserted that "that which is most important . . . and for the sake of which everything else is said, we defend today just as it was declared by Luther," and Calvin always considered the disagreements between the major reformers less significant than the "remarkable consensus among them on all that is essential to godliness"; he has been called not only the greatest but, in a genuine sense, "the only 'disciple' that Luther had."[13] Certainly there are important differences between Luther and Calvin, but it is incorrect to drive a wedge between them.

11. For Luther's rejection of asceticism, see Max Weber, *The Protestant Ethic and the Spirit of Capitalism*, trans. Talcott Parsons (1930; pap. rpt. New York, 1958), chap. 3; and Heinrich Bornkamm, *Luther's World of Thought*, trans. M. H. Bertram (St. Louis, 1958), pp. 176–94. C. S. Lewis's comments on "the beautiful, cheerful integration" of Tyndale's world are directly applicable to Luther, Tyndale's master (see *English Literature in the Sixteenth Century, Excluding Drama* [Oxford, 1954], p. 190). On Luther's Eucharistic theology, see Yngve Brilioth, *Eucharistic Faith and Practice, Evangelical and Catholic*, trans. A. G. Hebert (London, 1934), chap. 4; and Hermann Sasse, *This is My Body: Luther's Contention for the Real Presence* (Minneapolis, 1959).

12. For Cranmer's Eucharistic theology, see Peter Brooks, *Thomas Cranmer's Doctrine of the Eucharist* (London, 1965); for Herbert's, see the works cited in chap. 3, n. 6 below. For Herbert's tendency toward asceticism (with some speculation on its relation to his Eucharistic doctrine), see Richard Strier, "George Herbert and the World," *JMRS*, 12 (1981), 211–36.

13. Calvin, *A Defense of the Sound and Orthodox Doctrine of the Bondage and Deliverance of the Human Will against the False Accusations of Albert Pighius*, in B. A. Gerrish, "John Calvin on Luther," in Pelikan, *Interpreters of Luther*, p. 79; Calvin, *On Scandals*, in Gerrish, "Calvin on Luther," p. 83 (more literally translated as "remarkable agreement *about the whole substance of the faith*" [*In tota pietatis summa mirabilis fuit eorum consensus*] in John Calvin, *Concerning Scandals*, trans. John W. Fraser [Grand Rapids, 1978], p. 81). For the Latin, see *Joannis Calvini Opera Selecta*, ed. P. Barth and D. Scheuner (Munich, 1952), p. 215. For "the only 'disciple,' " see Peter Meinhold, quoted in Gerrish, "Calvin on Luther," p. 86.

I have also made use of a number of seventeenth-century English divines, some contemporary with Herbert, some a bit later. A number of the figures on whom I have drawn are classified as Puritans, some as radicals. In using these figures, I have tried to blur some of the distinctions that are normally drawn among English Protestants in the earlier seventeenth century. The distinction between "Anglicans" and "Puritans" has often, especially in literary scholarship, been crudely and unhistorically drawn. In the sixteenth and early seventeenth century, the distinction between Puritan and Conformist was not that of Calvinist versus non- or anti-Calvinist. Doctrinally, most religiously aware Englishmen in the period, whether satisfied or unsatisfied with the liturgy and organization of the established church, were Calvinists in the sense of holding the doctrines that Luther and Calvin shared.[14] While the term "Puritan" was in actual use in the period, the term "Anglican" was not, and a conception of "Anglicanism" derived mainly from the nineteenth century, partly from Walton's *Life of Herbert* and partly from misreading Herbert's "The British Church," has bedeviled Herbert criticism.[15] In using the writings of Puritans to gloss Herbert's poetry, I do not mean to call into question Herbert's loyalty to the established church. I do wish to suggest that the devotional and theological temper of men like John Cotton, John Downame, and Richard Sibbes was in many ways closer to Herbert's than was that of Richard Hooker, Archbishop Laud, or even Lancelot Andrewes.

In drawing on some works by radicals of the mid-century, I am, again, not suggesting that Herbert was himself a religious radical, even an incipient one. What I am trying to show is that the radicals—those who opposed all "ordinances" in the church—were developing strands that were genuinely present in the Reformation tradition and that Herbert's poetry helps us understand the continuum or inner connection between, for instance, Martin Luther and William Dell. Herbert's poetry expresses the central Reformation doctrines so richly that this continuity can be demonstrated through it. Luther and Calvin were always having their own words quoted at them by the anti-magisterial reformers. This was not accidental. However horrified the

14. See Charles H. George and Katherine George, *The Protestant Mind of the English Reformation* (Princeton, 1961), chap. 1; and Dickens, *The English Reformation,* pp. 313ff.

15. For "Anglicanism" as a term that "is best avoided altogether," being "unknown to the sixteenth [and seventeenth] century, and, as an indication of a distinct system of divinity, an invention of the nineteenth," see Patrick Collinson, *The Elizabethan Puritan Movement* (Berkeley and Los Angeles, 1967), p. 13; and Gordon Stevens Wakefield, *Puritan Devotion: Its Place in the Development of Christian Piety* (London, 1957), p. 1, n. 3. On the polemically anti-Puritan motives of Walton's *Life of Herbert,* see Clayton D. Lein, "Art and Structure in Walton's *Life of Mr. George Herbert,*" *UTQ,* 46 (1976–77), 162–76. On Herbert's "The British Church," see Richard Strier, "History, Criticism, and Herbert: A Polemical Note," *PLL,* 17 (1981), 347–52.

major reformers were by the radicals, the radicals were in traceable and authentic ways their kin, however distant. As Geoffrey F. Nuttall has demonstrated, the key to this kinship and continuity is the doctrine of the work of the Spirit, a doctrine that was part of the meaning of "justification by faith alone."[16] If this blurs and complicates our historical mappings, so much the better. The tradition that Herbert's lyrics embody is deeper than that celebrated in Walton's *Life of Herbert* or Keble's *The Christian Year.*

Scholarship has begun to acknowledge the extent of Herbert's Protestantism. Joseph H. Summers did the pioneering work in freeing Herbert from Walton and the High Church movement. In the superb biographical chapter of *George Herbert: His Religion and Art* (Cambridge, Mass., 1954), Summers demonstrated the Puritan and anti-Laudian connections of Herbert's patrons and associates in the church. In the chapter on religion, Summers both warned against the use of easy party categories and recognized, though not quite in so many words, the fact of Herbert's Calvinism. Summers's anxiety, however, to show that Herbert was never tempted toward the rejection of images or the senses prompted him to an emphasis on Herbert's commitment to order and forms that lead back, paradoxically, to the very position his biographical chapter debunked. Form rather than content became Summers's focus.

Two books roughly contemporaneous with Summers's, Rosemond Tuve's *A Reading of George Herbert* (Chicago, 1952) and Louis L. Martz's *The Poetry of Meditation: A Study of English Religious Literature of the Seventeenth Century* (New Haven, 1954; rev. 1962), put forth a strongly medieval and Anglo-Catholic Herbert. Since that time, the historical reliability of both these seminal works has been questioned. They have both been shown to ignore the impact and importance of the Reformation. The existence of a distinctly Protestant meditative tradition has been documented in England long before *The Saints Everlasting Rest* (the only Protestant meditative manual treated by Martz), and a distinctly Protestant understanding of typology (Tuve's theme) has been fully elucidated.[17] Meditation and typology remain topics

---

16. Geoffrey F. Nuttall, *The Holy Spirit in Puritan Faith and Experience* (Oxford, 1964). For a general survey of the "antimagisterial" reformers in the sixteenth century, see George Huntston Williams, *The Radical Reformation* (Philadelphia, 1962).

17. On Protestant meditation in England, see U. Milo Kaufman, *"The Pilgrim's Progress" and Traditions in Puritan Meditation* (New Haven, 1966); Norman S. Grabo, "The Art of Puritan Meditation," *SCN,* 26 (1968), 7–9; Barbara Kiefer Lewalski, *Donne's "Anniversaries" and the Poetry of Praise: The Creation of a Symbolic Mode* (Princeton, 1973), chap. 3; and Frank Livingstone Huntley, "Joseph Hall and Protestant Meditation," *Studies in the Literary Imagination,* 10 (1977), 57–71. For Protestant typology, see William G. Madsen, *From Shadowy Types to Truth: Studies in Milton's Symbolism* (New Haven, 1968); Barbara Kiefer Lewalski, *"Samson Agonistes* and the 'Tragedy' of the Apocalypse,"

deeply relevant to Herbert's poetry, but they have now been freed from medieval and Counter-Reformation contexts.

A view of Herbert as a fully Reformation poet would seem to have arrived with William Halewood's *The Poetry of Grace: Reformation Themes and Structures in English Seventeenth-Century Poetry* (New Haven, 1970) and Patrick Grant's *The Transformation of Sin: Studies in Donne, Herbert, Vaughan, and Traherne* (Montreal and Amherst, 1974). With regard to Tuve, Halewood criticized the exclusively continuity-oriented historicism of *A Reading of George Herbert*. With regard to Martz, Halewood pointed out the extraordinarily interesting *affinities* between Loyola's *Spiritual Exercises*, one of Martz's key texts, and the devotional theology of the reformers. Yet, like Summers, Halewood seems to resist the implications of his own insights. Despite the title and subtitle of his book, Halewood disparages the idea of trying "to claim Herbert for the Calvinists" and insists on the *differences* between Herbert and "his more extreme Calvinistic countrymen."[18] Grant simultaneously affirms Herbert's Protestantism and continues the endeavor of Tuve's *Reading* by attempting to link Herbert to the tradition of *medieval* Augustinianism as exemplified, especially, in the Franciscans. Not until 1979 was a scholar finally willing to "claim Herbert for the Calvinists" indeed. In *Protestant Poetics and the Seventeenth-Century English Lyric* (Princeton, 1979), Barbara Kiefer Lewalski, who had already been instrumental in identifying Protestant traditions of meditation and typology, is willing to state outright that "the individual-typical speaker of 'The Church' is Calvinist in theology" (p. 286). Lewalski's main concern, however, as her title indicates, is less with Protestant the-

---

PMLA, 85 (1970), 1050–61; idem, *Donne's "Anniversaries,"* chap. 5; and Sacvan Bercovitch, ed., *Typology and Early American Literature* (Amherst, Mass., 1972). For recent work disputing specific claims about Herbert's debt to medieval and Counter-Reformation modes and practices, see Ilona Bell, " 'Setting Foot into Divinity': George Herbert and the English Reformation," *MLQ*, 38 (1977), 219–41, and Richard Strier, " 'To All Angels and Saints': Herbert's Puritan Poem," *MP*, 77 (1979), 132–45; idem, "Herbert and Tears," *ELH*, 46 (1979), 221–47; idem, "Changing the Object: Herbert and Excess," *George Herbert Journal*, 2 (1978), 24–37.

18. *Poetry of Grace*, pp. 89, 91, 104. Halewood's claim that Herbert differed from "the Calvinists" or the "extreme Calvinists" in considering the eucharist "holy and an essential part of Christian worship" (p. 91) is historically misguided. Calvin certainly believed these things (see Ronald S. Wallace, *Calvin's Doctrine of the Word and Sacrament* [Edinburgh, 1953]; G. S. M. Walker, "The Lord's Supper in the Theology and Practice of Calvin," in *John Calvin*, ed. G. E. Duffield [Appleford, Abingdon, Berkshire, 1966], pp. 131–48; Killian McDonnell, *John Calvin, the Church, and the Eucharist* [Princeton, 1967]), as did the English Puritans (see Horton Davies, *The Worship of the English Puritans* [Glasgow, 1948]; and E. Brooks Holifield, *The Covenant Sealed: The Development of Puritan Sacramental Theology in Old and New England* [New Haven, 1974]). For comments on a specific passage Halewood adduces for his distinction between Herbert and "the strict Calvinist" (p. 104), see chap. 7, n. 80 below.

ology as such than with Protestant "poetics," with the rhetorical and aesthetic resources available in the English Protestant tradition. Like Summers, she is concerned to show that Herbert's Protestantism does not interfere with his having a very rich "conception of form."

Although my view of Herbert's theology is close to Lewalski's, the aims of my book have been most closely anticipated in a remarkable essay by Tuve, "George Herbert and *Caritas*" (*JWCI*, 22 [1959], 303–31; rpt. in Thomas P. Roche, Jr., ed., *Essays by Rosemund Tuve: Spenser, Herbert, Milton* [Princeton, 1970], pp. 167–206). Tuve there insisted that "we must discuss outright the Christian doctrinal positions enunciated or implicit in Herbert's poems" and asserted that the most important of these positions is Herbert's conception of love. She breaks up the rather monolithic sense of "the tradition" at work in *A Reading of George Herbert* by distinguishing a number of ways in which theologians and theological traditions have understood love in a Christian context. What is odd about Tuve's essay is that it virtually demonstrates the position it retreats from—the connection between Herbert and Luther.

Tuve calls her essay "George Herbert and *Caritas*" and yet convincingly shows that "Herbert celebrates in poem after poem God's love for man, Agape" (Roche, p. 182). The substitution of *caritas* for *agape* in the title is more than merely a shift from Greek to Latin. Tuve's understanding of *agape*, the New Testament word for love, derives primarily from Anders Nygren's *Agape and Eros*.[19] Nygren sees *agape*, the conception of God's spontaneous and "unmotivated" love for man, as the distinctive fundamental motif of Christianity. According to Nygren, quite soon in the patristic period and more markedly in the medieval church, the fundamental Christian motif of *agape* is obscured or weakened by being replaced or blended with the opposing fundamental motif of *eros*, acquisitive or value-inspired love. Luther, in Nygren's view, is the great post-Pauline exponent of *agape;* Luther's "Copernican revolution," made possible by the doctrine of justification by faith, was to restore the unmixed Christian concept. By using *caritas* rather than *agape* in her title, Tuve evades the prominence Nygren gives to Luther and suggests that Herbert's poetry remains within the Augustinian and medieval tradition which Nygren terms "the *caritas* synthesis," the most successful blending of *eros* and *agape*.

What is odd about this is that in the first part of her essay, Tuve follows Nygren closely in asserting that Augustine and Aquinas share an understanding of love from which Luther stands distinctly apart,

19. *Agape and Eros: Part I, A Study of the Christian Idea of Love; Part II, The History of the Christian Idea of Love*, trans. Philip S. Watson (1953; pap. rpt. New York, 1969).

and she then goes on to argue that in Herbert's poetry an emphasis on gratitude as "the primary constituent of man's love for God" is "more ubiquitous than [Aquinas's] emphasis upon desire for the *summum Bonum*," than Augustine's "upon *quies*, rest or peace in God,"than the emphasis Augustine and Aquinas share on "ultimate full happiness," or than a striving for mystical union, "whether in the terms of the Song of Songs as in Bernard, of the God who seeks man as in François de Sales, [or] even of the God whom man will 'en-joy,' as in Augustine" (Roche, p. 184). Yet just at this point, when the conclusion seems inevitable that Herbert stands, with Luther, outside the medieval-Augustinian tradition, Tuve recoils. Without any supporting quotations she adds that "much in Herbert does, however, closely resemble the *fruitio Dei* of Augustine." The remainder of the essay is a forced and sketchy attempt to show Herbert's position to be that of Augustine and Dante. A medieval Herbert again emerges. *Caritas* replaces *agape*.

An even more striking recoil occurs earlier in Tuve's essay. Having noted "Herbert's emphasis upon the absence of merit in himself and his stress upon *sola gratia*," Tuve disdainfully acknowledges that these emphases "would have the savour of sound doctrine to many a Lutheran"! She hastens to add, however, that she could easily show "how ancient a Christian position" this is (Roche, p. 182). This qualification again frees her from identifying Herbert with Luther and allows her not to consider the differences between the Reformation use of *sola gratia* and earlier uses in the Christian tradition. Tuve's refusal to identify Herbert with Luther leads her to ignore distinctions she began by insisting upon and, even more ironically in the face of her campaign for the "historical approach," to fail to relate the theology of Herbert's poems to its most obvious historical context. A seventeenth-century Englishman who insisted on faith alone did not mean to be identifying himself with the "Christian tradition" in general or with the medieval Franciscan tradition. He meant to be identifying himself with Saint Paul *as understood by the reformers*. His position would have "the savour of sound doctrine" only to deeply committed Protestants. Bellarmine would smell a rat. Ignatius Loyola warned against speaking too much and with too great emphasis on faith.[20]

The first five chapters of my book are concerned with the doctrine of grace alone conceived in distinctively Reformation terms. These chapters seek to demonstrate the centrality of the doctrine, so conceived, to Herbert's poetry. They attempt to proceed in a systematic

20. *The Spiritual Exercises of St. Ignatius*, trans. Anthony Mottola (New York, 1964), p. 141 (in number 16 of the "Rules for Thinking with the Church"). It should be noted that "grace alone" and "faith alone" are formulations identical in content. The former is more precise, but the latter is the historical battle cry.

way so that each chapter builds upon the previous one. Rather than providing a large section of "background" followed by analyses, I have tried to bind "background" and "foreground" together by linking the chapters and introducing ad hoc the theological and historical materials relevant to the topic of each chapter. Chapters 1–3 form a single unit. Chapter 1 demonstrates Herbert's commitment to the most fundamental Reformation position, the denial that man can merit salvation. This leads to a detailed consideration of Herbert's conception of sin. Chapter 2 argues that, like Luther, Herbert tends to conceive of sin and *concupiscentia* in psychological and intellectual rather than in sensual terms. Building on the conception of Herbert's antirationalism developed in chapter 2, chapter 3 is an "interlude" on the exact nature and implications of Herbert's attack on reason. It responds directly to the conception of this attack put forth with great vigor by Stanley Fish in *Self-Consuming Artifacts: The Experience of Seventeenth-Century Literature* (Berkeley and Los Angeles, 1972).

Chapter 4 locates Herbert's antirationalism in an immediate historical context. It seeks to show Herbert criticizing, from the point of view of the initial theology of the Reformation, a particular rationalistic tendency in the "advanced" Protestantism of his day, the movement that we know as "covenant theology." The chapter relies upon and provides independent evidence for Perry Miller's view of Puritan covenant theology (together with "preparationism") as subtly falling prey to the underlying tendencies of the rationalism this theology intended to oppose. This chapter should clarify Herbert's *theological* relation to the Puritans (his devotional relation is more complex): he is close to them when they sound the major note of the Reformation; he departs from them when they depart from it.

Chapter 5 examines Herbert's understanding of conversion or regeneration, a topic played down by the "preparationists." Coming to focus on Herbert's presentation of the phenomenology of conversion, chapter 5 serves as a transition to the final three chapters, which move from the central doctrine of the Reformation to the cosmological and psychological implications of the doctrine. Chapter 6 concerns inwardness, individualism, and functionalism, while chapter 7 concerns the privileged place Herbert gives to emotion. The attack on reason is shown to produce a parallel exaltation of "feeling." This seventh chapter builds on some of the insights into Herbert's respect for emotion suggested by Arnold Stein in *George Herbert's Lyrics* (Baltimore, 1968). The chapter provides a theological context for these insights and also relates them, as Stein does not, to the issue of Herbert's attitude toward art. Here, as in chapter 6, I establish the theological and attitudinal connections between Herbert and the radicals of the Reformation and English Revolution—connections that have to do, as I have already suggested, with the radical potentialities of the Reformation doctrines themselves. In chapter 8, I show that Herbert and the tradition in which he stands had a sense of the unreliability as well as of the integrity of immediate emotional experience. The chapter sees some of Herbert's most complex poems as expressing and dramatizing this double attitude.

Implicit in my study is a view not only of how poems, closely read, can be used in the service of intellectual history and of how intellectual history can determine the meaning and significance of the results of literary analysis, but also a view of how the "relevance" of poetry like Herbert's can be established. The demand for relevance can certainly be crudely put, but some form of it must be acknowledged as legitimate. Is a full appreciation of Herbert's poetry unavailable to those who do not share its (or any) religious perspective? Is Herbert a great poet or a great religious poet? Must we invoke the special category? Helen Vendler's *The Poetry of George Herbert* (Cambridge, Mass., 1975) has raised these questions sharply. Vendler attempts to distinguish the "human" from the doctrinal content of Herbert's poetry. My study suggests that we can grasp the human content of Herbert's poetry only through, not apart from, the theology. To grasp the human content of the poetry we must grasp the terms in which this content is expressed. Something like this is probably true of the encounter with almost any older literature, but my study would suggest that such an approach works particularly well with Herbert's poetry because the context into which, as I argue, Herbert fits was one that itself insisted on the experiential content of its major terms. Pauline theology as formulated by Luther can be seen as based upon or consonant with certain fundamental psychological insights. It is, I would claim, one of Herbert's distinctions to have recognized and dramatized this. The more deeply we understand the theology of the poetry the more deeply we understand its human content. The two are one.

1

Dust and Sin:
The Denial of Merit

Nothing is more basic to Reformation theology than the denial that man can in any way merit salvation. Where the most Augustinian form of medieval theology saw grace as a necessary condition of merit, the Reformers saw grace and merit as opposed. The general view of high medieval theology can be summed up in the coordinated axioms "without grace no merit" and "without merit no blessedness."[1] Grace made merit possible, but merit was a necessary condition of salvation. The Reformation view was that human merit of any kind was irrelevant to salvation because it was impossible. For Luther and Calvin, there was no greater obstacle to a proper relationship to God than the "opinion of righteousness," the belief that one could contribute to one's own salvation.[2] The only proper attitude was to despair of one's own powers and gifts completely and cast oneself on the mercy

1. See Nygren, *Agape and Eros*, pp. 621–25, relying, for the most part, on Aquinas, *Summa theologica*, 12ae, Q.109, Art. 1–10 (see *Nature and Grace: Selections from the Summa Theologica of Thomas Aquinas*, ed. and trans. A. M. Fairweather [Philadelphia, 1954], pp. 137–156). It should be noted that later medieval theology (that which immediately preceded the Reformation) granted much more to what man could do on his own powers (*ex puris naturalibus*). See Heiko A. Oberman, *The Harvest of Medieval Theology: Gabriel Biel and Late Medieval Nominalism*, rev. ed. (Grand Rapids, 1967), chaps. 5–6.

2. On the "opinion of righteousness," see Luther, *A Commentary on St. Paul's Epistle to the Galatians: A Revised and Completed Translation of the "Middleton" Edition of the English Version of 1575*, ed. Philip S. Watson (London, 1953), pp. 299ff.; *The Freedom of a Christian*, in *Martin Luther: Selections from His Writings*, ed. John Dillenberger (New York, 1961), pp. 57, 71–72, 85 (whenever a work appears complete in this collection, I will cite from it as "Dillenberger" followed by a page number). For Calvin, see *Institutes of the Christian Religion*, ed. John T. McNeill, trans. Ford Lewis Battles (Philadelphia, 1960), III.xii.4–7.

1

of God. Grace alone made salvation possible, and was sufficient as well as necessary. Man could not claim for himself ever so little without claiming too much. The whole conception of "merit" was to be renounced.

The denial of merit is truly, as Tuve says, omnipresent in Herbert's poetry.[3] "Sighs and Grones," for instance, is a direct appeal to God for mercy. It begins:

> O do not use me
> After my sinnes! look not on my desert,
> But on thy glorie![4]   [1–3a]

"My sinnes" and "my desert" are equivalent; only if God wholly puts aside the question of "desert" will He "reform / And not refuse" the agonized speaker (lines 3b–4a). It is a commonly accepted principle that a poet's translations often reveal his characteristic values. The only translation Herbert included in *The Temple* is of perhaps the most famous affirmation of trust in God in the entire Bible, Psalm 23. Herbert makes explicit the assertion of salvation by grace alone which he finds in verse three of the psalm:

> if I stray he doth convert
> And bring my minde in frame:
> And all this not for my desert,
> But for his holy name.   [9–12]

"All this not for my desert" is Herbert's own addition. No other known version includes it.[5]

In the third book of the *Institutes*, Calvin argues that "to this question we must apply our minds if we would profitably inquire" concerning merit: "How shall we reply to the Heavenly Judge when he calls us to account?" (III.xii.1). In "Judgement," Herbert "applies his

---

3. "Herbert and *Caritas*," p. 182.

4. All quotations of Herbert's poetry and prose unless otherwise indicated will be from *The Works of George Herbert*, ed. F. E. Hutchinson, corr. ed. (Oxford, 1945), hereafter cited as "Hutchinson." Page references for the English poetry will not be given. Page references for the prose will be given in the text following the shortened form of the title of the work in question: *CP* for *The Country Parson;* "Notes on Valdes" for "Briefe Notes on Valdesso's *Considerations*." As Joseph Summers notes, there is no intrinsic or textual authority for referring to *The Country Parson* as *A Priest to the Temple* (*Herbert*, p. 13).

5. For a convenient gathering of the English translations of the twenty-third psalm from the Great Bible of 1539 to the Authorized Version of 1611 (hereafter cited as AV), see Hyder E. Rollins and Herschel Baker, eds., *The Renaissance in England* (Boston, 1954), pp. 134–40. On the specifically Herbertian concerns in the translation, see Coburn Freer, *Music for a King: George Herbert's Style and the Metrical Psalms* (Baltimore, 1972), p. 132; Lewalski, *Protestant Poetics*, pp. 303–4.

mind" to this question. In the first stanza he speaks in general, stating the problem:

> Almightie Judge, how shall poore wretches brook
>> Thy dreadfull look,
> Able a heart of iron to appall,
>> When thou shalt call
> For ev'ry man's peculiar book? [1–5]

This is, of course, a rhetorical question; "poore wretches"—all men— shall not be able to "brook" the dreadfulness of the almighty Judge. God's call is relentless and individualized; no man, the stanza implies, can adequately answer it. In the second stanza, however, Herbert switches into the first person singular and adopts a mock-ingenuous tone. Rather than envisioning his own response to the judgment scene, he presents a rumor about certain "others":

> What others mean to do I know not well;
>> Yet I heare tell,
> That some will turn to thee some leaves therein
>> So void of sinne,
> That they in merit shall excell. [6–10]

Clearly this stanza contradicts the drift of the first. Suddenly there are "some" who, in "some" respects at least, are not "poore wretches." In the final stanza, the speaker does not stop to comment on the possibility of excelling in merit; instead he merely presents what *he* "[means] to do"—rather blandly, as simply the adoption of another alternative, a personal preference:

> But I resolve, when thou shall call for mine,
>> That to decline,
> And thrust a Testament into thy hand . . . [11–13]

The stanza comes to a full stop here (it is the only stanza in the poem which is not continuous in its syntax at this point), and the poem ends on a note of confidence and assertion rather than of resolution or fear and trembling. Referring to the "Testament," Herbert's speaker enjoins,

> Let that be scann'd. [14]

And, he informs the "almightie Judge,"

> There thou shalt find my faults are thine. [15]

"Judgement" is a studied personal and nonpolemical piece in its rejection of "the way of merit," yet anyone who feels the force of its

opening vision cannot possibly consider this way.[6] The only course
open to such a person (other than that of simply being "appalled")
is the more peculiar and paradoxical path obliquely and rather ob-
scurely presented in the final stanza. The whole purpose of the vision
of judgment, Calvin explained, was to eliminate the possibility of any
man considering himself in any respect or in any action "void of
sinne." Although the speaker of "Judgement" does not himself judge
the rumor he hears, the poem does. Like "Sighs and Grones"—an-
other poem in which the speaker imagines himself at, or feels himself
to *be* at, "the divine tribunal"—"Judgement" makes it clear that the
denial of merit and the doctrine of "faith alone" both follow from the
Reformation conception of sin. And this conception of sin, the poems
show, arises in the religious consciousness dialectically rather than
directly: it arises not merely from self-contemplation, but from self-
contemplation *coram Deo*, in the face of an ethical and metaphysical
Absolute "beside whose purity all things are defiled," "whose righ-
teousness not even the angels can bear."[7]

In the "Prayer before Sermon" with which Herbert ends his "char-
acter" of the country parson and in "Miserie," one of the darkest
poems in *The Temple*, we can see very clearly the way in which the
concept of sin arises dialectically from the contemplation of self *coram
Deo*. We see it, as Rudolf Otto says, "not springing from the con-
sciousness of some committed transgression, but rather [as] *an im-
mediate datum* given with the experience of the numen."[8] The "Prayer
before Sermon" begins:

> O Almighty and ever-living Lord God! Majesty, and Power, and
> Brightnesse, and Glory! How shall we dare to appear before thy
> face, who are contrary to thee, in all we call thee? for we are dark-
> nesse, and weaknesse, and filthinesse, and shame. [*CP*, p. 288]

6. Coleridge was surprised to find in "Judgement" "so open an avowal of the article
of merit" (Roberta F. Brinkley, ed., *Coleridge on the Seventeenth Century* [Durham, N.C.,
1955], p. 537.) His surprise, as Hutchinson points out (pp. 542–43), was based on a
textual corruption. In all the editions of *The Temple* from 1660 (N.B.) to the Pickering
edition of 1799 which Coleridge used, line 7 of "Judgement" reads "Yet I here tell"
rather than, "Yet I heare tell." On the basis of the text he had, Coleridge's reading was
justified. He interestingly related this "avowal of the article of merit" to the praise of
the desert fathers in "The Church Militant," lines 37–46.

7. On *coram Deo* as opposed to *coram hominibus* (or *coram nobis*), see Luther's *Römerbrief-
vorlesung*, in *D. Martin Luthers Werke kritische Gesamtausgabe*, ed. J. C. F. Knaake, et al.
(Weimar, 1883), LVI, 3, and passim (this edition will hereafter be cited as *WA* [Weimar
Ausgabe]); *Luther's Lectures on Romans*, trans. Wilhelm Pauck (Philadelphia, 1961), p.
5. For "beside whose purity," see Calvin, *Institutes*, III.xii.1 (paraphrasing Job 25:5 and
4:18).

8. Rudolf Otto, *The Idea of the Holy*, trans. John W. Harvey, 2d ed. (1950; rpt. New
York, 1958), p. 50.

"How shall we dare to appear before thy face" is quite close to *"how shall* poore wretches brook / Thy dreadfull look" in "Judgement." Not daring is one of the primary results of contemplation of God's majesty in *The Temple.*[9] In "Miserie"—the "Prayer before Sermon" continues, "Misery and sin fill our days"—Herbert exclaims:

> My God, man cannot praise thy name:
> Thou art all brightnesse, perfect puritie;
> The sunne holds down his head for shame,
> Dead with eclipses, when we speak of thee.   [31–34]

The stanza ends with a horrified question:

> How shall infection
> Presume on thy perfection?[10]   [35–36]

In general, however, Herbert does not present man in terms of "filthinesse and shame," and in general he does not present God in terms of "perfect puritie." Stein has noted that "social ills, *the faults of the flesh,* the lesser passions" do not move Herbert to distinguished expression.[11] Herbert does not generally present sin in terms of pollution or "infection." On the one hand this vocabulary is overly materialistic, and on the other it is overly suggestive of sensuality as the source and most characteristic manifestation of sin. Herbert's poetry is not entirely free of this strain, present in "Miserie" and strong in "Home," but it is not his distinctive emphasis. Herbert also does not normally present God in terms of majesty and brightness and glory. "The Authour's Prayer before Sermon" goes on to address God as "patience, and pity, and sweetnesse, and love." Herbert's most characteristic way of describing God is in terms of "power and love"— absolute power in the service of absolute love. The paired nouns are almost a formula in the poetry. They occur together in a single phrase, "thy power and love," in "The Temper" (I; line 27) and in "Provi-

9. On other contexts of "daring not" in Herbert, see Strier, " 'To All Angels and Saints': Herbert's Puritan Poem," pp. 139–40.

10. In *Self-Consuming Artifacts,* pp. 180–82, Fish has argued that the speaker of "Miserie" is a Pharisee who exempts himself from the condemnations of "man" in the poem. This argument seems to me misguided on a number of counts. First, it is not true that "nowhere in the body of the poem does the speaker acknowledge complicity in the sins he is indicting" (p. 180). The speaker uses the first person plural in line 34 (quoted above) and in line 39. Second, and more important, even when the speaker is using the third person—"How canst thou brook *his* foolishnesse?"—the horror of his tone and the pungency of the phrasing express a sense of being deeply implicated in the behavior he is describing (compare Stein, *Herbert's Lyrics,* pp. 88–89). The final line of the poem, "My God, I mean my self," becomes, in my view, not a turnabout but a sudden acknowledgment.

11. *Herbert's Lyrics,* p. 89 (emphasis mine).

dence'' (line 29), and they tend to attract one another in larger grammatical and structural units. In "The Method," Herbert reminds himself that *he* must be responsible for God's apparent unresponsiveness because

> Thy Father could
> Quickly effect what thou dost move;
> For he is *Power:* and sure he would;
> For he is *Love.*   [5–8]

Successive stanzas of "Prayer" (II) characterize God respectively in terms of "Ease, Power, and Love"; "The Flower" as a whole moves from "Lord of power" (line 15) to "Lord of love" (line 39); the proem to "The Church Militant" begins with "thy power" (line 3) but ends by praising "Not the decrees of power, but bands of love" (line 10). This brings us to a final reflection on this Herbertian "formula": the effort of Herbert's poetry is almost always to collapse the two terms into one, to see power as love. Herbert's God is ultimately, as he says in "Even-song," "all love." In the "Prayer before Sermon," after shifting from majesty to love, Herbert states: "Thou hast exalted thy mercy above all things" (*CP*, p. 288).

   If this conception of God is truly central to Herbert's poetry and the dialectic of *coram Deo* is at work in the poetry, Herbert's conception of man must emerge dialectically from this conception of God. The opposites of "power and love"—weakness on the one hand and malice or selfishness on the other—are the primary terms for characterizing man in the poetry of *The Temple*. The speaker of "Love" (III) offers what is essentially a Herbertian formula for man when he characterizes himself as "Guiltie of *dust and sinne.*" Almost all Herbert's comments on man in the poetry can be placed under these rubrics. Later in "Love" (III) Herbert provides us with an insight into what he means by the second of the terms. When pressed by his interlocutor, the speaker characterizes himself in more detail as, "I, *the unkinde, ungratefull.*"

   It is no accident that, as "Love" (III) proceeds, Herbert's focus shifts from the comprehensiveness of "dust and sinne" to a more particular focus on "sinne" (adumbrated in the oddness of "*Guiltie of* dust"). Herbert recurrently employs both ways of characterizing man in "The Church," but in general one or the other will dominate the coloration of any given lyric. There is a sense in which the two characterizations, while not inherently contradictory, tend in opposite directions: the one emphasizes weakness, the other perversity; the one stimulates pity, the other, horror. The differing emphases recur in differing emotional, rhetorical, and theological contexts. When he is writing out of the experience of painful, almost overwhelming contrition, Herbert tends to emphasize man's weakness and to suggest that it would be, so to speak, unworthy of God to put forth His power against so bruised, weak, and evanescent a creature. When he is attempting to *evoke* contrition and a sense of wonder at God's mercy or when he is attempting to justify "affliction," Herbert emphasizes sin, in particular sins against love.

Since the "man is all weaknesse" theme of "Praise" (I) runs throughout *The Temple*, one could, by selective but not altogether unfair quoting, create the impression that Herbert does not really have a sense of *sin* at all, merely an overwhelming feeling for human weakness—or, to use one of his favorite words, for "frailtie." Tuve seems to move in this direction when she says that Herbert's emphasis is generally "upon the vanity rather than the foulness of sin," and when she points to his recurrent characterizations of sin as "foolishnesse."[12] A poem like "Easter-wings" seems to support this view; foolishness seems to replace sin as a description of the Fall:

> Lord, who createdst man in wealth and store,
>   Though foolishly he lost the same,
>   Decaying more and more,
>   Till he became
>   Most poore:
>   With thee
>   O let me rise. [1–7]

Yet in the second stanza, when the history as well as the petition in the stanza is personal, Herbert states that God "didst *so punish sinne,* / That I became / Most thinne" (emphasis mine). "Repentance," another direct plea to God, seems to present man entirely in terms of weakness:

>   Oh! gently treat
> With thy quick flow'r, thy momentarie bloom;
>   Whose life still pressing
>   Is one undressing,
>   A steadie aiming at a tombe. [2a–6]

It seems to transform "foulness" into "vanity":

>   O let thy height of mercie then
>   Compassionate short-breathed men.

---

12. "Herbert and *Caritas,*" p. 185. John S. Coolidge has made the fascinating suggestion that "Herbert's use of 'foolishness' may be intentionally reminiscent of the Old Testament root *nbl,* as in the name Nabal in I Samuel 25:25, or in Psalm 14:1, or in Deuteronomy 32:6, etc., referring to something much more heinous than mere weakness of intellect."

> Cut me not off for my most foul transgression:
> I do confesse
> My foolishnesse.[13]   [13-17]

"Complaining" is entirely constructed in the mode of the opening of "Repentance." Each stanza draws a contrast between "Thou" and "I" on the basis of power:

> Do not beguile my heart,
> Because thou art
> My power and wisdome. Put me not to shame,
> Because I am
> Thy clay that weeps, thy dust that calls.
>
> Thou art the Lord of glorie;
> The deed and storie
> Are both thy due: but I a silly flie
> That live or die
> According as the weather falls.   [1-10]

"Sighs and Grones" presents the same contrast, but here the "flie" is a worm:

> thou onely art
> The mightie God, but I a sillie worm;
> O do not bruise me![14]   [3b-5]

The essential stance toward God of all these poems is articulated in "Discipline":

> Though man frailties hath,
> Thou art God:
> Throw away thy wrath.[15]   [30-32]

It is important to realize that, in spite of their pleas, these poems do not contest the appropriateness of God's wrath. On the contrary, they strongly assert it. We have already noted the denial of merit with which "Sighs and Grones" begins ("O do not use me / After my

13. The ease of movement from "man" or "men" to "I" and "me" in these poems should be noted. This movement works against some attempts to distinguish sharply between "personal" and "impersonal" modes in Herbert. See n. 10 above and Vendler, *Poetry of Herbert*, pp. 63, 151, and passim.

14. It is perhaps worth noting that the word "sillie" in these poems is used primarily in the older senses of "deserving of pity, compassion, or sympathy," "helpless, defenceless," "weak, feeble, frail, insignificant" (*OED* "Silly," adj., *1a, b; 2a, c*), rather than in the modern sense (though this is not entirely irrelevant).

15. The ending of "The Priesthood" uses this appeal on the basis of weakness in an avowedly strategic way; it relies, with mock cynicism, on a politic maxim, "The distance of the meek / Doth flatter power" (lines 39b–40a).

sinnes!''); "Repentance" begins, "Lord, I confesse my sinne is great; / Great is my sinne." "Complaining" does not question the justice of God's wrath but instead asks:

> Art thou all justice, Lord?
>   Shows not thy word
> More attributes?   [11–13a]

These poems are all spoken from a deeply humbled and penitent point of view. There is no question of merit in them. The speakers of these poems are already, in the terms of "Sighs and Grones," bruised and ground by their own awakened consciences. The intimacy and poignance of their language shows that they have all learned the lesson which, according to "The Flower," God's apparent wrath toward the regenerate is meant to teach:

> To make us see we are but flowers that glide.   [44]

Recall "Oh! gently treat / With thy quick flow'r, thy momentarie bloom." These poems stress the mercy man needs rather than the judgment he deserves. They are certain that God's word does have "more attributes" than justice, that He has "exalted [His] mercy above all things." They recall the promises of the gospel to the bruised reed and the smoking flax (Matthew 12:20), and they rely on the conception of God's love implicit in those promises.

In the poems that attempt to stimulate rather than express contrition, the case is altered. In these poems there is no doubt of Herbert's sense of sin. "Ephesians 4:30" is a meditation on both the necessity and the impotence of human penitence.[16] Its first stanza is an attempt to feel the force of the assertion that failures of love within the Christian community "grieve the Holy Spirit." Contemplation of these failures provokes horror, not pity. The stanza is particularly interesting in the context we have been developing. It contrasts man with God on the basis of both power and love and transforms an image which has been a hallmark of weakness into a parable of perversity:

> And art thou grieved, sweet and sacred Dove,
>   When I am sowre,
>   And crosse thy love?
> Grieved for me? the God of strength and power
>   Griev'd for a worm, which when I tread,
>   I passe away and leave it dead?   [1–6]

---

16. For a general treatment of Herbert's view of penitence, see Strier, "Herbert and Tears," pp. 221–47.

The speaker's aim in this stanza is not to present himself to God as a weak creature, "a sillie worm," but to feel the strangeness of God's care for man by contrasting this care with man's characteristic attitude toward worms. The second half of this stanza is a trap for the reader. The ontological contempt which "the God of strength and power / Griev'd *for a worm*" forces us to feel is transformed into moral self-contempt when ontological contempt turns out to be precisely the quality which establishes the final contrast between God and man. The instinctive contempt which the stanza has forced us to summon highlights by contrast God's mercy, the strangeness and wonder of His pity.[17]

"Giddinesse" begins as a general contemplation of "how farre from power" man is (line 1). In this poem, as its title indicates, power is conceived of primarily as the capacity to establish stability, "setled peace and rest" (line 2). The poem maintains a tone of detached, semisatiric presentation—"He builds a house, which quickly down must go" (line 13)—until it culminates in a final asseveration:

> Surely if each one saw anothers heart,
> There would be no commerce,
> No sale or bargain passe: all would disperse,
> And live apart.   [21–24]

There seems to be genuine moral horror here, a rather Swiftian sense of the advantages of being well deceived. The overall context makes it clear, however, that what men would see in each other's hearts is not malice but chaotic changeableness—"giddinesse." The previous stanza exclaimed:

> O what a sight were Man, if his attires
> Did alter with his minde;
> And like a Dolphins skinne, his clothes combin'd
> With his desires!   [17–20]

The Timon-like vision of universal dispersion and solitariness moves beyond sardonic comedy to sober moralizing, yet it remains within the framework of "frailty." As we have suggested, true moral horror

17. In only one other moment in his poetry does Herbert rely so directly on the fallenness of the reader and entrap the reader through it. In "A Wreath," God is addressed as being "more farre above deceit, / Then deceit seems above simplicitie" (7b–8). Here again the context is a sharp comparison of God's ways with man's, and here again, in order merely to understand the lines and work out the proportional analogy, we are forced to acknowledge intimate acquaintance with a perspective that literally damns us. For an analysis of similar (though more epistemologically oriented) effects in Milton, see Stanley E. Fish, *Surprised by Sin: The Reader in Paradise Lost* (New York, 1967), pp. 22–28.

for Herbert arises from the contemplation of man *coram Deo* rather than among men. The idea of looking into the heart naturally turns the poet's thoughts to God ("he sees hearts, as we see faces" [*CP*, p. 234]). The last stanza of "Giddinesse" is a prayer, and here (in contrast to "Miserie") it is true that only at the final moment does Herbert explicitly include himself in the vision he presents. "Lord," he prays,

> mend or rather make us: one creation
> Will not suffice our turn.   [25–26]

Herbert's use of *correctio* here (when we speak "as if we had not wel spoken so that we seeme to call in our word againe") is, as his use of this device almost always is, deeply significant theologically: men must be totally remade, not merely mended, by God.[18] As Tyndale said in a similar context, God "is no patcher."[19] In his "natural" state, man contains no salvageable materials. Even the notion of a single second creation is too optimistic:

> Except thou make us dayly, we shall spurn
> Our own salvation.   [27–28]

"We shall spurn / Our own salvation"—this is presented not as a speculation like "Surely if each one saw anothers heart," but as a fact, "we shall." The body of "Giddinesse" denies both the Augustinian optimism of "The Pulley"—man's lack of "setled peace and rest" does *not* "toss him to [God's] breast"—and the Stoic optimism of "Constancie"—being "some twentie sev'rall men at least / Each sev'rall houre," man has no stable self to which to be true. The final vision, however, breaks the "giddinesse" framework. What these lines assert is not, as the second stanza says, that man will sometimes seek salvation and sometimes "spurn" it, but that he will alwayo spurn it. The development of the poem explains this contradiction. In stanza two, Herbert is contemplating the unevenness of the psychological life of the regenerate Christian:

18. For the device of *correctio*, see George Puttenham, *The Arte of English Poesie*, ed. Gladys Doidge Willcock and Alice Walker (Cambridge, 1936), p. 215. In *The Poetry of Herbert*, Vendler presents self-correction or "reinvention" as Herbert's major procedural mode (chap. 2), but she tends to conceive of this phenomenon in psychological rather than in rhetorical or theological terms (see Richard Strier, " 'Humanizing' Herbert," *MP*, 74 [1976], 78–88).

19. *The Obedience of a Christian Man*, in Rev. Henry Walter, ed., *Doctrinal Treatises and Introductions to Different Portions of the Holy Scriptures by William Tyndale* (Cambridge, 1848), p. 135. Compare also, in the famous opening lines of Donne's "Batter my heart," "you / As yet but knock, breathe, shine, *and seek to mend*" (emphasis mine). Donne's sonnet, however, does not consistently maintain the Reformation perspective of its opening and closing.

> One while he counts of heav'n, as of his treasure:
> But then a thought creeps in,
> And calls him coward, who for fear of sinne
> Will lose a pleasure.[20]   [5–8]

As "Giddinesse" continues, however, it comes to focus on man's purely natural state, culminating in the somber sixth stanza ("Surely if each one saw anothers heart"). The final stanza continues the focus on nature. *Coram Deo,* it forces the darkest implications of the "state of nature" to emerge.

These implications are fully dramatized in "Sepulchre." Here God's love and man's malice face each other directly. "Sepulchre" particularizes the general vision of the final stanza of "Giddinesse." Completing the opening movement of "The Church" from Good Friday to Easter Sunday, "Sepulchre" is the definitive presentation of one of Herbert's favorite images for sin, the stony heart. In context, "Sepulchre" connects the personal hardness of heart lamented by the speakers of "The Altar" and "The Sinner" to the historical hardness of heart lamented by Christ in "The Sacrifice." In "Sepulchre," the "Jewish hate" portrayed in "The Sacrifice" is shown to be the normal and inevitable response of untransformed human nature; in this, too, "Their storie pennes and sets us down" ("The Bunch of Grapes," line 11).[21]

"Sepulchre" begins like an Ignatian meditation with a "composition of the place."[22] The speaker imagines himself at Christ's sepulchre after the crucifixion:

> O Blessed bodie! Whither art thou throwne?
> No lodging for thee, but a cold hard stone?   [1–2]

20. "The Collar" dramatizes at length the emergence of the type of "thought" mentioned here. This stanza of "Giddinesse" helps us to recognize the overall content of "The Collar."

21. For "Jewish hate," see line 1 of "Self-condemnation." This poem too tries (although in a more trivial context, that of greed) to show that "a Jewish choice" "may be thy storie" (lines 9 and 6). The difference in poetic quality between "Self-condemnation" and "Sepulchre" confirms Stein's observation (quoted on p. 5 above) on "the lesser passions" not moving Herbert to distinguished expression.

22. The first prelude to the first of the spiritual exercises is to form "a mental image of the place" (Saint Ignatius Loyola, *Spiritual Exercises,* p. 54). In *The Poetry of Meditation,* p. 27 and passim, Martz sees this practice as "of enormous importance" for English religious poetry in the seventeenth century. In " 'Setting Foot into Divinity': George Herbert and the English Reformation," pp. 219–41, Bell suggests that the opening sequence of "The Church" offers a critique of Ignatian methods of meditation. She does not treat "Sepulchre."

In the next lines, however, the poem immediately shifts to its real subject, human nature vis-à-vis Christ. The notion of "lodging" becomes entirely nonphysical:

> So many hearts on earth, and yet not one
>   Receive thee?   [3–4]

In these opening questions, the speaker, as Fish points out, assumes three things: that hearts are very different from "cold, hard stone"; that this difference makes them superior lodgings for the blessed body; and that hearts are capable of receiving Christ, if only they would (that, as Fish puts it, "the initiative in the situation rests with the heart").[23] Even within the initial questions, however, the assumptions on which they apparently rely seem naive. The absoluteness and the emphatic placement of "and yet not one" tend to undercut the possibility that hearts could "receive thee" if they would, and the proximity (reinforced by the half-rhyme) of "hard" to "hearts" works to associate rather than to distinguish these terms.

The naiveté of the opening becomes transparent in the second stanza. Continuing the mock-physical treatment of "hearts," the speaker argues that there must be "room within our hearts good store" since "they can lodge transgressions by the score" (lines 5–6). Herbert is intentionally presenting an odd and self-defeating argument (the third stanza rightly comments, "But that which shews them large shews them unfit"). He is also forcing us first to consider and then to reject a thematic possibility raised by a grammatical ambiguity—a technique which he will use again at a crucial moment in the poem. "Sure there is room within our hearts good store" is constructed in such a way as to leave the grammatical status of the words "good store" ambiguous. They can be taken either adjectivally, as modifying "room," or substantively, as part of the possessive phrase, "our hearts' good store" (the lack of the convention of identifying the possessive with an apostrophe allows the ambiguity). As the poem proceeds, however, it becomes apparent that the substantive sense is *only* a grammatical possibility, not a thematic one. That our hearts have no "good store" is the burden of the rest of the poem.

After commenting on the "argument" he advanced (or pretended to) in the second stanza, the speaker demonstrates the naiveté of his opening assessment of the relative value of sepulchre and heart as lodgings for Christ. When moral categories replace physical ones, he reverses his initial judgments. Sin replaces (literal) coldness and hardness as the source of unfitness:

23. *Self-Consuming Artifacts*, p. 170. Fish's discussion of "Sepulchre" extends from p. 170 to p. 173. I will not give specific page references within this discussion.

> What ever sinne did this pure rock commit,
> Which holds thee now? Who hath indited it
>   Of murder?   [10–12]

The strong positional, metrical, and rhetorical stress on "it" ("this pure rock") implies that someone *has* indicted us "of murder." The fourth stanza tells us who—the Jews who rejected and persecuted Christ. We are they. The thought of the technical moral purity of the literal sepulchre leads directly to the thought of the actual moral impurity of our hearts.[24]

John 10 tells us that when Jesus walked in the porch of the temple at the Feast of the Dedication, the Jews "took up stones again to stone him." Continuing the contrast between our hearts and the sepulchre, Herbert notes that:

> Where our hard hearts have took up stones to brain thee,
> And missing this, most falsely did arraigne thee;
> Onely these stones in quiet entertain thee,
>   And order.   [13–16]

"Our hard hearts *have took up* stones to brain thee." This is a plain statement of fact. In relation to Christ, the true horror of nature is revealed. These lines invite us to perceive our hearts as virtually being the stones taken up to "brain" Christ. "Hardness of heart" takes on its full potency of meaning.

The next stanza steps back from the "place" to make a generalized comment on the relationship between the Word and stone:

24. Fish argues that "this pure rock" in line 10 is an allusion to I Corinthians 10:4: "they drank of that spiritual Rock that followed them: and that Rock was Christ." I am not convinced that the context of the poem (as opposed to the pressures of Fish's argument) encourages us to make this connection. In insisting on this allusion here, Fish ignores his own excellent caveat (p. 211, n. 26) against "a mistake made often by the practitioners of a naive historical criticism, to proceed at once on the basis of what the seventeenth-century (eighteenth-century, nineteenth-century) reader [supposedly] knew." Fish argues that what distinguishes the informed contemporary reader from less able readers is his ability "to put clues together when they come to him," to produce relevant contexts when they are demanded. If this is true, as I believe it is, the proper critical question in relation to a potentially allusive line or passage becomes, "Are the 'clues' which will activate potential knowledge clearly present in this context?" The fact that the allusion to Christ as "that spiritual Rock" is "hardly recondite" does not count in any way for its relevance. Fish does not identify any "clues" (or cues) for this allusion in the text. Rather, he *assumes* the relevance of the allusion and then uses it to create problems in the text—"In the context of these allusions . . . the sense made by the syntax becomes problematical" (p. 171). The literal meaning and straightforward syntax of lines 10–12 of "Sepulchre," however, provide a fully coherent and powerful context for the emphasis which "this pure rock" receives in them.

> And as of old the Law by heav'nly art
> Was writ in stone, so thou, which also art
> The letter of the word, find'st no fit heart
> > To hold thee.   [17–20]

That God's Word encounters stone is presented here as the normal condition of divine-human interactions (with also a hint of Calvin's insistence that the Old Testament promises literally refer to Christ [see *Institutes* II.ix–xi]). Fish has claimed that "every reader" will recognize this stanza as a "near paraphrase" of II Corinthians 3:2–3, "Ye are our epistle written in our hearts . . . not in tables of stone, but in fleshy tables of the heart." But the point of the stanza is to *deny* the distinction Paul is there drawing between the old dispensation and the new, stone and heart. Herbert elsewhere makes this distinction, but he is not doing so here. The framework of this stanza is very similar to that of "The Sinner," another poem in the carefully ordered opening sequence.[25] At the end of "The Sinner," after acknowledging the hardness of a heart that "scarce to thee can grone," Herbert petitions God to "Remember that [He] once did write in stone." Here, as in "Sepulchre," Herbert does not want to make any distinctions between the way things were "of old" and the way they are "now."

The final stanza of "Sepulchre" begins with a temporal ambiguity:

> Yet we do still persist *as we began.*   [21; emphasis mine]

"As we began" in both the Old Testament and the New. The latter, however, is especially relevant: the Gospel accounts of the rejection and persecution of Christ. "And so," Herbert concludes in the next half-line, we "should perish" (22a). Both senses of "should" are relevant. The rest of the local context makes it clear that "should" is future conditional here, but the pressure of the poem as a whole makes us feel intensely the presence of the indicative sense. There is no doubt that we "should perish" from the moral point of view. It turns out, however, that this point of view is irrelevant, for

> > nothing can
> Though it be cold, hard, foul, from loving man
> > Withhold thee.   [22b–24]

The referential ambiguity of "as we began" and the grammatical ambiguity of "should perish" are germane, but what of the ambiguity of "loving man"? Grammatically, "loving" can be either a participial

25. Since "Sepulchre" does not appear in the Williams manuscript, it was probably added to *The Temple* after the completion of this manuscript (hereafter referred to as "W"). "Sepulchre" is one of the two poems Herbert added to the opening sequence of "The Church."

adjective modifying "man" or a gerund expressing the action of Christ. Fish sees "the pressure to resolve the ambiguity" as minimal here. Apart from the general constraints of his framework, Fish takes this position because he believes the recognition that Christ is "already in residence" in the speaker's heart to be central to the meaning of the poem. His insistence on this recognition leads him to brush aside as mere "surface rhetoric" the strong assertion of the stoniness of our hearts. Clearly, he says, it is only a "fleshy" heart, softened by the Word inscribed upon it, that can "produce laments and self-accusing poems."

But *does* the fact of the poem undercut its explicit statements, and are we free to read "loving man" either way, or both ways at once? Fish is certainly right that only a regenerate Christian could speak of and feel toward himself the way the speaker of "Sepulchre" does. He is also right in detecting a paradox here. Yet he misconceives the meaning and rhetorical aim of the poem. The paradox to which Fish is pointing springs from a fundamental Reformation doctrine, the doctrine of "imperfect sanctification" or "sin in believers." This doctrine is Article XV of the Anglican Articles of Religion ("Of Christ Alone without Sin"); its classical formulation is Luther's: "a Christian man is both righteous and a sinner [*simul justus et peccator*], an enemy to God and yet a child of God."[26] ("These contraries," Luther characteristically goes on to add, "no sophister"—meaning no Roman theologian—"will admit.") John Downame, a contemporary of Herbert's and the author of an extremely popular work of "practical divinity," expresses very clearly the paradox that Fish sees as undermining the "surface rhetoric" of "Sepulchre." "The deare children of God," Downame writes, "do oftentimes see and feele to their great grief, their hardness of heart."[27] "Yea, in truth," he continues, "this kind of hardness of heart *is incident unto them alone*" (emphasis mine). Unregenerate men, "though their hearts are most hard and obdurate . . . do not discerne" their condition.

The speaker of "Sepulchre," then, is a regenerate Christian, one of "the deare children of God."[28] Yet the poem is *about* the natural state and the natural impulses of the human heart. The regeneracy of the

26. *Commentary on Galatians*, ed. Watson, p. 226. For the Latin, *homo Christianus simul justus et peccator, sanctus, prophanus, inimicus et filius Die est*, see *WA*, XL[1], 368.

27. John Downame, *The Christian Warfare against the Devill, World, and Flesh* (1634), p. 230a.

28. This is true, of course, also of the speakers of "The Altar," "The Sinner," and the many other self-condemning poems in "The Church." This paradox serves as a fully sufficient answer to the charge (close to Fish's remarks on the "surface rhetoric" of "Sepulchre") that "The Altar" is incoherent because "a hard heart is one not likely to spend its time praising God" (Vendler, *Poetry of Herbert*, pp. 61–63). Halewood, *Poetry of Grace*, p. 104, falls into a similar mistake in describing the speaker of "Justice" (I) as "struggling *but unregenerate* (emphasis mine). Luther insisted that when Paul speaks

speaker is a fact about the poem but it is not part of the content of the poem (as it is, for instance, in "Sinnes Round"). The point of the poem, the "aim and mark of the whole discourse" to which all its parts are chained (see *CP*, p. 256), is the contrast between God's treatment of man and man's treatment of God. The poem does not function, as Fish suggests, to dissolve but rather to assert the distinctions "which would make one reading [of "loving man"] better than another—between loved and loving man, between the heart as agent and Christ as agent." Fish's analysis of "Sepulchre" entirely omits the stanza in which "our hard hearts have took up stones to brain thee." The whole effort of the poem is to demonstrate how far from "loving" man was and is toward Christ—"Yet do we still persist as we began." If "loving" were an adjective modifying "man," man should *not* perish, and "Sepulchre" as a whole would truly be a hopelessly incoherent piece. The point of the ambiguity is to force the reader to consider *and then rule out*, on strictly thematic grounds, a grammatically respectable, indeed inevitable reading. In the poem, man is only the object, not the subject of "loving." The relation between the phrase in its adjectival sense and the reality presented in the poem is meant to be bitterly and piercingly ironic. It is meant to renew our perceptions of both sin and grace, to make us feel the special strangeness of a love that is indifferent to the hostility of its object. "He took flesh, he wept, he died; for his enemies he died; even for those that derided him then, *and still despise him*" (*CP*, p. 288; emphasis mine). Nygren describes the "unmotivated" character of *agape* as "the most striking feature of God's love as Jesus represents it."[29]

When the speaker of "Love" (III) characterizes himself as "unkinde, ungratefull," he is speaking of his relation to God, not of his relationships in general. This is borne out not only by the immediate context of his characterization ("Ah my deare, / I cannot look on thee") but also by the two poems which Herbert wrote (perhaps had already written) specifically on the subjects of "unkindnesse" and "ungratefulnesse."[30] "Sepulchre" presents man only in relation to God; "Giddinesse" presents man's behavior toward God as continuous with his

---

of "the flesh [lusting] against the Spirit" in Galatians 5:16 and elsewhere, he is *not* speaking "in the person of the ungodly" (*Commentary on Galatian*, ed. Watson, p. 502). George Ryley was correct in characterizing the poems in "The Church" as providing "a description of the dispositions of *a sound member* of ye Church; wch is ye Body of Christ" ("Mr. Herbert's Temple and Church Militant Explained and Improved," ed. John Martin Heissler [Ph.D. diss., University of Illinois, 1960], I, 40 [emphasis mine]).

29. Nygren, *Agape and Eros*, p. 75.

30. Since "Love" (III), "Unkindnesse," and "Ungratefulnesse" all appear in "W," it is possible that Herbert had already written "Unkindnesse" and "Ungratefulnesse" by the time he composed "Love" (III).

general behavior, although only revealed in its true magnitude in relation to God. The speaker of "Unkindnesse" finds himself puzzled at the *lack* of continuity between his relations to God and his relations with men. The poem presents a speaker who simultaneously fulfills one of the highest classical ethical ideals, that of *philia*, disinterested friendship, and fails at the demands of Christian ethics. It thus serves as a comment both on the classical ideal in itself and on the possibility, important to Saint Thomas and other medieval thinkers, of using the Aristotelian ideal of friendship as a model for the ideal love of a Christian for God (*amor amicitiae* as opposed to *concupiscentiae*).[31]

"Unkindnesse" opens with the prayer, "Lord, make me coy and tender to offend." As the rest of the stanza makes clear, what this means is, "Make me feel and behave toward you, Lord, the way I do to my friends":

> In friendship, first I think, if that agree,
> Which I intend,
> Unto my friends intent and end.   [2–4]

This is the ideal. The speaker places his friends' "intent[s] and end[s]" before his own. In the final line of the stanza, which becomes, with variations, a refrain, the speaker uses his fulfillment of this ethical ideal as a measure of how different his relation to God is:

> I would not use a friend, as I use Thee.   [5]

Apparently the speaker does not give the same priority to God's intents and ends as he does to those of his friends. But there is no hint, at this point in the poem, as to why the speaker uses God in so unfriendly a way. The second stanza follows the model of the first and stresses Herbert's (the speaker's) concern for his friends' "good name" and, implicitly, Herbert's lack of concern for God's, but it too offers no explanation of the fact it contemplates—"I could not use a friend, as I use Thee" (line 10).

The third stanza hints at an explanation. The stanza is formally different from the previous ones in that it presents an example of the speaker's treatment of God rather than merely an exclamation asserting this "unkindnesse" after a four-line portrayal of ideal human friendship. The first line of the stanza is trivial ("My friend may spit upon my curious floore"),[32] but the rest is serious:

31. See Nygren, *Agape and Eros*, pp. 642–55, and Oberman, *Harvest of Medieval Theology*, pp. 134, 152–57.

32. The only interest in this remarkably weak line is what it tells us of Herbert's personal fastidiousness, a trait noted in contemporary accounts of him and in Izaak Walton, *The Life of Mr. George Herbert*, in *The Lives of John Donne, Sir Henry Wotton, Richard Hooker, George Herbert, and Robert Sanderson*, intro. George Saintsbury (London, 1927), pp. 270, 275, 305.

> Would he have gold? I lend it instantly;
>> But let the poore,
>> And thou within them, starve at doore.   [12–14]

These lines place Christian ethics strongly in contrast with *philia*. What they reveal is that *philia* is personal. The speaker is "instantly" responsive to the appeal of his friend, but unmoved by the plight of those who are merely objectively in need. Yet the distinctive feature of the ethics of the Gospels is precisely the insistence on transcending the personal, the local, and the tribal. "Thy neighbor as thyself" echoes parochialism in order to reject it. The parable of the good Samaritan is Jesus' answer to the shrewd and obvious question, "And who is my neighbor?" (Luke 10:25–37). Here, on the basis of Matthew 26:40—"Inasmuch as ye have done it unto the least of my brethren, ye have done it unto me"—Herbert strikingly identifies Christ and "the poore," so that the "double commandment" of Luke 10 ("Thou shalt love the Lord thy God with all thy heart . . . and thy neighbour as thyself") becomes single. As Luther puts it, "to love God *is* to love one's neighbor" (*amare Deum est amare proximum*).[33] This stanza of "Unkindnesse" echoes "Sepulchre": "Out of doore / [We] leave thee."

The fourth stanza returns to the ideal enunciated in the first; it gives an instance of the general principle of thinking "first" of the friend:

> When that my friend pretendeth to a place,
> I quit my interest, and leave it free.   [16–17]

In structure, however, the fourth stanza resembles the third rather than the first; its dimeter line, again beginning with an adversative, makes explicit the contrast between *coram hominibus* and *coram Deo:*

>> But when thy grace
>> Sues for my heart, I thee displace.   [18–19]

The key question is whether these lines make a judgment on the limits of the ideal presented earlier in the stanza parallel to the judgment the corresponding lines in stanza 3 make on that stanza's opening. I think the lines do work this way, though my argument rests on a nuance of phrasing (with Herbert one might hold that this makes for rather than against the point). If I am correct, lines 18 and 19 of "Unkindnesse" make a judgment on *philia* even more penetrating than the Gospel-oriented third stanza makes.

The rich nuance is the placement of the pronouns in "I thee displace" (line 19b). Given the phrasing and climactic position of this half-line, it is difficult not to read it as meaning that "I" displaces "Thee"—as, in other words, a description of irrepressible egotism

---

33. WA, *Tischreden*, No. 5906, V, 397; quoted in Nygren, *Agape*, p. 736.

and inability truly to renounce or transcend the self. But, the question must arise, what of all the examples of selflessness given in the poem—"I quit my interest"; "first I think, if that agree," and so forth? If my reading of "I thee displace" is correct, the argument of this stanza is that none of the examples of altruism which the poem has presented involves renunciation of self in the deepest sense. Herbert would not, I think, have been deaf to the note of self-satisfaction in "I quit my interest." Pleasure in the conscious exercise of virtue is a deeply Aristotelian conception and, of course, a deeply self-satisfied state of mind. In the course of the poem, the ideal of friendship, even in its highest form, has been shown not to demand a transcendence or transformation of human nature.[34] (There is perhaps a further hint of the prudential within the apparently altruistic in "Would he have gold? I lend it instantly" as opposed to the metrically equivalent "I *give* it instantly." This is, again, a nuance, but if the poem is a dramatic monologue, it is perhaps meant to be unconsciously self-revealing.)

If man's nature were not vitiated, man *would* love God *super omnia*[35]—certainly above any friend:

> Yet can a friend what thou hast done fulfill?
> O write in brasse, *My God upon a tree*
>   *His bloud did spill*
>   *Onely to purchase my good-will.*
> Yet I use not my foes, as I use Thee.   [21–25]

Suddenly an abyss opens. The question of why the speaker fails to treat God as a friend fades before the recognition that he treats Him worse than an enemy. The puzzlement of the previous stanzas—"I would not use a friend, as I use Thee'; "I could not"; "I cannot"—gives way to horror. The passive culpability of stanza three ("*let the poore* . . . starve at doore") is too weak. The movement is similar to that from "So many hearts on earth, and yet not one / Receive thee" to "our hard hearts have took up stones to brain thee" in "Sepulchre." Unlike "Sepulchre," however, "Unkindnesse" ends at this point—on a moment of horrified and baffled self-contemplation. The notion of "friendship with God" has been shown to be an ill-conceived and fanciful speculation, a speculation that does not take proper account of the corruption of nature proceeding from the Fall.

34. For some remarks by a present-day ethical philosopher on the limits of Aristotle's concept of friendship, see Alasdair MacIntyre, *A Short History of Ethics* (New York, 1966), pp. 79–80.

35. On *amor Dei Super omnia* in late medieval theology and its relation to "doing what is in one" (*facere quod in se est*), see Oberman, *Harvest of Medieval Theology*, pp. 133–34, 152–57, 184, 460, 468.

There is, however, a problem with the ending of "Unkindnesse." While its bleakness does not guarantee the badness of the piece,[36] "Unkindnesse" does seem, as "Miserie" puts it, to make "all the bloud of God to run in vain." The more closely one looks at the final stanza, the more contradictory it seems until one notices an ambiguity parallel to that of "loving man" in "Sepulchre," if less striking. As in "Sepulchre," the ambiguous line is the penultimate one: "Onely to purchase my good-will" (24). Here the thematic context forces into prominence readings of the line that would not otherwise have arisen. "Onely to purchase my good-will" would seem to mean, "solely for the purpose of inducing me to take a favorable attitude." But, as the chilling final line of the poem tells us, and as we already know from the previous stanzas, man (the speaker) does not take a favorable attitude, show "good will" toward Christ. Recognition of favors bestowed ("Yet can a friend what thou hast done fulfill?") does not, in this all-important case, result in good will. It seems, then, that Christ does not fulfill His purpose. If, however, the line means either "to *make* my will good" or "to purchase the Father's good will toward me," the stanza becomes fully coherent. The presence of either of these possibilities in the line again creates a heart-piercing irony. If the first is accepted, the ambiguity reminds us that the purpose of grace is to transform man's will, not to appeal to it through gratitude. If the second (and perhaps more likely) alternative reading is accepted, the ambiguity serves, together with the final line, to emphasize the contrast between God and man.[37]

Man is not a free agent; this is what the corruption of nature means. He is bound to sin (pun intended).[38] When God's grace "sues for" his heart, he *must* "displace" it with something more satisfying to his ego. As "Justice" (I), which occurs shortly after "Unkindnesse," puts it, "sinne the hand hath got" (the "other law in my members" of Romans 7:23). In Reformation theology, as in Paul's epistles, both sin and grace are conceived of as forces independent of the individual personality, though not external to it. Herbert consistently portrays them this way in his poetry ("still," in the following lines, means, as it generally does in Herbert, "always"):

36. For an argument of this sort, see Vendler, *Poetry of Herbert*, pp. 188–90 (discussing "Ungratefulness" and "Decay").

37. Interestingly, Article X of the Anglican Articles, "Of Free-will," contains a parallel ambiguity: "we have no power to do good works pleasant and acceptable to God without the grace of God by Christ preventing us, *that we may have* a good will, and working with us *when we have* that good will" (emphasis mine). Text from B. A. Gerrish, ed., *The Faith of Christendom: A Sourcebook of Creeds and Confessions* (Cleveland, 1963), p. 189.

38. See Luther, *The Bondage of the Will*, trans. J. I. Packer and O. R. Johnston (Westwood, N.J., 1957), pp. 239ff. and passim.

> Sinne is still hammering my heart
> Unto a hardnesse, void of love:
> Let suppling grace, to crosse his art,
>   Drop from above.   ["Grace," 17–20]

The final stanza of "Unkindnesse" reveals the depth of man's perversity by focusing on his inability to respond to God with the "natural" response of gratitude for favors.[39] Ingratitude is, above all, a failure of happy spontaneity. "Ungratefulnesse" addresses this in detail. Like Christ's self-descriptions in "Dialogue" and "The Bag," "Ungratefulnesse" is meant to break our hearts. Herbert knew that the more glowing his portrayal of God's bounty, the more horrified our sense of man's ingratitude. It is perhaps not irrelevant to note at this point that ingratitude was probably the vice most abhorrent to Shakespeare; in the premium he placed on generous spontaneity, and in his attitude toward prudential calculation, Shakespeare is very much in touch with the main outlines of Reformation, especially Lutheran, ethics.[40]

"Ungratefulnesse" begins as a paean to *agape*, God's unique love of man:

> Lord, with what bountie and rare clemencie
>   Hast thou redeem'd us from the grave!
>   If thou hads't let us runne,
>   Gladly had man ador'd the sunne,
>   And thought his god most brave;
> Where now we shall be better gods than he.   [1–6]

The central lines of this stanza (3–5) are devoted to making clear how fully man deserved the grave from which God's love redeemed him. These lines form the strongest assertion in "The Church" of the "naturalness" of idolatry.[41] One inevitably thinks of Caliban. Even the language is Caliban-like (Stephano is "a *brave* god" who Caliban

39. In *Paradise Lost*, unfallen Adam manifests this gratitude; see IV, 411–39 and V, 153–208.

40. There is a remarkable parallel in both context and rhetoric between a passage in the Elizabethan translation of Luther's *Commentary on Galatians* and the opening of Portia's famous speech on the unconstrained quality of mercy (*Merchant of Venice*, IV.i.182–84): "Like as the earth engendereth not rain, nor is able by her own strength, labour, and travail to procure the same, but receiveth it of the mere gift of God from above: so this heavenly righteousness is given us of God without our works or deservings" (Watson, ed., p. 23). All quotations of and line references to Shakespeare are from *The Complete Works*, the Pelican text, rev., gen. ed. Alfred Harbage (Baltimore, 1969).

41. Compare "The Church Militant," lines 111–12: "Ah, what a thing is *man devoid of grace*, / Adoring garlick with an humble face" (emphasis mine).

"*adores*" [*The Tempest*, II.ii.115, 136]).[42] In Shakespeare's play in praise of civilization, Caliban says that without books, Prospero is "but a sot" as he himself (Caliban) is (III.ii.89–90); in Herbert's Reformation poem, all men, left to themselves by God, are but sots like Caliban. Man would inevitably "rest in Nature" (see "The Pulley," line 14). "Now," however, "we shall be," as Jesus promises, "better gods" than the sun (see Matthew 13:43). This is "rare clemencie" indeed. "The rarer action is / In virtue than in vengeance"—*The Tempest*, V.i.27–28.

Stanza 1 of "Ungratefulnesse" celebrates the effects and the power of God's "bountie"; stanzas 2 through 4, the body of the poem, gaily and wittily explicate the nature of this bounty. "Thou hast," Herbert says to God, with playful theological daring, "but two rare cabinets full of treasure." These are "The *Trinitie* and *Incarnation*," and God has "unlockt them both" (lines 7–9) to provide a dowry with which to "betroth" man to Himself (here the suitor provides the dowry for His impoverished bride).[43] The next two stanzas are devoted to the "treasure cabinets," one for each. The Trinity is "the statelier cabinet"; Herbert stresses its inaccessibility to man prior to entering the kingdom of glory. Death will "blow / The dust into our eyes" that will remove their mortal film and "make us see" (lines 15–18).[44] Luther continually warned his readers and auditors against "speculation on the majesty" of God, against what he called "the theology of glory." He urged, instead, a theology of the cross. "Let the naked Godhead be," he insisted, "leave the majestic God alone" and focus instead on the God clothed in flesh, on the Incarnate Christ—"cleave to"

42. I am not suggesting any direct allusion, only that Shakespeare and Herbert were drawing on the same tradition in portraying fallen nature as inherently idolatrous.

43. In this paraphrase of the second stanza, it will be clear that I am taking "the work of thy creation" to refer *to man* ("Thou hast unlockt them both, / And made them jewels to betroth / The work of thy creation / Unto thy self in everlasting pleasure" [lines 9–12]). The content of the poem, its focus on God's redemptive "bountie" toward man, seems to me to make it impossible (together with the inherent unlikeliness of the conception) that Herbert is here speaking of God as "betrothing" the entire creation to Himself. For man as "*the* work of thy creation," see "Man," in which compared to him "All things are in decay," he is "ev'ry thing, / And more," "in little all the sphere," and "one world [with] / Another to attend him" (lines 5–7, 22, 47–48). In giving and making man treasure and pleasure, God is restoring man's prelapsarian state (see "Miserie," lines 67–72). For the place of "Man" in "The Church," see Richard Strier, "Ironic Humanism in *The Temple*," in Claude Summers and Ted-Larry Pebworth, eds., "*Too Rich to Clothe the Sunne*": *Essays on George Herbert* (Pittsburgh, 1980), pp. 34–39, and Stanley Fish, *The Living Temple: George Herbert and Catechizing* (Berkeley and Los Angeles, 1978), pp. 85–86.

44. "A common treatment of a horse or dog with bad eyes was to blow a powder into them to clear the film"; Hutchinson's note, p. 504.

His humanity.[45] This is precisely what Herbert does. From the dazzling "statelier cabinet," he is barred access ("sparkling light accesse denies") and he does not speculate upon it. He simply moves on, happily, from "the majesty" to "the other":

> But all thy sweets are packt up in the other;
> Thy mercies thither flock and flow:
> That as the first affrights,
> This may allure us with delights;
> Because this box we know;
> For we have all of us just such another.   [19–24]

As Herbert leaves the Trinity for the Incarnation, he feels pleasure, even relief ("the first affrights"). The humorous homeliness of the initial "cabinets" conceit is continued in "packt up" and purposely intensified when, in the fifth line of this stanza, the second "cabinet" becomes "a box"—a box, as Herbert says elsewhere, "where sweets compacted lie" ("Vertue," line 10). The Incarnation is presented as having been an act of divine "accommodation" to the limitations of the human capacity for response. We can be "allured" by the incarnate God because "this box we know; / For we have all of us just such another." God has put aside His majesty and made Himself approachable, even familiar.[46]

Thus far, "Ungratefulnesse" has been pure praise. The only ungratefulness the poem has envisioned—the affront of idolatry to God the Creator—has been presented as happily forestalled. All of stanza 4, especially the final long line ("For we have all of us"), is calculated to imply that "now," after revelation and Incarnation, it is natural, easy, almost inevitable that we love God. In the final stanza, however, Herbert turns from contemplating God's actions vis-à-vis man to man's vis-à-vis God. After all the evocation of "bountie" in the poem, of

45. For the distinction between "theology of glory" and "theology of the cross," see Luther's *Theses for the Heidelberg Disputation* in Dillenberger, pp. 502–3, and the "Proofs of the Theses," in *Luther's Works*, American edition, gen. eds. Jaroslav Pelikan and Helmut Lehman (Philadelphia, 1958), XXXI, 52–53 (this edition will be cited henceforth as *LW*). For a warning against "speculation on the majesty," see *Commentary on Galatians*, pp. 42–43 (*debeamus abstinere speculatione maiestatis; WA*, XL¹, 75). On leaving the majestic, "naked" Godhead alone, see Luther's commentary on Psalm 51 in *LW*, XII, 312 ff. (*WA*, XL², 329 ff.: *relinquat deum in Maiestate; Deum non nudum, sed vestitum . . . necesse est nos apprehendere*). On cleaving to the humanity of Christ as the opposite of speculating on the majesty, see *Commentary on Galatians*, pp. 42–45 (*haere in ista humanitate; WA* XL¹, 75).

46. It is typical of Herbert to stress God's accommodation to man's emotional rather than his epistemological limitations. For the more familiar cognitively oriented account of accommodation, see *Institutes*, I.xiii.1.

God's free unlocking of all He has to man (*"Thou hast but two* rare cabinets full of treasure"),

> man is close, reserv'd, and dark to thee. [25]

These are carefully chosen adjectives. They suggest the exact opposites of "bountie"—tightness, closedness, secretiveness, purposeful withholding. The next two lines explicate these adjectives (Herbert alters the rhyme scheme of the poem here to have its final stanza fall into two very tight, "close," and distinct grammatical and prosodic units, separated by a full stop):[47]

> When thou demandest but a heart,
> He cavils instantly. [26–27]

Man cannot simply accept and be grateful. Instead, he "cavils"— argues, sets up small objections and qualifications, wants an escape hatch or certain guarantees.[48]

That God "demandest but a heart" is Herbert's version of "Thou shalt love the Lord thy God with all thy heart, and all thy soul." This command, as Jesus insists, "is written in the law" (Luke 10:27–29, quoting Deuteronomy 6:5). The purpose of the Law in Pauline and Reformation theology is to "reveal sin," to make clear the corruption of man's nature and the exact character of this corruption (see Romans 3:20: "by the law is the knowledge of sin"). By making obedience to the Law "merely" a matter of inward disposition rather than particular acts, Jesus made obedience to the Law more, not less difficult. Luther warns that "you must not understand the term 'law' [in Saint Paul's epistles] in its everyday sense as something which explains what acts are permitted or forbidden. This holds for ordinary laws, and you keep them by doing what they enjoin, even though you have no heart in doing so. But God judges according to your inmost convictions; His Law must be fulfilled in your very heart." Again, in explaining why Saint Paul calls the Law "spiritual" (Romans 7:14), Luther argues that it is "spiritual" because "no one keeps it unless everything he does springs from his inmost heart"; "it is one thing," Luther says, "to do what the law enjoins, and quite another to *fulfil* the law"— "to *fulfil* the law we must meet its requirements gladly and lovingly." Those who think they can fulfill the law by doing or not doing specific

47. Until the final stanza, the rhyme scheme of "Ungratefulnesse" is A – B – C – C – B – A; in the final stanza, it is A – B – A – C – B – C. The syllabic pattern remains constant (10 – 8 – 6 – 8 – 6 – 10).

48. For the significance of the legalistic nature of this "caviling," see the analysis of "Obedience" and related poems, in chap. 4. For a Miltonic use of "cavil" in just Herbert's way (as expressing the nature of fallen consciousness), see Adam's self-rebuke in *Paradise Lost*, X.758–59.

things "are unaware how much the law demands; in particular, a heart that is free and eager and joyful." The demand for love and gratitude, for a heart that is "free and eager and joyful," reveals the inward "reluctance and unwillingness" with which man, by (corrupted) nature, always faces God.⁴⁹ "He cavils instantly." This inward reluctance is the deepest meaning of sin.

"Instantly" is Herbert's word for spontaneity (compare "Would he have gold, I lend it instantly"). Man cannot but cavil—instantly. He is incapable of even momentary self-transcendence. Nothing would seem more "natural" than to respond to bounty with gratitude, but this response is exactly what man's nature is incapable of. In the Fall, according to Calvin, man "shamefully spurned God's great bounty" (*Institutes*, II.i.4). The lines from "Ungratefulnesse" that we have been discussing illuminate and are illuminated by their parallel in "Unkindnesse": "When thy grace / Sues for my heart, I thee displace." Both passages point to the quality in man which Emerson called "mean egotism," to the quality which keeps him (us), in Luther's phrase, "curved in upon himself" (*incurvatus in se*) rather than open toward God, trapped in prudential considerations.⁵⁰ The "box" imagery of the fourth stanza of "Ungratefulnesse" associates man with Christ through Christ's assumption of a human body, but the final lines of "Ungratefulnesse" portray man as being properly represented only by a box-within-box construction:

> In his poore cabinet of bone
>   Sinnes have their box apart,
> Defrauding thee, who gavest two for one.   [28–30]

These lines further explicate "close, reserv'd, and dark." They give us the "place" that is properly so described. In a world of "bountie," where all good things "flock and flow" toward man, sin establishes a place "apart," a piece of private property, locked up. And this "place," sin's "box apart" in man, is, as the rhyme that links the two halves of the stanza tells us, the heart.

In the course of a discussion of Herbert's passion "to understand and to relate," Stein provocatively remarks that Herbert's "deepest sense of the God he would praise and love *requires* the images of

49. The quotations from Luther in this paragraph are from "Preface to Romans," Dillenberger, pp. 20–21, 31.

50. For Emerson's phrase, see "Nature," pt. 1, in *The Selected Writings of Ralph Waldo Emerson*, ed. Brooks Atkinson (New York, 1940), p. 6; for Luther's, see *WA*, LVI (*Römerbriefvorlesung*), 304–5, 356 ff. (*Lectures on Romans*, pp. 159–60, 218 ff.). For how Luther's use of *curvatus* differs from Augustine's apparently similar usage, see Nygren, *Agape*, p. 713, and Rupp, *The Righteousness of God*, p. 165.

reluctance and conflict he finds in himself" (emphasis mine).[51] Stein does not elaborate further and does not offer an account of why this should be so. *Agape* provides the explanation. In order for God's love to be recognized as utterly free, it must be clear that there is nothing at all in man which could merit or stimulate this love. As Nygren explains, "when God's love is directed to the sinner, then the position is clear; all thought of valuation is excluded in advance; for if God, the Holy One, loves the sinner, it cannot be because of his sin, but in spite of his sin."[52] The conception, then, necessitates a particular view of both God and man. In developing the implications of the conception, a writer or theologian can, at particular moments, place his emphasis on either one or the other pole of the dialectic, on sin or grace. In "Sepulchre," Herbert shifts from sin to grace in the final moment, so that the ultimate emphasis is on the wonder of God's love. In "Ungratefulnesse," Herbert shifts in the other direction, so the final effect is penitential rather than celebratory ("Sighs and Grones" immediately follows it).

Yet in the portrayal of one pole the other must also be present, at least by implication. "Ungratefulnesse" cannot be simply and solely a confession of sin. It must also contain the solution to the dilemma on which it ends. And it clearly does so. The solution is the very conception of "bountie" that so much of the poem celebrates and that reveals, by contrast, the inadequacy of man's responses. The bleak-ness of the finale is contradicted by the assertions with which each of the first three stanzas ends: "we shall be better gods than he"; "Unto thy self in everlasting pleasure"; "by that powder thou wilt make us see." Despite the rhetorical weight of its conclusion, the poem as a whole precludes believing that the God who redeemed the wretched potential idolaters of stanza 1 would allow Himself to be defrauded by man's caviling, however deep its roots in our nature. God does not expect to find in man what He expects to give him. A heart that is "free and eager and joyful" is given only by the Spirit. Only the Spirit gives us "that happiness and freedom at which the law aims."[53] The unique prerogative of God's justice is to know the heart. The unique prerogative of His love is to change it.

In the overall context of *The Temple*, "Ungratefulnesse" must be read with its complement, "Gratefulnesse," in mind. This later poem (it is not in "W") includes the knowledge of sin which "Ungrateful-nesse" teaches, but entirely absorbs this knowledge into a celebration of God's *agape*. In a remarkable rhetorical coup which gives us a kind

51. Herbert's *Lyrics*, p. 97.
52. *Agape and Eros*, p. 77. On pp. 72–75, Nygren discusses the Romantic position (as elaborated by Max Scheler) that "the sinner is in fact better than the righteous man."
53. "Preface to Romans," Dillenberger, pp. 21–22.

of double vision, Herbert has his speaker humorously present a plea
for growth in grace as a typical and recognizable instance of "cavil-
ing":

> Thou that hast giv'n so much to me,
> Give one thing more, a gratefull heart,
> See how thy beggar works on thee
> > By art.
>
> He makes thy gifts occasion more,
> And sayes, If he in this be crost,
> All thou hast giv'n him heretofore
> > Is lost.   [1–8]

Herbert's gift for tonal mimicry is at its peak here. These are the very
accents of caviling. Yet despite the intimacy of its knowledge of sin,
"Gratefulnesse" goes serenely on. In arranging man's salvation, God
has figured in the meanness of man's nature.

> But thou didst reckon, when at first
> Thy word our hearts and hands did crave,
> What it would come to at the worst
> > To save.   [9–12]

"At the worst" is a joke here. "The worst" is the ordinary and un-
varying state of unregenerate human nature.

2

The Attack on Reason

With "Ungratefulnesse" we come to the very center of Herbert's conception of sin. What is striking about this conception is how inward and psychologically intimate it is. It locates sin in the tiniest motions and impulses of the heart. Luther constantly inveighed against "the monks" and "the sophists" for understanding "the flesh" and "the concupiscence of the flesh" in Saint Paul as solely or primarily referring to the body and bodily lusts.[1] Luther insisted that in Pauline usage "the flesh" (*sarx*) did not signify a specific part or aspect of man's being but his entire spiritual state *coram Deo*; "flesh" refers to all aspects of fallen man's nature, "to everything that is born of the flesh, that is, *the entire self*, body and spirit."[2] Nothing in man is free of sin; no *scintilla* or citadel within him remains untainted and aloof. Moreover, the primary meaning of "flesh" for Saint Paul is "the very righteousness and wisdom of the flesh"; the primary lust of the flesh is pride.[3] The sophisters and schoolmen speak only of "outward and

1. *Commentary on Galatians*, ed. Watson, pp. 143–44, 212–13, 402, and, especially, 498: "the schoolmen take the concupiscence of the flesh for carnal lust" (see *WA*, XL², 83: *sophistae concupiscentiam carnis interpretantur libidinem*). See also *WA*, *Tischreden* 4, No. 5097 (*Illi inepti asini nullam sciverunt tentationem quam libidinis*), and *That These Words of Christ, 'This is my Body,' Still Stand Firm against the Fanatics*, LW, XXXVII, 96. Calvin picks up the theme in *Institutes*, II.i.8–9, and II.iii.1. For an extremely interesting treatment contemporary with Herbert, see Downame, *Christian Warfare*, who devotes an entire chapter (Pt. IV, bk. i, chap. 4) to refuting "the erroneous conceit of the Papists, who by the flesh understand the body and the sensuall faculties onely."

2. *Against Latomus*, LW, XXXII, 228 ff.; "Preface to Romans," Dillenberger, p. 25 (emphasis mine). See also *The Bondage of the Will*, p. 247.

3. *Commentary on Galatians*, ed. Watson, p. 212; *Lectures on Romans*, p. 218.

gross faults and unrighteousness." They do not consider the sins of
the mind and heart toward God, the "uncleanness and inward poison
lurking in the heart, as incredulity, doubting, contemning, and hating
of God." They especially do not "go to the very head of this beast
which is called Reason, which is the fountain and headspring of all
mischiefs."[4] For Luther (and, as Luther believed, for Saint Paul), sin
was primarily found in man's highest rather than his lowest faculties.[5]
Most of all, it was to be found in "natural reason."

Luther's attack on reason has been widely and sometimes wilfully
misinterpreted.[6] He was not attacking the faculty of reason as such,
the capacity to understand concepts or make inferences and distinc-
tions. He was attacking the way the faculty, left to itself, inevitably
operates in the realm of religion. Man deeply desires that God be
"reasonable," that the realm of religion be rationally apprehensible.
The fundamental assumption that reason leads man to make, the
assumption that brings the faculty itself into disgrace and leads Luther
to seek to cut off "the very head of this beast," is that there must be
some (humanly) intelligible basis for God's decision to save certain
men and condemn all others. For Luther, this assumption represents
a fundamental unwillingness to "let God be God," to believe that God
can be just and good "when he speaks and acts above and beyond
the definitions in Justinian's Code, or the fifth Book of Aristotle's
Ethics."[7] Reason assumes that there must be some basis *in man* for
God's decisions. It therefore produces "works-religion," the proudest,
most anxiety-producing, most perverse and utterly "natural" way of
conceiving of the path to salvation.

On the basis of reason, man wants the responsibility for his sal-
vation to lie with him. He therefore both puts an intolerable burden
on himself and "robs God of the glory" of saving man; ultimately,
this is self-worship, the worst form of idolatry.[8] Man's reason will not
let him give up his proud and idolatrous commitment to "the opinion
of righteousness," the twofold belief that salvation is to be attained
through righteousness and righteousness is to be obtained by obeying
laws and doing works. Only through grace can man escape from the
toils of "the beast which is called the opinion of righteousness" and

---

4. *Commentary on Galatians,* ed. Watson, p. 224.

5. *The Bondage of the Will,* pp. 251–52; *Commentary on Galatians,* p. 212.

6. See B. A. Gerrish, *Grace and Reason: A Study of the Theology of Luther* (Oxford, 1962),
chap. 1 and passim; also Rupp, *The Righteousness of God,* chap. 1.

7. In his *Disputation against Scholastic Philosophy* (Thesis 17), Luther asserted that "Man
is by nature unable to want God to be God (*LW,* XXXI, 10). To "let God be God" might
be said to be the entire message of *The Bondage of the Will* (see esp. pp. 209, 232–34,
252–53, 314–15). The quotation is from *Bondage of the Will,* pp. 232–33. The fifth book
of *Nicomachean Ethics* concerns justice.

8. *Bondage of the Will,* p. 252; *Lectures on Romans,* p. 220.

"come to a knowledge of the freedom of faith," that is, freedom from self-concern.[9] Reason works on the basis of self-interest. It seeks for some profit in everything it does. Whether the profit being sought was material or not made no difference in Luther's view.[10] The more spiritual the profit sought, the more perverse the endeavor. Man is so curved in upon himself through this kind of natural prudence that "he bends not only physical but also spiritual goods to himself, seeking himself in all things."[11] "Human nature and natural reason, as it is called," are wed by birth to self-seeking and "the opinion of righteousness"; "nature of itself cannot drive it out or even recognize it, but rather regards it as a mark of the most holy will."[12] Reason must seek to avoid the confrontation with God that produces the genuine sense of sin and the recognition of total dependence.

The theological attack on reason pervades Herbert's poetry. Herbert's language is not as hyperbolic as Luther's, but his theology is the same. It is no accident that in "Ungratefulnesse," caviling suggests perverse ingenuity as well as meanness of spirit. The image of sin's "box apart" also has this potential; as soon as the "box apart" is imagined as something *constructed*, the implication surfaces. This happens in "Confession," a poem about the power of "affliction" to penetrate even the "close, reserv'd, and dark" places in the psyche:

> O what a cunning guest
> Is this same grief! within my heart I made
> Closets; and in them many a chest;
> And, like a master in my trade,
> In those chests, boxes; in each box, a till:
> Yet grief knows all, and enters when he will.　　　[1–6]

This stanza praises "grief" for being more cunning than sin. In "Grace," Herbert prays for God to cross sin's "art"; in "The H Communion," God meets "sinnes force *and art*" (emphasis mine). In "Confession," art, making, is again associated with sin; there is no mistaking the self-contempt in "like a master in my trade." Herbert is not here speaking as a poet; he is speaking as a regenerate and sinful Christian. Everyone is a master of *this* trade. The imagery of craftsmanship here expresses the intensity and ineradicability of the "natural" human

9. *Commentary on Galatians,* ed. Watson, pp. 299 ff., and passim; *The Freedom of a Christian,* Dillenberger, pp. 71 ff.

10. *Freedom of a Christian,* p. 79. There is a remarkable instance of the attitude Luther was attacking in Joyce's portrayal of Stephen Dedalus, in an ascetic phase, feeling "his soul in devotion pressing like fingers the keyboard of a great cash register" (*Portrait of the Artist as a Young Man,* Penguin ed. [New York, 1976], p. 148).

11. *Lectures on Romans,* p. 219.

12. *Freedom of a Christian,* pp. 85, 72, respectively.

desire to withdraw or withhold from God, to establish and maintain a place in the self apart from Him. Ingenuity is equated with egotism and, most of all, with the attempt at evasion. The more cunning the art—and the more cunningly compact the description of it—the more intense the self-contempt: "In those chests, boxes; in each box, a till." Stein's talk of grief outwitting "man's ability to compartmentalize his feelings"[13] responds accurately to the tone and the imagery of the lines, but is misleading about what is at issue—evasion and "re-servedness," not compartmentalization (rather too modern and Romantic a sin).

In the second stanza of "Confession," "Gods afflictions" are "too subtill for the subt'llest hearts," where creaturely subtlety is clearly, as in the Mosaic characterization of the serpent, a negative value; in the third stanza we are told that "No smith can make such locks but they [God's afflictions] have keys." Ingenuity, subtlety, seeks to lock the heart, or some compartment in the heart, from God. The third stanza, which begins the praise of confession in the poem, is entirely built on the contrast between the open and the closed heart—"Onely an open breast / Doth shut them out" (the confession in question is, of course, directly to God). This stanza concludes:

> Smooth open hearts no fastning have; but fiction
> Doth give a hold and handle to affliction.   [23–24]

The word "fiction" here is the culmination of the associations between human art, craft, or ingenuity and evading, lying, or constructing pretenses. "Fiction" here has its root meaning of "something made." This couplet completes the association of ingenuity with the closed or "fastened" heart.[14]

The conception of sin in "Confession" parallels the anti-intellectual and antitechnological implications in the biblical account of the Fall. "Sighs and Grones" explicitly relies on these implications. Despite its rather hysterical and overheated quality, this poem too portrays sin in a surprisingly intellectual way. In characterizing himself as the ill steward who has abused his master's stock, "destroy'd [his] woods," Herbert goes on to confess:

> my head did ake,
> Till it found out how to consume thy goods.   [10b–11]

13. *Herbert's Lyrics*, p. 88.
14. On "the economy of the closed heart," see Edward Hubler, *The Sense of Shakespeare's Sonnets* (1952; rpt. New York, 1962), pp. 95–109.

Apparently a certain amount of ingenuity was necessary to effect this consumption of God's "goods" (the pun is surely intentional and adds an element of ungratefulness to the line). If Herbert had merely wanted an image of raging appetite, he would not have drawn attention to the speaker's head and would not have introduced language of calculation, of finding out how. The intellectuality of the process is intended, as is the speaker's presentation of his head as in "it" acting independently of his will—"My head did ake, / Till *it* found out." The next stanza continues this complication of the language of appetite, of *concupiscentia*, and is saturated in biblical imagery:

> I have deserv'd that an Egyptian night
> Should thicken all my powers; because my lust
> Hath still sow'd fig-leaves to exclude thy light.   [14–16]

The speaker is imagining for himself an internalized version of the punishment visited on pharaoh in Exodus because he continually—"still"—behaves like Adam in Genesis.

The allusion to Genesis purposely conflates two verses. In Genesis 3:7, Adam and Eve "knew that they were naked; and they sewed fig-leaves together, and made themselves aprons." This is a separate action from that described in the next verse: "and Adam and his wife hid themselves from the presence of the Lord God amongst the trees of the garden." Herbert's lines, by substituting the homonymous "sow'd" for "sewed," tightens the connection between technological ingenuity and the attempt to reject or escape from God. It eliminates any experience of shame *coram hominibus*, prior to God's demand for self-disclosure ("the Lord God called unto Adam, and said unto him, Where art thou?"). And, by making "my lust" the subject of "sow'd," Herbert presents the primary impulse of lust not as sexual but as the desire to establish a secret place, a place apart "close, reserv'd, and dark." Man, in this view, constantly uses his ingenuity to create a place where he can be happily "curved in upon himself," free from the demanding attentiveness of God's love.[15] This lust is an inevitable stimulus to ingenuity.

In revising and expanding *The Temple*, Herbert placed "Sighs and Grones" between "Ungratefulnesse" and another poem that also alludes to the fig leaf passage in Genesis. "The World" is an allegorical narrative in which four personified abstractions of increasing potency

---

15. Compare Stein, pp. 103–4, and Luther on Genesis 3:7 in *Luther's Commentary on Genesis*, trans. J. Theodore Mueller (Grand Rapids, 1958), I, 73.

are presented as attacking, in turn, a stately house which "Love built."[16] In the third stanza, the house (which began as "the world") becomes man, and the context becomes psychological:

> Then enter'd Sinne, and with that Sycomore,
> Whose leaves first sheltred man from drought & dew,
> Working and winding slily evermore,
> The inward walls and sommers cleft and tore.   [11–14]

The relation between sin and ingenuity is presented as one of subtle concomitance rather than of straightforward causality—"*with* that Sycomore"—but here, as in "Sighs and Grones," there is no mistaking the association. The suggestion seems to be that sin is the inevitable inward accompaniment of even the most innocent and "natural" acts of human ingenuity. Herbert is himself perhaps working rather "slyly" here since the construction of these lines makes it impossible for us not to begin by adopting a positive attitude toward "that Sycomore, / Whose leaves first sheltred man from drought & dew."[17]

The characterization of sin as "*working and winding* slily evermore" has resonances throughout *The Temple* (when Herbert says of the Bible that "this verse marks that, and both do make a motion / Unto a third, that ten leaves off doth lie," he is surely telling us how to read his own volume). In "Confession," God's afflictions are seen as working and winding into man ("No scrue, no piercer can / Into a piece of timber *work and winde,* / As Gods afflictions into man"), but it is clear in the poem that sin creates the conditions that force God to be thus cunning. In "Grace," death is presented as "working" in man, but, of course, sin and death are intimately related, and the image of the mole in "Grace"—"Death is still working *like a mole,* / And digs

16. Joseph Mede's caveat about the "fundamental Error" of commentators on Revelation in assuming that "the *Events* succeeded one another in the same *Series* and order as the *Visions* do" is also applicable to Herbert's "The World"—the progression of visions in the poem cannot be understood as historical or chronological (for Mede, I am indebted to an unpublished essay by Michael Murrin, "Revelation and Two Seventeenth-Century Commentators"). "The World" is best understood as a sequence in which the speaker-seer is presented with various threats to God's order and their respective antidotes. The narration represents the order of the appearance of these visions to the speaker-seer. Perhaps the chronology of the visions represents the development of the seer's religious consciousness: from Christian humanism ("Wisdom") in stanza one to total dependence on grace.

17. "Sycomore" was both "a species of fig-tree common in Egypt" and "a large species of maple introduced into Britain from the Continent, and grown as a shady ornamental tree" (*OED*, 1, 2). For a rather literal-minded account of why Herbert identified the fig tree of Genesis with a "sycomore," see Don Cameron Allen, "George Herbert's 'Sycomore,' " *MLN*, 59 (1944), 493–95. A very similar entrapment of the reader occurs in Spenser, *The Faerie Queene*, I.i.7, the beginning of the series of events that lead to Error's den.

my grave at each remove"—serves to emphasize further how thoroughly "Confession" is presenting God as, so to speak, beating sin at its own game: "We are the earth; and they [God's afflictions], / *Like moles within us*, heave, and cast about" ("Confession," lines 13–14). In general in *The Temple*, it is sin that is presented as "working and winding."[18] In "A Wreath," man's "crooked winding ways" are associated with deceitfulness and with worldly wisdom of a particularly politic sort while God's ways are associated with "straightness" and "simplicitie." The association of "winding" ways with the wisdom of the serpent is not a remarkable one, though (as in the "winding stair" of "Jordan" [I]), Herbert puts it to some interesting uses. His presentation of sin as "working" is more distinctive. He generally uses this word to express the terrible dynamism of sin ("Originall concupisence is such an active thing . . . that it is ever attempting, or doing, one mischief or other" [*CP*, p. 238]).[19]

Herbert's most important presentation of sin as "working" is "Sinnes Round." It is surely no coincidence that Herbert's two most formally and conspicuously interwoven and circular poems, "A Wreath" and "Sinnes Round," are both presentations of sin. "Sinnes Round" focuses on the dynamism of sin. The speaker of the poem is clearly a regenerate Christian since the poem begins and ends with an expression of penitence (lines 1 and 18): "Sorrie I am, my God, sorrie I am" (Luther argued that when Christ said, " 'Repent,' He called for *the entire life* of believers to be one of penitence").[20] But 1 and 18 are the only lines in the poem where the first person pronoun appears in the nominative case. In line 2, the possessive seems to separate out from the nominative ("my offenses course it in a ring"), and by the fourth line, the speaker has taken to characterizing his thoughts in the third person—"*their* cockatrice *they* hatch and bring." The pronouns of the poem are enacting the Pauline formula of Romans 7:15; "it is no more I that do it, but sin that dwelleth in me." Like "Justice" (I), "Sinnes Round" is concerned with what Richard Sibbes called the "mystery

---

18. The exceptions to this generalization are "Coloss. 3.3," where the conceit of the spiritual life having a "double motion" like the sun forces a change in the association of winding, and "The Starre," another poem exploring a conceit—"That winding is their fashion / Of adoration." It should be noted, however, that for the speaker of "The Starre," winding can be a "fashion / Of adoration" only after he is entirely "disengag'd from sinne and sicknesse"—that is, after he is dead. And in terms of the reader's experience, "Coloss. 3.3" does not, in fact, "wind toward" God. It proceeds toward Him in a "hidden" but straight line. The poem is not interwoven or circular in the way "A Wreath" and "Sinnes Round" are.

19. Compare Luther, *Against Latomus*, LW, XXXII, 253; Calvin, *Institutes*, II.i.8.

20. This is the first of the "95 Theses" (*Disputation on the Power and Efficacy of Indulgences*), Dillenberger, p. 490 (emphasis mine). For the significance, see Strier, "Herbert and Tears," esp. pp. 224–25.

of sinfulnesse." "Let us labour," Sibbes exhorted his auditors, "to have as deepe conceits in our understandings as we can of that mystery of sinfulnesse that is in us."[21] Luther held that the biblical conception of sin is the most difficult and fundamental doctrine in all of theology.[22]

"Sinnes Round" gives *thoughts* a striking priority in the genesis of sin and presents this genesis in a striking way.[23] Herbert's critique of ingenuity and "art" again emerges. He presents the process of sinning as a perverse act of generation or creation. His emphasis is not on the relation of thoughts to external stimuli but on the mysteriously "creative" power of the mind:

> My thoughts are working like a busie flame,
> Untill their cockatrice they hatch and bring:
> And when they once have perfected their draughts,
> My words take fire from my inflamed thoughts.   [3–6]

The cockatrice image brings serpents into the stanza by transforming the flame into a serpent (since cockatrices are hatched by serpents from cocks' eggs), but even more deeply relevant than the serpent association is the biblical context of the cockatrice itself. As Hutchinson points out in his note, the cockatrice appears in Isaiah 59:5: the wicked "hatch cockatrice' eggs, and weave the spider's webb." The Authorized Version glosses Isaiah 59 as treating "the nature of sin." The salient feature of this chapter is a constant movement from actions back to the heart and mind: the wicked "conceive mischief, and bring forth iniquity"; their thoughts are "thoughts of iniquity"; they are continually "conceiving and uttering *from the heart* words of falsehood" (and, of course, "their works are works of iniquitie"). We are very close to Herbert here, though it is deeply significant, as we have seen, that Herbert applies Isaiah's characterizations of "the wicked" to the regenerate.[24]

The emphasis in lines 3–6 of "Sinnes Round" is all on busyness and directed energy. Something is being created or is emerging into clarity in the foul rag-and-bone shop (or perhaps smithy) of the speaker's heart. The process in question is intensely teleological—"My thoughts are working . . . *Untill*." The pivotal line of the stanza is, "And when they once have perfected their draughts" (line 5). There

---

21. *The Fountain Opened, or the Mystery of Godliness Revealed*, in *The Complete Works of Richard Sibbes*, ed. Alexander Grosart (Edinburgh, 1862), V, 474.

22. *Commentary on Psalm 51, LW*, XII, 351.

23. Sibbes asserts the same priority in *The Fountain Opened*. The passage already quoted continues: "It is not to be conceived, what a depth of corruption is in this heart of ours, and how it issues out in sinful *thoughts, and speeches, and actions* every day" (emphasis mine).

24. See pp. 16–17 above.

is no mistaking the intellectuality of this; what is being created is a perfect conception or plan.[25] It is important to note that these "draughts" are conceived of as existing in a fully "perfected" mental state *prior* to their existence in verbal form: "And when they once have perfected their draughts, / My words take fire from my inflamed thoughts." "Words" and "thoughts" are being sharply distinguished. Each of the perfected "draughts" is what Sidney called an "*Idea* or fore-conceit" of a "work," and these draughts have a normative as well as a temporal priority ("any understanding knoweth that the skill of the artificer standeth in that *Idea* or fore-conceit of the work, and not in the work itself").[26] The connection between craftsmanship and this conception of "draughts" is a deeply entrenched one, deriving ultimately from the *Timaeus*, as in, "the craftsman maketh his worke by the patterne which he had erst conceyved in his mynde."[27] The Sidneyan analogy makes it clear that what Herbert is describing in stanza 1 of "Sinnes Round" is the perfection of the "imaginative ground-plot[s]" of a whole series of *unprofitable* inventions; he is describing the process of "invention" itself in sinister terms. His wit as well as his will is infected, and he can only contemplate with horror (and repent) "the vigour of his own invention."[28]

25. The possibility of an Empsonian ambiguity (third type?) in "draughts" should at least be mentioned. The *OED* lists forty-seven separate senses for "draught" as a noun. I have incorporated what I take to be the primary sense of the word in the poem into my discussion (*OED* sense 34, "a plan of something to be constructed, as a building"), but other potentially relevant senses are: sense 6, "tendency, inclination, or impulse"; sense 7, "the art of drawing a net for fish, or birds"; and compound sense 48c, "draught-holt," "a hole by which air is admitted to a furnace," which would connect the imagery of stanza 1 very tightly to that of stanza 2. It would also be interesting to know whether Herbert intended his readers to be aware of *OED* senses 46 and 47: "a cesspool, sink, or sewer" a privy. The context would certainly support this association. "Draught" is used in this sense in the AV translation of Matthew 15:17.

26. Sir Philip Sidney, *An Apology for Poetry*, ed. Geoffrey Shepherd (London, 1965), p. 101.

27. Philippe de Mornay, *Of the Trewnes of the Christian Religion*, trans. Sir Philip Sidney and Arthur Golding, in Albert Feuillerat, *The Prose Works of Sir Philip Sidney* (Cambridge, 1912), III, 268. The context is an account of Christ as the Logos of the Father; the sentence is quoted in Shepherd, ed., *Apology*, p. 158, as a gloss on the "*Idea* or fore-conceit" passage.

28. For "an imaginative ground-plot of a profitable invention," see Shepherd, ed., *Apology*, p. 124. On invention in rhetorical and poetic composition, as "the finding out of the matter," see Thomas Wilson, *The Arte of Rhetorique*, introduction by George Herbert Mair (Oxford, 1909), p. 6. For Sidney's distinction between man's erected wit and his fallen will, see *Apology*, p. 101. For praise of "the vigour of his [the poet's] own invention," see *Apology*, p. 100. Lawrence A. Breiner's fascinating suggestion that the "cockatrice" of Herbert's stanza is the fiery uroboros cockatrice of the alchemists and represents "the final stage in the procedure by which the philosopher's stone was achieved" is appropriate to the context of perverse ingenuity and "hatching" ("Herbert's Cockatrice," *MP*, 77 [1979], 10–17).

In the second stanza, the speaker's words "take fire" from the volcano of his thoughts (line 8), and the verbalization of the thoughts seems to stoke the furnace further—"by their breathing [the words] ventilate the ill" (line 10). The process begun in stanza 1 is not yet complete—"words suffice not, where are lewd intentions" (line 11). Again the emphasis is on the power and priority of the mental, of "lewd *intentions.*" The new transition, from words to hands, makes explicit the submerged analogy to craft:

> My hands do joyn to finish the inventions.   [12]

This movement from invention to inventions, leads Herbert to the second major antitechnological locus in Genesis:

> My hands to joyn to finish the inventions:
> And so my sinnes ascend three stories high,
> As Babel grew, before there were dissensions.   [13–15]

Herbert presents his thoughts, words, and hands as cooperating harmoniously to give material reality to the *Idea* or fore-conceit "hatched" in stanza 1. Herbert's sins ascend triumphantly to form a great structure. We are perhaps to conceive of the "furnace" in the poem as burning the bricks for this structure (Genesis 11:3: "And they said to one another, Go to, let us make brick, and burn them thoroughly"). The Babel image in these lines primarily emphasizes perverse cooperation, but the image necessarily brings with it associations of presumption and of challenging God—perhaps of perverse pride in creation.

Conceptually as well as grammatically, "Sinnes Round" comes to a full stop here, at line 15, in the middle of the third stanza. The process begun in stanza 1 has achieved its *telos.* The structure of the poem seems to leave room for a countermovement, and for half a line, it looks as if one has begun—"Yet ill deeds loiter not" (line 16a). Just at this point, however, the implications of the formal structure of the poem fully emerge. The optimism of "Yet ill deeds loiter not" does not survive the completion of the sentence, though it perhaps survives the completion of the line. "Yet ill deeds loiter not: for they supplie" still allows us positive expectations about what the deeds supply occasions for, that is, thoughts and acts of penitence. It turns out, however, that what the "yet" of line 16 contradicts is precisely the experience of closure which the culminating Babel simile and the summarizing "And so" construction have produced. The line turns out to be a trap. Denial of closure has been a pattern in the poem ("And when they once have perfected their draughts"; "But words suffice not where are lewd intentions") and this pattern continues. The "ill deeds loyter not" because "they supplie" "New thoughts of sinning" (line 17a). Instead of changing its direction, the poem curves in upon itself, forcing us truly to perceive the process it describes as a "ring" (line 2). Each link or step in the structure only leads forward— that is, backward—to the force which generates the whole, "thoughts of sinning." Once again the horror of the poem is located in the process it evokes rather than in the products of that process. Once again we come back to the *Ideas* or fore-conceits, the "working" thoughts.

One other poem in "The Church" forms part of the sinister "working and winding" constellation, "Jordan" (II), the original title of which was "Invention."[29] "Sinnes Round" and "Jordan" (II) are closely akin; seeing them together highlights the sinister implications of "Jordan" (II). Both poems focus on and attempt to dramatize the phenomenology of "invention." The particular psychology of elaborate poetic creation presented autobiographically in "Jordan" (II) closely parallels the general psychology of sinning presented abstractly in "Sinnes Round." Both focus on the peculiar independence of thoughts from conscious direction, a phenomenon which Herbert found deeply disturbing and for which he was deeply "sorrie." When, in "Jordan" (II), Herbert recalls and imaginatively recreates the time when he had "sought out quaint words, and trim invention" (line 3), he recalls that when he had done so, his thoughts "began to burnish, sprout, and swell" (line 4). The pun on "burnish"—as meaning both "to shine" (reinforced by the presence of "lustre" in line 2) and "to grow plump"— gives it the same odd mixture of terms relating to craft and terms relating to organic processes so prominent in the description of the speaker's "working" thoughts in "Sinnes Round."[30] In the lines that summarize the whole process evoked in "Jordan" (II), Herbert recalls that

> As flames do work and winde, when they ascend,
> So did I weave my self into the sense. [13–14; emphasis mine]

These lines parallel the "busie" serpent-flame and the sinister ascension of "Sinnes Round," and they point to an important connection between ingenuity, elaborate craft, and egotistical selfhood. They pick up the horror of the final "my self" of "Miserie," which immediately precedes "Jordan" (II). Again, as in "Confession" and "Sinnes Round," the brilliance of the phrasing signals self-contempt. There is no contradiction in these poems using wit to attack wit. The witty conceits of these poems—Herbert would have liked the pun—dramatize and

---

29. See Hutchinson, pp. 1v, 102; *Williams Manuscript*, p. 74r.

30. *OED* definitions "burnish," verb[1], 1 and verb[2], 1. On the phallic sexuality of "burnish, sprout, and swell," see Vendler's comments on "swelling through store" in "The Flower" (*Poetry of Herbert*, p. 51). Herbert views his erected wit with alarm.

exemplify sinister processes. Herbert is not exempting his own in-
genuity from that he is attacking.

Thus far, the attack on reason we have seen in Herbert's poetry
has mainly been an attack on ingenuity and craft and has mainly been
expressed through imagery and allusion. At times, however, Herbert
attacks reason, or its characteristic operations, more directly. The most
notable of the direct attacks are three late poems closely related in
imagery and theme: "The Agonie," "Vanitie" (I), and "Divinitie."
These poems all take science as a metaphor for the characteristic
operations of reason, and they lead us, more explicitly than the poems
we have so far examined, toward the theological core of Herbert's
attack on reason.

"Vanitie" (I) stresses the power and authority of the scientific method:

> The fleet Astronomer can bore,
> And thred the spheres with his quick-piercing minde:
> He views their stations, walks from doore to doore,
>   Surveys, as if he had design'd
> To make a purchase there: he sees their dances,
>   And knoweth long before
> Both their full-ey'd aspects, and secret glances.   [1–7]

The astronomer is shrewd and observant and totally at home among
the spheres. He is like an important customer carefully examining
merchandise. The suggestion of smugness is unmistakable, but there
is a further edge to "Surveys, as if he had design'd / To make a pur-
chase there." These lines are disposed in such a way that the first of
them stands as a thought in itself before the second completes it. As
we read line 4, "Surveys as if he had design'd," it is difficult not to
supply an object for "design'd"—"surveys" the spheres "as if he had
design'd" *them*. This reading momentarily brings God into the stanza
and recalls the condemnation of man in "Mattens"—"He did not
heav'n and earth create, / Yet studies them, not him by whom they
be." This effect is, as I have said, momentary. The next stanza con-
tinues the imagery of boring and piercing, of violently getting under
surfaces, though the piercing it describes is literal and physical rather
than metaphorical and intellectual—"The nimble Diver with his side /
Cuts through the working waves." The third stanza returns to science
and reinforces the first. It especially picks up the suggestions of "quick-
piercing"—that is, piercing to the quick:

> The subtil Chymick can devest
> And strip the creature naked, till he finde
> The callow principles within their nest:
>   There he imparts to them his minde,

> Admitted to their bed-chamber, before
> > They appeare trim and drest
> To ordinarie suitours at the doore. [15–21]

There is a sense of violation in this stanza, especially in its first three lines, but its main emphasis is on lordly smugness ("he imparts to them his minde") and on superiority to "ordinarie suitours"—as in stanza 1 where the scientist "knoweth long before" ordinary men do. The pride implicit in these descriptions of man's ability through science to penetrate the arcana of nature (subtly presented as a rape?) culminates in the ironic vaunt that opens stanza 4: "What hath not man sought out and found. . . ?" (line 22).[31] This is a parody of "Seek, and ye shall find"; the sentence continues, "But his deare God" (line 23a). With this damning qualification, the focus shifts from man's operations to God's. "Deare" signals this shift. The "deare God" of "subtil," "quick-piercing," "ventrous" man

> yet his glorious law
> Embosomes in us, mellowing the ground
> > With showres and frosts, with love & awe.
> > > [23b–25]

The whole framework changes, indeed mellows. The softness and lovingness of "embosomes," and the shift from mechanical to natural imagery, express Herbert's sense of the differences between the characteristic operations of God and man. Man is now object rather than agent, and the poem emphasizes the contrast between the way man treats the objects of his activity and the way God treats the object of His. Man is harsh, merciless, and supercilious; God is loving and gentle—even His "frosts" are aimed at "mellowing the ground." God is a gardener, man an oilwell rigger.[32] God's "glorious law" is the law of love, but man's nature leads him to follow his inquisitive (exploitative?) intellect rather than respond to the law intimately "embo-

---

31. The sense of misplaced ingenuity as well as violence is even stronger in the Bodleian manuscript ("B") version of the line, which substitutes "wrought" for "sought" (see Hutchinson, p. 85). For "B," see Hutchinson, pp. l–lii.

32. Herbert has a strong sense of the violence involved in man's conquest of nature. Stanza 1 of "The Pearl" speaks of "What willing nature speaks, *what forc'd by fire*" (line 6; emphasis mine). Vaughan re-creates this sense of science as violation in "Vanity of Spirit," his adaptation of "Vanitie" (I):

> I summon'd nature: peirc'd through all her store,
> Broke up some seales, which none had touch'd before,
> > Her wombe, her bosome, and her head
> > Where all her secrets lay a bed
> I rifled quite . . . [9–13a]

All quotations from Vaughan are from *The Works of Henry Vaughan*, ed. L. C. Martin, 2d ed. (Oxford, 1957).

somed" in his heart "So that [he] need not say, Where's this command."
Herbert comments:

> Poore man, thou searchest round
> To find out *death*, but missest *life* at hand.   [27–28]

  The deepest meaning of "Vanitie" (I) is the rejection of outward-
oriented activism in favor of inward response. Man's activism is per-
versity ("vanity" in the senses of both "waste" and "pride"). His
activities, searching, piercing, surveying, and so forth, lead him to
ignore the activities of which he is object, the "inner weather" by
which God mellows the ground of his heart.[33] The truly important
information does not have to be sought or wrought out high and low
with proud and determined effort. It is at hand, "embosomed in us."
It is found by letting go.[34]

  "The Agonie" begins where "Vanitie" (I) ends. It is a more directly
theological piece.[35] Its ironies are more explicit, and they work in a
direction complementary to but rather different from those of "Van-
itie" (I). Where "Vanitie" (I) stresses the commanding power and pen-
etrating force of man's intellect, "The Agonie" stresses its
comprehending powers, its ability to reduce and eliminate mysteries,

---

33. I have borrowed "inner weather" from Aldous Huxley on "The Flower" in *Texts
and Pretexts: An Anthology with Commentaries* [New York, 1933], p. 13.

34. It will be obvious at this point that I do not believe Vendler's talk of "fearful
repudiation" masked under "apparently detached criticism" (*Poetry of Herbert*, p. 182)
is appropriate with regard to "Vanitie" (I). The repudiation the poem expresses is
neither fearful nor masked. It is open and, as this chapter seeks to demonstrate,
theologically motivated. The conception of "letting go" implied in my analysis is rather
different from—more positive than—the conception Fish develops in "Letting Go,"
the chapter on Herbert in *Self-Consuming Artifacts*. For Luther's version of "letting go,"
see *Babylonian Captivity* (*Pagan Servitude*), Dillenberger, p. 299. The relation between
Luther's thought and the *Gelassenheit* of the mystics is a complex matter. See Jared
Wicks, *Man Yearning for Grace: Luther's Early Spiritual Teaching* (Wiesbaden, 1969), pp.
118–23, 143–52; Heiko A. Oberman, *"Simul Gemitus et Raptus:* Luther and Mysticism,"
in *The Reformation in Medieval Perspective,* ed. Steven E. Ozment (Chicago, 1971), pp.
220–51; Steven E. Ozment, *"Homo Spiritualis": A Comparative Study of the Anthropology
of Johannes Tauler, Jean Gerson, and Martin Luther (1509–16)* (Leiden, 1969); and Gordon
Rupp, *Patterns of Reformation* (Philadelphia, 1969), Parts II and III. Bengt R. Hoffman's
Luther and the Mystics (Minneapolis, 1976) is to be used with caution.

35. I do not mean to suggest anything here about the order of composition of the
two poems; neither is in "W." It is noteworthy that they are also very close in stanza
form. Their stanzas differ only in the interpolation of a short third "A" line between
the long closing "C" lines in "Vanitie" (I) ("Vanitie" [I] = A8 – B10 – A10 – B8 – C10 –
A6 – C10; "The Agonie" = A8 – B10 – A10 – B8 – C10 – C10). The short third "A"
line in "Vanitie" (I) does not entirely eliminate the sense of the stanza ending on a
final couplet, but the quatrain-couplet structure of "The Agonie" does produce an
effect of tightness and epigrammatic power.

to find exact, quantifiable solutions to the questions that concern it. "The Agonie" includes political as well as physical scientists:

> Philosophers have measur'd mountains,
> Fathom'd the depths of seas, of states, of kings,
> Walk'd with a staffe to heav'n, and traced fountains.　　[1–3]

As in the first and third stanzas of "Vanitie" (I), Herbert seems to be celebrating the intellectual mastery of Renaissance man. There is nothing in heaven and earth which is not "fathom'd" in his philosophy. Yet the second half of the stanza asserts that

> there are two vast, spacious things,
> The which to measure it doth more behove:
> Yet few there are that sound them; Sinne and Love.　　[4–6]

Suddenly the whole vocabulary of measuring and quantification becomes bitterly ironic. The tools and methods of discursive reason are clearly inadequate and irrelevant in the face of the two "vast" things in question.

The other two stanzas of "The Agonie" detail respectively the ways in which man *can* come to know sin and love. They are both constructed to emphasize the strangeness of what they teach. Stanza 2 offers no explanation of why it is that one comes to "know Sinne" when one (somehow) "repairs" to Mount Olivet and "sees" there "A man so wrung with pains, that all his hair, / His skinne, his garments bloudie be" (lines 9–10). The couplet of the stanza has the syntactic form of a definition but is so phrased as to compound the mystery under the guise of removing it:

> Sinne is that presse and vice, which forceth pain
> To hunt his cruell food through ev'ry vein.　　[11–12]

"Is this an explanation?" one cannot but ask. It is purposely cryptic. The stanza "defining" love is even more puzzling. It too gives directions for a procedure before providing a verbal "definition," and it too is disconcertingly empirical—even, in the vocabulary of its first line, scientific:

> Who knows not Love, let him assay
> And taste that juice, which on the crosse a pike
> Did set again abroach; then let him say
> If ever he did taste the like.　　[13–16]

For Herbert, it is science that is abstract and religion that is concrete and empirical. The "knowledge" described in stanza 3 is entirely a matter of immediate experience, not of conceptual formulation. Perhaps echoing "O taste and see that the Lord is good" (Psalm 34:8),

Herbert stresses tasting—"let him . . . *taste* that juice"; "If ever he did *taste* the like." Furthermore, the content (as opposed to the predicted effect) of this experience is extremely confusing. The scenes which "illustrate" sin and love are disturbingly similar. They are both scenes of extreme and bloody pain. Again the definition that ends the stanza compounds the mystery. The formulation is now explicitly paradoxical, and, for the first time in the poem, personal:

> Love is that liquor sweet and most divine,
> Which my God feels as bloud; but I, as wine.   [17–18]

The speaker is one of those "few" (line 6) who do "sound" the two vast, spacious things. He "knows" sin and love and is thereby privy not only to the pain of stanza 2 but, and primarily, to the mysterious jubilation of the final couplet.[36]

"The Agonie" demonstrates that for Herbert, as for Luther, religion exists in a realm inaccessible to reason. In religion, Herbert says, "the well is deep, and we have *nothing of our selves* to draw with" (*CP,* p. 228; emphasis mine). Here, says Luther, in speaking of religious truths, "we are altogether in another world, far from reason."[37] Sin and love, the essential terms of religion, cannot be "fathomed" in the way that seas and states and kings can. In "Divinitie," Herbert asserts not only the irrelevance of reason to religion but the deep impropriety of man's tendency to mix them. Like "Vanitie" (I), "Divinitie" suggests that science profanes the natural universe, but its main concern is the way in which the intellect profanes religion. The opening stanzas comprise an elaborate simile analogizing man's treatment of the natural world to his treatment of "divinitie." They present the fabrication of elaborate, imaginary, and faithless constructs as the fundamental operation of reason:

> As men, for fear the starres should sleep and nod,
>   And trip at night, have spheres suppli'd;
> As if a starre were duller than a clod,
>   Which knows his way without a guide:
>
> Just so the other heav'n they also serve,
>   Divinities transcendent skie:
> Which with the edge of wit they cut and carve.
>   Reason triumphs, and faith lies by.   [1–8]

---

36. Vendler (*Poetry of Herbert,* pp. 73–74) recognizes the similarity between the scenes that "illustrate" sin and love, but is mistaken, I think, in asserting that Herbert "does not want his bystander to 'know' Sin experientially, as he 'knows' Love."

37. *Commentary on Galatians,* ed. Watson, p. 228.

Herbert here owes something to "of Meridians, and Parallels, / Man hath weav'd out a net, and this net throwne / Upon the Heavens" in Donne's "First Anniversary" (lines 278–80), but Herbert's lines seem to stress the *motive* for man's scientific speculations—"for fear the starres should sleep and nod, / And trip at night." Herbert is joking here, making fun of theory-construction; he knows that this is not truly why men have "spheres suppli'd." But the joke has a point. It means to present man as ridiculous in his inability to see beyond himself, to acknowledge that anything can proceed in a way unfamiliar to him. In lines 1 and 2, reason is earthbound, oversolicitous, and meddlesome; in lines 3 and 4, it is impertinent ("As if a starre were duller than a clod"). The implication of the stanza as a whole seems to be that man cannot acknowledge the majesty and mystery of nature, but must demean it with complicated, earthbound rationalizations. The stars presumably know their way without a guide by, as Vaughan puts it, "some hid sense their Maker gave" ("Man," line 25). Fish's remark that in *Paradise Lost*, "the Ptolemaic system is scorned as an attempt to 'save appearances' by making the heavens conform to *man's* sense of order" is relevant to Herbert.[38]

The second stanza of "Divinitie" sees the theorizing of the first as betokening an inveterate tendency in man—"Just so the other heav'n they also serve." Herbert's real concern is with this tendency in relation to "the other heaven," the "transcendent" one. Science is merely a metaphor for and manifestation of this tendency. Man cannot leave things alone and accept a mystery but must bring his cutting and carving wit into play. The emphasis here shifts from supplying unnecessary explanatory constructs to making unnecessary and impertinent distinctions. The theologians of the schools ("having sharp and strong wits, and abundance of leisure")[39] were, of course, the "cutters and carvers" par excellence of "Divinities transcendent skie." Theology is the *science* of "divinitie." It is worth noting, in this context, that Luther and Calvin did not consider themselves "theologians" in the traditional sense. They were strongly against philosophical and speculative divinity.[40] Herbert presents analytical and speculative di-

38. *Surprised by Sin*, p. 138. Herbert also seems to share Milton's sense that the reality of the celestial operations is both grander and *simpler* than man's imaginations of it. Compare Raphael's vision of "the Sphere / With Centric and Eccentric scribbl'd o'er" (*PL*, VIII, 82–83).

39. Bacon, *The Advancement of Learning*, in Hugh G. Dick, ed., *Selected Writings of Francis Bacon* (New York, 1955), p. 183. Herbert was a friend of Bacon's, the dedicatee of Bacon's *Translation of Certaine Psalms* (1625), addressed three Latin poems to Bacon (Hutchinson, pp. 435, 436, 438), and helped to translate parts of the *Advancement of Learning* into Latin (see Summers, *Herbert*, p. 32 and Appendix B).

40. See chap. 1, note 45.

vinity as the crown of "natural religion": "Reason triumphs, and faith lies by." Faith and reason are inimical and directly opposed.

The remainder of "Divinitie" focuses on the nonanalytical character of true religion. Christianity is purposely not addressed to the mind or to the taste for elaborate subtleties (here "divinitie" yields an aesthetic):

> Could not that Wisdome, which first broacht the wine,
>   Have thicken'd it with definitions?
> And jagg'd his seamlesse coat, had that been fine,
>   With curious questions and divisions?   [9–12]

"Curious questions and divisions" brings us back again to the Schoolmen. The next stanza tells us that instead of "jagg[ing] his seamlesse coat" in this way, Christ ("that Wisdome") made sure that at least the part of His doctrine that is necessary to salvation—"At least those beams of truth which onely save"—was "clear as heav'n, from whence it came" (line 14). The difficulty with Christ's basic doctrine is not in *comprehending* it:

> *Love God, and love your neighbour. Watch and pray.*
>   *Do as ye would be done unto.*
> O dark instructions; ev'n dark as day!
>   Who can these Gordian knots undo?   [17–20]

The stanza following this, however, returns to the hesitation of stanza 4 about the "clarity" of Christian doctrine ("*all* the doctrine" in line 13 is changed to "At least those beams" in 15 and 16). Christianity does seem to involve matters that are quite unclear, for instance, "he doth bid us take his bloud for wine" (line 21). Provoked by this, Herbert asserts that whatever this instruction may mean in rational paraphrase,

>   Bid what he please . . .
> To take and taste what he doth there designe,
>   Is all that saves, and not obscure.   [22a–24]

Unfortunately, this is obscure, but the closeness of these lines to the end of "The Agonie" helps clarify them. Herbert's emphasis is again on experiencing (*tasting*) rather than on cognitively understanding. And what we are to "taste"—"what he doth there designe"—must be love. "Love is that liquor sweet."[41]

41. Traditional criticism of Herbert would take both this stanza and the end of "The Agonie" as Eucharistic (see especially Martz, *Meditation*, pp. 84–85 and 292). To do this, however, is to read "he doth bid us take his bloud for wine" backwards. Coleridge saw this. His comment on the line was, "Nay, the contrary: take wine to be blood" (*Coleridge on the Seventeenth Century*, p. 536). Herbert's phrasing, both here and in "The Agonie," is purposely general in its reference, pointing to the paradoxical status of the

The conclusion of "Divinitie" returns to astronomy as a model for false (speculative) theology, for rational "divinitie":

> Then burn thy Epicycles, foolish man;
> Break all thy spheres, and save thy head.   [25–26]

It is important to be clear on the identity of "foolish man" and the meaning of "epicycles" here. Herbert is not contrasting "the great wheele of the Church" with the vagaries of private judgment.[42] Here, the epicycles and the spheres together represent the efforts of reason in the realm of "divinitie." "Foolish man" here is every man who has not had the perverse leviathan of his reason "put to death" by faith; every Christian, said Luther, "is a true priest, for first he offereth up and killeth his own reason, and the wisdom of the flesh."[43] "Save thy head" in line 26 of "Divinitie" is a triple pun. It means: (1) save (i.e., rescue) thy head from damnation; (2) attain salvation ("*save* thy head"); and (3) relax, cease from incessant intellectual effort. In sense 3, "Break all thy spheres, and save thy head" in the final stanza of "Divinitie" is exactly equivalent to "Copie out onely that [love], and *save expense*" in "Jordan" (II). "Prayer" (II), which immediately follows "Jordan" (II), insists that God "dislikes not easinesse" (line 4). Like "Prayer" (II) and "Jordan" (II), "Divinitie" is recommending "ease."[44] Man is saved by ceasing from (intellectual) effort, which can only damn him. "Break all thy spheres, and save thy head" may also have a further implication. The two verbs, "break" and "save," are carefully balanced. This balance turns the spheres into shells, protective devices reminiscent, perhaps, of the boxes in "Confession." If this is true, the line enunciates a paradox like "Onely an open breast / Doth shut them out": only by discarding the mechanisms which you thought protected you, which you constructed to protect you, can you truly be protected.

---

crucifixion in the Christian scheme. The abstractness of tasting "what he doth there designe" militates strongly against a specifically Eucharistic reading of the line. Herbert frequently uses Eucharistic-sounding language—language of blood, wine, and tasting—metaphorically. The repeated caveats of Malcolm Mackenzie Ross against confusing rhetoric with doctrine in Eucharistic contexts should be heeded (*Poetry and Dogma: The Transformation of Eucharistic Symbols in Seventeenth-Century Poetry* [New Brunswick, 1954], pp. 62 ff., 100, 180). Nuttall has pointed out that even George Fox could use sacramental *language* (*The Holy Spirit*, p. 101).

42. See Sir Thomas Browne, *Religio Medici*, I.vi, in Sir Geoffrey Keynes, ed., *Sir Thomas Browne: Selected Writings* (Chicago, 1968), p. 11.

43. See Luther, *Freedom of a Christian*, Dillenberger, p. 72; *Commentary on Galatians*, ed. Watson, pp. 224, 227.

44. As C. S. Lewis has pointed out, Thomas More thought Protestantism made the religious life too easy. See "Donne and Love Poetry in the Seventeenth Century," in *Seventeenth-Century Studies Presented to Sir Herbert Grierson* (Oxford, 1938), p. 75; Saint Thomas More, *The Confutation of Tyndale's Answer*, ed. Louis A. Schuster, et al. (New Haven, 1973), I, 215, 432 ff.

The final lines of "Divinitie" provide the clearest instance in *The Temple* of Herbert equating reason with "the flesh":

> Faith needs no staffe of flesh, but stoutly can
>   To heav'n alone both go, and leade.   [27–28]

At this point in the poem, there can be no doubt about the meaning of "staffe of flesh."[45] Equivalent to the spheres and the epicycles, it represents the imaginary contributions of man's reason to a universe which is both simpler and more mysterious than his reason can allow. Man does not need to aid faith with reason just as he need not supply spheres for the stars, which know their way without a guide. Only man needs a guide (and is therefore, in the terms of stanza 1, "duller than a clod"). The "guide" which can lead man to heaven is super-natural and totally self-sufficient; being "stout" (strong) it needs no "staffe" to lean on. In the context of the poem, "Faith . . . alone" in the final stanza means both that faith can save man all by itself and that only faith can save man. Man can only "save [his] head" by refusing to rely on it. When he does rely on it, "Reason triumphs, and faith lies by."

Significantly, Herbert placed one of the direct attacks on reason, "The Agonie," early in "The Church." Like the final sequence, the opening of "The Church" remained virtually constant through Herbert's enlargements and revision of his manuscript. 'Sepulchre" and "The Agonie" are the only additions to the "W" opening.[46] This sequence focused on the *strangeness* of Christianity, and the additions intensify this focus. The crucifixion dominates these poems. "The Sacrifice," in which the crucifixion is fully described, devotes its energy to highlighting the paradoxes of the event, the mysteriousness, as it says, of both God's willingness to undergo such torments and man's desire to inflict them. Christ speaks:

> Ah! how they scourge me! yet my tendernesse
> Doubles each lash: and yet their bitternesse
> Windes up my grief to a mysteriousnesse.   [125–27]

---

45. The uncannily literal phallic dimension of "staffe of flesh" is again probably relevant (see n. 30 above). Herbert seems to have conceived of the intellect in terms of aggressive sexuality. This both embodies(!) Luther's understanding of *concupiscentia* very fully and supports Vendler's remarks on the desire to escape from masculine sexuality revealed in moments like this in the poetry.

46. Of the first fifteen poems in "The Church," thirteen appear at the beginning of "W" in close to the final order. See Hutchinson, p. liv; *Williams Manuscript*, pp. 15v–29r. Aside from the addition of "Sepulchre" and "The Agonie," the only other major change in the opening sequence is the extensive revision of the second part of "Easter" (Hutchinson, p. 42).

Immediately following "The Sacrifice," we witness an earnest and pious man puzzling over the question of what his response to the sacrifice is to be. The speaker of "The Thanksgiving" begins his meditations with a strong assertion of the uniqueness of Christ's experience; he addresses Christ with an appropriate title, and then immediately reflects on it:

> Oh King of grief! (a title strange, yet true,
> To thee of all kings only due).   [1–2]

At the heart of Christianity is something "strange, yet true." The next couplet raises the question of the speaker's relation to this "strange, yet true" phenomenon. He sees Christ as having already, in Eliot's phrase, "foresuffered all," endured everything he (the speaker) could offer to endure:

> O King of wounds! how shall I grieve for thee,
> Who in all grief preventest me?   [3–4]

At the end of "The Sacrifice," Christ demanded that "others say, when I am dead, / Never was grief like mine"; in "The Thanksgiving," the speaker fully acknowledges that "*My God, My God, why dost thou part from me?* / Was such a grief as cannot be" (lines 9–10).[47]

The speaker of "The Thanksgiving" knows that his grief can never be adequate, yet rejects the possibility that grief is not the proper response:

> Shall I then sing, skipping thy doleful story,
> And side with thy triumphant glory?
> Shall thy strokes be my stroking? thorns, my flower?
> Thy rod, my posie? crosse, my bower?   [11–14]

These are "rhetorical" questions in a sense in which the previous questions of the poem—"how shall I grieve for thee?"; "Shall I be scourged . . . ?"—were not. The contemptuous puns on "skipping" and "stroking" and the witty antithetical compactness of the second couplet make it clear that the speaker regards the possibilities he is contemplating in these lines as absurd, too ridiculous to be seriously considered. Suddenly his perspective is rationalistic; paradox is rejected out of hand as absurdity. He has come a long way from his initial acknowledgment of strangeness. The explicit rationalism of these lines, moreover, alerts us to the rationalism implicit in the open-

---

47. I am taking the primary meaning of the final line of "The Sacrifice" to be Christ's assertion of the uniqueness of his grief. This is the sense explored in the poems following. I do not, however, mean to deny the important double meaning which William Empson (*Seven Types of Ambiguity*, 3d ed. [New York, 1955], p. 258) finds in the line. See also Bell, "Setting Foot into Divinity," 227–29.

ing questions, in the assumption of appropriateness, the assumption that our normal sense of decorum (grief for grief, and so on) is applicable to the interactions between God and man. The final result of this assumption is articulated in the lines which immediately follow. Christ is a model to be imitated:

> how then shall I imitate thee, and
> Copie thy fair, though bloudie hand?   [15–16]

Imitatio Christi was the essence of medieval and, to a large extent, Erasmian piety.[48] Luther, on the other hand, inveighed against those who "set Christ out unto us as an example to be followed"; he saw the notion of Christ as an example as fundamentally misguided, as encouraging the anxieties and impieties of "works-religion"—"We will admit no examples," said Luther, "not even from Christ himself."[49] It is no accident that at the point in "The Thanksgiving" when the rationalism of the speaker emerges and culminates in the conception of "imitat[ing] thee," the mode of the poem becomes comic. The project of imitation is announced with the words:

> Surely I will revenge me on thy love,
> And trie who shall victorious prove.   [17–18]

Herbert is presenting the desire to imitate Christ as the essence of misguided good intentions. He does not have Luther's rancor, but he does have his theology. The speaker pledges (vows?) to reciprocate Christ's love through Christian use of His gifts:

> If thou dost give me wealth, I will restore
> All back unto thee by the poore.
> If thou dost give me honour, men shall see,
> The honour doth belong to thee.   [19–22]

These are clearly admirable and pious resolves.[50] They, together with the other projects listed in the poem, are clearly good things to do. The problem lies in the speaker's motives. The context of the opening questions leads us to perceive the speaker's resolves as intended to

48. For Erasmus's relation to the tradition and movement that produced Thomas a Kempis's *The Imitation of Christ*, see Albert Hyma's *The Christian Renaissance* (New York, 1924), and *The Youth of Erasmus* (Ann Arbor, 1930); also Roland H. Bainton, *Erasmus of Christendom* (New York, 1969), pp. 8–26.

49. *Commentary on Galatians*, ed. Watson, p. 270; "Preface to the New Testament," Dillenberger, p. 17, and *The Freedom of a Christian*, Dillenberger, p. 77; *Against the Heavenly Prophets in the Matter of Images and Sacraments*, LW, XL, 132.

50. Bell ("Setting Foot into Divinity," 232–233) interestingly relates these resolutions to "the election of the second week" in the *Spiritual Exercises*.

make him *feel worthy* of Christ's love, to make him feel that he has responded to this love appropriately.

At times the speaker of "The Thanksgiving" appears truly ridiculous, but Herbert is always careful to remind us that this speaker is, after all, an impressively earnest and serious character:

> For thy predestination I'le contrive,
> > That three yeares hence, if I survive,
> I'le build a spittle, or mend common wayes,
> > But mend mine own without delayes.   [31–34]

The speaker is at his most ludicrous in comparing his avowedly contingent resolves—"three yeares hence, *if I survive*"—with God's predestination, but before we have time to settle into smirks, the fourth line brings us sharply back into touch with this speaker's true moral earnestness—"But mend mine own without delayes." If imitation of Christ's life or His attributes (line 40) were the true Christian path, this speaker would be proceeding correctly, even excellently. But the cutting edge of "faith alone" is directed at those who are aspiring to piety wrongly rather than to those who are indifferent to it. The doctrine is most cogently enunciated, therefore, in relation to *sincere* attempts at "works." What is at issue in "The Thanksgiving" is not the sincerity of the speaker but the adequacy of his conception of the Christian life. A poem which began as a meditation on the crucifixion has gradually become, through the emergent rationalism we have traced, an enumeration of the speaker's resolutions. The sacrifice has fallen away from his consciousness, and with it the sense of strangeness.

Roughly midway through the poem the crucifixion returns to the speaker's mind; he is, however, too caught up in projecting to focus on it:

> As for thy Passion—But of that anon,
> > When with the other I have done.   [29–30]

"The other" here, although unremarked on by the commentators, is a bit of a puzzle. It is probably best taken as referring to Christ's life as opposed to His death; the life, as recorded in the synoptic Gospels, provides the ethical model to be imitated. The phrase, however, may refer to Christ's godhead as opposed to His manhood, since these lines are immediately followed by the reference to "thy predestination." In either case, the theology which the speaker is propounding is not a *theologia crucis*, a theology strongly focused on the uniqueness of the sacrifice. *Theologia crucis*, as Luther conceived it, is equally opposed to a theology of glory and a theology of practical imitation.[51]

One critic has characterized all the resolutions of "The Thanksgiving" as "chatty glibness."[52] This is, as we have seen, too easy, but it does seem to apply to the final resolutions beginning, "My musick shall finde thee, and ev'ry string / Shall have his attribute to sing" (lines 39–40).[53] The resolutions end with the claim:

> I will read thy book, and never move,
> Till I have found therein thy love,
> Thy art of love which I'le turn back on thee:
> O my deare Saviour, Victorie!   [45–48]

In this last outcry, piety and impiety totally merge. Christ is the speaker's "deare Saviour," but the note of self-satisfaction is clangorous. This cry crystallizes the element of righteousness implicit in all the resolutions. At this moment, when with "the other" he has done, the speaker returns to the crucifixion. He is at the peak of his self-confidence when he suddenly falters:

> Then for thy passion—I will do for that—
> Alas, my God, I know not what.   [49–50]

The speaker returns to the sense of strangeness. There is no obvious human analogue to the crucifixion—"such a grief as cannot be"—and in the face of it the whole question of doing falls away. Imitation falls away as an evasive and rationalizing fiction. When the speaker focuses his attention on the cross, his attitude turns from competition to awe.

The poem which follows "The Thanksgiving" was entitled "The Second Thanks-giving" in "W," and every commentator on these poems has noted their continuity. Picking up the submerged military metaphors in "The Thanksgiving," Herbert retitled the companion piece "The Reprisall." It begins by answering an obvious rationalistic objection to the finale of "The Thanksgiving": why can't the speaker imitate Christ's passion by sacrificing himself in a similar way? The speaker begins where he left off, but his tone is now more contemplative:

51. See chap. 1, n. 45; and see Nygren, *Agape and Eros*, pp. 613–37, 700–721.

52. Stein, *Herbert's Lyrics*, p. 95. Michael McCanles, in *Dialectical Criticism and Renaissance Literature* (Berkeley and Los Angeles, 1975), pp. 80–81, characterizes the resolutions as "breezy" but takes them to be "at least three-quarters sincere."

53. Nowhere else in Herbert is there this confidence in the adequacy of art to God's nature. Stein remarks that although lines 39–42 of "The Thanksgiving" do present "an authentic philosophical goal of the poetry of praise, Herbert's own authentic voice does not seem to carry beyond the first clause" (*Herbert's Lyrics*, p. 112).

> I have consider'd it, and finde
> There is no dealing with thy mighty passion:
> For though I die for thee, I am behinde;
> My sinnes deserve the condemnation. [1–4]

The second stanza is a variation and elaboration on the first, but the third pretends outrage: "Ah! was it not enough that thou / By thy eternall glorie didst outgo me? / Couldst thou not griefs sad conquests me allow?" The fourth and final stanza shows this outrage to be pretended; the speaker is assured in his knowledge of the proper, noncompetitive relation of man to Christ:

> Yet by confession will I come
> Into thy conquest: though I can do nought
> Against thee, in thee I will overcome
> The man, who once against thee fought. [13–16]

This is, I think, a true rather than an "incomplete" resolution just as the outrage of the third stanza is to be taken as mock outrage.[54] The difficulty is in seeing exactly what is being said. The stanza makes its claims without explicating or expounding them. Fish's paraphrase—"in other words, if you can't beat him, join him"—is crude in its formulation and misleading in its analysis of the tone of the stanza.[55] The main point seems to be that the reprisal which the poem envisions is taken by the speaker *against himself,* and the "mechanism" of this reprisal is confession. Confession here seems to mean the kind of acknowledgment of sin or inadequacy enacted by the end of "The Thanksgiving," the willingness to "let God be God" without arrogating anything to oneself in the process of salvation.[56] In the context of "The Thanksgiving" and the body of "The Reprisall," "I can do nought / Against thee" seems to mean, "I can do nothing similar in kind to what you have done for me," I cannot "revenge me on thy love" by equaling it. "In thee" is prominently placed in this stanza. The regenerate Christian becomes a "member" of the body of which

54. For the final stanza as "an incomplete resolution at best" and for the third stanza as one where "the speaker's impurity of motive surfaces to the point where even he almost recognizes it," see McCanles, *Dialectical Criticism,* p. 81. McCanles's reading seems to me to multiply ironies in a way the poem does not invite. It is, however, easy to see how McCanles was led to his reading. "The Reprisall" does not specify, as "The Holdfast," for instance, does, that the "confession" in question is a product of grace rather than of will, but I do not think that this lack of theological specification is intended to be part of the meaning of the poem. Herbert generally signals mistakes by his personae through humor or overstatement, neither of which are present here.

55. *Self-Consuming Artifacts,* p. 183.

56. On "let God be God," see p. 30 above.

Christ is the head, and is therefore "in" Christ.[57] At moments, the regenerate Christian can overcome his natural desire to participate in his own salvation, to do something that will show or make him worthy of love. "The man, who once against thee fought" is the man who wanted, on the basis of his native sense of appropriateness, to "imitate thee." To come into Christ's conquest, His special relation to grief, is not a matter of consciously imitating Him but rather of being conformed to Him.[58] Imitation does not "overcome / The man."

"The Reprisall" points us deep into the mysteries of Pauline and Reformation Christianity. "The Agonie" follows "The Reprisall." In context, it constitutes an implicit rebuke to the rationalism of "The Thanksgiving." To the skeptical questions,

> Shall thy strokes be my stroking? thorns, my flower?
> Thy rod, my posie? crosse,my bower,

"The Agonie" answers, "Yes." What God felt "as bloud," the Christian feels "as wine." In its rejection of the discursive, quantitative reason of the measuring and fathoming philosophers, "The Agonie" revels in its paradoxes. One poem later in the opening sequence, "Good Friday," part 1, seems to present the speaker of "The Thanksgiving" transformed into one of the "philosophers" of "The Agonie." This speaker is deeply concerned with measuring and counting:

> O my chief good,
> How shall I measure out thy bloud?
> How shall I count what thee befell,
> And each grief tell?   [1–4]

"How shall I . . . How shall I?"—we are back to "The Thanksgiving." But there is a difference. This speaker's questions are clearly rhetorical. He does not, as the rest of the poem demonstrates, expect to find a way of literally numbering or physically symbolizing Christ's griefs ("Or can not leaves, but fruit, be signe / Of the true vine?"). He concludes by first giving up the attempt at numbering—"Then let each houre / Of my whole life one grief devour; / That thy distresse through all may runne" (lines 13–15)—and then by turning this attempt on himself—"Or rather let / My severall sinnes their sorrows get" (lines 17–18).[59]

57. See "Aaron," and the discussion, pp. 127–33.

58. For a clear exposition of the distinction between imitation of and conformation to, see Regin Prenter, *Spiritus Creator: Luther's Concept of the Holy Spirit,* trans. John M. Jensen (Philadelphia, 1953), pp. 8–13.

59. This is perhaps the only instance in *The Temple* in which Herbert's use of a *correctio* at the end of a poem (see p. 11 above) provides a weaker rather than a stronger ending. The penultimate stanza of part 1 of "Good Friday" is more powerful than the

Part 2 of "Good Friday" also seems to begin in a rationalistic and presumptuous manner; its opening couplet is jauntily syllogistic:

> Since bloud is fittest, Lord, to write
> Thy sorrows in, and bloudie fight . . .   [1–2]

One assumes that what will follow is an offer by the speaker to "copie" Christ's "fair, though bloudie hand" in his own blood. The first half of the third line, "My heart hath store," bears out this assumption, but the rest of the line suddenly overturns it:

> My heart hath store, write there, where in
> One box doth lie both ink and sinne.   [3–4]

Christ rather than the speaker will do the "writing," and this writing will be done "right there" (the pun is Herbert's) in the speaker's heart. The speaker will be object rather than agent. Instead of a bold offer to imitate Christ in what is clearly the most appropriate way ("since bloud is fittest"), the poem turns out to be the most powerful assertion yet made in "The Church" of the speaker's dependence on grace. The second stanza is gay and witty, envisioning the crucified Christ as "dispossessing" sin of the speaker's heart ("sinne may say, / No room for me, and flie away"). The final stanza turns somber, and prays:

> Sinne being gone, oh fill the place,
> And keep possession with thy grace;
> Lest sinne take courage and return
> And all the writings blot or burn.[60]   [9–12]

At this point in "The Church," when we are again at one of "the dark and deepe points of Religion" (*CP*, p. 256), Herbert places "Redemption." "Good Friday" and "Redemption," both entitled "The Passion," had appeared together in "W," and Herbert kept them together through his final revisions and reorderings. "Redemption" is the first narrative by a fully dramatized fictional persona in *The Temple*. This persona is a commonsensical character indeed; everything he does makes perfect sense. Herbert uses the sonnet form to emphasize

---

final stanza and provides a richer ending for the poem. Herbert probably wanted the additional "My severall sinnes" stanza for its expression of conviction of sin, since the poems preceding and following part 1 of "Good Friday" emphasize this ("The Sinner" and "Good Friday," part 2).

60. It is interesting that Herbert's revisions of this poem made its ending much more somber and increased its sense of dependence on grace. In "W," the final stanza reads:

> Sinn being gone o doe thou fill
> The Place, & keep possession still.
> for by the writings all may see
> Thou hast an ancient claime to mee.

See Hutchinson, p. 39; *Williams Manuscript*, p. 24v.

this persona's "step-by-step" manner of proceeding. The first quatrain is a completely self-contained grammatical and narrative unit:

> Having been tenant long to a rich Lord,
>   Not thriving, I resolved to be bold,
>   And make a suit unto him, to afford
> A new small-rented lease, and cancell th'old.   [1–4]

There is nothing at all extraordinary here. The situation is an ordinary, immediately recognizable one, and the speaker's response to it is fully and immediately intelligible. The second quatrain narrates the immediate results of the speaker's resolve "to be bold." With the first words of this quatrain, the entire context of the poem changes; the "narrative" becomes a religious allegory.[61] Yet the speaker's tone remains perfectly even.

> In heaven at his manour I him sought,   [5]

the speaker recounts, and calmly goes on with his tale:

> They told me there, that he was lately gone
>   About some land, which he had dearly bought
> Long since on earth, to take possession.   [6–8]

The speaker has no difficulty seeking "him" in heaven; he has no particular interest in who "they" are; and he has no questions about the land "which he had dearly bought / Long since on earth." *We* may be puzzled at this point and realize that we are in the presence of a mystery (predestination), but the speaker is single-minded in pursuit of his stated goal. His only concern is the location of his Lord. "I straight return'd," the sestet begins, but the mode of the narration shifts slightly at this point. For the first time, Herbert has his persona explicitly state the assumptions governing his actions:

> I straight return'd, and *knowing his great birth,*
>   *Sought him accordingly* in great resorts,
>   In cities, theatres, gardens, parks, and courts.
>   [9–11; emphasis mine]

By having his speaker, right before the climax of the poem, not merely manifest common sense but also call attention to the fact that he is doing so, Herbert forces his readers to be fully aware of the presumptions implicit in common sense. In spite of the modified Shakespearean rhyme scheme of the sestet (effegg) Herbert divides it into

---

61. It is not quite accurate to say, with Vendler, that in "Redemption" Herbert "*immediately* gives his 'meaning' away" (*Poetry of Herbert,* p. 60, emphasis mine).

two tercets rather than a quatrain and a couplet; the final tercet con-
cludes the narrative:

> At length I heard a ragged noise and mirth
> Of theeves and murderers. There I him espied,
> Who straight, *Your suit is granted,* said, and died.   [12–14]

From the narrator's point of view, the essence of his experience is
that he finds his lord in neither a place nor a condition suitable to his
lord's "great birth." He finds him in totally unlikely and unsuitable
company performing a totally unlikely and unsuitable action—dying.
The point of the poem is precisely the strangeness of Christianity, its
affronting of natural reason and common sense. When natural reason
conceives of God, it can only do so in terms of majesty and power—
on the analogy, indeed, of earthly lords.[62] The conception of the most
glorious and powerful Being in the universe, the King of Kings, dying
a humiliating death among "theeves and murderers" violates deco-
rum in a fundamental way. Erich Auerbach has shown how basic to
classical thought and expression the concept of decorum is and how
thoroughly the doctrines of the Incarnation and Passion violate this
concept.[63] Like Augustine and Luther, Herbert (who was trained as
a rhetorician) knew this, but like Luther and unlike Augustine, he
was completely at ease with this violation.[64] In "Redemption," Herbert
is dramatizing the effect of the Christian revelation on a consciousness
committed to a natural (and classical) sense of decorum. What hap-
pens to the speaker makes no sense to him—that is Herbert's point.

The syntax of the poem enacts the breakdown of the speaker's
world picture. Until the final tercet, the speaker is clear on the reasons
for his actions and on the links between them: "Having been tenant
long . . . Not thriving, I resolved"; "They told me there . . . I straight
return'd"; "knowing . . . Sought him accordingly." He comes upon
his Lord, however, totally "accidentally" ("At length I heard"), and

---

62. In *That These Words . . . Still Stand Firm, LW,* XXXVII, 69–71, Luther insisted that
there was an absolute opposition between the Christian and the classical or "natural"
conception of glory.

63. See Erich Auerbach, *"Sermo Humilis"* in *Literary Language and Its Public in Late
Latin Antiquity and in the Middle Ages,* trans. Ralph Manheim (New York, 1965), pp. 27–
66, and *Mimesis,* trans. Willard R. Trask (Princeton, 1953), pp. 40–47, 72–76, 153–54,
and chap. 8 ("Farinata and Cavalcanti") passim.

64. For Augustine's lack of ease with violations of decorum, see his complex attitudes
toward traditional eloquence, toward Cicero, and toward "the vulgar manner of speech"
in *On Christian Doctrine,* trans. D. W. Robertson (Indianapolis, 1958), p. 134, and Book
4, passim. See also Joseph A. Mazzeo, "St. Augustine's Rhetoric of Silence," *Renaissance
and Seventeenth-Century Studies* (New York, 1964), pp. 1–28 (esp. pp. 2 and 13), and the
discussions in Stein, Introduction, *Herbert's Lyrics,* and Lewalski, *Protestant Poetics,* pp.
215–18.

achieves the goal of his quest, the granting of his suit, before he is
able to ask for it. In the last sentence of the poem there are no causal
connections at all—"I him espied, / Who straight . . . said, *and* died."
By the end of the poem, Christ rather than the speaker has become
the agent of the narrative, and the narrative itself has become abrupt,
mysterious, and paratactic. The end adopts the narrative mode which
Auerbach characterizes as distinctly biblical, while the body of the
poem, with its plethora of connectives, approximates the mode of
classical narration.[65] I see no reason not to credit Herbert with the
same insight into biblical style that Auerbach achieved. The poem
also seems to parallel another of Auerbach's observations on biblical
style, the prominence of direct discourse.[66] The one moment of direct
discourse in "Redemption" has, literally, the force of a revelation. It
is an absolute and "unmotivated" assertion of divine good will. It
seems to be modeled on those moments in the Gospels when Jesus
responds to the *thoughts* of his interlocutors.[67] The Lord's words come
"out of nowhere" to the speaker. They come to him independently
of all his efforts and give him freely what he has been misguidedly
struggling to attain.[68] "Redemption" dramatizes not only the strange-
ness of the means of grace but also the strange *givenness* of grace.

In the final order of *The Temple,* "Sepulchre" follows "Redemption,"
and we have already seen that the subject of "Sepulchre" is *agape.*
The opening sequence comes to an end with the two "Easter" poems
("Easter-wings" begins a sequence on the elements of the Christian
life—affliction, the sacraments, repentance, faith, prayer, the Scrip-
tures). The first part of "Easter" (or the first "Easter" poem) is inte-
grated into the opening sequence only insofar as it tacitly rebukes the
confidence in "my musick" of "The Thanksgiving" ("O let thy blessed
Spirit bear a part, / And make up our defects with his sweet art"),
and provides a positive answer to "Shall thy strokes be my stroking?"
("His stretched sinews taught all strings, what key / Is best to cele-
brate this most high day"). The second part of "Easter" is far more
significant; it functions, especially in its revised form, as the culmi-
nation of the opening sequence.[69] Part 2 of "Easter" combines the
competition motif of "The Thanksgiving" with the counting motif of
"The Agonie" and "Good Friday," part 1. As the poem opens, the
speaker is again, as in "The Reprisall," "prevented" by Christ:

65. See *Mimesis,* pp. 7–9, 75, and chap. 8.
66. Ibid., pp. 45–46 and chap. 8.
67. See, for instance, Matthew 9:3 and Luke 7:40.
68. See Grant, *Transformation of Sin,* p. 125.
69. For the revisions, see Hutchinson, p. 42; *Williams Manuscript,* p. 27r.

> I got me flowers to straw thy way;
> I got me boughs off many a tree:
> But thou wast up by break of day,
> And brought'st thy sweets along with thee.   [1–4]

Christ does not need the speaker's offerings. He was "up" before
him and brought along his own "sweets." The speaker is like the two
Marys who "brought sweet spices" with which to anoint the body of
Jesus on the Sunday following the Crucifixion. Although they came
to the sepulchre "very early in the morning . . . at the rising of the
sun," they discovered that Jesus was indeed "up" before they ar-
rived—"he is not here" (Mark 16:1–6). As Herbert's stanza progresses,
its focus shifts from "I" and his efforts ("I got me flowers . . . I got
me boughs") to "thou" and His nature. This nature becomes the
subject of the poem. Not only does it transcend and make nugatory
all the speaker's efforts, it transcends the whole order of created
nature. The resurrection was no ordinary rising:

> The Sunne arising in the East,
> Though he give light, and th' East perfume;
> If they should offer to contest
> With thy arising, they presume.   [5–8]

The speaker wholly accepts Christ's preeminence over nature. It is
no longer he who "offers to contest" with Christ but a dramatized
"They" (the sun and the "east").

In the first stanza, when Christ was "up by break of day," daybreak
retained its normal status as a marker in relation to Jesus' behavior.
The second stanza throws this status into doubt. The ordinary sunrise
must not "offer to contest" with Christ's arising, but we are left
wondering what this means. The third stanza tells us. It begins by
asking,

> Can there by any day but this,
> Though many sunnes to shine endeavour?   [9–10]

The way in which the sun could contest with Christ's arising is by
"claiming" that *its* rising causes day. "Day" ceases to be a temporal
term.[70] It has nothing to do with the sun's "endeavour" to shine. Our
ordinary sense of things is totally mistaken:

70. Stein identifies the main effect of Herbert's revisions as the transfer of emphasis
"from the 'I' (and its relations to the day) to the day itself and to the relations of that
day to time" (*Herbert's Lyrics*, p. 142).

We count three hundred, but we misse.   [11]

Where we habitually find many transitory particulars (three hundred "days"),

There is but one, and that one ever.   [12]

This ending is one of the most astounding moments in Herbert. A vista opens up in relation to which all our "countings" like all our acts of "natural piety" (getting flowers) fail, but we are here left contemplating the vista itself rather than our failures in relation to it. As befits its occasion, the poem is celebratory rather than penitential. It transposes the movement from "each houre" to a sun which is "one" and "all" in the missed climax of "Good Friday" into a key which "Is best to celebrate this most high day." The ending of "Easter" does not puzzle us with strangeness or break our hearts with poignance. It provides a moment of contemplative transcendence.

3

Interlude:
Theology or Philosophy?

In the rather dazzling light of "Easter," part 2, it looks as if we are forced to reformulate our account of the nature and aim of Herbert's attack on reason. The ending of "Easter" seems to be making an ontological claim and to be attacking not merely certain assumptions that man tends to make in his attitudes and behavior toward God, but the discursive intellect in general, the general procedure of "count[ing] three hundred." This interpretation of Herbert's attack on reason has recently been proposed and strongly argued by Stanley Fish. Fish sees Herbert as seeking to undermine "our reliance on discursive forms of thought," as rejecting "the dividing and distinguishing tendencies of the human consciousness" in general, "the distinctions of times, places, objects, persons—we customarily make as we move about in the world."[1] Herbert wishes to undermine these distinctions because they falsify his most fundamental sense of the nature of reality, what Fish calls "the insight of God's omnipresence" (SCA, p. 158).[2] Fish would see the assertion that "there is but one" as a seriously meant ontological claim central to Herbert's endeavor.

Although Fish could have based his argument on the ending of "Easter," part 2, he does not mention this poem. He relies instead on some closely parallel lines on how "we misse":

1. *Self-Consuming Artifacts*, pp. 163, 158, 156 (hereafter in this chapter this work will be cited as *SCA* in the text).
2. In *The Living Temple: George Herbert and Catechizing*, Fish shows greater historical awareness, but continues to insist on the importance of "the insight of God's omnipresence" to Herbert (*The Living Temple*, pp. 34, 85, 160).

We say amisse,
This or that is:
Thy word is all, if we could spell.

["The Flower," 19–21]

Fish takes these lines as ontological in their focus—concerned with what "is"—and as stating that the act of predication (saying or implying that "this or that" exists) violates the nature of reality, since God is "all" (*SCA*, p. 158).[3] Fish's reading depends on an equation, established through an allusion to the opening of the gospel of John ("and the Word was God"), of God's "word" with His substance (*SCA*, p. 156). But it is by no means clear that Herbert makes this equation. The lines can be seen as making a claim about God's power rather than His being. The stanza to which these lines form the coda begins, "There are thy wonders, Lord of power." In context, the mistake these lines identify is not to assert that "this or that" exists, but to assert or feel that this or that happens independently of God's (benevolent) will. To read the lines in this way makes them and Herbert's overall endeavor specific and theological rather than general and philosophical. By blurring this distinction, Fish blurs the focus of many of the poems. He transforms a functionalist framework into an essentialist one.

Fish's reading of "Thy word is all" is historically as well as contextually unlikely. Luther and Calvin were both quite clear on the difference between theological and philosophical distinctions, and between functionalist and essentialist frameworks (for them, in fact, the two distinctions were one). Luther was especially suspicious of Platonism and attempted to discourage ontological readings of the prologue to John. "St. John is not a Platonist," Luther thundered, "he is an evangelist."[4] Calvin explicitly warned against confusing God's will with His being. His remarks on Acts 17:28, another biblical text extremely important for Fish's argument, are illuminating. This verse contains one of the few quotations from a classical author in the Bible ("we are also his offspring"), and in commenting on the verse, Calvin accepts the fitness of Paul's quote from Aratus but warns that we must be careful to realize that the statement refers only to "quality,"

---

3. A. L. Clements ("Theme, Tone, and Tradition in Herbert's Poetry," *ELR*, 3 [1973], 264–83) reads the lines much as Fish does: "When rightly apprehended, all else ('This or that') is egoistic illusion" (p. 282).

4. *Sermon for the Principal Christmas Service on the First Chapter of John*, in *Luther's Church Postil*, trans. John Nicholas Lenker (Minneapolis, 1905), I, 209 (*WA*, X, I^1, 227); see also p. 190 for "human, Platonic, and philosophical thoughts, which lead us away from Christ." In *The Babylonian Captivity* (*Pagan Servitude*), Luther describes Dionysius the Areopagite as "very pernicious, being more of a Platonist than a Christian" (p. 343).

not to essence.[5] If we fail to distinguish between quality and essence, we fall into the "Manichaean errors" revived in Calvin's day by Servetus and Osiander. Calvin saw these theological radicals as promiscuously confusing God and the creatures in stating that God is "substantially" or "essentially" in us and all creatures, and that we and all things are therefore "portions" of God.[6] Fish's reading makes Herbert a "Manichee," a mystical pantheist like Servetus or some of the great Eastern and heterodox Western mystics.[7] Fish states that for Herbert, "To stop saying amiss is not only to stop distinguishing 'this' from 'that,' but to stop distinguishing oneself from God"—exactly what Calvin attacked in Osiander—"and finally to stop, to cease to be" (*SCA*, p. 157). Again on the basis of lines 19–21 of "The Flower," Fish sees what Herbert means by learning to "spell" as a process by which "the individual lets go, one by one, of all the ways of thinking, seeing, and saying that sustain the illusion of his independence, until finally he is *absorbed into the deity* whose omnipresence he has ac-

5. *Institutes*, I.xv.5. For the line quoted by Paul, see *The Phaenomena of Aratus*, trans. G. R. Mair, in *Callimachus, Lycophron, Aratus* (Cambridge, Mass., 1955), p. 207. Milton, much more involved with monist and materialist heresies than Herbert, related Aratus' line to Lucretius, *De rerum natura*, II.991–992: *caelesti sumus omnes semine oriundi; / omnibus ille idem pater est* (see Maurice Kelley and Samuel D. Atkins, "Milton's Annotations of Aratus," *PMLA*, 70 [1955], 1102). As Kelley and Atkins note, Milton echoed *Phaenomena*, 5, in *Paradise Lost*, V.503. The context of this echo is strongly "materialist." Fish quotes or alludes to the first half of Acts 17:28 ("in him we live and move and have our being") in *SCA*, pp. 157, 173, and in *The Living Temple*, pp. 73, 135.

6. *Institutes*, I.xiii.22 (on Servetus), III.xi.5–6, on Osiander's "Manichaean" doctrine of "essential oneness" with Christ. Luther's doctrine of the ubiquity of Christ's glorified body tended to place God literally "in" the creatures, but Calvin and all the Swiss Reformers rejected Luther's position on the Eucharist (which demanded the ubiquity of Christ's body). Herbert's Eucharistic theology is Reformed rather than Lutheran (see Robert Ellrodt, *L'Inspiration personnelle et L'Esprit du temps chez les poètes métaphysiques anglais* [Paris, 1973], Part I, Bk. ii, 325–441; and Jeanne Clayton Hunter " 'With Wings of Faith'. Herbert's Communion Poems," *Journal of Religion*, 62 [1982], 57–71). It should also be noted, however, that even in the context of his Eucharistic theology, Luther retained his focus on God's *will*. For Luther's Eucharistic theology, see Introduction, n. 11 above.

7. In explicating "the insight of God's omnipresence" Fish makes prominent use of a consciously playful and daring passage in Thomas Browne's *Religio Medici* (*SCA*, p. 158). Browne is a much more Platonic, heterodox, and theosophical writer than Herbert, yet even Browne, after speaking of "the ubiquitary and omnipresent essence of God," adds, "I hope I shall not offend Divinity" (*Selected Writings*, ed. Keynes, p. 41). Clements, in "Theme, Tone, and Tradition," quotes Eckhart ("God's is-ness [*istigkeit*] is my is-ness") in relation to Herbert's "paradoxical and profound realization of his being in God or God's being in him" (p. 283). On the close kinship between Eckhart's thought and that of one of the greatest Hindu mystics (Sankara), see Rudolf Otto, *Mysticism East and West*, trans. Bertha L. Bracey and Richenda C. Payne (New York, 1932), ch. 1. On Servetus and Osiander, see Williams, *The Radical Reformation*, pp. 322, 612 ff. (Servetus), 654–55 (Osiander).

knowledged"; Herbert's project is to "return" his poems "and every-
thing else" to God *"of whose substance they are"* (*SCA*, p. 157; emphasis
mine). This is truly close to the Manichaean doctrine of redemption.[8]

Yet if Herbert is not a mystical pantheist, and is more inter-
ested in disposition and will than in Being, what is to be made of
"There is but one"? Even if "Thy word is all" is not an ontological
assertion, surely "There is but one" is such, and surely part 2 of
"Easter" does undermine our normal framework of perceptual and
conceptual distinctions. What needs to be said is that the ending of
"Easter" dramatizes a perception of absolute *value*. As the poem pro-
ceeds, the great and miraculous—supranatural—fact of the resurrec-
tion seems to "dawn" on the speaker's consciousness more and more
fully until, in the final lines, it sweeps away all else. In relation to
this, nothing else matters. Mattering is precisely the point. Although
the language is apparently ontological, the drama of the poem is the
realization of a priority of value—of importance, not of being. The
rhetorical and psychological situation is closely parallel to that of one
of Donne's most famous hyperboles, "Nothing else is," in "The Sunne
Rising" (line 22). Surely no one would take Donne's line, in spite of
its syntax and its force, as a straightforward ontological assertion; like
Herbert's, it is an assertion and realization of value. Part 2 of "Easter"
is Herbert's "The Sunne Rising." Like Donne, he rejects "houres,
dayes, months, which are the rags of time" ("The Sunne Rising," line
10).[9] Herbert is dramatizing a consciousness which attains the con-
ceptual equivalent of true gratefulness to God:

> Not grateful when it pleaseth me,
> As if thy blessings had spare dayes,
> But such a heart, whose pulse may be
>   Thy praise.
>
> ["Gratefulnesse," 29–32]

8. See Hans Jonas, *The Gnostic Religion: The Message of the Alien God and the Beginning
of Christianity*, 2d ed., rev. (Boston, 1963), chaps. 8 and 9. It is also close to the doctrines
of Renaissance Kabbalism (see Gershom G. Scholem, *Major Trends in Jewish Mysticism*
[rpt., New York, 1961], chap. 7). Again, there is a greater likelihood of relevance to
Milton.

9. On "Nothing else is," see Wilbur Sanders, *John Donne's Poetry* (Cambridge, 1971),
pp. 72–73, and Brian Vickers, "The 'Songs and Sonnets' and the Rhetoric of Hyperbole,"
in A. J. Smith, ed., *John Donne: Essays in Celebration* (London, 1972), pp. 132–74. On
"the rags of time," it is interesting to recall that Donne himself later transposed this
phrase into a theological context. Donne reused the phrase in his Christmas Sermon
of 1624: "We begin with that which is elder than our beginning, and shall over-live
our end, the mercy of God. . . . The names of first or last derogate from it, for first
and last *are but ragges of time,* and his mercy hath no relation to time" (*The Sermons of
John Donne*, ed. Evelyn M. Simpson and George R. Potter [Berkeley, 1953], VI, 120).

Despite his own ontological and epistemological focus, Fish does recognize that Herbert's focus is ethical and dispositional. In a brilliant transitional move, Fish conflates the ethical with the ontological by arguing that in Herbert's poetry in general (as in "Sepulchre" in particular) Christ is discovered to be not only "the substance of all things," but also "the performer *of all actions*" (*SCA*, p. 173; emphasis mine). To be in a proper relationship to God, therefore, the individual must give up all pretense to "independent motion" as well as to independent existence (*SCA*, p. 173). Herbert is a total determinist as well as a thoroughgoing monist. Here again, Fish blurs a potentially valid point by overgeneralizing it, by ignoring the distinction between theological and philosophical claims.[10]

In support of his position, Fish quotes Joseph Summers as stating that for Herbert "the essential 'act' is that the individual should abandon the pretense that he *can* act in any way" (*SCA*, p. 173). But Summers's position is not identical with Fish's. What Summers wrote is that for Herbert, "the essential 'act' is that the individual should abandon the pretense that he *can* act in any way *pertaining to salvation*" (added emphasis mine).[11] This is a very different claim. It is not a general denial of free will but only of free will in regard to salvation. It is, in other words, a specifically theological rather than a philosophical claim. It is precisely what Luther meant by "the bondage of the will." In his famous treatise by that title, Luther conceded that although the "most religious" thing would be to drop the term "free will" entirely, "we may still in good faith teach the people to use it to credit man with 'free will' in respect not of what is above him but of what is below him"—that is, things of the world (money, possessions, and so on). However, "in all that bears on salvation or damnation," man has no free will.[12] Herbert echoed this position exactly when he asserted that "a man's fre-will is only in outward, not in spiritual things" ("Notes on Valdes," p. 313).

The major consequence of mistaking the theological for the philosophical in Herbert is that we thereby miss or distort the actual shape and force of many of the poems. "The Holdfast" is an important case in point. Fish sees "The Holdfast" as in many ways "the quintessential

10. Calvin argues that when Paul says "It is God who works all things in all" in I Corinthians 12:6, Paul is *not* "discussing universal governance" but speaking rather of "all good things in which believers excell" (*Institutes*, II.iii.6). On the distinction between theological and philosophical conceptions of divine causation, see Otto, *Idea of the Holy*, pp. 88 ff.

11. Summers, *Herbert*, p. 61. In the earlier version of "Letting Go," Fish acknowledged his truncation of Summers (*ELH*, 37 [1970], 482).

12. *The Bondage of the Will*, p. 107, and see also p. 289; *Commentary on Galatians*, p. 175.

Herbert poem" (*SCA*, p. 176). It dramatizes with particular clarity the conundrum that Fish sees at the heart of Herbert's vision: "the individual should abandon the pretense that he *can* act in any way"; and, says Fish, "the extent of the difficulty becomes clearer when we understand that this abandoning is itself an act for which the individual must disclaim responsibility, and that this disclaiming is itself an act . . . and on and on." Every withdrawal from a prideful claim "only reconstitutes it on the other side of the gesture" (*SCA*, p. 182). This process is, obviously, "infinitely self-perpetuating," and Fish sees it as still operative and pressuring in the poems where it is introduced when the poems themselves are formally complete (*SCA*, p. 179). Again and again, Fish refutes the endings of Herbert poems, asserting that they cannot have genuine resolutions.[13]

Fish is certainly correct that in "The Holdfast" and many other poems, Herbert confronts "the central question of the Christian life, What must I do to be saved?" Yet we need not accept Fish's recurrent assertion that Herbert sees this question as fundamentally *posing a dilemma* (*SCA*, pp. 174–75). "The Holdfast" is one of a series of poems in which Herbert dramatizes and celebrates the full implications of the Reformation doctrine of grace. Celebration is the key. The doctrine was meant, in the words of the Anglican Articles, to be "sweet, pleasant, and [of] unspeakable comfort."[14] Human insufficiency was only half of it. What made the gospel truly good news was the other half, the doctrine of grace. In not seeing "The Holdfast" as dramatizing the central doctrine of the Reformation, and in not fully confronting the implications of the doctrine, Fish overlooks two major and related facts about this poem: (1) that it is comic; and (2) that it is happy.[15] Fish makes the poem similar to Donne's earliest *Holy Sonnets*, poems which truly see faith alone as a problem rather than a

13. See *SCA*, p. 169 (on the ending of "Church-monuments"), p. 201 (on that of "A True Hymne"), and p. 223 (on that of "The Forerunners"). Again, Fish continues this practice in *The Living Temple* (see n. 50 below). For some interesting remarks on denials of closure in Shakespeare criticism, see Richard Levin, "Refuting Shakespeare's Endings," *MP*, 72 (1975), 337–49.

14. From Article XVII, "Of Predestination and Election," in Gerrish, ed., *Faith of Christendom*, p. 191. In Article XI, "Of the Justification of Man," the doctrine "that we are justified by faith only" is characterized as "most wholesome" and "very full of comfort" (Gerrish, ed., p. 189).

15. Summers does associate the poem with the doctrine of grace and does see that it is happy (*Herbert*, p. 61); compare also, Lewalski, *Protestant Poetics*, p. 286. In *The Living Temple*, Fish hints at the positive dimension of Reformation theology but still tends to talk primarily in terms of dilemmas and impasses (pp. 117, 132, and passim). He still tends to stress the anxiety-provoking rather than the "comfortable" aspects of the theology, though he is forced, occasionally and uncomfortably, to acknowledge the latter (see pp. 118 and 133).

solution.[16] The doctrine produces conundrums only in the absence of the conception of grace that it is meant to embody. In content, if not in poetic quality, "The Holdfast" is "quintessential." It dramatizes with particular clarity Herbert's understanding of and attitude toward the Reformation doctrine of grace.

Fish claims that the speaker and the reader of "The Holdfast" are put through parallel experiences, that for both speaker and reader the poem is an exercise in humiliation, the "discovery of personal insufficiency" (*SCA*, p. 175). This reading ignores both the ending of the poem and its overall narrative mode. "The Holdfast" does not present a dramatic action; its mode is retrospective as well as comic. In its first lines, indeed its first words, the reader is alerted that the poem depicts a former folly happily recollected in tranquility. We are thrown back to "The Thanksgiving":

> I threatned to observe the strict decree
> > Of my deare God with all my power and might.   [1–2]

"Threatned" immediately makes the depiction comic (as in "Surely I will revenge me on thy love" in "The Thanksgiving"), and there is no mistaking the depicted speaker's emphasis on his own "power and might." We already know at this point what the speaker's story will be; it will narrate how he came to see the limits of his "power and might." However, as in "The Thanksgiving," it is clear that at the time recollected in the poem the speaker was attempting to manifest genuine love of God (compare "the strict decree / *Of my deare God*" with "O *my deare Saviour*, Victorie!"). As in "The Thanksgiving," the problem to be explored or dramatized is not impiety—"threatening" God in a serious (Satanic) sense—but a mistaken attempt at piety by someone already regenerate (only the regenerate can love the Law).[17] Here, as in "The Thanksgiving," Herbert is sporting with follies rather than with crimes;[18] this is what allows the depiction to be comic. The geniality of the speaker's self-mockery leaves no doubt about the happy ending to which the recollected process has come.

Unlike "The Thanksgiving," "The Holdfast" does not recount the speaker's attempts at observing "the strict decree"; it is much more

---

16. See especially "Oh my blacke Soule!" (*Holy Sonnets*, 1633, no. 2). On the dating and grouping of the *Holy Sonnets*, see Helen Gardner, ed., *The Divine Poems of John Donne* (Oxford, 1952), pp. xxxvii–xlvii. On Donne's probable state of mind when writing the "1633" sonnets, see R. C. Bald, *John Donne: A Life* (Oxford, 1970), pp. 235–36. See also John Stachniewski, "John Donne: The Despair of the 'Holy Sonnets,' " *ELH*, 48 (1981), 677–705.

17. See Luther's "Preface to Romans," Dillenberger, pp. 20–24.

18. For this distinction as it applies to comic theory, see Jonson's Prologue to *Every Man in His Humour*, line 24.

stylized and theologically explicit than the earlier poem.[19] In the third line, the speaker recollects having been authoritatively informed that he *could not* observe the decree—perhaps, indeed, since the phrasing is absolute and impersonal, that no one can:

But I was told by one, it could not be.   [3]

Like "Redemption," "The Holdfast" is a sonnet, and again Herbert makes powerful use of the form. The opening quatrain ends with what seems to be the speaker's response to the blank negativity of line 3:

Yet I might trust in God to be my light.   [4]

The beginning of the next quatrain, however, shows that this line does not represent the speaker's conclusion, but is rather part of the report of what he was "told." It is line 5 that presents his response:

Then will I trust, said I, in him alone.   [5]

The ambiguity about the speaker of "Yet I might trust" prepares for the critique of "Then will I trust" that follows. The reassignment of line 4 makes us aware of the "I" as an agent in line 5 rather than as merely a recipient of information. "Will I" is very prominent in the line, and, in case we are not instantaneously suspicious, the interjected narrative tag ("said I") reminds us that the comic retrospect of lines 1 and 2 is continuing. Line 5 has a kind of comic vigor; it follows rather too quickly upon the previous line, with no interval of reflection depicted.[20] It also perhaps activates a submerged or potential pun; the thematic context works to associate the modal "might" of line 4 with the substantive "might" of line 2. We seem to be invited to conclude that the speaker took the mention of trust as an opportunity to exercise might.

These suspicions are immediately confirmed by the authoritative sixth line, which continues the abrupt mode of "it could not be":

Nay, ev'n to trust in him, was also his.   [6]

Within the narrative, the speaker's eagerness to turn trust into an action is explicitly rebuked, treated as another "threat." The next three

19. The movement toward stylization seems to be one of the characteristics of Herbert's development. Mary Ellen Rickey's work on the development, *Utmost Art: Complexity in the Verse of George Herbert* (Lexington, Ky., 1966), chap. 4, tends to support this observation.

20. For the conception of comic vigor here employed, I am indebted to the comments on *Astrophil and Stella* of David Kalstone in *Sidney's Poetry: Contexts and Interpretations* (Cambridge, Mass., 1965), chap. 5, and of Neil Rudenstine in *Sidney's Poetic Development* (Cambridge, Mass., 1967), chaps. 15–16.

lines, completing the octet and beginning the sestet (7–10a), duplicate the movement of lines 3–6. Just as line 4, "Yet I might trust in God to be my light," had seemed an escape hatch from the blank negativity of line 3 ("it could not be"), so line 7, "We must confesse that nothing is our own," appears to be an escape hatch from "even to trust in him, was also his." Line 7 even duplicates the narrative ambiguity of line 4; we do not know which voice speaks it. The quatrain ends as it began, with a resolution:

> Then I confesse that he my succour is.   [8]

"Then will I trust. . . . Then I confesse"—the parallel could hardly be more marked. In the face of it, Fish acknowledges—rather damagingly for his assertion of the identity of the reader's experience with that narrated in the poem—that the reader is likely at this point to be "wary of accepting" the new resolution as a viable one (*SCA*, p. 176). The reader is indeed wary at this point; Herbert can now dispense with narrative tags and allow the directly quoted resolution of line 8 to be directly answered. The confession that "he my succour is" is taken as fulfilling the demand to confess "that nothing is our own." The speaker apparently could not quite bring himself to say this, but he was, so to speak, given credit for having said it, and answered as if he had:

> But to have nought is ours, not to confesse
> That we have nought.   [9–10a]

The speaker "stood amaz'd at this" (10b).[21]

Although missing the retrospective mode of the narrative, Fish excellently describes the psychological content dramatized in the speaker's repeated resolutions: "he will agree to anything so long as some sphere of responsibility remains to him"; "what he will not do is to admit that nothing is required of him, for to do so would be to give up his sense of personal worth" (*SCA*, p. 174). It would seem that at this point Fish must begin to consider the Reformation doctrine of grace, but he does not. He presents the assertion that the poem is about "the opposition between faith and works" as one of the misconceptions which the poem deliberately fosters in order to reject (*SCA*, p. 175). That Fish takes this view is especially significant because it involves him in precisely the misapprehension of the opposition between faith and works that Herbert is dramatizing. Ironically, Fish

---

21. At a parallel moment in Bunyan, the speaker of a narrative like this exclaims, "Do! I could not tell what to do." See Hopeful's spiritual autobiography in *The Pilgrim's Progress*, ed. Roger Sharrock (New York, 1965), p. 180.

is "entangled" by this poem in a way which I do not think Herbert intended.

According to Fish, the poem moves from works to faith, from the old dispensation to the new, when it moves from speaking of "the observance of strict decrees" to speaking of trust in God.[22] He sees the poem as transcending the opposition between faith and works when it reveals that "ev'n to trust in him was also his" (*SCA*, p. 175–76). For Fish, the opposition between faith and works is that between internal and external acts. This misunderstanding of the doctrine is what the parallel units of "The Holdfast" dramatize. The "faith alone" formulation is ambiguous and open to the misapprehension in question, but essential to Reformation theology is the view that faith is a *result* of grace, something, as Luther says, "that God effects in us."[23] Faith alone means grace alone. Fish gets the emphasis exactly backwards when he speaks of "the supererogatory goodness of God which is so extensive that it finally claims responsibility not only for the deeds that are done, but for the impulse to do them" (*SCA*, p. 176). Man's impulses are what the doctrine of faith alone *primarily* concerns. It is because "God judges according to [our] inmost convictions" that no man fulfills "the strict decree" (the double commandment of Luke 10). The impulses are what faith transforms.[24]

Like Luther, Calvin, and all the strict maintainers of their theology, Herbert knew that the doctrine of grace alone was almost impossible to keep sharply and constantly in focus; he knew the belief that it merely advocated an internalized form of work would always haunt it. In "The Holdfast" and many other poems, Herbert dramatizes the difficulty of coming fully to terms with so utterly counterintuitive a doctrine—surely there is *something* we can do. But, like Luther and Calvin, he knew that the doctrine had to be maintained in its full force in order for it to have any force at all. His poetic practice shows Herbert to have shared Luther's conviction that "if we lose the article of justification, we lose all things together . . . most necessary it is, chiefly and above all things, that we teach and repeat this doctrine continually . . . it cannot be beaten into our ears enough or too much. Yea, though we learn it and understand it well, yet is there none that taketh hold of it perfectly."[25] A hundred years later, in defending "the article of justification" against what he saw as subtle but extremely

22. Fish blunts the New Testament flavor of "the strict decree" in line 2 of the poem by speaking of decrees in the plural, and he equates the opposition between faith and works with "what is required under the New Dispensation and the Old" (*SCA*, p. 175). From the Reformation point of view, however, salvation was always by faith.

23. "Preface to Romans," Dillenberger, p. 23; *Institutes*, III.ii.35 ff.

24. "Preface to Romans," Dillenberger, pp. 20, 24; *Freedom of a Christian*, Dillenberger, pp. 67–70, 74–75; *Babylonian Captivity (Pagan Servitude)*, Dillenberger, p. 275.

25. *Commentary on Galatians*, ed. Watson, p. 40.

pernicious modifications of it, John Cotton, a genuine Calvinist, insisted that "there is no promise of life made to those that wait and seek in their own strength, who being driven to it have taken it up by their own resolutions."[26] Summarizing Cotton's view, Perry Miller noted that if, in resisting the doctrine of grace alone, we should try "to reassure ourselves by reflecting that if we cannot work we can believe, or that if we cannot believe we can wait until we come to believe"—or at least "confesse / That we have nought"—Cotton, like Luther or Calvin (or Herbert), would have replied, "here is still the old root of Adam left alive in us, whereby men seek to establish their own righteousness."[27] "*To have nought* is ours," not to participate in the process of our redemption by confessing that we have nought. "It cannot be beaten into our ears enough or too much."

All this, however, is rather grim-sounding, and it is not, contrary to Fish's reading, where Herbert ends. At the moment of maximal intensity in the narrative, when Herbert allows us to overhear rather than hear about the recollected dialogue, Herbert reintroduces the mode of comic self-dramatization—"I stood amaz'd at this" (10b). The next line, however, introduces a note of unparodied emotion to which, in the recollected history, an interlocutor responded. The speaker was not only "amaz'd," but

> Much troubled, till I heard a friend expresse,
> That all things were more ours by being his.   [11–12]

Fish comments that when, in the second half of line 10, the speaker gave up holding fast to his own sense of personal worth, he prepared the way "for the revelation from without, the revelation that the solution, and indeed all else, is beyond him, but that it is well within the capacity and inclination of another." Fish has nothing more to say about the "revelation from without"; after this perfunctory summary of its content ("it is well within the capacity and inclination of another"), he goes on to assert that "the proper response to the dilemma the poem poses is discovered to be not action, mental or physical [i.e., faith or works in Fish's view], but humility and self-abnegation" (*SCA*, p. 175).[28]

---

26. *The New Covenant* (1654), pp. 196–97.

27. Ibid., p. 182; Perry Miller, " 'Preparation for Salvation' in Seventeenth-Century New England," *Nature's Nation* (Cambridge, 1967), p. 61.

28. Humility, in the Reformation view, is one of the *effects* of faith (not, says Calvin, that we are to imagine "some space of time in which it brings it to birth"). See *Institutes*, III.iii.1–2, 20–21; *Babylonian Captivity* (*Pagan Servitude*), Dillenberger, pp. 317–18. In *The Living Temple*, p. 45, Fish comes to a more positive view of the end of "The Holdfast," but he still seems to see humility as a precondition rather than a result of grace (see p. 116).

Fish ignores the force of line 12 and the very existence of the final couplet. In line 11, the authoritative "one" of line 3 has become "a friend" (presumably they are the same), and line 12 records, still in retrospect, a remarkable and paradoxical claim—"That all things were more ours by being his." This line contains another calculated ambiguity. In "Nay, ev'n to trust in him was also his" (line 6), the final pronoun refers ambiguously to both God and "one" in line 3, but the identification of the speaker of the statement ("I was told by one") is separated so far from the statement itself that the ambiguity is felt only faintly, if at all. Line 12 repeats the ambiguous possessive pronoun (which is also the rhyme word) of line 6, but here the identification of the speaker—"I heard a friend expresse"—is brought very close to this speaker's statement. The result of the collocation is that we realize in a flash much like a revelation that in line 12 the ambiguous pronoun refers to the "friend" of line 11; the friend who was speaking and the "one" of line 3 *are* the God whose "all things" are. The speaker had been encountering revelation all along. At this point the narrative ceases, and we are given a hymnlike, impersonal couplet culminating in a present that is both historical and actual:

> What Adam had, and forfeited for all,
> Christ keepeth now, who cannot fail or fall.   [13–14]

It is impossible to assign these lines. They either continue to report what the "friend" expressed or represent the speaker's conclusion in the present. The voices merge.

This couplet proclaims not merely that the solution to the speaker's "problem" is within the capacity and inclination of another, but that this other has in fact taken care of the matter—"What Adam had . . . Christ keepeth now." The couplet provides the positive content of the doctrine of grace: the experience of assurance. Christ cannot lose His innocence or God's favor. These lines provide a positive meaning for the title. Christ is the true "holdfast," the true agency by which we are held in place—as opposed to our own "power and might." The sense in which all things are "more ours" by being in Christ's keeping is that they are there *more secure* than they could be (or were) in our own. Luther explains that "as all things are in him [Christ], so through him we have all things."[29] "The Holdfast" does not pose a dilemma. It celebrates a—*the*—solution. And this solution is not undercut by ironies still operative and pressuring when the poem is formally complete. The formal completeness of the poem is genuine. The poem does not leave either its speaker or its reader stranded in amazement, much troubled. It ends on a note that demonstrates the

29. *Commentary on Galatians*, ed. Watson, p. 226.

proper response to what the poem "poses," the note of joy. Praise, not humility and self-abnegation, is the final note.

If "The Holdfast" is a quintessential Herbert poem in its dramatization of the strangeness and the wonder of faith alone, and if Herbert truly shared Luther's sense both of the absolute primacy of "the article of justification" and of how deeply this doctrine violates man's sense of decorum, we would expect Herbert's poetry to manifest an acute sensitivity to the many forms, including very subtle ones, in which what Cotton called "the old root of Adam" can assert itself. We have seen that the speaker of "The Holdfast," like the speaker of "The Thanksgiving," wants nothing more than to do good (*SCA*, p. 176). Almost all the retrospective narrative poems in *The Temple* dramatize threats *of this kind* to the article of justification. "Jordan" (II) presents a type of genuine piety—the desire of a poet to find words "rich" enough to express "heavenly joyes"—as deeply and fundamentally compromised. Their sense of decorum connects the speakers of "The Thanksgiving," "Jordan" (II), and "Redemption." Surely one must attempt to imitate Christ; surely only the finest words will suffice in religious poetry; surely the Lord will be found in places suitable to "his great birth." The notions of decorum in art and in social behavior are specialized applications of the concept of justice, of things or persons receiving their due (or perhaps decorum is the primary conception and justice a specialized form of it). The doctrine of faith alone outrages the demand for justice. "Human nature and natural reason," therefore, "can only condemn it."[30] Christ saves sinners, and He saves them *as sinners*. Damnation, or at least punishment, is more intelligible. The judgment of reason can only be that Christ is angry at sinners.[31]

In "The Holdfast," "Jordan" (II), "The Thanksgiving," and "Redemption," we see or hear of the activities and proposals of a persona who is suddenly, near or at the end of the poem, forced to refrain from effort and resolution, from the active attempt at righteousness. By the end of these poems, the speakers have been forced into a new passivity, into what "Prayer" (II) calls "ease." "Jordan" (II) and "The Thanksgiving" show their speakers striving to do things worthy of the favor which they feel; "The Holdfast" shows this impulse in a more internalized form. There are, however, even more subtle ways of avoiding the implications of faith alone, of insisting upon decorum. Both thematically and structurally, "The Holdfast" and "Love" (III), the final poem of "The Church," can be seen as companion pieces. In "Love" (III) Herbert dramatizes his awareness that the doctrine of

---

30. *The Freedom of a Christian*, Dillenberger, p. 85.
31. *Commentary on Galatians*, ed. Watson, pp. 226 ff.

faith alone can be undermined not merely by assertions of merit and cooperation, but by assertions of unworthiness as well. "Love" (III) shows that at the deepest level the two forms of assertion are the same.

Like "The Holdfast," "Love" (III) is a retrospective first-person narrative which begins with the announcement of an initiative immediately rejected: "I threatned to observe. . . . *But* I was told . . ."; "Love bade me welcome: *yet* my soul drew back." What gives "Love" (III) its special quality is that in this case the rejected initiative is divine. The dramatic situation is reversed, and, tonally, this makes all the difference. Herbert's presentation of the speaker's experience in "Love" (III) is a great deal more sympathetic than in "The Holdfast." The speaker of "Love" (III) is never presented as foolish, while the speaker of "The Holdfast" immediately mocks himself. If "Love" (III) is correctly described as a comic poem, it is definitely and in many senses comedy of manners, while "The Holdfast" tends toward farce. The dangers of *negative* self-assertion are not ones which Herbert was inclined to mock. They are too profoundly recognizable and too closely linked to genuine humility.

The courtesy-contest situation of "Love" (III), the guest-host framework, allows Herbert to dramatize with great precision the steps by which self-denial becomes self-assertion. The first stanza is entirely narrative and almost completely devoted to "Love's" actions and demeanor. The narrator had not yet said anything, and the only "action" he had taken was an infinitesimal and virtually involuntary one—"my soul drew back." The speaker acknowledges that this was an inappropriate response to having been "bade welcome"—"*Yet* my soul drew back"—but he proceeds in the short second line to finish the opening sentence with a justification, or at least an explanation, of his response. His soul "drew back,"

Guiltie of dust and sinne.   [2]

The moment of reluctance here being described (this drawing back, after all is internal—"*my soul* drew back") is presented as an immediate reflex of consciousness upon itself. It dramatizes the brute fact of self-consciousness. We have seen that for Herbert the words "dust and sinne" summarize the human condition;[32] in "A Nocturnall upon S. Lucies day," Donne notes that one of the characteristics of being human is that one "needs must know" that one is such. The speaker's soul draws back in "Love" (III) merely and precisely because he is human—and therefore conscious of being so, and therefore "guiltie."

32. See pp. 6–7 above.

Interestingly enough, however, the host-guest framework allows this moment of immediate self-consciousness *not* to be guilty within the fictional frame. It is very much part of ordinary courtesy (in the seventeenth century as now) to greet an unexpectedly gracious invitation with an initial demurrer. The self-consciousness in the stanza becomes almost *merely* social, "*guiltie of dust*" ("I am not dressed properly, I am dirty from the trip"). Herbert seems to want to allow his speaker (and himself, presumably) this moment. The fact that "Love" observes this reflex on the part of the speaker—"quick-ey'd Love, observing me grow slack . . . Drew nearer"—confirms its characterization as "quick-ey'd." In each of the long lines of the stanza (the stanza alternates pentameter and trimeter lines), Herbert has Love do something. It bids in line 1, observes in line 3, and finally draws nearer, "sweetly questioning" in line 5 (the use of the same verb for both the human figure and Love emphasizes the adverbs—"drew back. . . . Drew nearer"). So far, everything is perfectly courteous on *both* sides, and Love naturally asks the speaker how he can be accommodated. The stanza ends as it began, strongly focused on the graciousness of the host.

The next stanza, however, begins abruptly. The guest, hitherto existing in the poem only as a rather touching object of sympathy, suddenly speaks out (compare the movement from the first two stanzas to the third in Donne's "The Blossome").[33] The shift is made particularly striking by a change in the narrative mode and in the social situation. The guest is presented as answering the indirectly reported question of stanza 1. His answer is slightly jarring within the social situation, though perfectly intelligible psychologically. The question alluded to in stanza 1 ("What d'ye lack?") was more a gesture than a question, the guest, however, is presented as having chosen to disregard his awareness of the *kind* of utterance the host had made:

> quick-ey'd Love, observing me grow slack
> From my first entrance in,
> Drew nearer to me, sweetly questioning,
> If I lack'd anything.
>
> A guest, I answer'd, worthy to be here. [3–7]

33. See Clay Hunt's excellent comments on the shift in "The Blossome" in *Donne's Poetry: Essays in Literary Analysis* (New Haven, 1954), pp. 46–47. In general, I think it might be said that Herbert learned more from—or at least has a deeper poetic kinship with—Donne's "Songs and Sonnets" than Donne's *Holy Sonnets*. See also chap. 4, n. 47 below.

This is, as Stein says, a witty response ("a verbal clench"),[34] but it begins to put pressure on the social situation—though still remaining within the bounds of conventional courtesy ("Oh no, I couldn't . . . not me"). The guest has become the focus. The host's reply is placed in the short line; it is direct, almost curt:

> Love said, you shall be he.   [8]

The guest, however, cannot accept this. His reply takes up two lines and Herbert presents it as direct discourse, without any narrative tags:

> I the unkinde, ungratefull? Ah my deare,
> I cannot look on thee.   [9–10]

"I the unkinde, ungratefull" conceptualizes the reflex of lines 1 and 2. It begins to move, one might say, from shame to guilt. In its direct incredulity and insistence on its own view, it is a sharp, almost sarcastic rejoinder, but the poignance of the rest of the reply (moving back, once again, toward the realm of gestures—"I cannot look on thee") keeps it within the bounds of courtesy. After this burst of direct discourse, Herbert moves back to calm, past tense narration for the final long line of the stanza. As in the equivalent line of the first stanza, we are given Love's "actions" before, in the final short line, Love's words:

> Love took my hand, and smiling did reply,
> Who made the eyes but I?   [11–12]

The wit of this response and the smile accompanying it suggest that all of the guest's demurrers so far have been taken indulgently, in good part, as acceptable within the social situation. The opening of the third stanza again presents the guest responding not quite appropriately to a rhetorical question. Again the urgency of the human speaker's voice is represented by direct discourse (and again, as in the middle of stanza 2, his response is given two lines). He could not deny the host's assertion, but he could refuse to accept it as ultimate, as silencing further discussion—as it was clearly intended to be taken. Courtesy has begun to fall away here. The dialogue is becoming a debate:

> Truth Lord, but I have marr'd them: let my shame
> Go where it doth deserve.   [13–14]

---

34. *Herbert's Lyrics*, p. 193. Stein's discussion of "Love" (III) apears on pp. 191–95.

We start, at this point, to hear the note of caviling ("true, but . . .").[35] Love's reply is immediate, and the narrative tag, when it comes, is in the present tense:

> And know you not, sayes Love, who bore the blame? [15]

This question is the turning point of the stanza. From here until the end of the poem, Love is once again the focus. The human speaker appears only in the trimeters. As Stein remarks, each of the guest's moves calls forth "increased counterpressure" by the host, and this final question *is* an ultimate one. It is also, implicitly, a rebuke. It does not have the playfully witty quality of "Who made the eyes but I?" The auditory structure of the line increases its pointed quality; the stressed and alliterating plosives of "bore the blame" make it difficult to say that half of the line gently.[36]

At this point "Love" (III) approaches closely to the world of "The Holdfast" as an authoritative negation is immediately followed by a human resolve. We hear "Then will I trust" in "My deare, then I will serve" (16), although the mode of presentation is still not mocking but, as always in "Love" (III), psychologically naturalistic. In response to this assertion, Love ceases to be polite. The last line of reported dialogue in the poem, the last pentameter in the poem, is a direct command which will allow of no reply:

> You must sit down, sayes Love, and taste my meat. [17]

The source for this line, Luke 12:37, has something of the same quality of insistence: "he shall gird himself, *and make them to sit down* to meat . . . and serve them."[37] There is nothing left for the human speaker

---

35. On caviling, see p. 25 above. One of the biblical instances of caviling seems relevant to "Love" (III). In the version of the parable of the great supper told in Luke 14, the respectable guests invited "all with one consent began to make excuse." Verses 18–20 detail their excuses. For this analogue, see Chana Bloch, "George Herbert and the Bible: A Reading of 'Love' (III)," *ELR*, 8 (1978), 332.

36. Bloch, "Herbert and the Bible," seems to miss the auditory quality of the line in seeing it as "the quietest" in the poem (p. 335). This is part of Bloch's stress (contra Fish, *Living Temple*, pp. 132–33) on the gentleness of Love's voice in the poem.

37. Bloch has pointed out the analogy between this passage and the twenty-third psalm (p. 332). Herbert's version of that psalm is also oddly insistent—"Thou dost *make me* sit and dine" (line 17; emphasis mine). Fish rightly stresses the quality of insistence in the divine voice in the poem, but it does not follow from this perception that the poem is a sugarcoated "bitter pill" (*Living Temple*, p. 133). Both Fish and Bloch are right—the divine voice does have an edge of toughness and the poem *is* truly sweet. The toughness makes for the sweetness. In the episode of *Pilgrim's Progress* that parallels "Love" (III), Great-heart explains that although Mr. Fearing "had the root of the matter in him," his shaking and shrinking at the Gate made him a very "troublesome" pilgrim. Great-heart finally got him to come in "but I dare say I had hard work

to say. He has manifested and tried all forms of refusal from the barely
conscious to the fully rationalized. The end of the process which began
with Love's "welcome" is signalled by a final return to the calmly
reportorial mode of the opening.[38] All urgency falls away. Both the
human speaker's and the host's last words are prospective; the final
line, by returning to the narrative frame, reminds us that the whole
"scene" which has been evoked has already taken place. The tense
of the final trimeter is emphatically past:

So I did sit and eat.   [18]

Dialogue and argument have given way to narrative. The distinction
which "The Holdfast" makes between having nought and confessing
that we have nought makes it clear why "Love" (III) ends with a
vision of the speaker *actually doing* what he was told, and not with a
vision of him *resolving* to do so.

Critics have seen in "Love" (III) a dramatization of taking com-
munion and of the redeemed soul's entry into heaven.[39] These inter-
pretations are clearly valid: the "host-Host" pun is literalized in the
startling penultimate half-line—"and taste my meat"—and we have
already acknowledged the relevance of Christ's evocation of the final
banquet of the faithful. These readings can be coordinated through
Luther's remark that Christ "instituted the sacrament of the Supper
with a view to our entry into the future life."[40] The Eucharistic and
eschatological readings, however, are specialized forms of the mean-
ing of "Love" (III). "The Banquet," after all, precedes "Love" (III) by
only a few poems, and heaven is the subject (and title) of the poem
that immediately precedes it.[41] The primary subject of "Love" (III) is
truly what its title indicates. The poem is about *agape*. As Nygren
points out, *agape* is characterized not only by an indifference to value,
but also by a capacity to *create* value.[42] Luther expressed both con-

---

to do it." Great-heart notes that "my Lord . . . carried it wonderful lovingly to him"
(*Pilgrim's Progress*, pp. 302–4).

38. This shift in mode creates the effect to which Stein is responding when he says
that, by the end of "Love" (III), "the poem disappears" (*Herbert's Lyrics*, p. 195).

39. Martz, *Meditation*, p. 319; Summers, *Herbert*, p. 89.

40. *Babylonian Captivity (Pagan Servitude)*, Dillenberger, p. 358.

41. There is also, it should be noted, a further problem with taking "Love" (III) as
primarily Eucharistic in reference. The only people who actually *sat* and ate at com-
munion were some Puritans. Herbert explicitly rebuked the practice: "The Feast indeed
requires sitting, because it is a Feast; but *man's unpreparedness asks kneeling* . . . hee that
sits, . . . puts up to an Apostle (*CP*, p. 259; emphasis mine). For the guest to kneel
would break the frame of "Love" (III). This should alert us that the host-guest frame-
work is more central to the poem than representation of worthy receiving. For the
Puritans who sat and ate, see Davies, *The Worship of the English Puritans*, pp. 136–37.

42. Nygren, *Agape and Eros*, pp. 77–78.

ceptions with great clarity in his final thesis for the Heidelberg Disputation (1518):

The love of God does not find but creates its object (*Amor Dei non invenit sed creat suum diligibile*).[43]

The whole question of worth is irrelevant to the process of salvation; unworthiness is just as irrelevant as worthiness. This is what the human speaker of "Love" (III), out of a natural reluctance to accept a wholly unmerited gift, failed to understand. Human nature and natural reason cannot merely accept.

Confronted with being loved just as he is, "Guiltie of dust and sinne," the human speaker of "Love" (III) is preoccupied with worth— "A guest, I answer'd, *worthy to be here.*" Love's response to this demurrer is a direct assertion of the value-creating quality of *agape:* "You shall be he" (8). A more traditional politeness would have reassured the guest that he was worthy already, but Love, of course, could not do that. With the full implications of "You shall be he" in mind, the human speaker's next lines—"I the unkinde, ungratefull" can be recognized for what, at the deepest level, they are, a lack of faith, an unwillingness to believe that Love will keep His word. The human speaker "cannot look on" Love because he is so preoccupied with himself, with "*I* the unkinde, ungratefull." A contemporary philosopher has suggested that shame, the desire to avoid eyes, can easily manifest itself as an unwillingness *to recognize others* because "recognizing a person depends upon allowing oneself to be recognized by him."[44] This clarifies the emphasis on observation, looking, and eyes, in "Love" (III). The speaker "cannot look on" Love because of his own unwillingness to be looked upon. Cavell's insight also clarifies the relation between shame and pride: only the person who has a conception of his own possible worthiness would feel this desire to avoid eyes. The final words of Love in this stanza are intended to emphasize once again the irrelevance of value. "Who made the eyes but I?" implies: "I know everything about you, and it—everything that makes you ashamed—doesn't matter."[45]

---

43. *Theses for the Heidelberg Disputation,* Dillenberger, p. 503 (translation slightly amended); *WA* I, 354.

44. Stanley Cavell, "The Avoidance of Love: A Reading of *King Lear*," *Must We Mean What We Say?* (New York, 1969), p. 279.

45. Fish sees "Who made the eyes but I?" as another formulation of "the insight of God's omnipresence." He reads it as saying, "you cannot escape me because you are part of my substance" (*Living Temple,* p. 133). But again, the line says nothing at all about God's *substance.* Bloch ("Herbert and the Bible," p. 334) points out that the line is modeled on God's response to Moses' demurrer in Exodus 4:10–11.

The moment when courtesy breaks down in the poem, the climax of the guest's resistance to the host, is the moment when the human speaker most strongly insists that Love act according to his (the human speaker's) sense of decorum and justice—"let my shame / Go where it doth deserve" (13b–14). Here is when this speaker fully reveals himself as another character holding fast to something inappropriate. He is not merely recoiling into or onto himself, but making an assertion, a demand about how things, in the realm of salvation, ought to be. He is still expressing shame, but he is also now appealing to a principle, that of "desert"; he is still expressing what could legitimately be called humility, but Herbert has a strong sense of the arrogance implicit in this humility. The speaker is not only ashamed; he is also, in a sense, morally outraged. He would rather be damned than have his sense of propriety so deeply offended. The rationalism of his speaker is what Herbert is attacking; it is another refusal to "let God be God."[46] This rationalism would eliminate the mystery from God's dealings with man. It would eliminate *agape*.

The attack on rationalism implicit in "Love" (III) is clarified by another poem in *The Temple* which reveals humility to be arrogance. This poem, another loving conversation, is called simply "Dialogue." It begins at the point to which "Love" (III) comes:

> Sweetest Saviour, if my soul
> > Were but worth the having,
> Quickly should I then controll
> > Any thought of waving.   [1–4]

Once again, in an ordinary social or emotional situation, this would clearly be a plea for reassurance, and it would surely be responded to by a loving interlocutor with an assurance of worth—"you *are* worthy." But, again, this cannot be the response here, and in "Dialogue" the divine interlocutor is sharper and more direct in rebuking the human speaker than is the host of "Love" (III). In "Dialogue," the divine speaker explicitly points out the arrogance in the opening assertion of unworthiness. The frame of this dialogue is parent-child rather than host-guest, so it allows for a sharper tone:

> What, Child, is the ballance thine
> > Thine the poise and measure?
> If I say, Thou shalt be mine;
> > Finger not my treasure.   [9–12]

God declares that His decision to love is beyond human calculation. His love is "unmotivated," beyond "reasons," beyond "the fifth book

---

46. See p. 30 above.

of Aristotle's *Ethics*" or even the eighth and ninth books.[47] The affec-
tionate peremptoriness of the divine voice here is the perfect expres-
sion of the Reformation position and the perfect rebuke to tampering
human reason obsessed with the question of worth—"If I say, Thou
shalt be mine; / Finger not my treasure." We are very close here to
"*You* must sit down."

There is, however, an important difference between "Dialogue"
and "Love" (III), a difference that brings us back to the eschatological
dimension of "Love" (III) and to an aspect of its theological content
we have not yet touched upon. "Dialogue" ends on a moment of
conviction of sin within the celebration of *agape;* in response to God's
rebuke, the human speaker "lets go" of the whole question of worth.
He acknowledges that no aspect of God's benevolence toward him is
rationally intelligible, neither the initial acceptance nor the way in
which "you shall be he," neither grace nor sanctification:

> But as I can see no merit,
>   Leading to this favour:
> So the way to fit me for it
>   Is beyond my savour.
> As the reason then is thine;
> So the way is none of mine:
> I disclaim the whole designe:
> Sinne disclaims and I resigne.   [17–24]

The divine voice, now that of the Son, commends the human speaker
for his clarity before reminding him of his inability to hold there:[48]

> That is all, if that I could
>   Get without repining;
> And my clay, my creature, would
>   Follow my resigning.   [25–28]

He then describes His resigning; He did not worry about "desert":

47. *The Bondage of the Will*, p. 233. The eighth and ninth books of the *Nicomachean
Ethics* are on friendship. Aristotle there argues that since "not everything can be loved,
but only what is good," one cannot reasonably persist in loving a person who is no
longer worthy of being loved (that is, whose character has deteriorated). See *Nico-
machean Ethics*, 1165^b 15–23 (*Introduction to Aristotle*, ed. Richard McKeon [New York,
1947], p. 500).
48. Stein's reading of lines 17–24 of "Dialogue" as manifesting "open rebelliousness"
(*Herbert's Lyrics*, p. 125) is endorsed by Vendler (*Poetry of Herbert*, p. 124), but to read
the stanza in this way destroys the sequaciousness of the poem. Where Stein and
Vendler take "disclaim" in "I disclaim the whole designe" to mean "reject," I would
take it more literally as "claim none of." I would also not read "resigne" in the following
line as consciously ironic. McCanles's reading of this stanza captures its content while
still somewhat missing its tone (*Dialectical Criticism*, p. 85).

> I did freely part
> With my glorie and desert,
> Left all joyes to feel all smart . . .   [29–31]

The human speaker cannot bear this; he interrupts Christ's narrative with the cry:

> Ah! no more: thou break'st my heart.   [32]

The last stanza of "Dialogue" dramatizes the paradox by which, as Empson puts it, "the love of Christ [becomes] more painful than the law of Moses."[49] The final exclamation dramatizes the speaker's sudden emotional apprehension of the difference between Christ's "resigning" and his own.

"Love" (III), on the other hand, ends on a vision of human success, and there is no suggestion that the process it dramatizes will have to be repeated again and again. Its finality is what gives "Love" (III) its apocalyptic quality.[50] The speaker finally, as we have already noted, simply does what he is told—in silence. But this has further implications, apart from its eschatological ones. The shape of the conversation in "Love" (III) is determined by the human speaker's demurrers and resolves, but the outcome of the conversation is not so determined. It is, in fact, "none of" the speaker's. His reluctances and demurrers and resolves are all authoritatively overridden until finally he must endure the full burden of being loved and treated as a dignitary just as he is, for "no cause."[51] (This "burden" is the ultimate experience of joy; the ego naturally resists the suggestion that its deepest and most secret wish is about to be thoroughly fulfilled.)[52] The courtesy-contest of "Love" (III) is ultimately no contest; the outcome is never for a moment in doubt. Herbert is here dramatizing one of the great doctrines of the (original) Reformation: the doctrine of the irresistibility of grace.[53] This is a doctrine easily misrepresented.

49. "George Herbert and Miss Tuve," *KR*, 12 (1950), 736.

50. Fish equivocates on the matter of closure in "Love" (III). He wants the poem to represent "an exercise that has no natural cessation," but he cannot quite bring himself to assert that "Love" (III) "communicates no sense of closure." His solution is to observe that the closure in the poem is not earned but *imposed* (*Living Temple*, p. 136). One can grant this point and still not see it as making the poem bitter or unsatisfying.

51. I am borrowing this phrase from *King Lear*, IV.vii, a scene which dramatizes the human equivalent of *agape*. Much of its development is strictly parallel to that of "Love" (III).

52. Fish treats this "burden" as if it were merely painful. Vendler (*Poetry of Herbert*, p. 276) has a deeper insight into the wish-fulfillment content of the poem.

53. Fish is correct in saying that the human speaker "cannot escape" Love (see n. 45 above), but again, the reason for this has to do with God's will, not His substance, and the effect is joyous, not disturbing. McCanles captures the "double-valence" of the speaker's humility in "Love" (III), but mistakenly suggests that because of it the speaker "almost fails of salvation" (*Dialectical Criticism*, p. 76).

It seems to involve a violation of the human personality, a conception of God as an impersonal force, a steam-engine or a giant magnet. In the *Holy Sonnets*, Donne tended to conceptualize God in such ways "thou like Adamant draw mine iron heart"; "Batter my heart." But Herbert always conceived of God as a figure with whom genuine relationship was possible, a true "thou." He always, as in "Sepulchre," conceived of the irresistibility of grace in terms of love: "nothing can . . . from loving man / Withhold thee." In "Love" (III), the courtesy framework enabled him to give a fully humanly acceptable account of irresistibility. God is a host Who will not take no for an answer. In the courtesy framework, the graciousness of grace is one with its irresistibility.[54]

54. In "The Dawning," Herbert appears to suggest that grace is resistible: "Arise sad heart; *if thou doe not withstand*, / Christs resurrection thine may be" (lines 9–10; emphasis mine). The subject of "The Dawning," however, is not the relationship between the Christian and grace, but the problem of inappropriate gloom. The point of the poem is not that grace must be chosen but that Christianity is a joyful religion.

4

Vindiciae Gratiae
The Rejection of Bargaining

To say that Herbert believed in and gave appealing poetic embodiment to the doctrine of irresistible grace and to seek elucidation of his positions in the writings of Luther and Calvin are assertions and procedures that imply a particular view of Herbert's relation to his own period. He was writing, after all, over a hundred years after Luther's declaration of independence in the Reformation tracts of 1520 and over fifty years after the final version of Calvin's *Institutes*, and he was writing in a period of considerable ferment and development within the Reformed community. The Synod of Dort (1619) was the great theological event of his day. In making the claims I have made about Herbert's poetry, and in using the illustrative texts I have used, I have been implicitly asserting that Herbert was not an Arminian— not an Arminian, that is, in the *theological* sense as opposed to the general political sense in which the term is sometimes used.[1]

"I believe," wrote Arminius, "that many persons resist the Holy Spirit and *reject the grace that is offered.*"[2] Arminius denied as well the correlative doctrine of the perseverance of the saints (which, as we shall see, Herbert affirmed) and sought to put predestination on a rational footing by making it reflect foreknowledge of those who would accept grace and persevere in it and of those who would either not

---

1. For the use of "Arminian" to mean any one who supported the established church in the earlier seventeenth century, see Godfrey Davies, "Arminianism vs. Puritanism in England, ca. 1620–1640," *HLB*, 5 (1934), 157–79.

2. *A Declaration of the Sentiments of Arminius* in *The Works of James Arminius*, trans. James Nichols (London, 1825), I, 600 (emphasis mine).

84

accept or not persevere in it.[3] Arminius' rationalized view of predes-
tination follows straightforwardly from his doctrines of resistibility
and the possibility of falling from grace. Herbert, on the other hand,
accepted the "capricious" God of Augustinian and Nominalist piety,

Who gives to man, as he sees fit, $\begin{cases} \text{Salvation.} \\ \text{Damnation.[4]} \end{cases}$

In Herbert's day, however, Arminianism was not the only major
development within the Trinitarian and non-Anabaptist Reformed
community to lead away from the original theology of the Reforma-
tion. The original theology was, so to speak, being threatened from
the left as well as from the right. The decade between 1620 and 1630
was not only a period in which the Arminian controversy was intense;
it was also the period in which a number of eminent English divines
were developing the form of Calvinism which has come to be known
as "covenant theology."[5] The major English expounders of this the-
ological vocabulary (for it is more this than a set of doctrines) were
William Perkins, whose treatise on predestination led Arminius to
compose one of his important works, William Ames, Richard Sibbes,
and John Preston—the latter two exact contemporaries of Herbert.
All these men were notable "Puritans" whose works were well known
to the theological and political leaders of the New England Puritans
(Herbert's time was also that of the beginning of the Great Migration,
a fact on which he commented suggestively in his vision of religion
"readie to passe to the American strand").[6] Perry Miller has argued
at length and in various places that covenant theology is the very
marrow of Puritan divinity and that it represented, albeit uncon-
sciously, a rationalistic development parallel to the Arminianism which

3. For perseverance, see ibid., p. 602, and *Examination of Dr. Perkins's Pamphlet on
Predestination, Works of Arminius,* III, 470; on predestination, see *Declaration of Sentiments,*
pp. 589–90; *Examination of Perkins,* pp. 446 ff.
4. "The Water-course," line 10; see Lewalski, *Protestant Poetics,* p. 286.
5. See A. C. McGiffert, *Protestant Thought before Kant* (New York, 1919), pp. 153–54,
and, especially, Perry Miller, "The Marrow of Puritan Divinity," *Errand into the Wilderness*
(1956; rpt. New York, 1964), pp. 48–98; *The New England Mind: The Seventeenth Century*
(1939; rpt. Boston, 1961), ch. 13.
6. "The Church-militant," lines 235–36. In *The Life of Herbert,* p. 315, Walton states
that these "two so much noted verses" almost prevented *The Temple* from being li-
censed. The lines and their context are remarkably close to Sibbes's observation that
"The gospel's course hath hitherto been as the sun, from east to west, and so in God's
time may proceed yet further west" (*The Bruised Reed and Smoking Flax, Works,* I, 100).
In *The Puritan Origins of the American Self* (New Haven, 1975), Sacvan Bercovitch com-
ments interestingly on the relationship between Herbert's vision in these lines and
that of the American Puritans and their descendants (pp. 105, 129, 146, 235 n. 13).

it opposed and as deeply subversive of the initial emphases of the Reformation.[7]

There is no direct evidence that Herbert read Perkins, Sibbes, or Preston, though he might easily have heard as well as read the latter two. The strength of Herbert's connections to Cambridge together with the fame of the men and Herbert's professed addiction to "those infinite Volumes of Divinity, which yet every day swell, & grow bigger," make it unlikely that he would not have read (or heard) Sibbes and Preston, but this is merely plausible speculation.[8] A number of poems in *The Temple*, however, show Herbert aware of and consciously opposing, from the perspective of the original theology of the Reformation, the kinds of attitudes and emphases which Miller saw in Protestant covenant theology. Miller may have been wrong in some of his assertions about covenant theology, he may have overlooked one of its major and most surprising tendencies, and he is certainly faulty and vague on the origins of the movement; nevertheless, the poems in question show a deeply Protestant and theologically sensitive contemporary of Sibbes, Preston, and Thomas Hooker dramatizing and rejecting precisely those attitudes and emphases which Miller saw as the subversively rationalistic elements in the marrow of Puritan divinity.[9]

Covenant theology conceives of "the covenant" as the fundamental form of God's dealings with man, and the essence of this theology, according to Miller, is its conception of a covenant as a contract. What is new—or newly emphasized—in this version of Reformed theology is not the covenant vocabulary but the insistence that this term always specifies a contractual relationship.[10] "We must not," so the warning ran, "make Gods Covenant with man, so far to differ from Covenants

7. In addition to the works cited in n. 5 above, see also " 'Preparation for Salvation' in Seventeenth-Century New England." On the ironies of, for instance, Perkins's position in relation to covenant theology, see "Marrow," p. 57.

8. Letter to Sir John Danvers, 18 March 1618, Hutchinson, p. 365. On the importance of Cambridge to the Puritan movement, see William Haller, *The Rise of Puritanism* (1938; rpt. New York, 1957), passim.

9. For a perhaps overly enthusiastic review of revisions of Miller's work by recent historians, see Michael McGiffert, "American Puritan Studies in the 1960s," *William and Mary Quarterly*, 27 (1970), 36–67, esp. 47–50. For the tendency of covenant theology that Miller overlooked, see John S. Coolidge, *The Pauline Renaissance in England: Puritanism and the Bible* (Oxford, 1970), ch. 5. On the origins of seventeenth-century covenant theology, see Everett H. Emerson, "Calvin and Covenant Theology," *Church History*, 25 (1956), 136–44; and Jens G. Møller, "The Beginnings of Puritan Covenant Theology," *Journal of Ecclesiastical History*, 14 (1963), 46–67.

10. The argument of Jens G. Møller's essay, "The Beginnings of Puritan Covenant Theology," is that this view was implicit and sometimes explicit in the writings of the German-Swiss (Zwingli-Bullinger) line of Reformed theologians.

between man and man as to make it no Covenant at all."[11] The contract replaces the promise, so central to Luther's thought, as the central form of divine self-expression.[12] The terms of a covenant, in this view, must be limited, explicit, and specified in advance; the parties entering into it must know and understand the terms and freely bind themselves to their respective obligations; and, if the covenant is to remain intact, these obligations must be truly binding on the covenanting parties. If the covenant makes the performance of certain actions by one party contingent upon the fulfillment of certain conditions by the other, then the actions in question *must* be performed if the conditions in question have been fulfilled. If the relationship between God and man is a covenantal one in this sense, man must be capable of fulfilling his part of the agreement and God must be bound to fulfill His. Without going into the details of this theology—the differences between the Covenant of Works, demanding complete obedience to the moral law, which God established with Adam, and the Covenant of Grace, demanding earnest endeavor rather than perfection, which God established with Abraham—it is clear that in this framework the relationship between God and man has a legalistic cast. Grace becomes, as Miller puts it, "an opportunity to strike a bargain" on known and specified terms—and the reward, eternal life.[13]

In the poem entitled "The Pearl," Herbert presents a speaker who conceives of the religious life in just this way. He is deeply committed to doing his part, and he is an extraordinarily impressive character. As the title indicates, he takes his religious orientation from the parable of the pearl. He interprets the parable as treating the way to the kingdom of heaven rather than the value of the kingdom, and he has dedicated himself to doing what the merchant of the parable did— giving up all that he has. To him, this means giving up more than wealth. In successive stanzas we witness him renouncing three of the major goods of the world: learning, honor (meaning the courtier's life), and pleasure (especially sensual pleasure). His main aim in these

---

11. Thomas Blake, *Vindiciae Foederis; or, a Treatise of the Covenant of God Entered with Man-kinde* (London, 1653), p. 3 (quoted in Miller, *New England Mind*, p. 376). Compare Richard Baxter, *Plain Scripture Proof of Infants Church-membership and Baptism*, 3d ed. (London, 1653), p. 225: "That which is sealed by the Sacraments, is *a proper Covenant*, having a stipulation on our parts as well as a promise on God's part . . . the very definition of a proper Covenant (of which *Grotius de Jure belli*, and other Lawyers will inform you) sheweth as much that it must be *a mutual agreement*" (emphasis mine).

12. Baxter, for instance, in *Infants Church-membership* distinguishes sharply between "a proper Covenant" and a "meer Promise or Prophesie." For Luther's conception, see *The Babylonian Captivity (Pagan Servitude)* in Dillenberger; and see James Samuel Preus, *From Shadow to Promise: Old Testament Interpretation from Augustine to the Young Luther* (Cambridge, 1969).

13. *New England Mind*, p. 394.

stanzas is to establish the intimacy of his acquaintance with the realms he is renouncing. He clearly believes that the more exact his knowledge of the things he is renouncing, the more meaningful his renunciation. He begins, as I have said, with "Learning":

> I know the wayes of Learning; both the head
> And pipes that feed the presse, and make it runne;
> What reason hath from nature borrowed,
> Or of it self, like a good huswife, spunne
> In laws and policie; what the starres conspire,
> What willing nature speaks, what forc'd by fire;
> Both th' old discoveries, and the new-found seas,
> The stock and surplus, cause and historie:
> All these stand open, or I have the keyes:
>   Yet I love thee.   [1–10]

These lines do not sound like boasting, either "courtly" or "ostentatious."[14] They sound like sober demonstration. They manifest none of the sophistry, triviality, and arrogant scorn of Marlowe's Faustus surveying the disciplines in his opening soliloquy. The language of these lines demonstrates powerful intellectual (and syntactic) control. It is language of comprehensiveness and precise distinction—both this and that: "*both* . . . head / *And* pipes"; "What reason hath . . . borrowed" and what "of it self . . . spunne"; what "nature speaks" willingly and what must be "forc'd" from her; "*Both* th' old discoveries, *and* the new-found seas, / The stock *and* surplus." The conception of learning this stanza presents is close to Bacon's. Learning is not study or contemplation but the attempt to bring under human control ever larger realms of experience.[15] The speaker does not claim to know everything there is to know; he claims to know only the *kinds* of things that are to be known and the means to the various bodies of knowledge. The final short line comes with great power. Although the reader is probably, as Fish says, "neither surprised nor disconcerted" when he gets to this line, he is (or ought to be) impressed. The stanza is an impressive catalogue of the "wayes of Learning" in a number of senses, and it challenges the reader to grasp the distinctions which its speaker so compactly and magisterially makes. This speaker is outstanding in knowledge and command as well as in piety.

The stanza on "the wayes of Honour" is less resonant than the first; its terms of characterization are entirely negative. This is not necessarily a serious fault, since the speaker's claim is to know the

14. See Summers, *Herbert*, p. 151, and Fish, *Self-Consuming Artifacts*, p. 177. Fish's discussion of "The Pearl" appears on pp. 176–79.

15. For Herbert and Bacon, see chap. 2, n. 39 above.

"wayes" in question, not to admire them, and the details of the language again establish intimate knowledge. Like the first, this stanza relies upon the reader to fill in its images and abstractions out of his own knowledge of the activities in question. The detachment of the language, however, does take something from the force of the final "Yet I love thee" here; the opposing pull seems negligible. The third stanza makes up for this. A demonstration that one knows the "wayes of Pleasure" must rely on a genuine presentation of pleasure. The opening lines of this stanza are the most participatory in the poem:

> I know the wayes of Pleasure, the sweet strains,
> The lullings and the relishes of it. [21–22]

The imagistic vocabulary is musical here, but the implicit reference is sexual. "Sweet strains" blends both realms brilliantly and the reader's mind cannot help but fill in "it."[16] The speaker is concerned to establish his credentials as an ordinary human being, not a Stoic superman—"My stuffe is flesh, not brasse" (27)—and Herbert transfers to this speaker his own extraordinary capacity to dramatize "caviling" and sophistry:

> my senses live,
> And grumble oft, that they have more in me
> Than he that curbs them, being but one to five. [27b–29]

The repetition of "Yet I love thee" at the end of this stanza does not, as Fish asserts, begin to wear thin and become "praise of the self." It remains a simple, sober, and impressive assertion.

In the overall strategy of the poem, the rhetorical purpose of the first three stanzas is to give weight and authority to the opening of the fourth. The final stanza explains why the speaker has been detailing and demonstrating what he knows. The speaker has not forgotten the object of his address:

> I know all these, and have them in my hand:
> Therefore not seeled, but with open eyes
> I flie to thee, and fully understand
> Both the main sale, and the commodities;
> And at what rate and price I have thy love;
> With all the circumstances that may move.[17] [31–36]

16. For the musical terminology, see Summers, *Herbert*, p. 159. On the sexual side, perhaps a more pure-minded reader would not do what I have said at all. I am not sure. I believe Herbert to be consciously relying on his reader's fallen state here, using the "guilty reader" technique. I hesitate to suggest sexual meanings for "store" and "stuff" in lines 26–27, but see "swelling through store" in "The Flower" and Eric Partridge, *Shakespeare's Bawdy*, rev. ed. (New York, 1948), on "stuff" (p. 197).

17. I have adapted the Williams manuscript reading, "seeled," in line 32 here. It makes the antithesis in the line sharper. See Hutchinson, pp. 482–83.

For this speaker, part of the "rate and price" at which he has God's
love is that he "fully understand" what he is doing. He believes that
the terms on which he has this love demand not merely renunciation
of the world but fully mature and deliberate renunciation, renunci-
ation "with open eyes." Obadiah Sedgwick explained that one of the
reasons the covenant exists was "that we might know what to expect
from God, and *upon what terms*"(emphasis mine).[18] In Herbert's speak-
er's conception of the covenant, what God demands is precisely the
kind of mature and deliberate direction of the will that the speaker
has demonstrated.

Vendler responds to the impressiveness of this solemn dedication
of the self to God, while Fish sees these lines as "a nearly exhaustive
catalogue of the forms intellectual pride can take."[19] Fish's reading,
however, has the advantage of taking into account the fact that the
poem does not end here. At line 37, the speaker proceeds to another
"yet," this time incorporating the adversative into the body of his
stanza:

> Yet through these labyrinths, not my groveling wit,
> But thy silk twist let down from heav'n to me,
> Did both conduct and teach me, how by it
>   To climbe to thee.   [37–40]

These lines reveal the whole body of the poem to have been a trap.
The force of this final "Yet" depends upon the reader not having
anticipated it, upon the tone of the previous stanzas and the previous
part of this stanza not having been the crude, transparently self-
seeking and self-congratulatory one that Fish hears.[20] The point of
the poem, its aim and mark, is to reveal that even the most impressive
and sober attempt to "come to terms" with God is deeply misguided.
After the impressiveness and obvious intelligence of the speaker, "my
groveling wit" in line 37 is meant to come as a shock, almost an insult
to the reader. The poem ends on dependence rather than on dedi-
cation. They way in which the speaker has come, in the Scholastic
phrase, "to love God above all things,"[21] is through grace, not un-
derstanding. "By it" is emphatically placed. By God's "silk twist" let

18. Quoted in Miller, "Preparation for Salvation," p. 55.

19. *Poetry of Herbert*, pp. 181–82; *Self-Consuming Artifacts*, p. 178.

20. According to Fish, by the end of the third stanza, "the speaker and the reader
part company." Fish has the reader-speaker relationships established by "The Pearl"
and "The Holdfast" exactly reversed. "The Holdfast" does *not* trap the reader; "The
Pearl" does. Fish comments aptly on the way in which the "Yet" of line 37 works
against the previous three occurrences of the word, but then goes on to deny the
"stability" of this ending (see p. 66 above).

21. On *amor Dei super omnia*, see Oberman, *Harvest of Medieval Theology*, pp. 133, 153,
156, 460.

down to him rather than by his own powers has the speaker been enabled to love and "climbe to" God (Swift's joke about climbing and crawling is relevant here, as opposed to the dignity of "flying").[22] The poem is evidence, finally, not of what man can do but of what God has done. He "*Did* both conduct and teach me." The mutuality essential to the covenant-as-contract falls away.

What is implied by "The Pearl" is stated in "Obedience." Although the short, mobile, erratically lineated stanza of "Obedience" is at the opposite end of the formal spectrum from the massive, regular stanza of "The Pearl," the two poems are virtual companion pieces. The first stanza of "Obedience" meditates on written contracts within the framework of a prayer that God allow the poem to constitute such a contract:

> My God, if writings may
> Convey a Lordship any way
> Whither the buyer and the seller please;
> Let it not thee displease,
> If this poore paper do as much as they.   [1–5]

The tonal and thematic tensions of this stanza become explicit in the course of the poem. The first part of the stanza, the meditation on contracts (lines 1–3), stresses the power and freedom of ordinary contracts—"*any way* / Whither the buyer and the seller please"—while the second part, the prayer section (lines 4–5), is extremely tentative and humble—"Let it not thee displease"; "this poore paper." Implicit in the tentativeness of this conclusion is the suppressed or merely suspended recognition that the norms for dealings between man and man are *not* relevant to divine-human interactions. In the social context—"in respect . . . of what is below him"—man has power and can do as he pleases; in the other world of religion, he must worry about displeasing God.[23] The rhyme and juxtaposition of "please" and "displease" enforce the contrast.

The stanza ends, however, on a vision of what "this poore paper" *can* do—"Let it not thee displease, / If this poore paper do as much as they." The mixture of pride and humility in these lines is remarkable. By the end of line 5 "this poore paper" has taken on unquestionable strength; it is as powerful as an elaborate and formal "instrument." The opening of the second stanza continues the assertion of what the "poore paper" can do:

22. See "Thoughts on Various Subjects" in *Gulliver's Travels and Other Writings by Jonathan Swift*, ed. Ricardo Quintana (New York, 1958), p. 418.

23. On man's power in respect of what is below him, see p. 65 above; for religion as "another world" from that of ordinary life, see *CP*, p. 228.

On it my heart doth bleed
As many lines, as there doth need
To passe it self and all it hath to thee.   [6–8]

All the nervousness of stanza 1 has disappeared. Instead, there is an
extraordinary confidence about how many lines "there doth need"
to "passe" the heart to God. The stanza again divides after its third
line, and in the second half of this stanza, the speaker's full self ratifies
what his heart has spontaneously poured out:

To which I do agree,
And here present it as my speciall Deed.   [9–10]

The poem is clearly meant to be performative here; line 10 is meant
to establish the conveyance described in lines 6–8.[24] Hutchinson is
surely right in pointing out that this stanza imagines a pious parallel
to the demonic contract written in blood. As in the contract scene in
Faustus, the speaker presents himself as solemnly writing a deed of
gift in his own heart's blood. This conscious ratification of his heart's
spontaneous dedication is the speaker's "speciall Deed" (the pun, I
think, is fully intended by Herbert, though not by the dramatized
speaker). The mode of the poem is coming closer and closer to that
of "The Pearl":

If that hereafter Pleasure
Cavill, and claim her part and measure,
As if this passed with a reservation,
Or some such words in fashion;
I here exclude the wrangler from thy treasure.   [11–15]

The solemnity, the dignity, the psychological and social awareness of
this speaker all link him to the speaker of "The Pearl." Like that
speaker, the voice of this stanza fully understands what is at stake in
his actions. He wants his deeding of himself to be absolute, and he
solemnly discounts in advance all possible future talk of loopholes,
limitations, and mental reservations. "I here exclude the wrangler"
has all the dignity and weight of "I know all these, and have them
in my hand" in "The Pearl." Again the speaker presents his contract
as superior in quality to its worldly equivalents. He is a man, like the

24. On "performatives," see J. L. Austin, *How to Do Things with Words*, ed. J. O.
Urmson (1962; rpt. New York, 1965), Lecture 1.

speaker of lines 1–36 of "The Pearl," who could fully subscribe to Greville's chilling assertion, "I know the world and believe in God."[25]

There is, however, something else at work in line 15 of "Obedience," "I here exclude the wrangler from thy treasure." There is something paradoxical about the way it proceeds. Beginning with a strong assertion that places us firmly within the speaker's subjectivity, the line ends with a phrase that unexpectedly forces us to conceive of the acting and willing speaker as an object. With this shift the entire poem changes direction. Its focus becomes God's rather than the speaker's will. Instead of asserting and agreeing and excluding, the speaker suddenly turns to entreating—from acting and willing to asking God to act upon him. As the mode of the poem shifts from explanation to prayer, the relation of the syntax to the stanza also changes. The opening couplet becomes a complete exclamatory unit:

> O let thy sacred will
> All thy delight in me fulfill!   [16–17]

The speaker now presents himself totally as object. There is only one relevant will. The next lines are even more emphatic:

> Let me not think an action mine own way,
> But as thy love shall sway,
> Resigning up the rudder to thy skill.   [18–20]

There is no mistaking the emphasis on "Let me not *think*" here; it is metrical as well as rhetorical. The language of willing and contracting has once again been deceptive. The speaker does not want to steer himself to God but to be steered by God, to become an object on which and through which God's will—that is, His love—works.

The next stanza begins with another two-line exclamation, this time brought on by the thought of God's love. As in "Dialogue," it is only from God's inscrutable viewpoint that fallen man is a treasure. For two lines, Herbert writes a penitential psalm:

> Lord, what is man to thee,
> That thou shouldst minde a rotten tree?   [21–22]

Instead, however, of using this stanza as he did the previous one, making its second part expand upon its opening exclamation, Herbert here takes a rather different tack. Conviction of sin arises not only from the sense of the moral contrast between God and man but also

25. See Geoffrey Bullough, "Fulke Greville, First Lord Brooke," *MLR*, 28 (1933), 1. Bullough considers this assertion "a key to [Greville's] whole life." See also C. S. Lewis, *English Literature in the Sixteenth Century, Excluding Drama* (Oxford, 1954), p. 525.

from the sense of man's moral transparency to God ("He sees hearts as we see faces" [*CP*, p. 234]). In "Miserie," a poem entirely devoted to stimulating conviction of sin in its reader and writer, this transparency is a central theme: "Thou within [man's] curtains drawn canst see." In stanza 5 of "Obedience," Herbert tries to transform man's total visibility to God from a source of religious fear and shame into an argument for the loving control of man envisioned in the previous stanza:

> Yet since thou canst not choose but see my actions;
> So great are thy perfections,
> Thou mayst as well my actions guide as see.   [23–25]

Detecting in these lines "a lapse in Herbert's usual subtlety," Stein finds that the argument here "does not seem to point beyond itself" as Herbert's sophistical arguments elsewhere do.[26] But the key to these lines is their sophistry. They are so obviously sophistical as to be playful. There is no mistaking the "saintly impertinence" of "since thou canst not choose" and the jaunty quality of "Thou mayst as well."[27] The lines are playful because they are happy. The vision of God's directing love which burst into the poem in stanza 4 now dominates the speaker's consciousness. The sixth stanza makes this clear. It extends the jaunty mode of the second half of stanza 5 into an even more exaggerated casualness.[28] "Besides," it begins,

> thy death and bloud
> Show'd a strange love to all our good.   [26–27]

Besides! For a moment the manner of "Obedience" comes close to the delighted naiveté of "The Bag." In the three-line unit of the stanza, Herbert gives up some of this casualness in order to elaborate on "a strange love"—on *agape* manifested in the Cross:

> Thy sorrows were in earnest; no faint proffer,
> Or superficial offer
> Of what we might not take, or be withstood.   [28–30]

It is essential to this strange love that, like the Host in "Love" (III), it is "in earnest"—it cannot be refused or withstood. The whole contract notion has fallen away. The relation between God and man *is* a

---

26. *Herbert's Lyrics*, p. 128.

27. For "saintly impertinence," see Empson, *Ambiguity*, p. 238.

28. Compare Stein, *Herbert's Lyrics*, p. 53: "The whole poem ('Obedience') cultivates colloquial phrasing and other effects of casual raciness." But, Stein wisely adds, it does so "as part of the complex manner being developed."

matter of necessity, and necessity, as Samuel Willard points out, "destroys the very nature of a Covenant."[29]

Finally, having made this long digression from the opening "conveyance" framework, the speaker returns to it at the beginning of the seventh stanza: "Wherefore"—in the light of the *agape* of the Cross and the earnestness of God's love—"I all forgo" (line 31). This does not, however, seem to be an advance over stanzas 1 through 3 proportionate to the clarification which has been attained. Herbert is aware of this problem; the rest of the stanza deals with it explicitly:

> Wherefore I all forgo:
> To one word onely I say, No:
> Where in the Deed there was an intimation
> Of a gift or a donation,
> Lord, let it now by way of purchase go.   [31–35]

"The Deed" is the one described and "presented" in stanza 2 ("my speciall Deed"). The poet is taking back all suggestion that he had anything to do with God's possession of his heart. "By way of purchase" is the key phrase. The "purchase" here is the "price" Christ paid in the crucifixion ("thy death and bloud"). The conception of the "purchase-sale" embodied in Hutchinson's note from Littleton's *Tenures*, "Purchase is called the possession of landes or tenementes that a man hath by his dede or by his agreemente," is precisely the conception that Herbert is *denying*—the "intimation / Of a gift or a donation."[30] Through having been purchased by Christ is the only way a man's heart can be "passed" to God.

This stanza would seem to be a genuine conclusion, summing up and resolving the entire movement of the poem. It is similar in effect (though not in wit) to the final stanza of "Submission," which also begins with a resounding "wherefore" leading to a moment of heroic renunciation, and also ends on a very different note through a "slight" qualification of the initial resolution:

> Wherefore unto my gift I stand;
> I will no more advise:
> Onely do thou lend me a hand,

29. *The Doctrine of the Covenant of Redemption* (1693), p. 68 (quoted in Miller, *New England Mind*, p. 375).

30. Hutchinson, p. 514; see also Bernard Knieger, "The Purchase-Sale: Patterns of Business Imagery in the Poetry of George Herbert," *SEL*, 6 (1966), 109–24. Knieger presents Herbert's model of salvation as "a *bargain* or a *two-fold agreement*": God, "the party of the first part, agrees to be sold in order to discharge man's immediate debts (to Satan)"; in return, Knieger continues, "man, the party of the second part, agrees to pay God his soul and *to guarantee the worth of the merchandise by renouncing sin* and by otherwise following God's 'way' " (pp. 114–15; emphasis mine).

Since thou hast both mine eyes.
["Submission," 17–20]

"Obedience," however, does not end with its seventh stanza; it continues for two more. These stanzas seem to be an afterthought (though that they are such cannot be proven). They contradict the theological content and dramatic movement of the rest of the poem. Suddenly, perhaps because of the extraordinary self-consciousness of the poem ("this poore paper"; "As many lines"), Herbert begins thinking about its human reader. What seems to happen, under the pressure of this concern, is that Herbert's intense desire for his poems to do some religious good overwhelms his care for his theology. The situation is analogous to that of the Calvinist preacher whose zeal to encourage righteousness leads him to frame exhortations in ways not fully consonant with his theology.[31] In thinking of his human reader, Herbert returns to the conception he has just renounced:

He that will passe his land,
As I have mine, may set his hand
And heart unto this Deed, when he hath read;
And make the purchase spread
To both our goods, if he to it will stand.

How happie were my part,
If some kinde man would thrust his heart
Into these lines; till in heav'ns Court of Rolls
They were by winged souls
Entred for both, farre above their desert!   [36–45]

The final reference to transcending desert cannot eradicate the emphasis throughout these stanzas on the importance of human ability and resolution in the divine-human transaction—"*He that will* passe his land . . . *may* set his hand*." Everything depends upon whether the human partner "will stand" to the bargain with God. Again compare "Wherefore unto my gift *I stand,*" the transcended heroic ending of "Submission."[32]

Poems like "Obedience" and "The Pearl" reject the assumptions underlying covenant theology without ever rising to complete theological clarity. They are probably to be seen as reflecting the state of Herbert's theological development during the period in which they were written (they both appear in "W"). "Miserie" is another poem

31. Compare Miller, *New England Mind*, pp. 261–62.
32. Vaughan's response to "Obedience" in "The Match" (*Works*, pp. 434–35) responds literally to the final stanzas. Vaughan's sensitivity to theological tensions was not notable.

of this sort. It presents "the best of men" as incapable *ex puris natu-ralibus* of any steadiness in devotion or morality:

> The best of men, turn but thy hand
> For one poore minute, stumble at a pinne.[33]   [19–20]

And it presents these same best men as incapable of maintaining a bilateral agreement with God:

> They quarrell thee, and would give over
> The bargain made to serve thee.   [25–26]

Only God's love "holds them unto it,"

> Not suff'ring those
> Who would, to be thy foes.   [29–30]

Herbert here seems to agree with John Cotton that "it is . . . a manifest error, to make the agreement or consent on man's part essential to a Covenant between God and man."[34] "Miserie," however, suffers from a number of theological and attitudinal inconsistencies in both its presentation of sin and its use of hortatory and bargaining rhetoric—"Thou pull'st the rug, and wilt not rise, / No, not to purchase the whole pack of starres."

The poem in which Herbert's rejection of the premises underlying covenant theology comes to full definition is "Artillerie," one of a series of powerful and theologically explicit poems written after the compilation of the "W" manuscript. Although recent criticism has largely ignored it, "Artillerie" is one of the major lyrics of "The Church."[35] It begins as a retrospective first-person narrative and creates a fully dramatized allegorical world. The opening gives us a character, a setting, and an "event":

> As I one ev'ning sat before my cell,
> Me thoughts a starre did shoot into my lap.   [1–2]

---

33. It is significant that John Wesley, committed to a revisionist view of sanctification, marked these lines with an emphatic "NO!" (see Elsie A. Leach, "John Wesley's Use of George Herbert," *HLQ*, 16 [1953], 194).

34. *The Grounds and Ends of the Baptisme of the Children of the Faithfull* (1647), p. 65. Cotton makes use of Luther's *coram hominibus* / *coram Deo* contrast (see chap. 1, n. 7 above): "with men indeed, mutuall agreement and consent is necessary to a Covenant, but with God, *God's appointment maketh a Covenant, whether the creature consent to an agreement or no*" (p. 64; emphasis mine).

35. "Artillerie" has been treated at length only in Clements, "Theme, Tone, and Tradition," and in William V. Nestrick, " 'Mine and Thine' in *The Temple*," in Summers and Pebworth, eds., *"Too Rich to Clothe the Sunne,"* pp. 121–26.

As always in Herbert's narrative poems, the focus of the imagined situation is the speaker's response to it. The remainder of the quatrain gives us this response:

> I rose, and shook my clothes, as knowing well,
> That from small fires comes oft no small mishap.   [3–4]

Only an inexperienced reader of Herbert would fail to detect the satisfied reliance on prudential wisdom expressed in these lines. Within the imagined situation, the speaker, like his distant cousin the protagonist of "Redemption," is acting perfectly naturally and perfectly reasonably. There can be no doubt of this speaker's worldly wisdom; his expression of it takes on virtually proverbial form—"from small fires comes oft no small mishap." The singsong of the meter reinforces the smug and proverbial effect, as does the ostentatiously balanced construction.

The second half of the stanza also contains four lines but departs from the pattern of cross-rhymed decasyllabics; it rhymes in couplets and contains three octosyllabic lines before a final decasyllabic. Here the expected rebuke of the speaker occurs and the allegory is explicated. The first octosyllabic is a narrative transition from the speaker's perspective to direct quotation from an authoritative "one":

> When suddenly I heard one say,
> *Do as thou usest, disobey,*
> *Expell good motions from thy breast,*
> *Which have the face of fire, but end in rest.*   [5–8]

The shooting star was a "good motion." There is no doubt that Herbert believed in "motions," in what Milton called "intimate impulse[s]" from God. Herbert seems, however, to have believed that "restraining motions" like those depicted in "The Method" were more common than "inviting motions" of the sort depicted here.[36] The "good motion" in question clearly involved some danger or discomfort for the speaker ("the face of fire"), but only as a means toward a final good. The speaker's immediate and prudential response—"I rose, and shook my clothes"—and his generalizing of this response were completely inappropriate and irrelevant. Perhaps, as in "Redemption," the contrast between the strangeness of the situation (the speaker's "Lord" lives in heaven; a star shoots into someone's lap) and the banality of the response itself tells the story. Once again, Herbert is attacking natural reason, and once again he is attacking it for assuming that *its*

36. For "intimate impulse," see *Samson Agonistes,* lines 222–23; for Herbert's assertion that "restraining motions are much more frequent to the godly, then inviting motions," see *Notes on Valdes,* p. 313. In "The Method," Herbert presents himself as having recently ignored "a motion to forbear" something he was about to do (lines 22–24).

rules and assumptions are relevant to the realm of religion. Once again he is, as Luther expresses it, putting a difference between the two worlds "to the end that manners and faith, works and grace, policy and religion should not be confounded, or taken the one for the other."[37] The most natural of responses—self-preservation and the avoidance of pain—turns out to be opposition to God ("Do as thou usest, disobey").

The second stanza begins by continuing the narrative:

> I, who had heard of musick in the spheres,
> But not of speech in starres, began to muse.   [9–10]

The self-mocking comedy of lines 3 and 4 ("I rose and shook my clothes") seems to continue here. The speaker, an educated man who had heard of "musick in the spheres," is more taken by the fact that "a starre" seems to have spoken to him than by the content of what it said. The rest of the stanza, however, does not continue in this mode. A counter-movement begins in the third line, and its development fills out the stanza:

> But turning to my God, whose ministers
> The Starres and all things are; If I refuse,
>   Dread Lord, said I, so oft my good;
>   Then I refuse not ev'n with bloud
>   To wash away my stubborn thought:
> For I will do or suffer what I ought.   [11–16]

The content of the divine rebuke, recognized as such, *has* affected the speaker. His turn from himself to God, from musing to declaration, is signalled by a burst of powerfully biblical language and perception—"whose ministers / The starres and all things are"—and by a burst of guilt and willingness to suffer. The tone of these lines is extremely difficult to capture for analysis. There is no doubt of their sincerity. They seem close to the self-resignation that emerges in stanza 3 of "Dialogue" ("Sinne disclaims, and I resign"), but they contain a more problematic element. There is still an incipient rationalism in them, a rationalism dramatized by Herbert in the neat balance of the "If I refuse . . . then I refuse not" construction and in the speaker's assumptions that he *can* "do or suffer" what he ought and that by so doing can "wash away" the sin of his previous disobedience and frivolity. I do not mean to portray this speaker's gesture as cruder than it is. It is very close to the genuine resignation of "The Crosse," but it is still, at least in its form of expression, tainted in the ways suggested. Heroism, in Herbert, even when genuine, is always so.

37. *Commentary on Galatians*, Watson, p. 24.

By the end of the stanza, the speaker of "Artillerie," like the companions of the young Donne, is "hungry of an imagined martyrdom."[38]

Whatever the precise tonal and attitudinal content of the second stanza, the gesture made there does not represent the speaker's final position in the poem. The third stanza begins with a potentially ominous "But." Whatever the ultimate value of the position at which stanza 2 arrives, it is certainly an enormous advance over the prudential and openly self-satisfied mode of stanza 1, and it is certainly not to be lightly disregarded. The third stanza lightly disregards it. The tense of the poem shifts; the speaker drops retrospective narration for present assertion. By extending the artillery metaphor implicit in the "shooting star" incident, he is able to insist that he need not, as he had thought in the guilt-stricken moment recreated in stanza 2, merely stand and wait. He can take an active role:

> I have also starres and shooters too,
>   Born where thy servants both artilleries use.   [17–18]

The next lines of the quatrain (now, as in stanza 1, used as a unit) explicate the "starres and shooters . . . both artilleries" metaphor and define the actual dramatic situation of the poem:

> My tears and prayers night and day do wooe,
>   And work up to thee; yet thou dost refuse.   [19–20]

The dramatic situation is the same as that in "Deniall," "Church-lock and key," and "The Method"—God's ears seem "locked"; "no hearing." The speaker of "Artillerie" has conjured up the "shooting star" incident in order to use the metaphor it provides *as a way out of his present situation.*

Before making his major move, however, this speaker has a moment of caution, both rhetorical and theological, in the three octosyllabics. He does not mean to be impious:

> Not but I am (I must say still)
> Much more oblig'd to do thy will,
> Than thou to grant mine: but because
> Thy promise now hath ev'n set thee thy laws.   [21–24]

This is a rather elliptical construction; it ends before telling us what God is "oblig'd" to do. It only tells us why He is obliged. What God is obliged to do, of course, is to grant the speaker's will, his prayers. This is the point of the "to do" / "to grant" parallel. That this stanza

---

38. "The Preface," *Biathanatos*, facs. with a Bibliographical Note by J. William Hebel (New York, 1930), p. 17. In stanza 10 of "A Litanie," Donne notes that "to some / Not to be Martyrs, is a martyrdome."

means to establish what John Preston termed "a kinde of equality" between God and the speaker, however parenthetically hedged, emerges clearly at the beginning of the final stanza.[39] The artillery metaphor yields its final harvest:

> *Then we are shooters both,* and thou dost deigne
> To enter combate with us, and contest
> With thine own clay.   [25–27a; emphasis mine]

Although the sentence which ends the pentameter quatrain begins with an adversative, it extends rather than calls into question the development of the artillery metaphor; it offers a "bargain":

> But I would parley fain:
> Shunne not my arrows, and behold my breast.   [27b–28]

The speaker assimilates the whole poem into these lines. He returns to stanzas 1 and 2. The bargain or parley runs thus: If you, God, will not be unresponsive to my prayers, then I will be obedient to the "motions" which you send, however painful on "the face" of them they may be. We have come back to the end of stanza 2—"behold my breast" is exactly equivalent to "I will do or suffer what I ought." But the speaker now has more definite and more positive expectations: he expects God to respond in accordance with the laws to which His promise has "now" committed Him (line 24). The speaker sees, in other words, the posture into which he remembers being thrown by the divine rebuke as the answer to his current dilemma.

"God's covenant," William Perkins explained, "is his contract with man, concerning the obtaining of life eternall, upon a certain condition. This covenant consists of two parts: God's promise to man, man's promise to God. God's promise to man is that whereby he bindeth himselfe to man to be his God, if he performe the condition. Man's promise to God is that whereby he voweth his allegeance unto his Lord, and to performe the condition betweene them."[40] Bishop Hooper, a good deal earlier, called the covenant "the condition of the peace between God and man"—in other words, a "parley."[41] The artillery metaphor provided Herbert with a way of presenting the exact mechanism as well as the exact attitude of covenant theology. Covenant theology was, after all, developed most fully by men who thought of themselves as Calvinists. It was not intended to derogate

---

39. *The New Covenant, or The Saints Portion,* 4th ed., corr. (1630), p. 331.

40. *A Golden Chaine, or the Description of Theologie,* in *The Workes of . . . William Perkins* (London, 1626), p. 32a.

41. "Unto the Christian Reader," *A Declaration of the Ten Holy Commandments,* in *The Early Writings of John Hooper,* ed. Samuel Carr (Cambridge, 1848), p. 255 (quoted in Møller, "Beginnings," p. 55).

from God's majesty. The theological center of the position, as Miller
has shown, is the assertion that God has freely and of His own mys-
terious good pleasure chosen to bind Himself to the covenant. He
alone, as Miller puts it, "of His own unfettered will, proposed that
He be chained."[42] God did not have to enter into a covenant with
man. As with "humiliations" normally preceding "joyes," God has
not "tied himself to this manner of dealing upon any necessity, but
. . . hath expressed it to be his good pleasure so to dispense himself."[43]
Preston presented God as saying to man in the Covenant of Grace:

> I will not onely tell thee what I am able to doe, I will not onely
> expresse to thee in generall, that I will deal well with thee . . . if
> thou walke before me and serve me . . . but I am willing to enter
> into Covenant with thee, that is, *I will binde myselfe*, I will ingage
> my selfe, *I will enter into bond*, as it were, I will not bee at liberty
> any more, but I am willing even to make a Covenant, a compact
> and agreement with thee . . . There shall be a mutual ingagement
> betweene us.[44]

Herbert's "Thy promise now hath ev'n set thee thy laws" captures
the accent as well as the position of covenant theology. The "now"
and the "ev'n . . . thee" (all in positions of metrical prominence) are
very much part of the temper of this theology, in contrast, for instance,
with Richard Hooker's more Thomistic assertion that the *being* of God
"is a kind of law to his working."[45] The covenant theologians sidle
up to the assertion that God is "bound" by the covenant in just the
same way that Herbert's speaker does—"Not but . . . (I must say still)
. . . but because. . . ." However, the final result of the covenant ar-
rangement, thus interpreted, must be that God is bound, that the
terrifying God "whose ministers / The starres and all things are" has
set Himself laws, has deigned by His promise to treat with man, His
creature, as it were on equal terms—"hee is in heaven, and wee are
on earth; hee the glorious God, we dust and ashes; hee the Creator,
and wee but creatures; and yet hee is willing to enter into Covenant,
which implyes," as we have already heard Preston saying, "a kind
of equality betweene us." Then we are shooters both. The syntax of
the Preston passage, like the syntax of Herbert's third stanza, is itself

42. *New England Mind*, p. 379.

43. Thomas Hooker, *The Application of Redemption by the Effectual Work of the Word, The
Ninth and Tenth Books*, 2d ed. (London, 1659), p. 337 (quoted in Miller, *New England
Mind*, p. 379; "Marrow," p. 64 n). Miller's use of this passage is slightly misleading in
that he creates the impression that Hooker is directly referring to the Covenant here.

44. *The New Covenant*, p. 316 (quoted in part in Miller, "Marrow," p. 63); emphasis
mine.

45. *Of the Laws of Ecclesiastical Polity*, I.ii.2, intro. Christopher Morris (New York,
1965), I, 150.

significant. There is always an "and yet" in this theology. And, needless to say, the "promise" to which Herbert refers in "Thy promise now hath ev'n set thee thy laws" *is* the Covenant.

The practical result of the covenant arrangement was that if man did his part, he could call upon God to do His. It is this to which God is "bound"—if man does his part, God *must* do His. In the Covenant, "you may sue him of his own bond, written and sealed, and he cannot deny it."[46] When Herbert's speaker says, "behold my breast," he clearly expects God to respond by keeping His side of the bargain (as He does not seem to be doing in refusing to respond to the speaker's "tears and prayers"). Through abandoning his initial refusal of suffering, the speaker has put himself, he apparently feels, into a proper relationship to God.

The octosyllabics of the final stanza reveal the speaker's recognition—equivalent to the turnabout in "The Pearl," though more eloquent and satisfying—that he has been deeply misguided in his covenantal "artillerie" conception. As opposed to the mock adversative, "But I would parley faine," at the end of the quatrain, the reversal presented here is genuine. "Shun not my arrows," the speaker had cried, suing God of His bond, before suddenly realizing that he is not in a bargaining position—even with his breast exposed. Each of the final lines of "Artillerie" is a complete assertion, and each assertion adds a nail to the coffin of the covenant conception:

> Yet if thou shunnest, I am thine:
> I must be so, if I am mine.
> There is no articling with thee:
> I am but finite, yet thine infinitely.   [29–32]

"There is no articling with thee"—the rejection of a contractual covenant conception could hardly be more explicit.[47] God is not to be conceived of as in any way bound or obliged to keep particular terms with men. There is all freedom on the one side and all obligation on

46. Preston, *The New Creature, or A Treatise of Sanctification* (1633), p. 23 (quoted in Miller, "Marrow," p. 72).

47. The literary ancestry of "There is no articling with thee" is interesting. This line, together with line 29 of "Artillerie" ("Yet if thou shunnest, I am thine"), seems to be drawn from one of Donne's "Songs and Sonnets." In the relevant stanza of "Loves exchange," Donne gives up demanding anything from Love. The stanza begins, "If thou [love] give nothing, yet thou art just" (line 22), and moves to the conclusion, "I may not article for grace" (line 27). Arnold Stein's comment on "Loves exchange" (*John Donne's Lyrics* [Minneapolis, 1962], p. 130) illuminates the connection with "Artillerie." Stein argues that in this poem, Donne managed "to create and stay wonderfully close to a genuine inner pattern of tragedy, and to unite that pattern with an ironic, triumphant humility, and to make *authentic religious feeling* bear on a pagan and secular theme" (emphasis mine). See chap. 3, n.33.

the other. "Hee is in heaven, wee are on earth; hee the glorious God, wee dust and ashes; hee the Creator, and wee but creatures"—and no "and yet." The initial concession before the appeal to the covenant in stanza 3—"Not but I am (I must say still) / Much more oblig'd"— turns out to be true in an absolute rather than a concessive sense, and the relationship between man's obligation to do God's will and God's obligation to grant man's turns out not to be a matter of degree at all ("*more* oblig'd to do thy will, / Then thou to grant mine: but . . ."). Man is infinitely bound. He has only obligations, no rights—except, that is, the "right" of being his own *because* he is God's.[48] In a sense, then, "Artillerie" ends with a new version of the complexly resonant assertion which ended its second stanza. "I am but finite, yet thine infinitely" expresses all the reverence of "I will do or suffer what I ought" without any of the self-regard and rational calculation that slightly vitiate the earlier assertion. The distinction is parallel to that between having nought and confessing that we have nought in "The Holdfast." "I am but finite, yet thine infinitely" expresses the profound feeling of creaturehood, of ontological distance and moral obligation, which Rudolf Otto took as central to the human experience of the holy.[49]

In its assertion of the utter absoluteness of God's sovereignty, "Artillerie" is close to "To all Angels and Saints."[50] The dynamics of the poem, the emergence into prominence of the mutual obligation conception, seem to have provoked Herbert to this response, to an assertion of the Nominalist terror at the core of Calvinist piety. "Artillerie" is therefore also like "To all Angels and Saints" in not being, in content, thoroughly characteristic of Herbert. In spite of the playfulness and comedy of its opening and the occasional resurgence of comedy in the development of the title conceit, "Artillerie" becomes, by the time it concludes, a grim, if moving, piece. The rejection of the covenant conception is normally more joyous for Herbert, as the poems on irresistibility demonstrate. Central to the assertion of irresistibility (which the covenant conception obfuscates) and central to the entire endeavor of the Reformation was the doctrine of assurance. Covenant theology intended to articulate the doctrine of assurance; in this regard too, however, it subverted what it intended to bolster. Since covenant theology stressed man's duties under the covenant, it tended to regard the performance of these duties (or the heartfelt attempt at them) as evidence of election, of inclusion in the covenant. This is "the Doctrine of Marks and Signs," the search for evidences of election which cre-

48. This conception is implicit in "The Holdfast" and fully articulated in "Clasping of hands," a poem that denies the contractual conception potentially implicit in its title.
49. *The Idea of the Holy*, pp. 8–30.
50. See Strier, " 'To All Angels and Saints: Herbert's Puritan Poem," pp. 135–45.

ated the paradox by which, as Empson puts it, salvation by faith came to give an intolerable importance to works.[51]

"Assurance," one of the series of theologically explicit poems written after the completion of "W," manifests and explains the joy Herbert normally found in the rejection of the covenant idea. Technically, the mode of "Assurance" is dialogue or address, but in effect the poem is a soliloquy since the addressee in the opening and closing stanzas is a "thought." The whole poem is a dramatic response to a thought which the speaker is presented as having just had—indeed perhaps as continuing in some sense to "have" throughout the course of the poem (our vocabulary for talking about the mind's relations to particular "thoughts" is very crude). The speaker of the poem seems less a persona, a dramatized consciousness with particular characteristics, than a direct projection of Herbert's own consciousness. Although "Assurance" is not a comic poem, it is, as we shall see, a resoundingly triumphant one.

The thought in question must, we gather from the title, be a threat to the speaker's assurance, but Herbert dramatizes his response to the thought before revealing its content. He seems too horrified to verbalize that content. The opening is exclamatory, almost sputtering, as if Herbert were trying to banish the thought by execrating it, calling it names:

> O spitefull bitter thought!
> Bitterly spitefull thought! [1–2a]

Aside from the showy chiastic effect, what is striking about these parallel exclamations is not their evocation of the painfulness of the thought, but their ascription of malice to it. This is an odd way to speak of one's own thoughts; it makes the "thought" a conscious and independent agent. Yet this seems to be precisely the suggestion Herbert wants. He experiences this "thought" as a consciously malicious attack on him, a suggestion that is intensified by the major previous instance of spite in the poetry, the torture of Christ in "The Sacrifice"—"See how *spite cankers* things" (line 109, emphasis mine; see also lines 85 and 245).

After the opening exclamations, "Assurance" moves to an exclamatory question that continues to express Herbert's sense of the "spitefull thought" as independent of his will:

> Couldst thou invent
> So high a torture? Is such poyson bought? [2b–3]

---

51. For the "Doctrine of Marks and Signs," see John Cotton, *Gospel Conversion* (1646), p. 35; for the Empson remark, see *Ambiguity*, pp. 258–59.

The addressee is the personified "thought," but the questions are also, inevitably, self-address. They express Herbert's sense that the peculiarly poisonous thought could not have come to him in any of the ordinary ways thoughts "come to" people. "Invention" and "buying" are possibilities among these ordinary ways ("invention" suggests self-generation, "buying" suggests obtaining from someone else); the rhetorical and positional parallel of the two reinforces the catalogue effect. The next line is declarative and presents itself as an answer to the questions. It seems a nonsequitur only if we have not been following Herbert's drift:

> Doubtlesse, but in the way of punishment.   [4]

Herbert is answering the questions; he has come to an intellectual realization about the provenance of the spiteful thought. It comes, directly or indirectly (by command or by permission, as Herbert says in "Providence"), from God "in the way of punishment" for actions or thoughts for which he, Herbert, is culpable. He has "bought" this poison in a way which the previous line did not envision. This realization, implying, as it does, a rationality in the universe of the psyche, serves momentarily to stabilize the speaker's state of mind. After the opening rash of exclamations and questions, it allows him to regain equilibrium that is reflected in the form of the stanza, a concluding octosyllabic couplet. From his new position the speaker can reflect on the general mechanism by which a poisonous thought is produced. He is still thinking (feeling?) its spitefulness; spite is addressed:

> When wit contrives to meet with thee,
> No such rank poyson can there be.   [5–6]

The peculiarly "rank" quality of the thought is apparently tied up with its intellectuality ("when *wit contrives*").

Herbert can now bring himself to articulate the thought:

> Thou said'st but even now,
> That all was not so fair, as I conceiv'd,
> Betwixt my God and me; that I allow
> And coin large hopes, but that I was deceiv'd:
>   Either the league was broke, or neare it;
>   And, that I had great cause to fear it.   [7–12]

The speaker can barely believe the event has happened—"Thou said'st but even now"—but the key feature of the stanza is the tone of the voice it recalls, a voice that is calm, modest, and above all, reasonable. This is the voice of prudence, good advice, and common sense, the voice of realism gently but gravely alerting the speaker to his unrealistically sanguine conception of his standing vis-à-vis God. The voice does not want to overstate its case—"all was *not so fair,* as I conceiv'd . . . Either the league was broke, *or neare it.*" It does not positively *say* that Herbert will be damned; it only suggests that he has "great cause to fear it." It offers a word to the wise, a call to necessary prudence and self-examination. The aim and mark of its discourse is not that Herbert entirely give up hope but that he moderate his (counterfeit? self-generated?) "large hopes" and reopen the question of his relationship to God. It implies that Herbert's sense of regeneracy is a dangerous self-deception. "The ungodly," Luther noted, "declare that no man can be certain of the forgiveness of his sins."[52]

The evocation of this voice sends Herbert back to exclamatory questions:

> And what to this? what more
> Could poyson, if it had a tongue, expresse?   [13–14]

Poison is Herbert's dominant image for the advice outlined in stanza 2; this is its third occurrence. The next questions, however, go beyond stanza 1 in specificity:

> What is thy aim? wouldst thou unlock the doore
> To cold despairs, and gnawing pensiveness?   [15–16]

Reopening the issue of his own salvation would unlock this door; it would throw Herbert into a state of chronic anxiety. "Gnawing pensiveness" has an almost clinical exactness about it. This speaker sees the implications of his situation very clearly. He characterizes the modest and reasonable voice of stanza 2 as diabolic and ends his new reflections on the power of the voice with an assertion that, despite the intensity of his reactions, he is not a novice in the spiritual life:

> Wouldst thou raise devils? I see, I know,
> I writ thy purpose long ago.   [17–18]

Like the first, this stanza ends on a moment of clarity.

Being clear about the problem, however, is not the same as having a solution. Herbert's solution reveals his theological orientation. The state of mind which the "spitefull thought" was attempting to induce in Herbert was a familiar one in the Protestant tradition; we must take the intensity of his response to it seriously. Luther called this state of mind the experience of *Anfechtung,* a word, says his modern biographer, for which there is no English equivalent—it "may be a trial sent by God to test man, or an assault by the Devil to destroy man" (or both); it is "all the doubt, turmoil, pang, tremor, panic,

---

52. *Babylonian Captivity (Pagan Servitude),* Dillenberger, p. 296.

despair, desolation, and desperation which invade the spirit of man."[53]
Bunyan's spiritual autobiography, *Grace Abounding,* is primarily, even
obsessively, concerned with this kind of experience. Doubt of one's
own election was the great plague of the Protestant tradition; it was
an issue to which reformed theologians were more and more fre-
quently addressing themselves in the seventeenth century. Bunyan's
stress on it is no accident. "How a man may know, whether he be
the child of God, or no?" was one of the great topics of English
Protestantism in the seventeenth century.[54] "How to know" books
and sermons and treatises abounded.

I have already suggested the relationship between covenant the-
ology and the search for "evidences of election": the fulfillment of
the covenant conditions was evidence of grace. That God proceeds
in an orderly manner in regenerating men was one of the special
emphases of the covenant theologians.[55] And since God proceeds in
this orderly way, one can safely reason backwards from the fulfillment
of the conditions to election. George Downame explained that "the
conditions of the Covenant are the bottom ground, not of salvation,
but *of our evidence* of our interest in salvation" (emphasis mine).[56] Since
the primary condition of the Covenant of Grace was sincerity rather
than perfection (as in the Covenant of Works), good works were
certainly evidence of election, but their goodness was defined by the
sincerity with which they were performed. To be assured, therefore,
men had to examine not only their actions but also their motives.
Since examination of behavior could never by itself discriminate the
truly elect from the righteous-seeming hypocrite, the only genuine
means to assurance was for Christians to "descend into themselves,
and to examine how it is with them within."[57] Richard Baxter, though

53. Roland H. Bainton, *Here I Stand: A Life of Martin Luther* (New York: Mentor, 1950),
p. 31.

54. The quotation is part of the title of a pamphlet by William Perkins, *A Case of
Conscience, the greatest that ever was; How a Man may know, whether he be the childe of God,
or no* (1592), in *Workes of Perkins,* pp. 421–38.

55. See John Downame, *The Christian Warfare,* pp. 119–20; Thomas Hooker, *The Ap-
plication of Redemption, Books One through Eight* (1657), pp. 33, 165. On Hooker's insist-
ence on the *ordo salutis,* see Sargent Bush, Jr., *The Writings of Thomas Hooker: Spiritual
Adventure in Two Worlds* (Madison, 1980), chaps. 7–10.

56. *The Covenant of Grace* (Dublin, 1651), p. 161 (quoted in Coolidge, *Pauline Renais-
sance,* p. 125).

57. Quoted in Coolidge, *Pauline Renaissance,* p. 132. Coolidge remarks on the paradox
of a position that "appeals to an anxious self-interest to motivate an intense self-
scrutiny, to which the reward of assurance [is promised] if it reveals a motive that is
not self-centered." It is, Coolidge notes, "like straining every nerve in an effort to relax"
(p. 132). In *The New Covenant,* Preston exhorted his auditors, "labour to get assurance"
(p. 333). Thomas Hooker constantly spoke this way (see Bush, *Writings of Thomas Hooker,*
pp. 151 ff. and passim).

perhaps not a covenant theologian, was very deeply concerned with the question of "signs of Sincerity."[58] Baxter is thoroughly at one with the covenant theologians in his assertion that "the great means" to conquer doubt of one's salvation is self-examination, "the serious and Diligent trying of a man's heart by the Rule of Scripture." Baxter argues that since Scripture describes the elect and "what be their properties by which they may be known," Christians in doubt about their election must proceed to "search carefully their own hearts" until they find out "whether they be those men or not."[59]

Herbert, however, faced with the same doubt (or the possibility of it) does not proceed in this way. He neither examines his behavior nor descends into himself. Instead, he takes the "antinomian" position; he turns wholly outside of himself—to God.[60] Having asserted that he knows the full diabolical purpose of the doubts with which he is afflicted, he ceases to talk about himself entirely and refuses to treat the situation as a battle between *himself* and the devil:

> But I will to my Father,
> Who heard thee say it. [19–20a]

This is the first time in the poem that a stanza has begun with a declaration. The speaker refuses to doubt God's favor. The reference to God as the speaker's "Father" perhaps momentarily identifies the speaker with Christ, and this too is not theologically irrelevant; Luther insisted that Christ, like David and the other saints, had his *Anfechtungen*.[61] The rest of the stanza, together with the two that follow it, consists of what Herbert's speaker says to his Father in this moment of *Anfechtung*. His first gesture is to deny, in vehement terms, that he can find anything in himself on which to base his assurance:

> O most gracious Lord,
> If all the hope and comfort that I gather,
> Were from my self, I had not half a word,
> Not half a letter to oppose
> What is objected by my foes. [20b–24]

58. *The Saints Everlasting Rest*, 7th ed., rev. (1658), p. 44.

59. Ibid., p. 404r (verso pages are not counted in the pagination of this edition from 402 to 409).

60. Baxter castigates as "antinomians" those who say "it must be the Spirit that must Assure us of our Salvation, and not our Marks and Evidences of Grace, that our comfort must not be taken from any thing in our selves, that our Justification must be immediately believed, and not proved by our Signs of Sanctification" (*Everlasting Rest*, p. 406r). See also p. 408v.

61. See Luther's reading of Psalm 21 in *Operationes in Psalmos*, 1519–21, WA, V, 602–3.

The speaker does not "coin" hope but gathers it, and he gathers not only hope but comfort, a new term in the poem. Since the stanza ends with so strong an assertion of the speaker's lack of resources in himself against his foes—"not half a word, / Not half a letter"—the poem must go on to specify what and where his resources are. The fifth stanza begins like the fourth with a "But" followed by a stark assertion. This time the assertion is wholly contained in the opening trimeter line: "But thou art my desert" (line 25). There is no mistaking the metrical prominence of "thou" here.

In order to regain his comfort, Herbert must reject the way in which the diabolical voice implicitly conceived of the "league" between Herbert and God. Herbert can have "great cause to fear" only if his own moral condition is relevant to the stability and permanence of this league. The only "great cause to fear" can be Herbert's unworthiness. The contemplation of this would certainly produce "cold despairs, and gnawing pensivenesse." Herbert retains the league vocabulary, but refuses to conceive of this league as bilateral:

> And in this league, which now my foes invade,
> Thou art not onely to perform thy part,
> But also mine . . .   [26–28a]

Herbert does what the covenant theologians warned against. He makes the league between man and God "so far to differ from Covenants between man and man, as to make it no Covenant at all."[62] "Thou art not onely to perform thy part, / But also mine." This is a mystery, not a transaction. This "league" is totally one-sided. Moreover, Herbert insists that it was always so, in the initiation as well as the sustaining of it. As in "Obedience" and "The Pearl," he wants to avoid any "intimation / Of a gift or a donation" on his part:

> as when the league was made
> Thou didst at once thy self indite,
> And hold my hand, while I did write.   [28b–30]

There is another mystery here. "At once" means not only "both" but also literally "at once," simultaneously. The two gestures are one.

Having clarified the nature of the "league," Herbert can proceed to triumph. Again a "thou" in a stressed position is the key. Like the fourth and fifth, the sixth stanza of "Assurance" begins with a complete assertion; it draws a conclusion on the basis of the previous stanzas:

> Wherefore if thou canst fail,
> Then can thy truth and I.   [31–32a]

62. See n. 11 above.

The stability of the "league" is guaranteed by the stability of God. His stability becomes the focus:

> while rocks stand,
> And rivers stirre, thou canst not shrink or quail.   [32b–33]

Herbert, of course, *can* "shrink or quail." The words are purposely chosen for their recognizably human (and animal) character. God is associated with the most permanent and enduring features and processes of nature. These lines, however, are a "set-up." Nature is employed as a measure of stability only to be immediately rejected. At this point in the poem, Herbert too is beyond shrinking or quailing. As in "The Holdfast," he is holding fast to "that which is good," to the one who "cannot fail or fall." His faith extends beyond nature— temporally as well as ontologically. His voice takes on the ringing and fearless quality of apocalyptic affirmation. In this mood he can contemplate the end of nature with complete equilibrium, "nor spare a sigh" though the whole world turn to coal:[63]

> Yea, when rocks and all things shall disband,
> Then shalt thou be my rock and tower,
> And make their ruine praise thy power.   [34–36]

This stanza has moved from if and while to when and shall. Its mode is no longer conditional. It expresses the living and unshakeable confidence that Luther meant by faith[64]—"Then shalt thou be my rock and tower." In these lines Herbert adopts the most striking feature of the diction of the English Protestant Bibles and frames his assertion in directly biblical terms. The only other place in his poetry where Herbert uses "Yea" is in his translation of the twenty-third Psalm. The most notable use of God as "rock and tower" in the Bible occurs in another psalm. Psalm 18 (A.V.: "David praises God for manifold blessings") begins: "I will love thee, O Lord, my strength. The Lord is my rock, and my fortress, and my deliverer; my God, my strength, in whom I will trust; my buckler, and the horn of my salvation, and my high tower." In borrowing these images, Herbert's voice even takes on something of the joyous ferocity of the psalm ("then did I beat them small as the dust"). "Disband" is a rather light and colorless word in "when both rocks and all things shall disband," its force being largely conceptual (a unity breaking up), but the final line of the stanza insists on glorying in the "ruine" of "all things," and in the relationship between "their ruine" and God's power. The structure of the line virtually equates the two phrases ("their ruine . . .

---

63. See "Vertue," line 15; Hopkins, "Spring and Fall," line 7.
64. "Preface to Romans," Dillenberger, p. 24.

thy power") and the "make" construction ("make their ruine praise thy power") emphasizes the use of force, as does the final resting on "thy power."

Herbert adopts biblical imagery and biblical phrasing in this stanza not only to lend greater force and dignity to his assertion of faith but also to suggest the object of his faith. Luther habitually defined faith in terms of believing that God is "true," that He will keep His promises.[65] Herbert's emphasis on God's power is an assertion of His ability to keep His word—"if thou canst fail, / Then can *thy truth*, and I." Herbert takes his stand on God's truth. In the throes of a potentially corrosive doubt, Herbert relies on God's promises. He reminds himself that the "league" between himself and God rests entirely upon God's promises and not upon a "covenant." Miller notes that the covenant theologians practically did away with the conception of God as merely promising and that where these theologians saw God's statement of "terms," Calvin had seen an assertion of the permanence of His promises.[66] Herbert dealt with the experience of *Anfechtung* in the way Luther did, not in the way Preston, Bulkeley, or Baxter did. Significantly, the nonbiblical text which "Assurance" most strongly recalls is Luther's most famous assertion of assurance, the hymn "Ein' feste Burg." We can perhaps understand and appreciate "Assurance" better by recalling, as Roland Bainton points out, that "Ein' feste Burg" was composed in the year of Luther's worst *Anfechtungen* (1527).[67] "Thou shalt be my rock and tower" and "Thou art my desert" are exactly the stance of Luther's hymn (though in the hymn the assertions of faith are in the plural).

I am not forgetting that "Assurance" does not end on the apocalyptic note of its sixth stanza. It returns, as is Herbert's wont, to the immediate dramatic situation. The final testimony to the speaker's assurance is his changed attitude toward his present situation. He has not blotted out the poisonous thought; he has, through theological clarity and a reassertion of faith, changed his relationship to it. He is no longer vulnerable. He can now glory in his imperviousness to the despair-inducing thought and take a grandly condescending attitude. He can see it as foolish rather than terrifying:

> Now foolish thought go on,
> Spin out thy thread, and make thereof a coat
> To hide thy shame . . .   [37–39a]

---

65. See, for instance, *Babylonian Captivity (Pagan Servitude)*, Dillenberger, p. 274.

66. "Marrow of Puritan Divinity," pp. 61–62 (citing *Institutes* II.viii.21). Compare Baxter, *Infants Church-membership and Baptism*, p. 225: "the Absolute promise is not a proper Covenant."

67. *Here I Stand*, p. 290.

This conceit, apparently so casually arrived at—from "spin" and "thread" to "coat" and covering nakedness—serves to link the thought with which the poem deals to the initial doubting thought which caused the Fall of Man. The significance of these lines, however, is in their gaiety and wit, their attitudinal rather than their conceptual content. The sudden burst into conceit here is a token of renewed joy, freedom, and, as in "The Flower," relish of "versing." The rest of the quatrain continues in this vein, explaining more fully why the thought is foolish. On the one hand, the thought only compounds its "shame," on the other,

> thou hast cast a bone
> Which bounds on thee, and will not down thy throat. [39b–40]

The bone of contention which the thought has attempted to cast has turned out to be a boomerang. It serves, as the poem has demonstrated, only to choke itself by eliciting a reassertion of Herbert's faith. "Assurance" ends as "The Holdfast" does, on an impersonal and hymnlike note, here an assertion of the "causelessness" and creativity of *agape*. For the first time since the opening stanza, the octosyllabic couplet is an independent assertion:

> What for it self love once began,
> Now love and truth will end in man.   [41–42]

"In man" here means both *for* man (Love began the process "for it self" which it will end in man) and *within* man: through God's power and love, man will be made capable of love and truth, that is, steadfastness, holding to the Word—as in this poem.

5

The New Life: Conversion

Nothing more strongly links Herbert to the initial impulses of the Reformation than his insistence on assurance as the essential Christian experience and his conception of assurance as dependent wholly upon God's nature and Word, and not, in any respect, upon man's actions, efforts, or mental states. The source of all the hope and comfort Herbert gathers is located entirely outside himself. The poems which celebrate this "alien righteousness," as Luther called it, are the true companion pieces of "Assurance" in *The Temple*. Their movement is always from anxiety to peace. To relieve anxiety, to set tormented consciences at rest, was the essential pastoral motive of the Reformation. Luther insisted that there is no comfort of conscience so firm or sure as the doctrine of alien righteousness.[1] In regard to covenant theology, Coolidge remarks (with an irony similar to that with which Miller viewed the doctrine), that "for the likes of Peter or David, or of young Martin Luther, the method of seeking assurance of God's favour from the evidence of one's own sanctification may leave something to be desired, but for ordinary decent folks it is good to have something tangible to refer to for assurance, even at the cost of a certain fretfulness."[2] This fretfulness is what Luther, young and old, sought to eliminate.

The poems in which Herbert most clearly and powerfully expresses the conception and the joy of "alien righteousness" are "Justice" (II) and "Aaron." Before proceeding to these, however, we must consider

1. *Commentary on Galatians*, ed. Watson, pp. 22, 160 ff., and passim; compare Calvin, *Institutes*, III.ii–iv (esp. III.ii.15–16).
2. *Pauline Renaissance*, p. 127.

two other late (non-"W") poems which seem to relate directly to the matter of assurance, "Conscience" and "The Discharge." "The Discharge" ends on the very note of the early Reformation:

> Away distrust:
> My God hath promis'd; he is just. [54–55]

The notion of faith as a discharge, a release from a tormenting obligation, is one of Luther's central positions and is part of what he meant by the freedom of a Christian. As a whole, however, "The Discharge" does not constitute a theologically relevant piece. The anxiety with which it is primarily concerned is focused on the speaker's future *in the world*. The religious point of the poem would seem to be that the speaker should not concern himself about his future because he and it are in God's hands. Yet the poem as a whole does not adopt the vein of "Take no thought for the morrow." Although it seems to be heading in this direction in stanzas 3–5 ("Thy life is Gods. . . . Onely the present is thy part and fee / . . . happy thou, / If . . . Thou couldst well see, / What present things requir'd of thee"), as the poem proceeds, its arguments against worrying about the future become increasingly pragmatic and prudential: "Dig not for woe / In times to come"; "Either grief will not come: or if it must / Do not forecast." *Che serà serà* rather than "consider the lilies of the field" is the dominant attitude. Most of the poem does not offer a *discharge* from anxiety but merely a dissuasion from it. The triumphant ending of the poem—the "discharge"—is almost a nonsequitur in this context.[3]

"Conscience," on the other hand, seems strongly reminiscent of Luther. It seems to have Luther's boldness of address and Luther's scorn for legalism. It begins by saying to conscience, "Peace, pratler, do not lowre" (line 1). In the 1531 commentary on Galatians, a book which Bunyan found "excepting the Holy Bible, before all books I have ever seen, as most fit for a wounded conscience," Luther repeatedly rebukes the Law for accusing him of sin: "Trouble not me in these matters, for I will not suffer thee . . . to reign in my conscience"; "trouble not me, not Conscience, I say, which am a lady

---

3. It is interesting that as the critique of anxiety in "The Discharge" becomes more and more prudential, the poetry becomes more and more proverbial, epigrammatic, and hortatory: "Man and the present fit"; "God chains the dog till night"; "Raise not the mudde / Of future depths"; "Do not forecast." The one note of Reformation piety, the ending, is the only first person utterance in the poem. These styles inhabit and express different worlds; the presence of one or the other in a Herbert poem helps us tell which world we are in. The mode of a poem like "Charms and Knots" tells us something about its content. It is significant also that "The Discharge" starts off talking about the heart and to the heart ("Busie enquiring heart, what wouldst thou know?"), but loses the particularity of both its subject and its addressee as it proceeds.

and a queen and have nothing to do with thee."[4] But "Conscience"
is not a work of theological power equal to "Assurance" or to the
many dialogues with the Law in Luther's Galatians commentary. As
with "The Discharge," the anxiety which it confronts is not doubt of
salvation. The anxiety in "Conscience" is over the use and enjoyment
of the things of the world. Its general movement—from a disturbance
within the self to "The bloudie crosse of my deare Lord" (line 23)—
allies it to the Reformation attack on anxiety, but its content, as the
language of the poem itself suggests, is less serious. The antagonist
in "Conscience" is a louring "prattler" who would steal the poet's
"eyes and eares," not a terrible poison that would corrode his hope
and comfort; the poet is annoyed by this antagonist, not tortured by
it. Insofar, however, as "Conscience" rejects a view of the Christian
life which sees all ordinary pleasures as dangerous, it is one of the
very few poems in *The Temple* that shares Luther's antiasceticism.[5]
Viewing the carping and catching conscience as profoundly antago-
nistic to the meaning of Christianity seems necessarily to bring some-
thing of Luther with it.

"Justice" (II) is a virtual transcription of one of the most famous
passages in Luther, his account of the conversion experience which
altered his understanding of Christianity.[6] The only critic who has
made the connection, Coburn Freer, nevertheless reads "Justice" (II)
as portraying the *weakness* of its speaker's faith. Freer sees the poem
as an example of "tentative form"—its "bathos" and "irresolution"
show how well Herbert could "follow the curve of his own reflexes."[7]
Vendler's reading is similar. She acknowledges that "Justice" (II) seems
to be a conversion poem, but insists that it does not tell "of a change
of *heart*."[8] Needless to say, to consider "Justice" (II) in the context of
the doctrine of assurance is not to see it as betraying weakness and
irresolution or as failing to tell of a change of heart. "Justice" (II) can
be seen as fully and successfully appropriating the experience which
Luther described, as very much telling of a change of heart.

Luther's conversion experience centered on the interpretation of
"the righteousness of God"—*justitia Dei*—in Romans 1:17: "therein

4. *Grace Abounding to the Chief of Sinners*, intro. G. B. Harrison (Everyman's Library;
New York, 1969; rpt.), par. 130; *Commentary on Galatians*, ed. Watson, pp. 28, 161.

5. On asceticism in *The Temple* and Herbert's relation to Reformation antiasceticism,
see Strier, "Herbert and the World," pp. 211–21.

6. See Luther's "Preface to the Latin Writings" (1545), in Dillenberger, pp. 10–12.
Unless otherwise noted, all references to this account are to these pages in Dillenberger.
At times the translation is slightly amended.

7. Freer, *Music for a King*, pp. 208–9 (his discussion of "Justice" [II] appears on pp.
204–9). Halewood, *Poetry of Grace*, p. 105, oddly treats "Justice" (II) in a context of
distinguishing Herbert from the early reformers.

8. *Poetry of Herbert*, p. 77.

[in "the gospel of Christ," Romans 1:16] is the righteousness of God revealed." Before his transforming experience, this verse seemed to Luther to make the gospel a more demanding form of the Law. He vividly recalls how he hated the righteousness of God, which he understood "philosophically" as referring to the "formal or active righteousness, as they call it, with which God is righteous and [because of which He] punishes the sinner." Luther felt that though he lived as a monk without reproach, God was not placated by his "satisfactions." Because of the boundless demands he felt upon him, he hated the righteous God Who had punished sinners under the Law and then added pain to pain by intensifying His demands in the gospel.[9] Finally, "by the mercy of God, and meditating day and night," Luther came to focus on the second rather than the first half of the verse: "For therein is the righteousness of God revealed *from faith to faith: as it is written, the just shall live by faith.*" Putting the two halves together (seeing their inner connection, as Harbison translates it), provoked the breakthrough: the "justice of God" revealed in the gospel is not the "active righteousness" with which God punishes the sinner but the "passive righteousness" with which "God clothes us when he *justifies us*" by faith (emphasis mine).[10] The righteousness of God, in other words, is a gift rather than a demand; it refers to what God does for the elect rather than to what He is. The emotional impact of this shift in exegesis was dramatic: "I felt that I was altogether born again and had entered paradise itself through open gates." With his new understanding of *justitia Dei,* "a totally other face of the entire Scripture showed itself" to Luther, and his feelings about *justitia* did a turnabout: "I extolled my sweetest word with a love that was as great as my hatred had been."

"Justice"(II) is about this shift from a "philosophical" to a "Christian" understanding of *justitia Dei.* Like "Love" (III) and "The Holdfast," "Justice" (II) is retrospectively narrated from the point of view of one who has already come through. It begins as direct address:

> O dreadfull Justice, what a fright and terrour
> Wast thou of old . . .   [1–2]

The opening phrase and perhaps the whole opening line could be taken as exclamatory, but this tone weakens at the beginning of the second line and vanishes as it proceeds. The lines are disposed in such a way as to prevent lingering over the first of them; the syntactic momentum, the absence of terminal punctuation, and the feminine

9. On the "natural" hatred of the Law, see also "Preface to Romans," Dillenberger, pp. 20 ff. On "satisfactions," see Strier, "Herbert and Tears," pp. 223–29.

10. For E. Harris Harbison's translation, see the *Christian Scholar in the Age of the Reformation* (New York, 1956), p. 120.

ending all push toward the second line. And even taken by itself, the first line is calmer and more analytical than a genuinely exclamatory address like "O spitefull bitter thought," the opening of "Assurance." "Dreadfull Justice" is a present "fright and terrour" for one nonend-stopped line. By the end of the second line, the past being spoken of turns out to be distant. The mode of the stanza is musing rather than exclamation.

We do not yet know when "of old" was. It looks as if the third line, since it begins with "When," is going to specify this (*contra* Freer, the syntactic movement of the stanza is anything but "slow"), but what we get is something rather different. The normal way to read "of old" (especially in the seventeenth century) would be to give it a historical content, making it refer to the period of the Law, the Old Testament. What follows the "When" of line 3, however, is not any historical entity but two abstractions—"sinne and errour." This surprise is followed by another; "of old" is "When sinne and errour / Did show and shape thy looks *to me*" (lines 3–4; emphasis mine). The period in question is not historical but personal. The first two lines establish an association which the next two purposely complicate. Formally the two units are balanced antitheses: a grammatically continuous long and short line ending in a phrase of adverbial effect followed by a short and long line with the same syntax. Herbert (or his "speaker") is stressing both his personal experience of the dread of justice and the fact that this experience is past. Moreover, both the prominence of the "terrour-errour" rhyme and the insistence of "show and shape" suggest that to see justice as a "fright and terrour" is not only a view that the speaker has transcended but one that was in itself mistaken. The next line completes the opening sentence and further emphasizes the mistakenness of the speaker's "old" view. "Sinne and errour" shaped the look of justice to him by being the medium through which he perceived it (compare Bacon's enchanted glass):[11]

> sinne and errour
> Did show and shape thy looks to me,
> And through their glasse discolour thee!   [3–5]

The speaker is recalling a nightmare which has passed but which is still vivid to him. Most of his effort thus far has gone into analyzing the mechanism by which the nightmare was produced. One would think that at this point Herbert would give voice to the relief which underlies the retrospective analysis and would indicate the true view of justice. Instead, the stanza ends on a line that evokes the experience

---

11. *The Advancement of Learning*, in *Selected Writings*, p. 295.

of "fright and terrour" in a way that the epistemological and other-directed emphases of lines 3–5 do not. Those lines come to rest on a feeling of the *irreverence* rather than on the terror of the transcended view. The final line is a sentence in itself and virtually independent, structurally, of the rest of the stanza; it opens a new vista:

> He that did but look up, was proud and bold.   [6]

We are suddenly within the world of "fright and terrour" and the terms have shifted from epistemological to moral ones. We have also moved from how things seemed to how things were—"He that did but look up, *was* proud and bold." The line gives us our first specific insight into the world "of old," and its generalized formulation reinforces the conflation of the personal and the historical implicit in lines 1–4.

The essential characteristic of the world of old seems to have been that it allowed no access to God. Even the most tentative approaches—"but look[ing] up"—were classed as unacceptable and treated as what would seem to be their opposite. If this seems a resentful line describing an irrational and indeed *unjust* world, it is meant to seem so. We are meant to hear something of Luther's anger at the unapproachable and "convicting" righteousness of God—"thus I raged, with a fierce and troubled conscience." Herbert's line, however, does not seem to include the subjective experience of the troubled conscience. It does not assert that in the world of dreadful justice, "he that did but look up" *felt* "proud and bold" rather than merely being arbitrarily classified as such.

To make this assertion is the purpose of the second stanza. The stanza gives a strong and immediate sense of how justice appeared to the terrified conscience. Herbert adopts the perspective of him "that did but look up," and presents this figure's relation to justice in terms of his response to an emblem of justice, a hand holding a balance. Justice is identified with its emblem, and Herbert is at pains to separate the "thing itself," the balance, from the speaker's past perception of it. Everything of justice that the speaker saw reminded him of Hell and torment. The description of the balance proceeds from bottom to top, extending the principle of line 6. As he who looked up continued to do so, what he saw became more and more terrifying:

> The dishes of thy balance seem'd to gape,
> > Like two great pits;
> > The beam and scape
> Did like some torturing engine show.   [7–10]

Finally, at the very top, "Thy hand above did burn and glow" (line 11).

This is justice perceived through guilt and fear of punishment. As the description proceeds, it becomes more and more "actual." In the opening lines of the stanza, the dishes *"seem'd* to gape, / Like two great pits"; in the second two-line unit, the beam and scape "Did like some torturing engine *show"* (there is less distance between the appearance and the "reality" here and less grammatical insistence on this distance); in the final line, the hand above *"did* burn and glow." This progression, together with the hallucinatory vividness of the images, creates an impression which has led to mistaken accounts of the structure of the poem as a whole. The retrospective point of view is easily overlooked.[12] We have seen in "The Holdfast" and "Love" (III), however, that Herbert's retrospective narratives tend to move more and more into the present as they proceed—only to return suddenly, at the height of the "action," to an awareness of the original narrative perspective.

The line which ends the second stanza of "Justice"(II) is not quite as independent as that which ends the first, but it too represents a shift in mode from a visual to a moral and psychological perspective. Here, however, the effect is to decrease rather than to increase the intensity. After the hallucinatory visual description, the final generalization seems calm. It records the effect of the vision on two types of men:

> Danting the stoutest hearts, the proudest wits.   [12]

This is rather different from line 6. "He that did but look up" is not clearly a heroic or venturous figure, but the stout hearts and proud wits clearly are so—they truly are what "he that did but look up" was classified as. They *are* the proud and the bold. Ostensibly, the fact that even these types are daunted merely emphasizes further the terror and the power of the "old" view of justice. There is, however, a moral ambiguity in the line that slightly but significantly complicates our response to it. "Danting the stoutest hearts" seems morally neutral in its immediate context (more so, probably, than if Herbert had retained "bold" from stanza 1), but the same cannot be said of "Danting . . . the proudest wits." The "daunting" of "proud wits" can certainly be seen as morally positive. For a moment, then, at the end of two very negative stanzas on the "old" view, there is a brief and implicit suggestion that this view of justice also had a positive function—to inculcate humility as well as, or along with, terror. This recognition also perhaps casts a shadow of moral dubiety retroactively

---

12. According to Freer, *Music,* p. 204, the first two stanzas describe "the torture awaiting the poet" and the second two "his hoped for redemption." Vendler's account is similar (*Poetry of Herbert,* p. 77). Her discussion appears on pp. 75–79.

back upon "the stoutest hearts." Perhaps the dreadful vision of justice is calculated to reduce to nothing the highest pretensions of human nature. The Homeric provenance of the image of the divine balance daunting stout hearts (*Iliad*, VIII) perhaps reinforces this suggestion.

The ambiguity of line 12 is a conceptual flicker: the emotional and dramatic arc of the poem moves directly from "Thy hand above did burn and glow" to the triumphant assertion of the present perspective at the beginning of stanza 3. There is, however, one further point to be made about stanza 2. Seeing the "beam and scape" of the emblematic balance as a torturing engine obviously produces an image of a cross, and this "double image" has, as Tuve has shown, an ancient lineage in the Christian tradition. The concept of the Father weighing human sin against the sufferings of Christ produced images like Deguilleville's "Upon the balance of the Cross there was the treasure weighed."[13] Tuve was content to demonstrate—often, as here, successfully—that traditional materials are used in Herbert's poems. She was not concerned with *how* they are used. Failure to ask what Herbert does with his materials leads to misreadings. Relying on Tuve's account of the traditional content of the image of the cross-as-balance while noting that "it is hard to ignore the infernal tendencies" of the image in "Justice" (II), Freer concludes that Herbert's picture "of *both* sides of the balance as gaping pits is not indicative of a right-thinking Christian spirit." The poem therefore expresses Herbert's fears more strongly than his faith.

Yet surely Herbert did not intend us to ignore the infernal tendencies of the imagery of his second stanza, and it would truly be odd for Herbert to have drawn no comfort whatever from an allusion to the sacrifice. *Herbert* has not put Christ into this stanza. From the perspective being presented, the cross is merely a "torturing engine"; it is merely part of the balance. If Christ is perceived at all from this perspective, it is as Judge rather than as Savior—"as if indeed," said Luther, recreating his preconversion state of mind, "it were not enough that miserable sinners, eternally lost through original sin, are crushed by every kind of calamity by the law of the decalogue, without God having to add pain to pain by the gospel." We see the redemptive possibilities in the cross image just as *we* see the daunting of the proud wits as positive, but the figure in whose conscience-stricken perspective the dishes of the balance gape like pits does not so see it. What happens in stanza 3 is precisely that the speaker proclaims his ability "now," in the present of the poem, to see Christ rather than the naked cross—or, rather, he proclaims his ability to see the

13. *A Reading of Herbert*, pp. 165–68; for the quote from Deguilleville, see p. 167.

balance-cross *through* Christ. Herbert's emphasis, as Halewood puts it, is "abstract and functional" rather than concrete and literal.[14] There is no description or evocation of the crucifixion, as there is in the medieval use of the conceit ("there was never gold nor silver so busily examined, for they enforced him so sore to the weight till the cords bursted of the balance, that were the sinews and veins of his blessed body").[15] Herbert's emphasis is theological rather than descriptive; he relies on the epistle to the Hebrews rather than on the synoptic Gospels. In contrasting the old with the new dispensation, the author of Hebrews proclaims that the veil before the Holy of Holies in the temple has been replaced by the "new and living" veil of the Incarnation (10:20). Herbert uses the veil image as a medium of sight. He opens the third stanza with a strong two-line unit:

> But now that Christs pure vail presents the sight
> I see no fears.   [13–14]

This veil is "pure" in an epistemological as well as a moral sense. It is not simply a new medium but an undistorting one; it is not rose-colored but transparent. The fearless view is the true view. The next line eliminates all suspicion that one distorting medium has merely been substituted for another. Herbert takes advantage of the color scheme implied in Hebrews (the literal veil before the Law was "of blue, and purple, and crimson" [II Chron. 3:14]) in order to transform the most terrifying aspect of the old, false vision into an emblem of benevolence. The speaker can now look up freely and see that "Thy hand is white" (line 15). Suddenly reality replaces appearance. "Christs pure vail" *presents* the sight; being replaces seeming—"thy balance *seemed* to gape" but "Thy hand *is* white." With the removal of error, terror also disappears. The rest of the stanza "presents" the transformed view of the emblem. Analogy takes on a different function. Where before it had emphasized subjectivity, it now serves merely as a manner of speaking, a way of conceptualizing the reality:

> Thy scales like buckets which attend
> And interchangeably descend,
> Lifting to heaven from this well of tears.   [16–18]

This vision is very similar to that of the transformed bogey of "Time." "Time" is an entirely comic piece in which the speaker, a saintly *naif*

14. *Poetry of Grace,* p. 105.

15. Quoted in Tuve, *A Reading Of Herbert,* p. 167. Herbert's closest approach to this is in "Easter," part 1, lines 11–12: "His stretched sinews taught all strings, what key / Is best to celebrate this most high day." Even there, however, Herbert's treatment is abstract and functional. For Herbert's relation to medieval and Counter-Reformation visualization, see Strier, "Herbert and Tears," pp. 239–45.

lecturing time for its slackness, explains in his leisurely way that time is "now," since Christ's coming, blessed in the blessing of man:

> For where thou onely wert before
> An executioner at best;
> Thou art a gard'ner now, and more,
>   An usher *to convey our souls*
>   *Beyond the utmost starres and poles.*   [14–18;
>   emphasis mine]

Lifting to heaven from this well of tears.

Unlike "Time," however, the primary concern of "Justice" (II) is not the ultimate effect of grace but rather the impact of grace on the earthly life of the individual. The overall movement of "Justice" (II) is horizontal and temporal rather than vertical and spatial, and its closest analogue among the transformed bogeys is not "Time" but "Death." In "Death," the movement from the transcendental back to the historical is even more pronounced. The address to death as a grinning bumpkin of bones culminates in the vision of a time when "all thy bones with beautie shall be clad," but this is only a prologue to the actual conclusion. As Stein points out, "a quiet 'Therefore' " at the beginning of the final stanza converts a striking conclusion into mere transition."[16] In "Justice" (II), after a vision of being lifted to heaven, the equivalent quiet word is "For." Herbert turns from the emblem (of which he has perhaps grown slightly tired and which has led him in a slightly inappropriate direction) back to the initial perspective of the poem, the address to *Justitia Dei* in the abstract.[17] Triumphantly, and for the first time in the poem, Herbert uses the first half of the stanza as a complete unit:

> For where before thou still didst call on me,
>   Now I still touch
>   And harp on thee.   [19–21]

This is exactly parallel to Luther's account of the immediate result of his religious and exegetical breakthrough: "I extolled my sweetest word [*justitia*] with a love that was as great as my hatred had been." The repetition of "still" in Herbert's lines (meaning "always") dra-

---

16. *Herbert's Lyrics*, p. 42.

17. The real poetic energy of the third stanza of "Justice" (II) can perhaps be said to end with "Thy hand is white." The filling out of the transformed emblem is a structural necessity, but not a task that truly captures Herbert's imagination. The second half of the stanza, while certainly good enough, is rather perfunctory. The poem takes fire again at the beginning of stanza 4. In "Death," on the other hand, the transcended climax (lines 16–20) is dazzling. There are other formal similarities between "Justice" (II) and "Death." Both poems have 24 lines and turn on their thirteenth with a "But" followed by a temporal indicator referring to the Incarnation.

matizes the change in his condition—"where before *thou* still . . . /
Now *I* still. . . ." Under the rule of "sinne and errour," Herbert had
continually felt God calling on him for an account just as He "called
unto" Adam after the original sin (Genesis 3:9). This first rebuke to
sinful man echoes continually through history in the conscience stricken
by the Law. "But now" it is Herbert who continually touches and
harps on this justice, this demand for an account. The puns on "touch"
and "harp" here mark the emotional high-point of the poem. Not
only does Herbert insist on justice, but he plays on it (*toccare*); he
makes the music of the angels with it, the music of faith.[18]

We are now in a position to see the inappropriateness of concluding
that the poem has a missing middle term because it does not mention
faith or tell of a change of heart. "Justice" (II) does not have to mention
faith or tell of a changed heart because, like "Death" and "Time," it
dramatizes and manifests these things. Only the man of faith can
joyfully "harp on" God's justice and see it with "no fears," just as
only the man of faith can peacefully "go die as sleep" (compare Donne's
"Valediction: forbidding Mourning"). To the man who has not ex-
perienced conversion, God's justice—and therefore God—must al-
ways be a fright and terror from which, like Adam or Marlowe's
Faustus, he seeks to hide. Only the man of faith can truly love God
because only the man of faith experiences God as lovable.[19] And since
God *is* lovable, and supremely so, this means that only the man of
faith sees God correctly, without the error implied in the guilty man's
terror. Luther explains that

> If you have true faith that Christ is your Saviour, then at once you
> have a gracious God, for faith leads you into and opens up God's
> heart and will, that you may see pure grace and overflowing love.
> This it is to behold God in faith: that you are able to look upon his
> fatherly, friendly heart, *in which there is no anger or ungraciousness.*

Luther goes on to observe that:

> He who sees God as angry does not see him rightly but looks only
> on a curtain, as if a dark cloud had been drawn across his face.[20]

He who sees God as angry does not see him rightly—this is the
"epistemology" of Herbert's poem.

In the final lines, Herbert addresses and harps on justice further,
exercising the boldness and full assurance recommended in the verses

---

18. The connotation of nagging in "harp on" is also perhaps relevant; it is, as we
shall see in chap. 7, one of the privileges of the Christian. William Veeder alerted me
to this connotation here.

19. Luther, "Preface to Romans," passim; Calvin, *Institutes*, III.iii.2, 15; III.iv.34.

20. Sermon on Matthew 5, *WA*, XXXII, 328. I have slightly amended the translation
in Bainton, *Here I Stand*, p. 50 (the emphasis is mine).

of Hebrews which immediately precede and follow that on "Christs pure vail":[21]

> God's promises have made thee mine;
> Why should I justice now decline?
> Against me there is none, but for me much.   [22–24]

Herbert is glorying in his faith, exercising what Luther called "a certain holy pride."[22] "Justice" (II) could not be further from fear or irresolution. Its final stanza does not assert the speaker's need of or hope for God's mercy but his possession of this mercy, his state and experience of being justified. "To have the law on our side," Luther explained, "is the very nature of freedom from sin and the law."[23] There is no puzzled, self-questioning declarative ("Why do I decline it?") lurking, as Freer says, within "Why should I justice now decline?" In context, the line celebrates the fact that "now" the speaker need not *and does not* "decline" justice. The line does not "wobble out" until reaching the stress on "decline," but is metrically and thematically stabilized by the realized stress on "now." The essence of conversion is to divide a life into "now" and "then."

Freer sees his point as a modest one. He notes that notwithstanding its tentative form, "Justice" (II) does not express doubt about the "ordering principle . . . only about its application." Nothing, Freer continues, "has been 'put in doubt' . . . except the speaker's immortality." He assures us that Herbert did not doubt "the general assumptions of his faith." These are remarkable assertions. *Only* the benevolence of God to the speaker is in doubt! In Reformation theology, belief in the personal application of redemption is the essence of faith—believing not merely that God will save some people but that god will save you, that "God's promises" are yours.[24] Even the devil believes "the general assumptions." Herbert goes out of his way in the second half of "Justice" (II) to make his affirmations personal.

21. "Having therefore, brethren, boldness to enter into the holiest by the blood of Jesus, By a new and living way, which he hath consecrated for us, through the veil, that is to say, his flesh; . . . Let us draw near with a true heart in full assurance of faith. . . . Let us hold fast the profession of our faith without wavering; for he is faithful that promised" (Hebrews 10:19–23).

22. *Commentary on Galatians*, ed. Watson, p. 164.

23. "Preface to Romans," Dillenberger, p. 29.

24. See *The Freedom of a Christian*, Dillenberger, p. 66: "Rather ought Christ to be preached to the end that faith in him may be established that he may not only be Christ, but be Christ for you and me." Robert Barnes, one of the first English Protestants, explained that "the faith that shall justify . . . must . . . make me believe that God, the maker of heaven and earth is not onely a Father, but also my Father" (quoted in E. G. Rupp, *Studies in the Making of the English Protestant Tradition* [1947; rpt. Cambridge, 1966], p. 191). In *Grace Abounding*, Bunyan could not derive full comfort from the words "thy grace is sufficient" while the words "for thee" were still left out (par. 206).

The nominative case of the first person pronoun emerges in the poem only in the first short line of the second half, "*I* see no fears" (line 14). In the final stanza, the corresponding line is "Now I still touch" (line 20). The ending is emphatic in its pronouns: "God's promises have made *thee mine*; / Why should *I* justice now decline? / Against *me* there is none, but for *me* much" (emphases mine).

Finally, the issue of agency must be dealt with. If the poem is truly an account of conversion parallel to Luther's, the issue is central. Vendler offers a "humanistic" reading of "Justice" (II). She strips away its "religious imagery" to reveal its "true" moral and humanistic import—"that self-regard yields a mistaken perception of reality." The poem, she says, "denies the value of a self-centered view of 'reality' '' and "chooses rather an upward glance, that very glance forbidden (line 6) by the false humility of self-regard." Why the humility of that line is false and how it expresses self-regard remain unclear, but the most troublesome aspect of Vendler's reading is her emphasis on choice. Her language is quite insistent: as the poem proceeds, Herbert "*chooses* to look not on his deserts . . . but rather on God's love"; when he "saw himself at the center of his vision and pondered his own sin and error, the universe (to him, as later to Carlyle) seemed a torture-house," but when Herbert "*ceased* looking at his own soul and *looked instead at* Christ, he saw through Christ another vision of the universe" (emphases mine).

This misrepresents the content of the poem as seriously as the view of it as "irresolute" does. Carlyle is a red herring. Unlike Carlyle, Herbert is not concerned with "the universe" (Carlyle's conversion experience altered his view of nature),[25] and, more important, "Justice" (II), unlike *Sartor Resartus*, is not a work recommending strenuous and willful renunciation of the self. The most striking feature of the speaker's role in "Justice" (II) is passivity. In both of the worlds presented in the poem he is passive. In the "old" world, sin and error shaped the looks of justice to him; now Christ's pure veil "presents the sight." The speaker is notably absent from this pivotal line. Except when he "did but look up," he is never seen as actively choosing or turning; he is seen as responding. His situation has changed; therefore what he sees has changed. There is no suggestion of initiative on his part. The response to God's justice that he manifested "of old" was not merely plausible, as Vendler says, but necessary. The experience which altered his relation to God *was provided by God*. The agents are named: "Christs pure vail" in stanza 3; "Gods promises" in 4. These

25. See "The Everlasting Yea" in *Sartor Resartus*, intro. W. H. Hudson (Everyman's Library; New York, 1965), p. 142.

are actual agents as well as grammatical ones. "*Faith* did change the scene."[26]

Yet there is something valid in the intuition that "Justice" (II) is not, in some sense, theologically complete. While the speaker of the poem is surely not, as Vendler sees him "as full of sin and error" in the present as he was before, the poem does not clarify the speaker's present relation to *sin* as opposed to error. The problem with "Justice" (II) to which the intuitions of Freer and Vendler point is that its epistemological stress is so powerful as to overwhelm its moral content. In the poem, the primary meaning of the purity of Christ's veil is epistemological. The poem does not clarify the moral content of what it means for the speaker to be "justified," for justice now to be his. It gives little expression to the moral content of Christ's mediation. The whole matter of righteousness is left vague.

Luther remarked that when he read Augustine's *On the Spirit and the Letter*, he was delighted to find that Augustine too interpreted *justitia Dei* in the "passive" rather than the "active" sense, but he goes on to note that Augustine "did not explain all things concerning imputation clearly."[27] Imputation is the concept that is missing from "Justice" (II). It provides the explanation of the way in which "through" Christ, God's promises have made justice Herbert's. Herbert's clearest presentation of "the righteousness of faith," of imputed or, as Luther would say, Christian (as opposed to philosophical) righteousness, is "Aaron," another late poem. The subject of "Aaron" is the nature of the true or good priest, but since the main characteristic of the true priest is holiness, the poem becomes an exposition and celebration of how the Christian attains holiness or righteousness—in more technical terms, justification. Since Herbert speaks, as always, as one of the regenerate, the poem becomes a credo, another demonstration of the nature of faith. Herbert is very much in line with the Reformation tradition in presenting the conditions for being a "true priest" as basically identical with those for being a true Christian. As we shall see, Herbert's main claim for his adequacy as a priest is his regeneracy.

The first stanza of "Aaron" characterizes the true priest in terms of Aaron's garments in Exodus 28. Herbert pretends to be following this account literally, but from the beginning his own descriptions of the priest's "clothing" hover on the border of allegory:

---

26. "Faith," line 39. As Vendler suggests (p. 78), "Faith" is intimately connected to "Justice" (II).

27. "Preface to Latin Writings," Dillenberger, p. 12. See Augustine, *On the Spirit and the Letter*, chap. 50, in *Saint Augustine's Anti-Pelagian Works*, trans. Peter Holmes and Robert Ernest Wallis, rev. Benjamin Warfield, *A Select Library of the Nicene and Post-Nicene Fathers*, ed. Philip Schaff (1887; rpt. Grand Rapids, 1971), V, 104–5.

> Holiness on the head,
> Light and perfections on the breast,
> Harmonious bells below, raising the dead
> To leade them unto life and rest:
> Thus are true Aarons drest.   [1–5]

Lines 1 and 2 seem to be following the Mosaic description as generally interpreted—though Herbert substitutes abstractions for named articles of clothing—but the long central line to which the others build and from which they recede, makes an astounding claim, a claim that cannot have to do with literal bells on a priestly hem unless this is a magical conception indeed. These "harmonious bells" have a power which is exclusively identified as Christ's in the gospels, the extraordinary power of "raising the dead." The next line, by making "raising the dead" merely instrumental to leading them "unto life and rest," weakens the claim of line 3 somewhat and tends to make "the dead" in question metaphorical, but there is no mistaking the sudden ingress of Christ into the stanza. The plural of line 5—"Thus are true Aarons drest"—also tends to point away from Christ as the single fulfillment of the Old Testament priesthood, but here too the suggestion lingers even as it is being dismissed.

The true Aaron is the powerful preacher. He "is not witty, or learned, or eloquent, but Holy" (*CP*, p. 233), and his words are agents of conversion ("raising the dead / To leade them unto life and rest"). However, as in "The Windows," to which "Aaron" is closely related, the thought of the "glorious and transcendent place" of the preacher leads to thoughts of the unfitness of man for it. What "The Windows" treats generally—"Lord, how can *man* preach thy eternal word? / *He* is a brittle crazie glasse"—"Aaron" treats personally. Herbert compares himself, point by point, with a true Aaron:

> Profanenesse in my head.
> Defects and darknesse in my breast,
> A noise of passions ringing me for dead
> Unto a place where is no rest:
> Poore priest thus am I drest.   [6–10]

This state of affairs seems totally hopeless, and the format of the comparison intensifies the dilemma. The reader is forced to be aware of the *systematic* nature of the contrasts because, at this point in the poem, he had no reason to expect the repetition of the rhyme words and their order from stanza 1. The first function of the special form of the poem is to establish the absoluteness of the initial contrast. Moreover, the terms in which Herbert describes himself, while certainly personal, are not merely personal; they are general and abstract.

Herbert is describing himself here, but he is describing himself as natural man. The contrast between the "true Aaron" of stanza 1 and the "poore priest" of stanza 2 is that between God and man. "The Authors Prayer before Sermon" is relevant ("Aaron" might be subtitled, "the Author's Meditation before Sermon"):

> O Almighty and ever-living Lord God! Majesty, and Power, and Brightnesse, and Glory! How shall we dare to appear before thy face, who are contrary to thee in all we call thee? for we are darknesse, and weaknesse, and filthinesse, and shame.   (*CP*, p. 288)

There is nothing within Herbert to make him a "true Aaron"; the help must come, in Luther's terms, from without—"when we had sinned beyond any help in heaven and earth, then thou saidest, Lo, I come!" (*CP*, p. 288). In "The Windows," God is presented as solving the problem of man's unfitness to minister the Word by conforming the minister to Christ—"thou dost anneal in glasse thy storie, / *Making* thy life to shine within / The holy Preachers." The emphasis of "The Priesthood" is similar; God makes the "foul and brittle" earth and clay (the "brittle crazie glasse") of particular men into curious and holy vessels. In "Aaron," Herbert presents the solution to the problem of man's unfitness in terms of an even deeper mystery, a mystery which emphasizes Incarnation rather than power and skill, the Pauline conception of "membership" in Christ. This conception emphasizes the intimacy of the union of believers with Christ and with one another. Stanza 3 of "Aaron" begins with the word which Herbert characteristically uses when he wants to provide an unexpected loophole out of a seemingly absolute dilemma:

> Onely another head
> I have, another heart and breast,
> Another musick, making live not dead,
> Without whom I could have no rest:
> In him I am well drest.[28]   [11–15]

Again, as in "Assurance," "all the hope and comfort" Herbert gathers is not from himself. He could hardly emphasize "another" more strongly—"another head," "another heart and breast," "Another musick." The middle line of this stanza (line 13)—which is also the middle of the poem as a whole—testifies that the speaker has himself had the experience of being resurrected by "musick" that stanza 1 portrays the true Aaron as able to induce. The metaphor of being dressed in

---

28. With "*Onely* another head / I have," compare "*Onely* a sweet and vertuous soul" in "Vertue" and "*Onely* since God doth often vessels make" in "The Priesthood." The celebratory quality of "Aaron" is underscored when we notice that its "onely" comes in the middle rather than, as in "Vertue" and "The Priesthood," at the end.

another's clothes (here another's being—"*In him* I am well drest") is one of the most ancient and standard ways of talking about imputed merit, as in Donne's "So in his purple wrapp'd receive mee Lord," in Luther's talk of "the righteousness [of Christ] with which God *clothes us* when he justifies us," and in Ambrose's explication of Jacob being blessed in his brother's coat (highly approved by Calvin).[29]

"Onely another" in "Aaron" is parallel to the pivotal "But now" of "Justice" (II). Herbert is announcing his actual spiritual condition as a regenerate Christian personally and unequivocally—"another head / *I have* (the enjambment and caesura here are powerful). "In" the other alluded to, Herbert can claim to be alive ("not dead"), at rest, and "well drest" (the final permutation of Herbert's "gentile humour for Cloaths").[30] Herbert could easily go from this stanza to his conclusion ("So holy in my head, / Perfect and light in my deare breast"), but he chooses not to do so. He adds a stanza (thereby guaranteeing that the poem will have five) in which he names the other referred to in stanza 3 and uses "onely," now meaning "sole" rather than "except," in the same emphatic position in which he had used "another" in the previous stanza.[31] He insists, as Vendler well puts it, that Christ is "a substitute for the natural" rather than merely an alternative to it.[32] Herbert wants to make it clear that insofar as he lives "in" Christ, he dies to himself. Again the central line of the stanza, the line which alludes to music or noise and ends with "dead," justifies its structural prominence:

29. Donne, "Hymne to God my God, in my sicknesse," line 26; Luther, "Preface to Latin Writings," Dillenberger, p. 12; Saint Ambrose, *On Jacob and the Happy Life*, quoted in *Institutes*, III.xi.23.

30. See Walton, *Life*, p. 275.

31. I am not, in general, a devotee of mystical mathematics, but groups of five are so prominent in "Aaron" as to make it plausible that the number is intended to be significant. The poem has five stanzas with five lines visually arranged to emphasize the centrality of the middle line. If it is true that "Aaron" is about the "Christian meaning" of righteousness or justice, then what Sir Thomas Browne called "the ancient conceit of five surnamed the number of justice" (as in Book V of *The Faerie Queene*) may be relevant to it (*The Garden of Cyrus*, chap. 5[!], *Selected Writings*, p. 205). Browne's association of the number five with justice through the position of the number as the midpoint of the digits is perhaps paralleled in the structure of Herbert's stanzas. Browne also saw the number five as "the first sphaerical number . . . the measure of sphaerical motion" (ibid., p. 185). The circle, of course, is an emblem of perfection. "Aaron" might be said to be circular in a number of senses: it is cyclical in its repetitions, and it ends where it began (on the image and description of the "true Aaron"). Puttenham associates the "roundel or spheare" with poems that begin and end on similar words and have pivotal central lines as well as with poems that are visually shaped like spheres (*Arte of English Poesie*, pp. 98 ff.). The middle stanza of "Aaron" is pivotal.

32. *Poetry of Herbert*, p. 120. Vendler's discussion of "Aaron" appears on pp. 117–121.

Christ is my onely head,
My alone onely heart and breast,
My onely musick, striking me ev'n dead,
That to the old man I may rest,
And be in him new drest.   [16–20]

This is again emphatic writing, with "alone onely" and "ev'n dead."[33] Herbert does not want his point to be missed. He wants the sharp opposition between the holy and the natural expressed in the contrast between stanzas 1 and 2 to continue through the poem. The central line of this stanza, with the metrical and rhetorical prominence of "me," is the clearest statement in Herbert's poetry of the conception of selfhood as sin, although this conception is implicit in "Jordan" (II) and darkly expressed in "Clasping of hands." Herbert wants to eliminate from the poem any possibility that he "participates" in Christ as natural man. He wants to insist that the world into which he enters "in him" is not merely good—"In him I am *well* drest" (line 15)—but utterly new—"to the old man I may rest, / And be in him *new* drest" (lines 19–20). In a sense, Herbert is merely expounding "in him." The movement from having "another head" to being "in him" is a movement toward greater intimacy and unity. Herbert wants to deny that he has any genuine life outside of Him (compare "If I without thee would be mine" in "Clasping of hands"). When he wrote "Aaron," Herbert had already written a poem on the second half of Colossians 3:3, "your life is hid with Christ in God," but had not yet made use of the beginning of the verse: "For ye are dead."[34] Where the third stanza of "Aaron" emphasized imputation—the Christian being justified by the merits of "another"—the fourth stanza emphasizes regeneration, becoming a new creature.

Herbert had to make the fourth stanza emphatic in order to make his conclusion unambiguous. He does not want us to think, even momentarily at the opening of the final stanza, that he is claiming anything for himself when he returns to the initial description and concludes:

So holy in my head,
Perfect and light in my deare breast,
My doctrine tun'd by Christ, (who is not dead,

---

33. There is an interesting and relevant parallel to the first of these phrases in the 1575 English translation of Luther's *Commentary on Galatians:* "There is none but Christ *only and alone,* which taketh away the law, killeth my sin, destroyeth my death in his body" (Watson, p. 162).

34. "Coloss. 3.3" appears in "W." "Aaron" does not.

> But lives in me while I do rest)
>   Come people; Aaron's drest.   [21–25]

Vendler, once again seeking to make Herbert "humanistically" appealing, sees this stanza as dramatizing a moment in which "self-hatred has turned to self-tenderness." It is "a resurgence of the natural" in which Christ becomes "a normative principle to the human rather than an alternative or substitute one"; Herbert is rejecting the "harsh" and "immoderate" Pauline metaphor of being struck dead. The poem as a whole, for Vendler, is a dramatization and critique of the "excesses of self-reproach and enthusiasm that beset the experience of conversion." What this reading ignores, stanza 4 exists to assert. Stanza 4 insists that Christ is Herbert's "onely head," his "alone onely" heart and breast, so that when Herbert speaks of "his" head and breast in stanza 5, we will understand that he is speaking of his "alone onely" head and breast—that is, *of Christ*. Stanza 5, beginning as it does with a summarizing "So," is continuous with the stanza which precedes it; stanza 4 instructs us how to read stanza 5. Neither the tenderness nor anything else in stanza 5 is *self*-directed. Christ, "in" Whom and only "in" Whom Herbert spiritually lives and is holy, is as always Herbert's only "deare"—"Perfect and light in my deare breast."

For Vendler, the fact that Herbert's "own doctrine" is "tun'd" by Christ (line 23) is part of the "self-acceptance" of the final stanza. But surely the poet who expressed such horror at "th' old sinnes and *new doctrines* of our land" ("The Priesthood," line 33) was not celebrating his presentation of original doctrine to his congregation, doctrine that was "his own" and merely "tun'd" by Christ (whatever this would mean). Line 23—the central line of the final stanza—confirms the suggestion of the opening stanza that the poem is about preparation for preaching. What Herbert is in fact imagining in "Aaron" is the fulfillment of the prayer which he encouraged his country parson to make while preaching: "Oh my Master, on whose errand I come, *let me hold my peace, and doe thou speak thy selfe*" (*CP*, p. 233; emphasis mine); "My doctrine tun'd by Christ, (who . . . *lives in me while I do rest*").[35] Christ is the true Aaron after all, since He "only and alone" has all the required attributes and can perform the required function—

---

35. The connection of "Aaron" with preaching is strengthened by its position immediately before "The Odour." "The Odour" is based upon a Pauline passage on the acceptability to God of true preachers who do not "corrupt the word" (II Corinthians 2:14–17). The central phrase in "The Odour," "My master," also connects "The Odour" to Herbert's account of the parson preaching: "Oh *my Master*, on whose errand I come. . . ." Like "Aaron," "The Odour" can be read as a meditation on the meaning *for the preacher* of this prayer in "The Parson preaching."

"raising the dead / To lead them unto life and rest."[36] In this final stanza we learn that for Herbert to be "in" Christ is also for Christ to be "in" him. In both ways of formulating the relationship, Herbert's ordinary self is obliterated. I do not think that Herbert would have worried about having (or thought it possible to have) what Vendler calls "*an excess of humility* vis-à-vis the glories of Christ" (emphasis mine). The poem does not distinguish the resting of the self described in stanza 5 from the death in which the self "may rest" in stanza 4— a distinction crucial to Vendler's argument. Both are phrases for what Luther called "the fulfillment of the sign or sacrament of baptism," that is to say, regeneration, spiritual "death and resurrection."[37] When Herbert needs to reassure himself of his worthiness to preach, he reminds himself of the meaning of regeneration.

We return again to assurance. We have by now heard a great many assertions of assurance ("Then shalt thou be my rock and tower"; "Against me there is none"; "another head / I have") and we have repeatedly heard the source of this assurance identified ("Thou art my desert"; "Gods promises have made thee mine"; "Christ is my onely head"). Assurance is the defining quality of faith, but what of the experience that produces the assurance? We have thus far seen only its effects. We have glimpsed regeneration itself as primarily cognitive and epistemological, an experience of knowing and seeing. What would fill out and deepen our account would be to find a poem or a group of poems in *The Temple* describing the phenomenology of conversion, presenting conversion as felt as well as understood. It would be odd if the poet who found those "demonstrations" most evident and clear that fetched their proofs "ev'n from the very bone" should not have left in his poetry some direct account of his own conversion.[38]

36. One reader of this analysis has raised the question of whether, in the view I am attributing to Herbert, we are to say "that the preacher is inspired just as the writer of the Gospel." I am suggesting that Herbert would say "yes" to this, with the important proviso that the preacher is inspired *with the same message* as the writers of the New Testament. To ignore this proviso would incur Herbert's censure against opposing "the teaching of the spirit to the teaching of the scripture, which the holy spirit wrote" ("Notes on Valdes," p. 317). The Spirit's (and Christ's) teaching is everywhere the same. Thus the horror at "new doctrines." As the passage in "The Parson Preaching" makes clear, the result of Christ speaking in or through the preacher is to make the preached gospel efficacious, "for thou art Love, and when thou teachest, all are Scholers" (*CP*, p. 233).

37. *Babylonian Captivity* (*Pagan Servitude*), Dillenberger, pp. 301–3. Vendler is correct that "Aaron" involves "an elaborate interweaving of conversion, baptism, and resurrection" (*Poetry of Herbert*, p. 119). This "interweaving" is the essence of Luther's baptismal theology (see p. 141 below).

38. For "Plain demonstrations, evident and cleare, / Fetching their proofs ev'n from the very bone," see "Dotage," lines 10–11. These lines are very close in both thought

The first stanza of "The Glance" is such an account. "The Glance"
clarifies Herbert's theology of assurance by locating the experience of
regeneration within the overall spiritual history of the Christian. "The
Glance" is even richer than "Aaron" in its interweaving of motifs.
The first stanza of "The Glance" describes a moment in Herbert's
experience—again I see no reason to distinguish Herbert from "the
speaker"—a datable event which he can recall as such, as a moment.
The stanza form is elaborate and lyrical; the syntax is flowing:

> When first thy sweet and gracious eye
> Vouchsaf'd ev'n in the midst of youth and night
> To look upon me, who before did lie
>   Weltring in sinne;
> I felt a sugred strange delight,
> Passing all cordials made by any art,
> Bedew, embalme, and overrunne my heart,
>   And take it in.   [1–8]

As Halewood has noted, this stanza presents God as embracing
man "in his worst condition"—"Weltring in sinne."[39] This is *agape*,
unmotivated by its object and transforming it (the poet "*before* did
lie / Weltring in sinne"). Herbert's emphasis is on God's freedom, on
the bestowal of grace as a gesture of lordly and "gracious" conde-
scension. Vouchsafe, in Herbert, is always a word that indicates gra-
cious and utterly unimaginable condescension. In "The Priesthood,"
Herbert wonders at the men who "serve him up, who all the world
commands: / When God *vouchsafeth* to become our fare." In "Marie
Magdalene," which follows shortly upon "The Glance," Herbert pre-
sents Mary as having "known" in an especially deep way "who did
vouchsafe and deigne / To bear our filth."[40] "Vouchsafe and deigne"
clarifies the force of "vouchsafing" in Herbert. "Ev'n," in line 2 of
"The Glance," is another strong word for Herbert. Mary knew "that
her sinnes did dash / Ev'n God himself"; in "The Bunch of Grapes,"
the speaker sees "Ev'n God himself being pressed for my sake." "Ev'n
in the midst of youth and night" emphasizes how totally unprepared
for grace Herbert was at the moment that was decisive in his life—
decisive *for*, not by him.

---

and phrasing to Keats's famous remark on "axioms of philosophy" not being axioms
"until they are proved upon our pulses" (letter to J. H. Reynolds, May 3, 1818, *The
Letters of Keats, 1814–1821*, ed. Hyder E. Rollins [Cambridge, Massachusetts, 1958], I,
279). I do not know whether Keats had access to the Pickering edition of *The Temple*
(1799).

39. *Poetry of Grace*, p. 103.
40. See Strier, "Herbert and Tears," pp. 229–39.

The experience described in the opening of "The Glance" is sudden or "catastrophic" conversion. In presenting conversion in this way, Herbert again allies himself with the early Reformation and against many of his Reformed contemporaries. One of the major corollaries of covenant theology was the doctrine of "preparation for grace." When regeneration was conceived of as a gradual rather than a sudden process, commencing, as Miller puts it, with "an initial stage of negotiation," it became possible and reasonable to assert "that men should undergo a preliminary state of 'preparation' before they were called."[41] Thomas Hooker endorsed the position that very often a man cannot tell exactly when faith was born in him.[42] Herbert, as "The Glance" shows, could tell, and he did not allow for any stage of negotiation. Again Herbert stands with John Cotton, who held that "a man is as passive in his Regeneration, as in his first generation."[43] "To works of creation," Cotton explained, "there needeth no preparation."[44]

Lines 1–4 of "The Glance" treat *agape;* lines 5–8 treat man's experience of it, and this experience is presented as primarily affective. Structurally, the eight-line stanza of "The Glance" is divided in half; the fifth line is very prominent: it follows the one full stop in the stanza at the end of the short fourth line, and it constitutes the point at which the stanza "turns." Line 5 of "The Glance" begins, "I felt." For the first time, Herbert presents himself as subject rather than object, and his role as subject is to feel. What he feels is "a sugred strange delight." For Herbert, as for Shakespeare, "strange" is a numinous word.[45] Herbert generally uses it only for sin and grace. In "Miserie," he speaks of the "strange wayes" of sinful man; in "Obedience," the crucifixion shows "a strange love to all our good"; in "The Bag," Herbert's persona describes—and tells—the Incarnation and Passion as "a strange story." By speaking of his delight in "the glance" as *strange,* Herbert is insisting on its numinous quality. The only other "strange delight" in Herbert's poetry is in "The H. Scriptures" (I), where the scriptures contain "infinite sweetness . . . a masse / Of *strange delights."* "The Banquet" also presents a strange delight—"Thy delight / Passeth tongue to taste or tell"—though Her-

41. "Preparation for Salvation," p. 55, and passim. See also Norman Pettit, *The Heart Prepared: Grace and Conversion in Puritan Spiritual Life* (New Haven, 1966), although this work is to be used with caution (see chap. 6, n. 3 below); and Bush, *Writings of Thomas Hooker,* chaps. 7–10.

42. Preface to John Rogers, *The Doctrine of Faith,* quoted in Miller, ibid., p. 59.

43. *The New Covenant,* p. 55.

44. *Gospel Conversion* (1646), p. 5.

45. For Shakespeare, see, for instance, *A Midsummer Night's Dream,* V.i.1; *Hamlet,* I.i.64, I.iii.220, I.iv.164 (all in reference to the ghost); *Pericles,* III.ii.106.

bert does not there use the phrase. And in "The Banquet" as in "The Glance," the strangeness of the delight is so important to Herbert that he goes out of his way to assert its transcendence. In "The Banquet," he hypothesizes two mock naturalistic explanations for the special sweetness of the Eucharist (lines 10–18) only to dismiss them out of hand ("Doubtlesse, neither starre nor flower / Hath the power / Such a sweetness to impart" [lines 19–21]). In "The Glance," he similarly insists that he felt "a sugred strange delight, / *Passing all cordials made by any art.*"

The final lines of the first stanza of "The Glance" present the glance as not only transcendently "sweet" but also as transcendently powerful. He felt the "strange delight . . . Bedew, embalme, and overrunne [his] heart" (line 7). This series represents increasingly powerful action on the heart—from sprinkling ("bedew"), to more thorough penetration ("embalme"), to the obviously overwhelming "overrunne."[46] Herbert presents the experience with detailed mock physicality. The dimeter final line of the stanza provides a rhyme for the dimeter final line of the first half and shifts quietly into a more abstract vocabulary. The vision of being washed, perfumed, practically drowned in a "cordial" of surpassing sweetness gives way to the "drier" image of entering a new realm: "I felt a sugred strange delight . . . Bedew, embalme, and overrunne my heart, / *And take it in.*" This almost anticlimactic line is Herbert's transition to the second stanza—one might almost say the second movement—of "The Glance." The second stanza describes Herbert's life in the realm to which he was brought by "the glance."

The stanza begins rather grimly. Herbert emphasizes the fact that the moment described in the first stanza took place long before the period in which he is writing. Herbert is no longer "in the midst of youth." "Since that time,"

> many a bitter storm
> My soul hath felt, ev'n able to destroy,
> Had the malicious and ill-meaning harm
> His swing and sway.   [9–12]

The emphasis is still on feeling—"My soul *hath felt*"—but now on negative and recurrent feelings rather than on a unique and overwhelmingly positive one. The ascription of malice to the potentially soul-destroying experiences in question inevitably recalls the opening of "Assurance." The recurrent "storms" are *Anfechtungen*, crises of faith. In this stanza, the emphatic "ev'n" (also in the second line)

---

46. "Embalme" is used here strictly in *OED* sense II.2: "to salve or anoint with aromatic spices, oils, etc."

points to the power of the storms Herbert's soul has felt—"ev'n able to destroy"—rather than to the benightedness from which he has been redeemed ("ev'n in the midst" [line 2]). But the structural parallel is itself encouraging when taken together with the knowledge that Herbert and his soul have obviously not been "destroyed" by the ill-meaning harms and the formal recognition of this knowledge in the counterfactual of line 11—"*Had* the malicious and ill-meaning harm."

The fifth-line turn of stanza 2, like so many of Herbert's turns is signaled by a "But." At the parallel moment in "Assurance," we hear "But I will to my Father." In "The Glance," Herbert makes a very different assertion, though one that perhaps explains how the assertion of "Assurance" is possible. We know that what must follow the adversative in line 13 is an assertion that God kept the "malicious" doubts from having their "swing and sway." What we are not prepared for is the central assertion of the poem, both thematically and structurally, the claim that the counterforce to the elements which threaten Herbert's soul is not any new infusion of grace but *the same* "infusion" dramatized in stanza 1. The delight of that time long ago "in the midst of youth" turns out to have been not "once upon a time" but "once and for all." The "many a bitter storm" would have destroyed Herbert,

> But still thy sweet originall joy,
> Sprung from thine eye, did work within my soule,
> And surging griefs, when they grew bold, controll,
> And got the day. [13–16]

Here again, "still" means "always." The "sweet originall joy" remained with Herbert always, not as a possession or a memory, but as a power, an active presence working within his soul. Whether or not Herbert was directly conscious of this controlling presence in his soul is not a question that "The Glance" answers. He is certain, however, that it *must have* been there on the basis of what he knows— "has felt"—of the power and destructiveness of "griefs" (compare "Hadst thou not had thy part, / Sure the unruly sigh had broke my heart," and "if but one grief and smart / Among my many had his full career, / Sure it would carrie with it ev'n my heart").[47] Herbert's assertion of the continuous working of the "originall joy" within his soul is a credo, not a report—or rather it is both, a credo *as* a report.

The main effort of the rest of stanza 2, the lines which follow the turn, is devoted to enriching the continuity between this stanza and

47. "Affliction" (III), lines 5–6; "Josephs coat," lines 56–57. Interestingly, this conception seems to be characteristic only of Herbert's late poems. In spite of its place in the "Affliction" series, "Affliction" (III), like "Josephs coat," does not appear in "W" ("Affliction" I, IV, and V do).

the first. To the perfectly clear reference of "thy sweet originall joy,"
Herbert adds the logically superfluous specifying phrase, "Sprung
from thine eye." He wants to bring into this stanza as full an allusion
as possible to the emotional and imagistic context of stanza 1, to the
remarkable "glance."[48] Stanza 2, however, never becomes fully joy-
ous. Like "Josephs coat" and like "Bitter-sweet," the poem which
precedes "The Glance" in *The Temple*, stanza 2 of "The Glance" pre-
sents the Christian life as complex, a mingled yarn, bittersweet—
"passions intermingled with comforts," as Sibbes said.[49] The final lines
of the stanza begin to take on a triumphant tone, especially if we give
"controll" its seventeenth-century meaning of "prohibit" rather than
its weaker modern meaning, but the language of victory here remains
rather abstract, and the terms of the victory are double negative rather
than fully positive. In the stanza as a whole, we are more aware of
the power of the "sweet originall joy" than of its joyousness. What
the soul "hath felt" in the stanza is only pain and the mysterious
surcease of it at the very moments when it seemed invincible. After
the powerful action of "controll"—in the syntax as well as the nar-
rative—the final dimeter of the stanza, "And got the day" (line 16),
again seems loose and almost anticlimactic, a colorless and cliché
addition to a much more strongly worded claim.

The third stanza of "The Glance" transforms power back into love;
it brings back the sweetness of "the glance." Beginning as a meditation
on stanza 2, on the power of the "originall joy" in the life it establishes,
the third stanza draws a conclusion on the basis of this meditation.
Thus far, the poem has been entirely concerned with God's first
"glance" at Herbert, with Herbert's "originall" Christian joy. Now,
Herbert meditates,

> If thy first glance so powerfull be,
> A mirth but opened and seal'd up again;
> What wonders shall we feel, when we shall see
> Thy full-ey'd love!   [17–20]

This is explicitly apocalyptic. The elect receive a foretaste of heaven—
but only a foretaste.[50] This stanza envisions the ultimate stage of the
process which stanza 1 dramatized beginning. And this apocalypse
is emotional and affective rather than epistemological. Herbert uses

48. In this context it is perhaps worth noting the difference between "The Glance"
and "The Glimpse." "The Glance" concerns *God's* glance at Herbert; "The Glimpse"
concerns one of Herbert's sporadic glimpses of God's favor.

49. *The Soul's Conflict with Itself, Works*, I, 131 (characterizing the Psalms).

50. See Tyndale, *Parable of the Wicked Mammon, Doctrinal Treatises*, p. 65: "in believing,
we receive the Spirit of God, which is the earnest of eternal life, and we are in eternal
life already, and feel already in our hearts the sweetness thereof."

the Pauline image of seeing "face to face" in a context closer to that of "Love" (III) than to that of "Justice" (II). He uses it in a context of love rather than of illumination.[51] Herbert imagines in heaven the greatest and most moving of "recognition scenes." He purposely keeps his emphasis affective by reversing the verbs in line 19: "What wonders shall we *feel,* when we shall *see* / Thy . . . love." We shall feel the wonders when we see the love.[52] Herbert does not desire to "see wonders" in heaven.

The prominence of the transposition of seeing and feeling in lines 19 and 20 of "The Glance" alerts us to the play with these concepts that has been going on throughout the poem. Herbert's reliance in the final stanza on the human experience of being loved as the most adequate way of conceptualizing God's relationship to the regenerate has been operative throughout. The reformers insisted that grace was not a quality or substance imparted to the soul but rather the experience of a change in God's *attitude.* It was not to be spoken of in terms of "infusion" but in terms of relationship. It designated, for the reformers, not a *qualitas* but a *voluntas.*[53] Melanchthon stated the position in an aphorism—"Grace," he said, "is not medicine but favor."[54] Like "Love" (III), "The Glance" is very much in this tradition. All the physicality of stanza 1, all the talk of grace as a surpassingly "sugred" and powerful "cordial," is mock physicality. Grace is cordial the way a person is, not the way a liqueur is. An attitude, a gracious glance, can be spoken of as if it were a medicine or a "cordial" because it can be as powerful and affecting as one—or more so. The mock

51. It is eloquent of the difference between Herbert and Vaughan that when Vaughan uses this passage from Corinthians (I, 13:12) he does so in a strongly epistemological context. See "Resurrection and Immortality," lines 51–56.

52. It is also deeply significant that in this final stanza, when Herbert is imagining glory rather than testifying to grace, he switches from the singular to the plural form of the first person pronoun ("What wonders shall *we* feel"). Like John Milton and John the Divine, Herbert expects to be among "sweet societies" in heaven (see "Lycidas," line 179).

53. See Luther, *Against Latomus,* LW XXXII, 227, "Here, as ought to be done, I take grace in the proper sense of the favor of God, not a quality of the soul" (*WA,* VIII, 106: *Gratiam accipio hic proprie pro favore dei, sicut debet, non pro qualitate animi*); and *Commentary on Galatians,* ed. Watson, p. 227: "They imagine that righteousness is a certain quality poured into the soul." Aquinas argues against the view that to say that a man has the grace of God is merely to say that he has the favor of God and for the view that "there is something supernatural in him, which God bestows," a "habitual gift" that is "infused" into the soul in *Summa Theologica,* Question 110, Articles 1–2 (in *Nature and Grace,* pp. 156–60).

54. Quoted in Gerrish, *Grace and Reason,* p. 129. See *De gratia, Loci Communes,* 1521, *Melanchthons Werke,* ed. Hans Engelland et al. (Gutersloh, 1952), II.1, 85–88, where the distinction between the Reformation position and the Catholic (Thomist) one is well discussed.

physicality of "The Glance" (and of many of Herbert's poems) makes this point. *Agape* is the greatest of heartwarmers. This line of development in "The Glance" culminates in the astounding turn-line of stanza 3:

> When thou shalt look us out of pain.   [21]

The process by which the joy that "sprung from" God's eye controls grief culminates here. The double negative becomes overwhelmingly positive when it is phrased as an absolute. Keeping to his central metaphor of "the glance," Herbert eliminates all suggestion of physicality from the most moving of the apocalyptic promises: "And God shall wipe away all tears from their eyes . . . neither shall there be any more pain" (Revelation 21:4).

The final lines of "The Glance" alert us to another strand of imagery in the poem which would probably otherwise go unnoticed. Herbert draws upon another great apocalyptic promise: "And there shall be no night there . . . neither light of the sun; for the Lord God giveth them light" (22:4). The verse immediately preceding this in the Apocalypse begins, "And they shall see his face." To "we shall see / Thy full-ey'd love" and "thou shalt look us out of pain," Herbert adds (brilliantly continuing both the face and the glance imagery):

> And one aspect of thine spend in delight
> More then a thousand sunnes disburse in light,
> > In heav'n above.   [22–24]

This staggering burst of supernal (de-)light (Herbert plays on this again in the poem entitled "Heaven") reminds us of the pattern of light-and-darkness imagery present throughout the poem. The opening describes the first beam of sunshine in a dark night ("ev'n in the midst of youth *and night*"), the second stanza describes a day, albeit a very stormy one. The final stanza envisions "More then a thousand sunnes disburse in light" and retrospectively taps the metaphorical potential of the anticlimactic "And got *the day*" by revealing the full extent of this victory.

The poem ends, as Herbert almost always does, on a quiet rather than an exuberant note. The final dimeter, "In heav'n above," is syntactically ambiguous. If it is read (as the pause created by the comma and the line break allows) as modifying "one aspect of thine" in line 22, it continues the description of glory. If, however, it is read as syntactically continuous with the line that precedes it, it modifies the thousand ordinary "sunnes" of line 23 and creates the image of a man looking up at or thinking about the literal sun. This reading, which is probably the primary one (with the other as a definite pressure), ends the poem with a reminder of the speaker's earthly status, a reminder that the vision of the previous lines is still in the future tense. The ending becomes similar to that of "Grace"—"Remove me, where I need not say, / *Drop from above*." We are reminded of the actual position of the speaker. The assertions of stanza 3 are, after all, faith, not knowledge.

One final "aspect" of "The Glance" remains to be considered. The language in which it presents conversion in the first stanza is strongly baptismal—"Bedew, embalme, and overrunne my heart." In attacking the Roman sacrament of penance, the reformers took what they thought of as a strong view of baptism. They inveighed against those who "weakened and diminished the force of baptism," who asserted that the sinning Christian needed "a second plank" after the ship-wreck of falling into sin. The reformers held that "[what] baptism signifies operates as long as we live" once it is activated by faith.[55] The essence of this view is its insistence on the continuity and *permanent* efficacy of baptism activated by faith—its insistence, in fact, on precisely the kind of continuity and permanent efficacy portrayed in "The Glance." Whenever Herbert asserts the continuity of grace, his language recalls his sonnet on baptism. The final quatrain of his version of the twenty-third psalm (which immediately follows "The Glance") begins: "Surely thy sweet and wondrous love, / Shall *measure all my dayes*." "In you," Herbert wrote of baptism, "Redemption *measures all my time*." Moreover, baptism, for the reformers, was not only efficacious throughout life but also eschatological. "The Glance" is Herbert's clearest affirmation of this. Luther asserted not only that what baptism signifies "operates as long as we live," but also that "we are continually being rebaptized [by faith] until we attain to *the completion of the sign at the last day*" (emphasis mine).[56]

This theology of baptism is a way of formulating another of the major Reformation doctrines which, like the irresistibility of grace and unconditional election, was being attacked in Herbert's day by the followers of Arminius, the doctrine of the perseverance of the saints.[57] "The Glance" is an assertion of this doctrine—"still thy sweet originall joy . . . did work within my soul"; "If thy first glance so powerfull be. . . . What wonders shall we feel, when we shall see / Thy full-ey'd love!" The doctrine of perseverance, like all the other major Reformation positions, was meant to be "full of sweet, pleasant, and unspeakable comfort to godly persons" and was meant to release the

---

55. For references and a fuller explication of this view, see Strier, "Herbert and Tears," pp. 223–29.

56. *Babylonian Captivity* (*Pagan Servitude*), Dillenberger, pp. 302–3. Both sacraments are eschatological for Luther (see p. 78 above for the Eucharist as eschatological).

57. For references in Arminius's writings, see chap. 4, n. 3 above.

Christian from anxiety.[58] We can appreciate the significance of "The Glance" more fully if we recall a story told about Oliver Cromwell. On his deathbed Cromwell is reported to have inquired whether grace, once enjoyed, could ever be lost. He is said to have died happy when assured that it could not be. "For I know," he is reported as saying, "that I was once in grace."[59]

58. Article XVII of the Anglican Articles ("Of Predestination and Election"), *Creeds*, ed. Gerrish, p. 191.

59. Quoted in Christopher Hill, *Puritanism and Revolution* (1958; rpt. New York, 1964), p. 248.

6

The Heart Alone:
Inwardness and
Individualism

"The Glance" presents an inward, private, and emotional experience as central to the entire Christian life. The first two stanzas of the poem are very close to the sort of "experimental account" of the work of grace in the believer's soul "whereby he (or she) is convinced that he is regenerate and received of God" that the "gathered churches" of the seventeenth century came to demand of their members.[1] The extraordinarily strong stress on individual inner experience in Herbert's poetry—together with his presentation of this experience in both its positive and negative forms as independent of his own volition—helps us to understand the appeal of Herbert's poetry to Puritan and Dissenting readers in the seventeenth and eighteenth centuries, and, more generally, as I have already suggested, the continuity of the Protestant tradition as a whole.[2]

It is easy to demonstrate the continuity between the "right" and the "left" of the Protestant tradition on both historical and theological grounds. The key to this continuity is the doctrine of the work of the

1. John Rogers, *Ohel or Beth-shemesh, a Tabernacle for the Sun . . . An Idea of Church-Discipline, in the Theorick and Practick Parts* (1653), p. 354. For the late development of this practice, see Edmund S. Morgan, *Visible Saints: The History of a Puritan Idea* (New York, 1963), chaps. 1–3.

2. On the appeal of Herbert's poetry to Puritan and Dissenting readers, see Hutchinson, *Works*, pp. xxix–xlvii; Summers, *Herbert*, chap. 1; Robert Ray, "George Herbert in the Seventeenth Century: Allusions to Him, Collected and Annotated" (Ph.D. diss., University of Texas at Austin, 1967); Sebastian Koppl, *Die Rezeption George Herberts im 17. um 18. Jahrhundert* (Heidelberg, 1978). For the continuity of the Protestant tradition, see pp. xv–xvi above.

Spirit.[3] In support of his view that "Christianity is founded on faith in Christ and the gift of his Spirit only, and not at all on Humane Learning," William Dell constantly appealed to Luther.[4] When Anne Hutchinson was accused of antinomianism by the Boston magistrates, she appealed to the teachings of Cotton on the witness of the Spirit; when Cotton himself was queried on this matter, his response was, "Let Calvin answer for me."[5] The doctrine of the direct working of the Holy Spirit on the hearts of believers was essential to the theology of the Reformation. It explained what the reformers meant by faith. "Faith," as Calvin puts it, "is the principal work of the Holy Spirit."[6]

There is no deeper misunderstanding of the Reformation than to view it as fundamentally concerned with the understanding or clarification of theological abstractions. Even the view so ably castigated by C. S. Lewis—that historical Protestantism was essentially gloomy or ascetic—is less serious a misunderstanding than this.[7] Early in the Reformation, Luther complained that many people missed the point when they heard of faith alone, conjuring up "an idea which they call 'belief,' which they treat as genuine faith" but which, nonetheless, "is but a human fabrication . . . without a corresponding experience in the depths of the heart."[8] "The Word of God is not received by faith," said Calvin, "if it flits about on the top of the brain, but when it takes root in the depths of the heart."[9] The work of the Spirit is to apply the Word to the heart in this way. Again, assurance is the key. Anyone can pretend to—or have—an intellectual assent to the status of the Bible as the revealed Word and to the historicity of the events described therein, but only the regenerate can feel the "inward testimony of the Spirit" to the truth of the Word, and, more centrally, only the Spirit can provide the human heart, "in its infirmity and

3. See Nuttall, "Historical Introduction," *The Holy Spirit in Puritan Faith and Experience,* and passim. Pettit's assertion that Richard Rogers's interest in the doctrine of the Holy Spirit was something new in the Reformation tradition is entirely misleading (*The Heart Prepared,* p. 10). Pettit cites Nuttall without seeming to grasp his argument.

4. William Dell, *A Plain and Necessary Confutation of . . . Sir Sydrach Simpson* (1654), p. 20 and passim. Dell appends an epilogue of "The Testimony of Martin Luther" to this work.

5. "The Examination of Mrs. Anne Hutchinson at the Court at Newton," in David C. Hall, *The Antinomian Controversy, 1636–1638: A Documentary History* (Middletown, Conn.; 1968), pp. 320–24, 333, 346–47; Cotton, *Gospel Conversion,* p. 22 (and see p. 30: "And surely for the Doctrine in hand, Calvin is as clear as my hearts desire is to God wee all might be"). See Miller, "Preparation for Salvation," pp. 60–68.

6. *Institutes,* III.i.4.

7. *English Literature in the Sixteenth Century,* pp. 33–35, 162, 190–91; "Donne and Love Poetry in the Seventeenth Century," *Seventeenth-Century Studies Presented to Sir Herbert Grierson* (Oxford, 1938), pp. 74–75.

8. "Preface to Romans," Dillenberger, p. 23.

9. *Institutes,* III.ii.36.

consciousness of sin," with an absolute assurance of its own salvation.[10] Calvin explained that the power of the Spirit is more clearly manifested in relation to the heart than to the mind because "the heart's distrust is greater than the mind's blindness."[11]

The distinction which we have already examined between a general faith and a personal one, is also, therefore, a distinction between a general and, using Tyndale's term, "a feeling faith."[12] The stress on experience is central to historical Protestantism. "Saints have an experimental knowledge of the work of grace, by virtue of which they come to know it as certainly—as we dispute against the Papists—as by feeling heat, we know fire is hot; by tasting honey, we know it is sweet."[13] "Experience, we say, proves principles," explained John Rogers; Sibbes asserted that "experience is the life of a Christian," and asked, rhetorically, "What is all knowledge of Christ without experience?"[14] Herbert is in the major Reformation tradition (and very close to Calvin's formulation) when he notes that "A generall apprehension, or assent to the promises of the Gospell by heare-say, or relation from others, is not that which filleth the heart with joy and peace in believing." What does so fill the heart is "the spirits bearing witness with our spirit, revealing and applying the generall promises to every one in particular" with a permanent and transforming "sincerity and efficacy" ("Notes on Valdes," pp. 308–9).

We can now see that what distinguished the radicals from orthodox Protestants—from everyone, that is, who believed in a learned ministry and established ordinances (preaching and the sacraments)—was not that the radicals stressed experience and the orthodox did not. The radicals stressed experience and the Spirit *alone*—apart from the Word. When Herbert rebukes Valdes for opposing "the teaching of the spirit to the teaching of the scripture," and tending to "overthrow all means," he is not doing anything particularly Anglican. He

10. For the "inward testimony of the Spirit," see Calvin, *Institutes*, I.vii.4; for "infirmity and consciousness of sin," see Luther, *Babylonian Captivity (Pagan Servitude)*, Dillenberger, p. 293.

11. *Institutes*, III.ii.36.

12. William Tyndale, *An Answer to Sir Thomas More's Dialogue*, ed. Rev. Henry Walter (Cambridge, 1850), pp. 50 ff. The "sundry English divines" who composed the Westminster *Confession* noted that "brain-knowledge [may be] in the worst of men, nay, in the worst of creatures, the devils themselves . . . in such eminency, as the best of saints cannot attain to," but only the saints, the regenerate, can have "an inward, a savoury, an heart knowledge . . . that spiritual sense and feeling of divine truths the Apostle speaks of" (*Church of Scotland, Confession of Faith* [Edinburgh, 1815], p. 5). See p. 125 above.

13. Thomas Shepard, *The Parable of the Ten Virgins Opened and Applied*, in *The Works* (1659; rpt. Boston, 1853), II, 222 (quoted in Miller, *New England Mind*, p. 51).

14. Rogers, *Ohel or Beth-shemesh*, p. 355; Sibbes, *A Learned Commentary . . . upon II Corinthians 4*, in *Works*, IV, 412.

is asserting that the Spirit works through the Word—applying it to our hearts—in just the way that Luther asserted this to the Spiritualists of his day, Calvin to the Spiritualists of his, and, during the Commonwealth and Protectorate, all the orthodox divines from "Anglican" to Independent did in the face of the great outcropping of "spiritual religion" then.[15]

As Summers has noted, what makes Herbert's notes on Valdes particularly interesting is not their horror at the Spanish reformer's "unsufferable" opinion of Scripture, but their obvious attempt "to read Valdesso charitably." Summers does not consider *why* Herbert would have wanted to exercise this charity, although Herbert himself is quite explicit on this.[16] What Herbert says he especially valued was: Valdes's understanding of imputation ("the intent of the Gospell in the acceptation of Christs righteousness . . . a thing strangely buried, and darkned by the Adversaries"); Valdes's devotion to Christ; and Valdes's notes on "Gods Kingdome within us and the working thereof"—of which, Herbert remarks, "he was a very diligent observer" ("Notes on Valdes," pp. 304–5). Needless to say, this last is the comment of one "diligent observer" thereof on another. One of the things that we can learn from Herbert's poetry and prose, as from the writings of Luther, Cotton, and perhaps even Calvin, is that the Reformation doctrines of grace and "Gods Kingdome within us" cannot be expressed in undiluted form and still be entirely freed from the spectre of radicalism.

One of the essential impulses of the "radical Reformation"was toward the internalization of religion, the replacement of external or institutional realities with internal or spiritual ones.[17] Where the orthodox called for correlation, the radicals called for replacement. A very clear demonstration of the difference between these orientations is provided by Herbert's "The Church-floore." This poem opens as if

15. For Luther's relation to the "Spiritualists," see Gordon Rupp, "Word and Spirit in the First Years of the Reformation," *Archiv für Reformationsgeschichte*, 49 (1958), 13–25; and Prenter, *Spiritus Creator*; for Calvin, see Wallace, *Calvin's Doctrine of the Word and Sacrament*; for the Commonwealth and Protectorate, see Nuttall, *Holy Spirit*. On the unhistorical nature of the term "Anglican" for the sixteenth and early seventeenth century, see p. xv above.

16. Summers, *Herbert*, p. 67. Grant, on the other hand, vastly overstates the importance of Valdes to Herbert (*The Transformation of Sin*, ch. 4), apparently suggesting that the notion of justification by faith came to Herbert *from Valdes*. For Valdes, see "Evangelical Catholicism as Represented by Juan de Valdes," in George Huntston Williams and Angel M. Mergal, eds., *Spiritual and Anabaptist Writers* (Philadelphia, 1957), pp. 297–394.

17. See Williams, *The Radical Reformation*; *Spiritual and Anabaptist Writers*, ed. Williams and Mergal; and, in somewhat popularized form, Rufus M. Jones, *Spiritual Reformers in the Sixteenth and Seventeenth Centuries* (1914; pap. rpt., Boston, 1959).

it were going to be a textbook case of the "Anglican" attitude toward the places and physical accoutrements of worship. Without ascribing holiness to the physical structure—which would be seen as the Roman attitude—the poem seems to see the physical structure as a help toward meditation on spiritual virtues. As Richard Hooker explains, "albeit the true worship of God be to God in itself acceptable, who respecteth not so much in what place, as with what affection he is served . . . manifest notwithstanding it is, that the very majesty and holiness of the place, where God is worshipped, hath in regard of us great virtue, force, and efficacy, for that it serveth as a sensible help to stir up devotion."[18] In "The Church-floore," Herbert seems to be instructing us how to use the church building as a "sensible help" to meditation:

> Mark you the floore? that square & speckled stone,
> 　　Which looks so firm and strong,
> 　　　　Is *Patience*.　　　　　　　　[1–3]

One would have to be a dull student indeed not to catch on to the trick here: as our guide "points out" to us various physical aspects of a church that we are to envision—"*that* square & speckled stone, / Which *looks* so firm and strong"—we are to consider the virtue which has the equivalent properties and functions in the Christian life. Reading along, we grow more and more confident that we have mastered the game (perhaps not entirely accidentally, the answer to the easiest of the riddles is *Confidence*). In the final riddle, however, Herbert seems to depart somewhat from the rules:

> But the sweet cement, which in one sure band
> 　　Ties the whole frame, is *Love*
> 　　　　And *Charitie*.　　　　　　　[10–12]

There is an appropriateness in the way Charitie serves as the cement to tie the whole frame of this section together "in one sure band" of rhyme (tying line 12 to line 6), but the description presented here is not equally applicable to both the physical and the moral terms. "Sweet cement" simply will not do as literal description. Moreover, Herbert seems overly eager to give the solution to the riddle here—it occurs at the end of the second as well as in the required third line. As readers, we note these departures from the norm but tend to take them merely as bespeaking the lecturer's eagerness to make his final point rather than as calling into question the whole procedure which has apparently been at work in the poem. There is some "cognitive dissonance" here, but not enough to make us seriously uneasy.

18. *Laws of Ecclesiastical Polity*, V.xvi.2 (II, 52).

The second section of the poem increases the dissonance. Suddenly a personified abstraction enters the "place" which we have been contemplating. "Hither sometimes Sinne steals" (line 13a). Where before the abstractions had existed merely as reference points, here an abstraction is presented as an agent. We begin to lose our sense that we are imaginatively contemplating an actual church or church floor. To be told that "Sinne . . . stains / The marbles neat and curious veins" does not quite restore the building's physical existence to us. "Stains" is too easily read as merely metaphorical. The next line, however, does restore the building to us—"But all is cleansed when the marble weeps" (line 15). By referring to a well-known, if semi-mythical, property of marble, Herbert restores our sense that he is really talking about marble as well as about penitence here, that he is still exploiting analogies between spiritual and physical phenomena. He has given up the riddling expository mode of the first section for a narrative mode of exposition, he has shifted from permanent to occasional properties of the building and from entities (and categories conceived as entities) to recurrent processes, but the overall strategy and point seem the same.

The next three lines follow the syntactic and narrative model of the previous ones so closely that we are again confident we know how to read them:

> Sometimes Death, puffing at the doore,
> Blows all the dust about the floore:
> But while he thinks to spoil the room, he sweeps. [16–18]

The insistent definite articles—"the doore," "the dust," "the floore," "the room"—together with the homeliness and familiarity of the terms themselves work to keep the scene literal and visualizable, but the "action" being depicted is on the miraculous side (the wind sweeping rather than dirtying a room), and the suspended syntax of the final line seems on the edge of turning from exposition to celebration. Moreover, the spiritual signification of this scene is by no means transparent. It requires more effort to "translate" these lines than any others in the poem.

Here, when we are at our moment of greatest puzzlement—and perhaps of wonder—Herbert produces his final couplet. The oddest thing about this couplet, and the key to its extraordinary power, is that it comes as a surprise. Developing the triumphant note implicit in the structure of line 18 though disguised by its matter-of-fact tone, Herbert fully shifts from exposition and narrative to praise:

> Blest be the *Architect*, whose art
> Could build so strong in a weak heart. [19–20]

We have been caught off guard. Formally, we should have been expecting another couplet to balance that of lines 13–14 ("Hither sometimes Sinne steals, and stains / The marbles neat and curious veins"), but Herbert has constructed this section to make its syntax and stanza form work against its rhyme scheme, producing the effect of parallel tercets rather than of a couplet followed by a quatrain. Substantively, Herbert has been so successful at keeping us and apparently himself occupied with the task of finding spiritual equivalents for material objects or physical equivalents for spiritual processes ("all is cleansed when the marble weeps") that we had not thought to ask where the spiritual facts and processes exist or how they are brought into existence. Paradoxically, the "concreteness" of the poem (the pun is almost unavoidable) has led us to conceive of the virtues and spiritual processes "depicted" in it abstractly. We have been led into misplaced abstractness as well as (*pace* Whitehead) misplaced concreteness. Being apparently given such a definite place to contemplate, we lost our sense of the true locus of significance.

The final word of the poem entirely eliminates the visual and material from its concerns. There is nothing to see here. There is no literal church floor. What we are left contemplating is not the capacity of a physical structure to suggest spiritual meanings but the unique ability of God to create imperishable spiritual virtues in the human heart—virtues which enable the regenerate Christian to achieve true penitence and escape fear of death. But there has been no "image," no place all along. Herbert has misled us, but we have allowed ourselves to be misled. It is we, after all, who read "Is like *Patience*" when Herbert wrote "Is *Patience*," who made the poem analogical rather than metaphorical. It is we who disregarded the hint implicit in "the sweet cement," and, as we cannot fail to realize by the end of the poem, missed the literal referent of "neat and curious veins." Yet even though, as Fish says, "The Church-floore" leads us "to interpretive strategies that are subsequently challenged,"[19] the point of the poem is less to rebuke us than to focus our attention where the poet's is focused—on the work of God in the individual Christian's heart.

Summers has noted that Herbert "nearly always presents the institutional as a hieroglyph of the personal rather than *vice versa*," and that "the hieroglyph of 'The Church-floore' has pictured primarily the marvellous art of God in decreeing the perseverance of the saints rather than His art in the construction of the church."[20] Summers goes on to add, however, that "those two arts are related; once raised, the image of 'The Church-floore' as the foundation of Christ's church is

19. *The Living Temple*, p. 39.
20. *Herbert*, p. 126.

relevant," and he asserts that the couplet "is also a reminder that the structure which God has built within the heart is truly the 'floore' of both the Church Militant and the Church Triumphant." Fish complains that the trouble with this reading is that "it stops unfolding too soon." This is in line with Fish's general concern to obliterate rather than to maintain distinctions, but in fact the trouble with Summers's reading is that it does not stop soon enough.[21] It proceeds to connect the personal with the institutional and outward in a way that the poem itself does not. Unlike Summers's analysis, the poem ends when it reveals the individual heart as the center of Christianity. The poem does not "picture *primarily* the marvellous art of God in decreeing the perseverance of the saints," it "pictures" *only* this. Summers's "but's" and "yet's" are precisely parallel to Hooker's "albeit . . . manifest notwithstanding it is" in the passage quoted above in which Hooker sidesteps the apparent force of the biblical testimony against "places." The poem, however, does not so sidestep. It "stops unfolding" at the moment of revealing the inward and personal.

"The Windows," which follows "The Church-floore" and presents preachers enabled by God to enact their messages as the true "stained glass" of the church, could have been written by an iconoclast; "Aaron," with its delineation of the purely spiritual "vestments" of the "true Aaron," could have been written by an antivestiarian (one who believed that "ministers should show their calling by life and character rather than by apparel"); just so "The Church-floore" could have been written by one who, like Milton or George Fox, believed that "all corporeal resemblances of inward holiness and beauty are now past."[22] "The Church-floore" does not show that Herbert was an incipient Quaker; it does show how deeply, despite his care for the physical structure at Bemerton, Herbert felt some of the impulses that led to Quakerism. This poem should caution us against too easily assimilating the personal to the ecclesiastical in Herbert's poetry. Tuve presents the view that Herbert's lyrics are "about his state of mind *and* about *anima* as *ecclesia*" as the only alternative to seeing Herbert as a Romantic or modern poet interested in psychological exploration per se; Heather Asals follows and extends Tuve in presenting the voice

21. *Living Temple*, p. 40. In commenting on some of the instances of "temple-language" that he cites, Fish himself seems to realize that the key question is to recognize *in which direction* the temple of the heart/temple-as-building or community trope is being run in any particular case (see *Living Temple*, pp. 70–71).

22. "Answer to the Archbishop's Articles (1584)," in *The Second Parte of a Register*, ed. Albert Peel, Preface by C. H. Firth (Cambridge, 1915), I, 180; *The Reason of Church Government Urged against Prelaty*, in Merritt Y. Hughes, *John Milton: Complete Poems and Major Prose* (Indianapolis, 1957), p. 673; George Fox, *The Journal*, ed. Rufus M. Jones (1904; rpt. New York, 1963), pp. 76, 140, 153–56.

of "The Church" as not that of an individual but of Christ as the Head of His Mystical Body.[23]

To insist on the personal nature of the poetry of "The Church" does not have to be anachronistic. Certainly Herbert was not a Romantic individualist. He was, however, a Protestant one.[24] We have already seen the emphasis that Protestant theology placed on personal experience. Protestant exegetical theory followed suit, seeing the Bible as a source of experience as well as of doctrine, laying extraordinary stress on what medieval fourfold exegesis called the "tropological" sense of Scripture—the application of Scripture to the individual's life.[25] Luther's decisive breakthrough can be put in precise exegetical terms. It came when he recognized the tropological sense of "the righteousness of God"—its application to the individual—as faith.[26] In the Reformation view, Scripture applied to the individual by being applied to him—not by his own effort but by the Spirit "bearing witnesse with our spirit, revealing and applying the generall promises to everyone in particular."

This sense of the special, individually directed dynamism of Scripture is powerfully expressed in the second of Herbert's sonnets on "The H. Scriptures." The poem begins with a prayer for understanding, a longing to know not merely each individual part of the Bible, but also and especially, all the complex ways the parts fit together— "Seeing not onely how each verse doth shine, / But all the constellations of the storie" (lines 1–4). The next quatrain, however, takes a different tack. It emphasizes the activity of the biblical verses among themselves and the power of this activity over man. It develops the "book of starres" conceit in terms of astrology rather than astronomy:

> This verse marks that, and both do make a motion
>   Unto a third, that ten leaves off doth lie:
>   Then as dispersed herbs do watch a potion,
> These three make up some Christians destinie.   [5–8]

The quatrain of the sestet makes the general assertion personal:

23. Tuve, *A Reading of Herbert*, p. 143; Asals, "The Voice of George Herbert's 'The Church,' " *ELH*, 36 (1969), 511–28.

24. In "Herbert and *Caritas*," p. 189, Tuve rebukes George Herbert Palmer for recognizing Herbert's individualism and linking him to Bunyan. Tuve characterizes Palmer's assertion that to Herbert "the personal relationship of God to the soul is the one matter of consequence" as "one of the most inexplicable remarks ever made about Herbert"(!) and professes surprise that it should have come from one who knew the poetry so well.

25. See Lewalski, *Donne's "Anniversaries" and the Poetry of Praise*, chap. 5, and *Protestant Poetics*, chap. 4; Preus, *From Shadow to Promise*, chap. 15.

26. See Warren A. Quanbeck, "Luther's Early Exegesis," in *Luther Today* (Decorah, Iowa, 1957), pp. 56–57, 74–75. On Luther's breakthrough, see pp. 116–17 above.

> Such are thy secrets, which my life makes good,
>   And comments on thee: for in ev'ry thing
>   Thy words do finde me out, & parallels bring,
> And in another make me understood.   [9–12]

The explicit passivity of the speaker in line 11—"thy words do *finde me out*"—helps us give proper emphasis to both "make" and "me" in line 12. Bunyan's experience of being "pursued" or seized upon by biblical texts is only a more melodramatic representation of what Herbert is describing here.[27]

The Reformation emphasis on the tropological sense also transformed the traditional study of typology, of the ways in which persons, objects, and events in the Old Testament prefigure events or objects in the life of Christ. Reformation typology treated the "types" tropologically, so that they prefigure the regenerate individual as well as Christ. To see Christ as Head of His Mystical Body speaking in "The Church" is to follow Augustine's commentary on the Psalms and to assume that Herbert did so as well. But Luther and Calvin interpreted the Psalms much less ecclesiologically than did Augustine. Luther saw the Psalms as "a faithful record of what the saints did and said: how they communed with God in the old days, *and how such men still commune with him*"; Calvin, following Athanasius, called the Psalms "an Anatomy of all the Parts of the Soul" and took the occasion of a prologue to his commentaries on the Psalms to write his own spiritual autobiography.[28] In this view, as Donne put it, "David was not onely a cleare Prophet of Christ himselfe, but a Prophet of every particular Christian."[29]

---

27. See *Grace Abounding*, pars. 64, 141, and passim. Lewalski's account of "H. Scriptures" (II) as merely recounting "the recommended exegetical procedures of collating related texts and applying all of them to the self" (*Protestant Poetics*, p. 105) misses the essential religious content of the poem, the idea of the exegete *as passive* in relation to "application."

28. Luther, "Preface to the Psalms," Dillenberger, p. 38; Calvin, "The Author's Preface," *Commentary on the Psalms*, trans. James Anderson (Edinburgh, 1845), I, xxix–xlix. For Athanasius, see "A Letter to Marcellinus on the Interpretation of the Psalms," in *Athanasius: The Life of Antony and the Letter to Marcellinus*, trans. Robert C. Gregg (New York, 1980), pp. 111, 126. It is interesting in relation to the problem of defining the predominant "voice" of "The Church" that Hermann Gunkel saw "the gravest error made by students of the Psalms" as being that they misunderstood this personal poetry "and have taken the living 'I,' which means the poet himself, as a mere figure of speech meaning the people" (quoted in George S. Gunn, *God in the Psalms* [Edinburgh, 1956], p. 122).

29. Sermon on Psalm 63.7 in *The Sermons of John Donne*, ed. Evelyn Simpson and G. F. Potter (Berkeley and Los Angeles, 1954), VII, 51. Compare Calvin, *Commentary on the Psalms*, II, 122.

Herbert fully accepts the reality of postfiguration.[30] He makes the same use of biblical as of institutional materials. The opening poem of "The Church" announces the emphasis on the inward and personal. In "The Altar," as Lewalski has noted, Herbert makes "radically personal" use of his biblical materials: Herbert (or his "speaker") "is made the primary antitype [fulfillment] of all the types, in that *the heart, not the New Testament church altar,* is the direct antitype of the altar of unhewn stones which figures so prominently in the divine prescriptions for the altar of sacrifice in the Old Testament."[31] Again Herbert's focus is noninstitutional.[32] Echoing the praise of "a broken and a contrite heart" in Psalm 51, he takes a position more radical than that of the Psalmist. Whereas the Psalmist promises a literal altar to God after the walls of Jerusalem have been built (verses 18–19), there is no reference to any material altar in Herbert's poem—except, of course, that which the poem typographically presents.

By placing "The Altar" at the head of his volume, Herbert immediately presents the individual heart as the locus of the two great mysteries of Christian life, sin and grace:

> A *Heart* alone
> Is such a stone,
> As nothing but
> Thy pow'r doth cut.　　　　　　[5–8]

The placement of "The Altar" before "The Sacrifice" establishes Herbert's main interest as the "application" rather than the history of redemption. He prays to receive the benefits of Christ's sacrifice before he presents his narrative of the sacrifice. And the narrative itself distinguishes the New from the Old Dispensation primarily in terms of the special psychological immanence of the New. As Empson says of a stanza in "The Sacrifice" which first separates and then equates Moses and Caesar, "both the earthly power of the conqueror and the legal rationalism of the Pharisees are opposed to the profounder mercy of the Christ and the profounder searchings of the heart that he causes."[33]

30. The term is Murray Roston's in *Biblical Drama in England* (London, 1968), pp. 69–78.

31. "Typology and Poetry: A Consideration of Herbert, Vaughan, and Marvell," in Earl Miner, ed., *Illustrious Evidence: Approaches to English Literature of the Early Seventeenth Century* (Berkeley and Los Angeles, 1975), pp. 45–46 (emphasis mine).

32. Summers, *Herbert*, pp. 140–41, notes the irony of "The Altar" being cited to prove Herbert's "Anglo-Catholicism."

33. *Ambiguity*, p. 360. In *A Reading of Herbert*, pp. 27–28, Tuve insisted that Empson's interpretation was unhistorical, that from a historical point of view, on the basis of the traditional typological identification of Moses and Christ, the point could only be the ironic contrast between Moses and Caesar—"*He* clave the stonie rock, when they were

The inward and personal emphasis of Protestant tropology and typology could have radical implications when both the Old and the New Testament were treated as merely "typical" of events in the soul. Through their concentration on the inward equivalents of biblical events, the radicals of the Reformation were led back, as William Madsen puts it, to the "Egypt of allegory" from which the original reformers saw themselves as escaping.[34] For Gerrard Winstanley, for example, the whole scriptures "are but a report of spirituall mysteries."[35] The Quakers were constantly being accused of declaring "that Christ is spiritual—that Christ, God and man, is within us, that his birth, his life, his death, his burial, his resurrection, his ascension are wrought within us," so that although they say, "Christ was born at Bethlehem and died at Jerusalem," they "intend in truth and reality no other birth nor life nor death but what may be extant and wrought in the heart of man."[36]

The possible conflict between history and postfiguration can be seen in two of Herbert's lyrics, "Christmas" and "The Bunch of Grapes." In "Christmas," Herbert adopts what one scholar calls "Luther's most vivid expression" for the personal character of the Bible, the second advent of Christ (the first is the Incarnation; the third, His coming in glory; the second advent is the entry of Christ into the individual believer's life).[37] In the sestet of "Christmas," Herbert prays:

> O Thou, whose glorious, yet contracted light,
> Wrapt in nights mantle, stole into a manger;
> Since my dark soul and brutish is thy right,

---

drie" (line 122). She overlooked the reorienting effect of the next line—"But surely not their hearts, as I well trie"—and the fact that typology was used to establish disjunctions as well as continuities between the New Testament and the Old. Both uses are equally historical. On the two uses of typology, see Sacvan Bercovitch, "Typology in Puritan New England: The Williams-Cotton Controversy Reassessed," *AQ*, 19 (1967), 166–91, and Lewalski, *Protestant Poetics*, pp. 130–31.

34. *From Shadowy Types to Truth*, pp. 35–48; and see Jackson I. Cope, "Seventeenth-Century Quaker Style," in *Seventeenth-Century Prose: Modern Essays in Criticism*, ed. Stanley E. Fish (New York, 1971), pp. 200–235. Lewalski's disagreement with Madsen's "reading of the evidence" (*Protestant Poetics*, p. 123) reflects the different evidence they are using. Although Lewalski works in much greater detail, she deals with a narrower spectrum of the Protestant tradition than does Madsen.

35. *Truth Lifting up Its Head above Scandals*, in *The Works of Gerrard Winstanley*, ed. George H. Sabine (Ithaca, N.Y., 1941), p. 116 (quoted in Madsen, *From Shadowy Types to Truth*, p. 45).

36. Roger Williams, *George Fox Digg'd out of His Burrowes* (1676), in *Publications of the Narragansett Club* (Providence, R.I., 1872), V, 70; see also p. 78–82. For earlier attacks on Quaker allegorization, see Baxter, *The Quakers Catechism* (1655), p. 30, and *One Sheet against the Quakers* (1657), p. 3. In his attack on the Quakers, Williams associated himself with Baxter (*Fox Digg'd*, 3d pref. epistle).

37. Quanbeck, *Luther's Early Exegesis*, p. 89.

> To Man of all beasts be not thou a stranger:
>   Furnish & deck my soul, that thou mayst have
>   A better lodging than a rack or grave.

In part 2 of "Christmas," Herbert purports to see the biblical nativity
narratives as a challenge—"The shepherds sing; and shall I silent
be?"—and then proceeds to establish, in rather mechanical detail, the
analogies between the shepherd's physical situation and his own
spiritual one ("My soul's a shepherd too; a flock it feeds / Of thoughts,
and words, and deeds. / The pasture is thy word.")

"The Bunch of Grapes" is a complex and difficult poem. On the
one hand it provides the clearest instance in Herbert of Protestant
"correlative typology," the establishment of equivalences between the
state of believers under the Old and New Dispensations;[38] on the
other hand it shows the problems Reformation typology can cause
when divorced from the Reformation doctrine of grace. The poem
presents a speaker who uses typology as a way of at once under-
standing his own experience and gaining leverage on God—all in an
attempt at cheering himself up. The speaker sees his problem as lying
in his relationship to joy. He addresses this abstraction in a comically
exasperated tone, as if it were a wayward child or a stray cat:

> Joy, I did lock thee up: but some bad man
>   Hath let thee out again.   [1–2]

Significantly for the poem as a whole, it is impossible to tell here
whether the speaker views joy as something positive or negative—
as something which he had sought to avoid by locking away from
himself or as something which he wanted to keep locked up as a
treasure. The sense seems to favor the former, but the intimacy of
the address suggests the latter.

Thus far, the whole thing seems rather lighthearted. "Some bad
man" is too self-conscious a joke to express any really disturbing self-
loathing. Slowly, however, the stanza becomes more serious:

> And now, methinks, I am where I began
>   Sev'n yeares ago: one vogue and vein,
>   One aire of thoughts usurps my brain.   [3–5]

"Sev'n yeares ago" transforms the stylized narrative of the first two
lines into genuine autobiography; the other lines seem to explain what
it means for joy to have gotten "out again." The speaker finds himself
taking joy in worldly things, or at least in the contemplation of them
("One aire of thoughts"). "Methinks" seems to allow the possibility

38. See Lewalski, "*Samson Agonistes* and the 'Tragedy' of the Apocalypse," pp. 1055–
57; *Protestant Poetics*, pp. 130–31.

that the speaker is wrong, that he is not merely "where [he] began," but the concluding couplet of the stanza confirms this view by seeing it as expressing a familiar pattern:

> I did toward Canaan draw; but now I am
> Brought back to the Red sea, the sea of shame.   [6–7]

These lines show quite clearly how, for Protestant autobiographers of the seventeenth century, "Israelite history became a kind of map on which believers could plot their exact spiritual position."[39] The speaker seems close here to seeing the Old Testament narrative as "a report of spirituall mysteries." Allegory seems to be displacing event.[40] The speaker quickly, however, works to defuse this implication and to insist on the historicity of both the Old Testament narrative and its connection to his own experience. He shifts from describing his own psychological and spiritual situation to elucidating the parallel to it which he has adduced. His mode becomes generalized, explanatory, and impersonal:

> For as Jews of old by Gods command
> Travell'd, and saw no town:
> So now each Christian hath his journeys spann'd.   [8–10]

The rest of the stanza explains why "Their storie pennes and sets us down" (line 11). A special property of God's works is to be "wide, and let in future times" (line 13). Tuve quotes the line that precedes this in the stanza—"A single deed is small renown"—to show that in "The Bunch of Grapes" Herbert has a purpose beyond "the mere conveyance of a particular individual's emotion at a given time, that thin subject with which modern readers have to be content."[41] But the whole point of this line in context is to provide a historical and religious *validation* of Herbert's concern with his own experience. "Each Christian" is now as much a focus of God's works as previously the whole community of the Jews was. The implications of the stanza are exactly the opposite of those demanded by Tuve's antimodernist polemic.

The final line of the stanza explains what is behind the historical mechanism the speaker has described. God's works are "wide" because neither He nor men have changed: "His ancient justice overflows our crimes" (line 14). We return here, albeit in generalized form, to the emotional note on which the first stanza ended. Fish perhaps

---

39. Owen C. Watkins, *The Puritan Experience* (London, 1972), p. 211.

40. I have borrowed this contrast from R. P. Hanson, *Allegory and Event: A Study of the Sources and Significance of Origen's Interpretation of Scripture* (London, 1959).

41. *A Reading of Herbert*, p. 117. Tuve's treatment of "The Bunch of Grapes" appears on pp. 113–17.

correctly perceives a liberating potential in this language of overflowing to which the speaker is not responding, but the problem does not, as Fish suggests, lie in a failure to understand typology. Typology was properly used in establishing continuities as well as contrasts between Old and New Testament experience.[42] The Old Testament records mercies as well as judgments. At the beginning of the third stanza, the speaker reminds himself of this and has to acknowledge:

> Then have we too our guardian fires and clouds;
>   Our Scripture-dew drops fast . . .   [15–16]

He cannot, however, maintain this focus (already rather strained) on the Christian equivalents of God's blessings on the Hebrews. He attempts to keep the parallels properly balanced, but he cannot keep from returning to the darker aspects of the Hebrews' experience in the desert:

> We have our sands and serpents, tents and shrowds;
>   Alas! our murmurings come not last.   [17–18]

Despite the mention of "our guardian fires and clouds" (unexplicated) and "our Scripture-dew," the focus of the poem remains penitential. The exclamation in line 18 is the first emotional outburst in the poem since the turn to exposition, but it remains rather lofty and generalized. The next line, however, returns to the personal note of the opening. The movement of the verse becomes animated and choppy; an enjambed series of questions replaces the calm, end-stopped assertions of the first half of the stanza. Herbert alludes, finally, to "the bunch of grapes," an element in the Numbers narrative which he has been suppressing:

> But where's the cluster? where's the taste
> Of mine inheritance?   [19–20a]

Having asked this, Herbert (or his "speaker") builds a personal plea on the basis of it:

> Lord, if I must borrow,
>   Let me as well take up their joy, as sorrow.   [20b–21]

There is, as Tuve says, "almost a pert defiance" in the questions, and the prayer is based on an extremely grudging acceptance of the way in which the Hebrews' story "pennes and sets us down"—"Lord, *if I must* borrow." Recalling the joy of "The H. Scriptures" (II) in being

---

42. Fish makes, in other words, the opposite mistake from that of Tuve discussed in n. 33 above. For his treatment of "The Bunch of Grapes," see "Catechizing the Reader: Herbert's Socratean Rhetoric," in *The Rhetoric of Renaissance Poetry*, ed. Thomas O. Sloan and Raymond B. Waddington (Berkeley and Los Angeles, 1974), pp. 180–85.

found out by Scripture further highlights the grudgingness here. Yet "The Bunch of Grapes" never explicitly presents its own questions as instances of "murmurings" and never fully transcends the grudgingness of "If I must borrow." The opening of the final stanza is meant to be a turn, yet instead of personal testimony it provides a generalized rhetorical question. The speaker views his situation from the outside, as a case—"But can he want the grape, who hath the wine?" (line 22). The phrasing is ostentatiously witty, and its impersonality lends a note of dutifulness to "I have their fruit and more" (line 23).

The problem is compounded by the rest of the stanza. Continuing the "bunch of grapes" imagery, the speaker blesses "God, who prosper'd Noah's vine," for the history recorded in the Old Testament (lines 24–25), and then develops the "and more" of Christianity:

> But much more him I must adore,
> Who of the Laws sowre juice sweet wine did make,
> Ev'n God himself being pressed for my sake.   [26–28]

Putting aside the awkwardness of the distinction between God and "him" (resolved in the final line), the problem with this conclusion is that it retains the element of compulsion, of recognizing a necessity—"But much more him *I must* adore." We have not come very far from "I must borrow." The final revelation that God *is* "the bunch of grapes," that the whole drama of biblical history exists "for the sake of" the speaker, is meant to dissolve all sense of grudging in contemplation of the sacrifice, yet even this line remains rather abstract. We are too conscious of it as a stroke of wit, as an announcement rather than an appropriation of a mystery. The intimate "knowledge" of sin and love manifested in "The Agonie" before its similar final line is absent here. Again the personal note seems almost official, almost (like "I have their fruit and more") a deduction from a general truth.

The literary problems with "The Bunch of Grapes" relate directly to theological problems. The poem is plagued by a sense of effort. First, the speaker must work up a theological exposition (this is why Herbert cannot make him, as Fish says, "deliberately naive") and then he must attempt to use this exposition not merely to analyze but also to transcend his immediate situation. The poem cannot present the speaker's efforts at personal application of typology as "murmurings" because it intends, finally, to make this application. We must heed Robert L. Montgomery's intuition that there is a problem in the relation between the expository and the dramatic elements in the poem.[43] Missing from "The Bunch of Grapes" is any recognition

---

43. Robert L. Montgomery, Jr., "The Province of Allegory in George Herbert's Verse," *TSLL*, 1 (1960), 464.

of the way in which, as Lewalski puts it, "the Protestant sense of the desperate condition of fallen man" shifted the focus of tropological exegesis "from a moralistic *quid agas*"—what *you* must do, the medieval focus—to "*opus Dei*, what God does."[44] There is no sense in "The Bunch of Grapes" of the work of God on the speaker's inner life. This speaker is finding out Scripture, not being found out by it. This is why the final joy of the poem seems forced and why the poem as a whole seems to lack interiority. The speaker sees himself falling into a predetermined pattern but does not feel *God* creating that pattern in his life ("some bad man / Hath let thee out again") and does not feel that pattern as entirely benevolent. Theologically as well as psychologically, there is an essential problem in the attempt to argue oneself into joy.

"The Bunch of Grapes" begins a sequence on joy. The poem that immediately follows, "Love unknown," directly responds to the problems in "The Bunch of Grapes." "Love unknown" fully expresses the interiority and internal power which Herbert saw as the special features of the new dispensation. It presents a world of literalized and realized typology in which the whole point of the fulfillment of the Old Testament types is to affect the heart of the individual Christian. It also serves to relate Herbert's emphasis on God's exclusive concern with the heart to another central topic of *The Temple*—the place of "affliction" in the Christian life.

"Love unknown" solves the problems of "The Bunch of Grapes" by truly presenting a speaker who is naive. He is even duller than the speaker of "Redemption"—to whom, as we shall see, he is directly related. With the possible exception of the irascible speaker of "Hope," the speaker of "Love unknown" can claim the distinction of being the least percipient in *The Temple*. He has received all the benefits of the Christian life without being able to perceive or experience them as such. The creation of this figure allows Herbert to expound these benefits quite fully while at the same time exploiting the ironies involved in not perceiving them. The speaker of "Love unknown" is the quintessential murmurer. Herbert recreates in him the very tone of the Old Testament murmurers—of those, for instance, who after seeing "the bunch of grapes," concluded: "Because the Lord hateth us, he hath brought us forth out of the land of Egypt, to deliver us into the land of the Amorites, to destroy us" (Deuteronomy 1:27).

The speaker of "Love unknown" is above all a man with a story. Herbert presents him as at once eager to tell his story to his dear friend and certain that this telling will not be productive:

44. Lewalski, *Donne's "Anniversaries,"* p. 161; Preus, *Shadow to Promise*, pp. 233–34.

> Deare Friend, sit down, the tale is long and sad:
> And in my faintings I presume your love
> Will more complie than help.   [1–3a]

We immediately know: (1) that this speaker (like the speaker of the
first stanza of "The Bunch of Grapes"?) is wrong about his tale being
a "sad" one; (2) that his manner of narration is blandly self-drama-
tizing and complacently pedantic ("Will more complie than help" is
a distinction without an obvious difference); and (3) that he is not a
man who has a very high regard for the efficacy of love, even though
he is speaking to his "deare friend."[45] He describes his situation in
rather mysterious terms which he seems to take as straightforward
("A Lord I had, / And have, of whom some grounds, which may
improve, / I hold for two lives"), and then gets to his tale:

> To him I brought a dish of fruit one day,
> And in the middle placed my heart. But he
>   (I sigh to say)
> Lookt on a servant, who did know his eye
> Better than you know me, or (which is one)
> Then I my self. The servant instantly
> Quitting the fruit, seiz'd on my heart alone,
> And threw it in a font, wherein did fall
> A stream of bloud, which issu'd from the side
> Of a great rock: I well remember all,
> And have good cause: there it was dipt and dy'd,
> And washt, and wrung: the very wringing yet
> Enforceth tears.   [6–18a]

Finally, at the memory which "yet / Enforceth tears" of what he
has undergone, this breathless narrator comes to a full stop. He is
not interested in the meaning of his story, only in the pain he has
endured. We seek the meaning, though the main details of it are
transparent. In offering "a dish of fruit" with his heart "in the mid-
dle," the speaker seems to have been making some sincere gesture
of devotion, either ethical or ceremonial. The Lord, however, is in-
terested in the "heart alone." Herbert is presenting the typological
fulfillment of Moses's rock in Christ's side as a means of working on
the speaker's heart—washing, wringing and "dyeing" it (there is
perhaps a pun here). He is presenting baptism as regeneration—or
rather, more accurately, he is presenting regeneration as baptism.[46]

45. The speaker's problem is not that he presumes *too much*. See Ira Clark, " 'Lord,
in Thee the Beauty Lies in the Discovery': 'Love Unknown' and Reading Herbert,"
ELH, 39 (1972), 577.
46. See stanza 1 of "The Glance" and pp. 141–42 above.

The emphasis, both Herbert's and the speaker's, is on the pain of the process and on the speaker's passivity in it ("Quitting the fruit, *seiz'd on* my heart alone").[47] The internality of the process is assumed, though not, given the nature of the fiction, here explicitly asserted.

The only genuinely puzzling details in the account are the identities of the servant and the friend. The speaker presents these figures in a proportional analogy which he immediately qualifies—"a servant, who did know his eye / Better than you know me, or (which is one) / Then I my self." The servant is to the Lord as the friend is to the speaker. The emphasis is on the intimacy of the relationships, but the qualifying phrase, with its own internal qualification, transforms the relationships from intimacy to identity—the servant and the Lord are one, just as the friend and the speaker are. When the speaker indicates that "you" and "me" are equivalent to "I" and "my self," Herbert is clarifying the strategy of this poem. The speaker of "The Bunch of Grapes" has been divided up into two figures: an autobiographer with his "sad" tale ("And now, me thinks, I am where I began") and an authoritative commentator ("Your heart was foul, I fear," the friend remarks in the second half of line 18).[48] Herbert has freed himself from the elements of strain and (Sartrian) bad faith which always seem to arise in presenting a figure, however intelligent and responsible, cheering himself up.[49]

The narrator of "Love unknown" represents not the sinful but what might be called the childish aspect of the regenerate Christian, the point of view which evaluates experience only in terms of immediate pleasure and pain. When the "friend" speculates on the foulness of the narrator's heart before it was "dipt and dy'd," the speaker does not demur. He accepts the truth of the observation and even adds to it, but he is not interested in it. What he is interested in is his story:

> Indeed 'tis true. I did and do commit
> Many a fault more than my lease will bear;

47. Clark's claim that the narrative shows that the speaker is "legally required to sacrifice his contrite heart to God" ("Lord, in Thee the Beauty Lies," p. 570) seems to mistake the theology of the poem. For Clark, the speaker must learn to repent "and thus *instigate the redemptive pattern* of justification by faith" (p. 578; emphasis mine). But the meaning of "justification by faith" is that only God can instigate it. Repentance, in the Reformation view, was a *result* rather than a cause of grace (see *Institutes*, III.iii.1–6). In *Protestant Poetics*, Lewalski notes that in "Love unknown" Herbert's speaker "does not cooperate actively with what happens to his heart but is surprised and shocked by the treatment it receives" (p. 206).

48. I do not mean to be suggesting anything about the order of composition of the two poems, only about the effect of their juxtaposition.

49. Here, as earlier in my analysis of "The Bunch of Grapes," I am drawing on T. S. Eliot's outrageous and haunting remarks on Othello's final speech ("Shakespeare and the Stoicism of Seneca," *Selected Essays of T. S. Eliot* [New York, 1932], p. 111).

> Yet still askt pardon, and was not deni'd.
> But you shall heare.   [19–22a]

Like "The Glance," the speaker's tale moves from regeneration, the beginning of the Christian life, to its ordinary course:

> After my heart was well,
> And clean and fair, as I one even-tide
> > (I sigh to tell)
> Walkt by my self abroad, I saw a large
> And spacious fornace flaming, and thereon
> A boyling caldron, round about whose verge
> Was in great letters set AFFLICTION.   [22b–28]

The speaker's response to this brings us back to the world of "Redemption"; "The greatnesse shew'd the owner" (line 29) is very close to "knowing his great birth" in "Redemption" (line 9). "Love unknown," however, explicitly focuses on the connection between this type of thinking and belief in the efficacy of works. "So," the speaker continues, with that same self-conscious reasonableness he shares with the speaker of "Redemption,"

> I went
> To fetch a sacrifice out of my fold,
> Thinking with that, which I did thus present,
> To warm his love, which I did fear grew cold.[50]   [29b–32]

We know this fear was groundless, but as far as the speaker himself is concerned, things go from bad to worse. What happened to the dish of fruit happens to the sacrifice:

> as my heart did tender it, the man,
> Who was to take it from me, slipt his hand,
> And threw my heart into the scalding pan.   [33–35]

The speaker again acknowledges the justice of the friend's observation that his heart "was hard" (line 37) and adds that not only was his heart "scalded" of "callous matter," but also treated with "holy bloud, / Which at a board, while many drank bare wine, / A friend did steal into [his] cup for good" (lines 41–43). This drug "taken inwardly," the speaker notes, was "most divine / To supple hardnesses." We will

---

50. It is interesting (as Clark, "Lord, in Thee the Beauty Lies," p. 561, notes) that Herbert has his speaker offer both Cain's and Abel's sacrifices. This would seem to imply the view that God is indifferent to the kind of works offered to Him. Luther insisted that it is absurd to think that there was anything *materially* wrong with Cain's offering (*Lectures on Genesis, LW*, I, 251). See also Calvin, *Commentary on Genesis*, trans. Rev. John King (Edinburgh, 1847), I, 196.

return later to why Herbert goes out of his way to present a strongly receptionist view of the Eucharist here ("many drank bare wine"), but the central point is again his conception of the religious life as entirely a matter of "the heart."

The final narrated episode concerns the speaker's desire to go to bed and "sleep out all these faults" (line 49). He finds that "with [his] pleasures ev'n [his] rest was gone," and that his Lord had "stuff'd the bed with thoughts, / I would say *thorns*" (Herbert is playing with us here, reminding us how little investment he has in maintaining a consistent allegorical or emblematic fiction).[51] The friend identifies the issue now as dullness of heart, which the narrator immediately equates with merely formal worship—"a slack and sleepie state of minde . . . so that when I pray'd, / Though my lips went, my heart did stay behinde." The narrator notes that even this was not "charged" against him ("all my scores were by another paid") and then merely stops, in midline, having no more "tale." His interlocutor provides an end for the narrative in both senses, a conclusion and a purpose (*"Mark the end"*).[52] He defines the speaker's situation as a case of "love unknown" (*"Truly, Friend, / For ought I heare, your Master shows to you / More favour then you wot of"*) and summarizes the points he has already made:

> The Font did onely, what was old, renew:
> The Caldron suppled, what was grown too hard:
> The Thorns did quicken, what was grown too dull:
> All did but strive to mend what you had marr'd.   [64–67]

One of the most important facts about "Love unknown" is that it does not stop here. The end of the poem, the aim and mark of the whole discourse, is not understanding or even acceptance, but joy.

---

51. Vendler (*Poetry of Herbert*, p. 60) comments on this phenomenon. She notes, using I. A. Richards's terminology, that Herbert regularly let his vehicles give way to their tenors. Herbert was always more interested in the analysis than in the image (see Strier, "Herbert and Tears," pp. 243–44). Rosemary Freeman (*English Emblem Books* [London, 1948], p. 153) notes that "pictures could add nothing essential to Herbert's verse" but remains rather uneasily committed to the view that Herbert had a positive relation to the emblem tradition. Lewalski's repeated association of Herbert's images with emblems (e.g., *Protestant Poetics*, pp. 200–206, 308–9) does not take the complexity of Herbert's practice into account. For the complexity of a strongly Protestant relation to (literal) visual images, see Ernest B. Gilman, "Word and Image in Quarles' *Emblemes*," *Critical Inquiry*, 6 (1980), 385–410.

52. That Herbert saw the two notions of the "end" of a narrative as connected is shown by "Affliction" (I), in which the speaker cannot conclude his story, or even tell it properly, because he cannot see its point or *telos*. For some speculations on these and related matters, see Barbara Leah Harman, "George Herbert's 'Affliction' (I): The Limits of Representation," *ELH*, 44 (1977), 267–85, although I cannot agree that "Affliction" (I) shows a "resistance to closure" (p. 279) rather than a longing for it.

Explanation yields to exhortation; the summary is merely prelude to
a mandate and a vision:

> *Wherefore be cheer'd, and praise him to the full*
> *Each day, each houre, each moment of the week,*
> *Who fain would have you be new, tender, quick.*   [68–70]

God does not work upon man to get him to do certain things but to
get him to be a certain way. He "would fain have you be new, tender,
quick"—in a state, that is, of complete and total responsiveness. "Love
unknown" demonstrates the relation between Herbert's rejection of
works and his focus on the inner life. The whole dynamic of the poem
lies in the shift in the meaning of "tender" from its use in line 33 to
its use in the final line—from tendering sacrifices to God to being
made tender by Him. In this context, the pointlessness of effort be-
comes apparent. We can also now understand the reasons for the
strong receptionism of the section on the Eucharist in the poem.
Herbert does not want to present taking communion as either a good
work in itself or a way of cooperating with God in suppling the heart.
"With a richer drug than scalding water / *I bath'd it* often" seems to
imply the latter view, but Herbert's insistence on the action of a friend
in stealing the "holy bloud" into the speaker's cup eliminates all
suggestion of cooperation. This experience, too, is a gift to the chosen
individual.[53]

   Both quickness and tenderness in "Love unknown" seem to consist
in sensitivity to pain. "Tender" in the final line seems to mean acutely
sensitive to pressure, acutely "irritable" in the biological rather than
the psychological sense. The first *OED* citation for "tender" in this
sense links it with quickness in a brilliant analogy from the *Ancrene
Riwle*—"Vor his flesche was al *cwic* ase is þe *tendre* eien." "Love un-
known," of course, is referring to an inner tenderness, a tenderness,
in a phrase we no longer have, of conscience. To be tender-consci-
enced is to be extremely sensitive to the possibility of sin.[54] "Lord,"
Herbert prays at the beginning of "Unkindnesse," "make me coy and
tender to offend." This kind of "tenderness" is not unrelated to ten-
derheartedness (an early Protestant coinage that we have kept), but
this connection is not one that Herbert explicitly develops in "Love

---

53. See Calvin, *Institutes*, IV.xvii.34. Herbert's view seems close to Calvin's here.

54. See *OED* "tender-conscienced." See also Donne, *Devotions upon Emergent Occasions*
(Ann Arbor, 1959), p. 66; Bunyan, *Grace Abounding*, par. 33 and 41 (where "tenderness
of heart" seems virtually synonymous with tenderness of conscience); and Fox, who
constantly speaks of tenderness of conscience, *Journal*, pp. 70, 82, 91, 135, 225. In the
chapter on Christian liberty in *The Country Parson* (chap. 31), Herbert shows how the
parson works to keep tormenting scruples from "pious minds, which are ever *tender*,
and delicate" (*CP*, p. 273).

unknown" although it is there in the final emphasis on gratitude and spontaneity.

Herbert keeps the focus on pain in "Love unknown" in order to suggest that the duality drawn in "The Bunch of Grapes" between "sweetness" and "sourness" is overly simple. The other poems in the sequence continue this development. "Mans medley," which follows "Love unknown," is primarily concerned with natural pleasure, but the penultimate stanza of "Mans medley" abruptly turns from man's pleasures to his pains, and the final stanza finds happiness in the uses of adversity:

> Happie is he, whose heart
> Hath found the art
> To turn his double pains to double praise.   [34–36]

"The Storm," which follows "Mans medley," presents an instance of this "art" at work; it descants upon the value of stormy times in life, both internal and external. The sequence culminates with "Paradise," which follows "The Storm." The speaker of "Paradise" is entirely "happy" in the sense which the end of "Mans medley" defines. The poem could be called "Love known." Its speaker recognizes himself as one of the elect (lines 1–3) and understands fully that the alternatives to the pain of God's attention are, in the present, the greater torment of His indifference ("Be to me rather sharp and TART, / Then let me want thy hand & ART") and, in the future, the horror of being cut off rather than merely "pruned" (lines 10–12). The "sharpness" which God shows to the regenerate, Herbert concludes, "shows the sweetest FREND." Such "cuttings" are beginnings which "touch their END"—that is, heaven. Luther remarked that the Kingdom of God is not being prepared for us, but rather, we are being prepared for it.[55]

The tiny lyric entitled "Bitter-sweet" shows how completely Herbert can resolve the dichotomy between "sweetness" and "sourness." It also shows very clearly the way in which man's "job" in relation to God is not to act but to feel. It begins where "Paradise" ends, but arrives, in the course of its first stanza, at an oddly competitive conclusion:

> Ah my deare angrie Lord,
> Since thou dost love, yet strike;
> Cast down, yet help afford;
> Sure I will do the like.   [1–4]

---

55. *The Bondage of the Will*, p. 182.

This conclusion would be truly disturbing if it were not so obviously self-mocking ("consciously glib," as Stein puts it)[56]—"Since thou . . . Sure I." In spite of the strong stress on "do," however, what Herbert actually vows to do in the second stanza is not to act but to respond. "I will complain, yet praise," the stanza begins; as it proceeds, the distinction between the two activities falls away until the adversative is replaced by a conjunction:

> I will bewail, approve:
> And all my sowre-sweet dayes
> I will lament, and love.   [6–8]

The voice which we hear in this poem is the essential "voice of George Herbert's 'The Church.' " Baxter described the Herbert of the poems as "a man who speaks to God like one that really believeth a God, and whose business in the world is most with God."[57] "The Church" is primarily the record of an intimate relationship. Baxter is right that Herbert generally speaks *to* rather than *of* God. Even more than the Psalter, "The Church" is the record and the dramatization of a single I-thou relationship. The intensity of Herbert's focus on the "evangelical nexus" has some consequences which have not been sufficiently noted. The first of these is in his relation to philosophical theology. Stein alone among Herbert's critics has recognized that "not all of the comprehensive demands to which [Herbert] responds can be quieted with ideas of harmonious correspondences" and that "some of the standard sources of answer" do not speak to Herbert "most effectively in the moments of crisis." Stein has also noted a contrast between the way in which God is known through His works in "Providence" but through His presence in a poem like "Mattens."[58]

This contrast can be put more sharply and located in a historical context. Throughout the history of Christian thinking, there has been a potential conflict between the biblical conception of God and, in Tertullian's phrase, "the God of the philosophers"—or, in other terms, between the God of devotion and the God of philosophical theology.[59]

56. *Herbert's Lyrics*, pp. 81, 86.

57. "The Epistle to the Reader," *Poetical Fragments* (1681), facs. with a note by V. de Sola Pinto (Westmead, 1971), sig. A⁷v. Baxter goes on to describe his volume as "Heart-Imployment with God and It Self," and to echo "Bitter-sweet": 'The Concordant Discord of a Broken-healed Heart. Sorrowing-rejoicing, Fearing-hoping, Dying-living."

58. *Herbert's Lyrics*, pp. 115, 121, 104. Stein's point of view contrasts with that of McCanles, who suggests that "Providence" is, "in a sense, the kind of poem the persona of *The Temple* aspired to write all the time" (*Dialectical Criticism*, p. 93).

59. Tertullian, *Adversus Marcionem*, ed. and trans. Ernest Evans (Oxford, 1972), II.27 (I, 162). For the distinction between the God of devotion and the God of philosophical theology, see Charles Hartshorne, *Man's Vision of God and the Logic of Theism* (New York, 1940), chaps. 1 and 3; Otto, *Idea of the Holy*, chaps. 10 and 12.

One of the historical *loci* of this conflict is the conception of the "anger" of God. The more one accepts this notion—prominent in the Old Testament and directly contrary to the position which Cicero describes as "common to all philosophers, that God is never angry"[60]—and the more literally one accepts it, the more antagonism or lack of sympathy will one feel for "the God of the philosophers." Lactantius argued that if God could not be angry, He could not be kind.[61] Luther laid extraordinary stress on both the objective reality and the psychological experience of God's wrath; he saw the experience of this wrath as necessary to the experience and understanding of God's love. He also saw philosophical theology as a form of the "theology of glory" which directly opposed the "theology of the cross."[62]

For Herbert, as "Bitter-sweet" shows, God's love and His wrath are intimate and related experiences. Herbert's orientation is fundamentally devotional. Stein rightly points to the relevance of "Mattens" in this regard. "Mattens" celebrates God's extraordinary attendance on man; "I cannot ope mine eyes," it begins, "But thou art ready there to catch / My morning-soul and sacrifice" (his happiness at seeing the sunlight?). "Then," Herbert adds with mock ruefulness, "we must needs for that day make a match" (lines 1–4). The next stanza turns to the central mystery:

> My God, what is a heart?
> Silver, or gold, or precious stone,
> Or starre, or rainbow, or a part
> Of all these things, or all of them in one?   [5–8]

After this playful listing of "answers" which merely serve to reveal further the speaker's puzzlement and wonder, he simply asks the question again, more sharply:

> My God, what is a heart,
> That thou shouldst it so eye, and wooe,
> Powring upon it all thy art,
> As if that thou hadst nothing els to do?   [9–12]

"As if that thou hadst nothing els to do" is a joke. God obviously does have other things "to do." The important point is that Herbert

60. *De Officiis*, trans. Walter Miller (Cambridge, Mass., 1913), p. 378: *commune est omnium philosophorum . . . numquam nec irasci deum nec nocere.*

61. *The Wrath of God (De Ira Dei)*, in *Lactantius: The Minor Works*, trans. Sister Mary Francis MacDonald (Washington, D.C., 1965), chaps. 4, 5, 17, 24.

62. On God's wrath, see *Commentary on Galatians*, ed. Watson, pp. 300 ff., 501 ff.; *Lectures on Jonah*, LW, XIX, 58, 75–76; "Commentary on Psalm 90," LW, XIII, 92–93; TR 4777 (on *Anfechtungen*; trans. in part in Bainton, *Here I Stand*, p. 283). See also Lennart Pinomaa, *Der zorn Gottes in der Theologie Luthers* (Helsinki, 1938), and Rupp, *The Righteousness of God*, chap. 5. On theology "of glory" and of "the cross," see chap. 1, n. 45 above.

is not very interested in these other things. A moment closely related to this suggests that the thought of these other things is not merely irrelevant but threatening to Herbert's deepest concerns. "Praise" (III) presents a tension between "the God of the philosophers," whose "skill and art" are shown in His orchestration of the cosmos (see stanza 10 of "Providence") and the God of devotion. The stanza which shifts from general to personal consideration of providence manifests this tension. The stanza begins by considering what God has "to do":

> Thousands of things do thee employ
> In ruling all
> This spacious globe: Angels must have their joy,
> Devils their rod, the sea his shore,
> The windes their stint: [19–23a]

"And yet," the stanza continues,

>   when I did call,
> Thou heardst my call, and more.   [23b–24]

This "and yet" is crucial. The vision of God "ruling all / This spacious globe" is perceived and presented here as a potential threat to His concern with the particular human individual. There is an edge of resentful weariness in "Angels *must have* their joy," and the list which follows seems to go on just a bit too long. The enumerated items are presented as—*salva reverentia*—God's menial chores. When George Herbert calls, God drops everything. As the stanza moves from "all" to "I," its tone becomes triumphant; the cosmological "all" dwindles in the face of the devotional "and more." As the focus narrows, the speaker exults. The next stanza begins, "I have not lost *one single tear.*" The poem suddenly becomes intimate; it is no accident that at this moment Christ rather than the Father emerges as the addressee. The Crucifixion, the next stanza tells us, guaranteed this intimacy. We move from glory to the cross.

From a cosmological point of view, the truth of the matter is that Herbert's deepest religious impulses require an empty rather than a "full" cosmos, a cosmos that is "empty" because it is so thoroughly filled with a single "I-thou" relationship. Herbert's empty cosmos is anything but lonely. The idea of a "full" cosmos, of the universe as (necessarily) containing all possible entities, is what A. O. Lovejoy has called "the principle of plenitude."[63] As Lovejoy has shown, this principle is the first of the major assumptions needed for the "great chain of being" conception as a total ontological scheme. In its world-

---

63. *The Great Chain of Being: A Study of the History of an Idea* (1936; rpt. New York, 1960), p. 52.

affirming aspect, the great chain conception sees diversity and variety as ultimate values. Aquinas asserts that "the perfection of the universe is attained essentially in proportion to the diversity of natures in it," and argues that if "all possible grades of goodness"—that is, being— were not filled up, "the supreme beauty would be lost to the creation."[64] Richard Hooker follows Aquinas closely in holding "the general end of God's external working" to be "the exercise of His most glorious and abundant virtue"—which abundance, Hooker continues, "doth shew itself in variety."[65]

The tension between this conception of plenitude and the immediate demands of personal piety can be seen in the relation between "Providence," which does celebrate the beautiful variety of all things, and some stanzas of "Longing," which show clearly why the harmonies of "Providence" do not speak effectively in moments of crisis. "Providence" is largely impersonal in mode; Herbert speaks not for himself but "all the creatures both in sea and land" (lines 5–28). He may not be adequate to the task of praise—"But who hath praise enough? nay, who hath any?" (line 141)—but in this case, as Stein says, "the failure will not be felt as a personal one."[66] Even in "Providence," however, Herbert does not seem wholly at ease with the aesthetics of "fullness." "Providence" is oriented remarkably strongly toward use rather than beauty. "A rose," Herbert hastens to add, "besides his beautie, is a cure" (line 78). This orientation recalls Miller's comments on the Puritan conception of beauty as "order and efficiency," beauty "as applied to the handicrafts and not to the fine arts."[67] At times the poem is strangely uninterested in the fullness of the creation as compared with its order and efficiency ("And as thy house is full, so I adore / Thy curious art in marshalling thy goods" [lines 93–94]). Nevertheless, the summary stanza on the creation as a whole enunciates the central features of the great chain conception— plenitude, continuity, and unilinear gradation:

> Thy creatures leap not, but expresse a feast,
> Where all the guests sit close, and nothing wants.
> Frogs marry fish and flesh; bats, bird and beast;
> Sponges, non-sense and sense; mines, th'earth & plants. [133–36]

This vision of the creatures constituting "a feast, / Where all the guests sit close, and nothing wants" is a positive poetic presentation

---

64. Quoted in Lovejoy, *Great Chain of Being*, p. 77.
65. *Laws of Ecclesiastical Polity*, I.ii.4 (I, 152).
66. *Herbert's Lyrics*, p. 102
67. *New England Mind*, p. 215.

of a closed and full universe.[68] "Longing" makes it clear how far this vision is from the devotional center of Herbert's concerns. An anguished and personal plea for God to respond to the speaker's abject need, "Longing" bursts, about halfway through, into two stanzas of rhetorical questions, the first personal, the second on God's relation to the cosmos as a whole and men in general:

> Hast thou left all things to their course,
>   And laid the reins
>   Upon the horse?
> Is all lockt? hath a sinners plea
>   No key?   [44–48]

The appalling vision of a God who has left the world to itself, who has ceased to govern the universe actively and involve Himself in the workings of second causes, is followed by the even more appalling vision of a God who is indifferent to human suffering and desire. A cosmological yields to a devotional horror. The movement of the stanza is back toward the personal—from "all things" to an unspecified "all" to "a sinner." The succeeding stanza answers the questions of this one, but what is striking about the stanza of answers—and deeply revelatory of Herbert's attitude toward the great chain conception— is that the answers to the second two questions are presented as antithetical to the answer to the first. The cosmological problem and the devotional one demand and receive different solutions. "Indeed," the affirmative stanza begins:

> the world's thy book,
> Where all things have their leafe assign'd:
>   Yet a meek look
>   Hath interlin'd.
> Thy board is full, yet humble guests
>   Finde nests.   [49–54]

The syntax of this stanza is the key to its meaning. Where we expected a strongly positive assertion, we are given a concessive ("Indeed"), and, as the stanza proceeds, each time a positive assertion is made, its implications are immediately denied: "all things have . . .

68. Lovejoy quotes the stanza (*Great Chain of Being*, p. 60). There is an interesting pun in the second line—"Where all the guests sit close, and *nothing wants*." On the one hand, the reference is ontological—"there is no creature missing"; on the other, it is use-oriented—"no creature lacks what it needs." The former is certainly primary, but in support of the latter as a competing possibility, see lines 49–53, in which God's "cupboard fills the world" and ensures that "Nothing ingendred doth prevent [its] meat." If the pun is admitted, even in this stanza Herbert has difficulty keeping a purely ontological focus. The succeeding stanza's concern with God's freedom is also interesting. As a whole, "Providence" is hardly perfect as an example of "the analogical imagination" conceived in Thomist terms (McCanles, *Dialectical Criticism*, p. 92 n.).

Yet a meek look / Hath . . .''; "Thy board is full, yet. . . ." The vision
of the world as God's book, "Where *all things* have their leafe as-
sign'd," directly answers "Hast thou left *all things* to their course?"
"All things" have an ordained place in the cosmos. The world as book
is an image clearly cognate with that of the great chain (as in Dante's
climactic use of it),[69] and the notion of the fullness of God's cosmos—
"a feast, / Where all the guests sit close, and nothing wants"—recurs
in this context: "Thy board is full." The trouble with these images,
from the point of view of the second two questions of the previous
stanza, is that they still leave the world "lockt." The idea that the
place of everything has been assigned by an all-powerful God does
not relate to the speaker's emotional and devotional needs any more
than the vision of a godless nature does—"Indeed," they are related.
They both stress the finality of the situations they describe, that is,
of nature: "all things" either blindly take "their course" or are sys-
tematically "assign'd." Meanwhile the speaker stands outside of both
cosmic visions, groaning for grace.[70]

The models of the cosmos as chain or book are not personal, dy-
namic, or responsive enough, and it is personal response, above all,
that the speaker craves—"My love, my sweetnesse, heare!" (line 79).
His interest, ultimately, is not in "all things" and the grand patterns
and regularities of the cosmos, but in the possibility of radical and
decisive change, of interlining the book and finding a place in spite
of the fullness of God's "board." The contrast between the active
verbs which relate to the speaker's devotional needs and the "have"
and "is" of the cosmological lines is significant. It reflects the differ-
ence between the static cosmos of philosophical theology and the
dynamic world of practical devotion. A full cosmos leaves no room
for movement or response; ultimately it is incompatible with the con-
ception of a God who enters into intimate personal relationships with
men, a God who Himself is as He wants His chosen to be—"new,
tender, quick."[71]

69. *Paradiso*, XXXIII, 85–90. For the history of this image, see E. R. Curtius, *European Literature and the Latin Middle Ages*, trans. Willard Trask (1953; rpt. New York, 1963), chap. 16.

70. I have borrowed this last phrase from Luther, *Lectures on Romans*, pp. 87, 208 (WA, LVI, 235, 346). See also Calvin, *Institutes*, II.i.3.

71. A later stanza in "Longing" shows how little consolation Herbert's speaker de-
rives from the fact that God "do[th] reigne, / And rule on high" (lines 56–57). The speaker finds it ironic that he should be called *this* God's child (lines 59–60). The God he is truly interested in "left [His] throne" (line 61). The poem that follows and directly answers "Longing," "The Bag," tells the "strange storie" of the descent of God. Ven-
dler's argument for God's promises (line 68) as the "elusive intermediary" in the poem (*Poetry of Herbert*, p. 264) is interesting but misses the incarnational focus of the final appeal to Christ as person ("My love, my sweetnesse, heare!").

The stanzas in "Longing" and "Praise" (III) that we have examined should lead us to think again about those moments in Herbert's devotional lyrics which seem to adopt or rely on traditional cosmological solutions. The final stanza of "Mattens" seems to envision the success of one of the great traditional answers, the ascent to God *per scala creaturarum:* "Then by a sunne-beam I will climbe to thee." What is noteworthy about Herbert's use of this conception is that he presents the process as realizable only through grace, not through disciplined mental effort. Herbert assimilates the intellectualism and optimism of "natural theology" to his own framework of grace and feeling. The final vision is part of a prayer:

> Teach me thy love to know:
> That this new light, which now I see,
> May both the work and workman show:
> Then by a sunne-beam I will climbe to thee.   [17–20]

Only through grace can Herbert "see" God in the sunlight to which he awakes. The question which dominates the poem, "My God, what is a heart," takes on added poignance when Herbert explains, in the penultimate stanza, that man's "natural" tendency is, as he says in "The Pulley," to "rest in Nature, not the God of Nature"; man

> did not heav'n and earth create,
> Yet studies them, not him by whom they be.   [14–15]

The grudgingness which seemed merely a joke in stanza 1—"Then we *must needs* for that day make a match"—turns out to have been fully serious. If God had not "prevented" Herbert by being "up" before him (as in "Easter"), Herbert would not have made this match. Once again we see God "not suff'ring those / Who would, to be [His] foes" ("Miserie," lines 29–30). What Herbert means by knowing God's love in the final prayer is not an abstract but an affective knowledge. The ascent envisioned in the final line is a matter not of effort but of spontaneity.

The one poem in *The Temple* which explicitly mentions the great chain is "Employment" (I). The poem as a whole is a prayer that God "extend" the speaker "to some good," put him, that is, to some use. The speaker feels, as Halewood says, like a "useless anomaly in a creation dedicated to use and function."[72] The final stanza summarizes this feeling before making its petition:

> I am no link of thy great chain,
> But all my companie is a weed.

---

72. *The Poetry of Grace*, p. 108. Halewood treats "Employment" (I) on pp. 108–9.

> Lord place me in thy consort; give one strain
> To my poore reed. [21 24]

Halewood notes that "the great chain conception is explicitly rejected for man" here, yet Halewood's own talk of a creation dedicated to use suggests a more subtle, and perhaps, revealing way in which the poem undermines the traditional great chain conception. The ontological framework which is the original and primary domain of the great chain idea has been entirely replaced by a functionalist framework.[73] Again what the poet is ultimately interested in is not the contemplation of a static hierarchy but the possibility of being the object of a decisive action—"Lord place me in thy consort." Again Herbert is concerned not with the grand scheme of things but in the possibility of individual "interlining" through grace.

73. M. M. Mahood's treatment of lines 21–24 of "Employment" (I) in *Poetry and Humanism* (1950; rpt. New York, 1970), p. 33, obscures this distinction. My use of this distinction draws on Michael Walzer, *The Revolution of the Saints: A Study in the Origins of Radical Politics* (1965; rpt. New York, 1969), chap. 5, esp. pp. 150–71.

7

The Heart's Privileges:
Emotion

Herbert's rejection or reformulation of the great chain of being is a matter of emphasis rather than of position. It might almost be classed as an unintended consequence of his intense devotional focus.[1] "I am no link in thy great chain" is, after all, a hyperbole not a straightforward assertion. Herbert's rejection of other traditional conceptions—in particular, of certain standard ways of admonishing man and conceiving of God—is explicit and explicitly warranted by his theological position. What leads Herbert to these radical consequences (and brings him close to some of the actual radicals in the English revolution) is his assertion of the special status of emotion in the relationship between man and God. His emphasis on personal experience is also an emphasis on emotional experience. We have already seen the privileged place which both Luther and Calvin gave to emotion in their treatment of faith.[2] Herbert certainly shared this view. Baxter summed up his comments on Herbert's poetry by saying, "*Heart-work* and *Heaven-work* make up his Book." This is an accurate assessment of "The Church" if we understand that for Herbert, if not so clearly for Baxter, "heaven-work" *was* primarily "heart-work."[3]

1. On the concept of "unintended consequences," see Karl Popper, *Objective Knowledge* (Oxford, 1972), pp. 159–60. For a somewhat problematic attempt at a literary application of the concept, see Ralph W. Rader, "Fact, Theory, and Literary Explanation," *Critical Inquiry*, 1 (1974), 245–72.

2. See pp. 144–45 above. For Calvin there is a useful discussion in Terrence Erdt, "The Calvinist Psychology of the Heart and the 'Sense' of Jonathan Edwards," *Early American Literature*, 13 (1978), 165–80.

3. See Baxter's *Poetical Fragments*, sig. A⁷v. Baxter is a complex figure in this context. On the one hand he is a partisan of "feeling," on the other he is a consciously antien-

Together with his stress on interiority, Herbert's stress on experience, especially emotional experience, is his strongest link with the radicals. Only one of Herbert's critics has been willing to acknowledge that "Herbert is in many ways an enthusiastic poet."[4] Summers is constantly on the verge of this acknowledgment, but equally constantly, as in his discussion of "The Church-floore," draws back from it. Lewalski's magisterial survey of Protestant rhetorical theory in the seventeenth century stops short after William Perkins with the remark that "the radical sectarian position represented, for example, by William Dell need scarcely concern us here," that is, in a literary context.[5] Over forty years ago, Perry Miller noted that "something less than justice" has been done to men like William Dell "possibly because historians, who belong for the most part to the scholarly caste, entertain the same prejudices in favor of that caste as did the Puritan clergy."[6] If we are going to see Herbert's poetry clearly, we must abandon our prejudice in favor of the scholarly caste and our assumption that Herbert shared this prejudice. The issue comes to a head with Herbert's poems on poetry. We must be willing to acknowledge the possibility that as gifted and intelligent a poet as Herbert could have believed that art and learning, including his own, were not of ultimate importance. A fuller appreciation of the value Herbert placed on emotional experience will allow us to take his "apparent" rejections of art at face value. We must acknowledge his connection to men like William Dell.

Although Stein is unwilling to take Herbert's statements about art at face value, he remains the only critic to speak directly and at length of Herbert's extraordinary respect for "the dignity and force of human desire."[7] Stein has also noted that in Herbert's poetry "the language of complaint enjoys within its body of laws the advantages of special privilege." In regard to "Longing," Vendler has remarked that "the childish repetition of 'heare, heare,' the repeated poignant self-descriptions, the persistence in demand in spite of all seemliness, are

thusiastic and rationalist figure. *The Saints Everlasting Rest* shows both currents very clearly. In his autobiography, Baxter refused to give a "particular account of heart-occurrences, and God's operations on me" despite the fact that he knew his audience wanted such an account (*Reliquiae Baxterianae: or, Mr. Richard Baxter's Narrative of the Most Memorable Passages of His Life and Times* (1696), I, 124. In *British Autobiography in the Seventeenth Century* (New York, 1969), Paul Delany characterizes the *Reliquiae* as "more akin to Mill's autobiography than Augustine's" (p. 72).

4. Halewood, *The Poetry of Grace*, p. 102.

5. *Protestant Poetics*, p. 266.

6. *New England Mind*, p. 77.

7. For Stein's nervousness about Herbert's devaluations of art (commented on by Fish, *Self-Consuming Artifacts*, p. 220), see chap. 1 of *Herbert's Lyrics;* for "the dignity and force of human desire" in Herbert, see ibid., pp. viii, 134, 210.

the qualities that make Herbert, in this vein, one of our most accurate poets of expostulation, pain, outcry, wounded hopes, and stratagems of emotion."[8] These insights can be extended and given a historical basis. They can also be related to Herbert's attitude toward the value of art.

"The advantages of special privilege" and "in spite of all seemliness" are the crucial points. One of the major corollaries of Herbert's focus on what he called "Gods Kingdome within us, and the working thereof" ("Notes on Valdes," p. 305) is the insistence that he does not have to suppress or deny anything he is feeling in order to address God. When Baxter praised Herbert for speaking to God "like one that really believeth a God," he was praising Herbert's passion and sincerity—"he speaketh things by words, feelingly and seriously, like a man that is past jest."[9] The context of Baxter's comments on Herbert is a defense of himself for publishing in a state of passion (grief for his wife's death) poems that "were mostly written in various passions," and a defense of the place of the passions in life and in religion. Baxter treasured *The Temple* "next the Scripture-poems" for precisely the quality that Luther emphasized in "the Scripture-poems" (that is, the psalms)—their expression of the whole range of human feelings with unparalleled vividness.[10]

One of the main assertions of Reformation theology was that the regenerate, who have "received the Spirit of adoption" (Romans 8), are entitled and encouraged to address God boldly and familiarly. As Sibbes, following Calvin closely, explained, "there is great deal of familiarity in the spirit of adoption"; there is "an inward kind of familiar boldness in the soul, whereby a Christian goes to God."[11]

---

8. *The Poetry of Herbert*, p. 265. Norman Maclean has remarked that "Herbert sure felt free to belly-ache a lot" (private communication to the author). In regard to Herbert's cultural position as a normative Anglican, it is worth pointing out the contrast with Keble's insistence on "a sober standard of feeling" in the "Advertisement" prefixed to *The Christian Year: Thoughts in Verse for the Sundays and Holydays* (Oxford, 1827), p. v. For a perceptive comparison of Herbert and Keble, see Elbert N. S. Thompson, "*The Temple* and *The Christian Year*," *PMLA*, 54 (1939), 1018–25.

9. *Poetical Fragments*, sig. A⁷v. In this context of speaking "things by words," Baxter likens Herbert to Seneca. Baxter is aligning himself with the emphasis of the anti-Ciceronian movement in the sixteenth and seventeenth century on *res* rather than *verba*. See Morris W. Croll, " 'Attic' Prose in the Seventeenth Century," "Muret and the History of 'Attic Prose,' " and "Attic Prose: Lipsius, Montaigne, and Bacon," in *Style, Rhetoric, and Rhythm: Essays by Morris W. Croll*, ed. J. Max Patrick, Robert O. Evans, John M. Wallace, and R. J. Schoeck (Princeton, 1966); George Williamson, *The Senecan Amble: A Study in Prose Form from Bacon to Collier* (1951; rpt. Chicago, 1966), esp. chap. 9; A. C. Howell, "*Res et Verba*: Words and Things," *ELH*, 13 (1946), 131–42.

10. "Preface to Psalms," Dillenberger, pp. 39–41.

11. "Christ's Sufferings for Man's Sins," *Works*, I, 364; *A Commentary on the First Chapter of the Second Epistle to the Corinthians*, *Works*, III, 457.

What God demands from the regenerate is not seemliness but sincerity. This is particularly relevant to expressions of pain and longing. Luther and Calvin both strongly attacked Stoic deprecation of the emotions, especially of complaint. Calvin asserted that "patiently to bear the cross is not to be deprived of all feeling of pain"; it is not to be "as the Stoics of old foolishly described 'the great-souled man,' one who, having cast off all human qualities, was affected equally by adversity and prosperity, by sad times and happy times—nay, who like a stone was not affected at all." Luther held that the ideal of being unmoved by temptations, passions, and grief had corrupted the theology of the Roman church, so that "the saints of the Papists are like the Stoics, who imagined such wise men as in the world were never yet found."[12]

Just as the reformers insisted that the regenerate are not and cannot be free from sin, they insisted that the regenerate are not and cannot be free from ordinary human emotions. A large part of the liberty the reformers saw themselves as providing was a freedom from impossible demands. They saw the "iron philosophy" of Stoicism condemned in the Scriptures by both word and example—Job, the psalmist, Jeremiah, Saint Paul. And, "if all weeping is condemned, what shall we judge concerning the Lord himself. . . . If all fear is branded as unbelief, how shall we account for the dread with which, we read, He was heavily stricken? If all sadness displeases us, how will it please us that He confesses His soul sorrowful even to death?" (*Institutes*, III.viii.9). As John Downame summarizes the matter, "It hath been the continuall practice of all the saints to sorrow and mourne in their afflictions."[13] The purpose of asserting this was always the same—"to recall godly minds from despair" at the fact that, as Calvin put it, "they cannot cast off their natural feelings of sorrow" (*Institutes*, III.viii.10).

The reformers were willing to go very far in defense of the "natural feelings" against what they saw as a dangerous and despair-inducing perfectionism. They were willing to acknowledge that the regenerate can even appear to fall into lack of faith. In commenting on the verse from Psalm 22 which Jesus quotes on the cross in Mark and Matthew—"My God, my God, why has thou forsaken me?" (Psalm 22:1)—Calvin explains that "this verse contains two remarkable sentences, which, although apparently contrary to each other, are yet ever entering into the minds of the godly together" (the psychological experience of "the godly" in all ages is constant). "When the Psalmist speaks of being forsaken and cast off by God," Calvin concedes, this "seems

---

12. Calvin, *Institutes*, III.viii.9; Luther, *Commentary on Galatians*, ed. Watson, p. 512.
13. *The Christian Warfare*, p. 796b.

to be the complaint of a man in despair," and yet, he continues, "in calling God twice his own God, and depositing his groanings in His bosom, [the psalmist] makes a very distinct confession of his faith." As he asks about a similar moment in another psalm, if the psalmist had truly lost faith in God, "how could he direct his prayers and groanings to Him?"[14]

Whether or not Herbert ever actually said that he intended his volume "for the advantage of any dejected poor soul," there is no doubt that he would have seen it as ideally serving this "comfortable" function.[15] Herbert's acceptance of the perspective we have been discussing is writ large in "The Church." Titles like "Complaining," "Longing," and "Sighs and Grones" speak for themselves. "Longing" makes especially clear Herbert's grasp of the paradox Calvin expounded. Herbert finds the psalmist's experiences of being "poured out like water" (22:14), "Smitten, and withered like grass" (102:4) recapitulated in himself:

> My throat, my soul is hoarse;
> My heart is wither'd like a ground
>   Which thou dost curse.   [7–9]

In the final words of the stanza, Herbert draws attention to the fact that He is nonetheless "depositing his groanings" in God's bosom:

> Lord, I fall,
>   Yet call.[16]   [11b–12]

Herbert never relinquished his right to call and to complain in times of affliction. Even in poems of loving resignation like "Bitter-sweet," Herbert recognizes that lamenting will always be as much part of his life as loving. This commitment to calling upon God and "groaning" to Him was one of the duties as well as one of the prerogatives of

14. *Commentary on the Psalms*, I, 357; I, 182 (on Psalm 13). See also *Institutes*, III.ii. 21.

15. For Walton's account of Herbert's deathbed comments, see *Life of Herbert*, p. 314. Bunyan stated on his title page that *Grace Abounding* was "for the support of the weak and tempted people of God." Isaac Pennington stated that he wrote *Babylon the Great Described* (1659) because "what I have seen and known I testifie for the relief of others" (sig. A⁴v). Baxter's title page proclaims his *Poetical Fragments* "for the Use of the Afflicted." The relevant general principle is stated by Thomas Goodwin: "That God pardon'd such a Man in such a Condition, is often brought home unto another Man in the same Condition" (*Memoir of Thomas Goodwin, Works* [Edinburgh, 1861], II, lxii). Delany notes how closely the statement of intention attributed to Herbert by Walton parallels those of later, *non-Anglican* spiritual autobiographers (*British Autobiography*, p. 54).

16. The maternal suggestions of "God's bosom" in Calvin become explicit in Herbert. The next stanza begins: "From thee all pitie flows. / Mothers are kinde, because thou art" (lines 13–14).

the Christian. John Downame argued that a "chiefe end why the Lord afflicteth us, and why he also deferreth to deliver us at the first [is] because he would have us more urgent and instant in our prayers."[17]

Herbert not only accepted this perspective but also recognized its peculiarity, its flouting of decorum. To be "urgent and instant" is hardly to be polite. A number of important poems explore this recognition. Along with "The Altar" and "The Church-floore," "Sion" is one of the major "architectural" poems in *The Temple*, one of the major expositions of the living temple topos. What makes "Sion" particularly interesting is that it presents the inner-outer dialectic, so characteristic of Herbert's treatment of institutional and typological materials, in terms of another dialectic, that between the animate and the inanimate, and it locates the essence of "animation"—of "quickness"—in man's emotional life. It unites "The Church-floore" with "Love unknown." Presenting the heart not merely as the locus of inwardness but also as the locus of the emotions, "Sion" allows Herbert to develop the dynamism that was created in the narrative section of "The Church-floore" but thwarted by the return of the epiphanic couplet to a revised version of the opening descriptions. Examining "Sion," we can distinguish Herbert's from Milton's sense of what it means for God to choose the heart as His special dwelling, for in Herbert we shall see that God does not choose the heart "before all Temples" because it is "upright" or "pure." Humanistic and Reformation interiorization diverge here.[18]

Some of the richest materials for typological exegesis were the elaborate descriptions of Solomon's temple in first Kings (6) and second Chronicles (3–4), and the equally elaborate visionary description in Ezekiel (40–46). Herbert sees the temple as characteristic of the way in which God was served "of old." He begins "Sion" with a tone of naive wonderment; he is impressed by the biblical accounts:

> Lord, with what glorie wast thou serv'd of old,
> When Solomons temple stood and flourished!   [1–2]

He is struck by the richness of the materials used ("most things were of purest gold"), and by the quality and nature of the art displayed. This art was not only ornate but symbolic:

> The wood was all embellished
> With flowers and carvings, mysticall and rare.   [4–5]

The last line of the first stanza presents itself as summary:

17. *Christian Warfare*, p. 821b.
18. For "th' upright heart and pure" as the Spirit's preferred dwelling, see *Paradise Lost*, I, 17–18. For the historical distinction, see Bainton, *Here I Stand*, p. 199; *Erasmus of Christendom*, chap. 8.

All show'd the builders, crav'd the seeers care.   [6]

The tone remains wondering and eulogistic, but the meaning is om-
inous. The "care" which completes both halves of the line and both
halves of the artistic transaction described is directed at the art of the
temple, not at the object of the art. We are close here to the end of
the first stanza of "Jordan" (II) in which the description of another
past effort at elaborate art ("Curling with metaphors a plain inten-
tion") culminated in another subversive summary, "Decking the sense,
as if it were to sell" (also line 6).

Herbert surely intended "Sion" to recall "Jordan" (II), which occurs
only three poems before. Both poems present God as fundamentally
uninterested in the "expense" which they describe. The second stanza
of "Sion" begins:

> Yet all this glorie, all this pomp and state
> Did not affect thee much, was not thy aim.   [7–8]

God, in Herbert's account, saw "all this glorie" and effort to have
been a cause for human discord. Herbert leaves this vague—"Some-
thing there was, that sow'd debate"—but it seems impossible to miss
the suggestion of a psychologically inevitable connection between the
motives involved in the creation of elaborate art, however ostensibly
devotional, and the impulses which lead to human discord. Calvin's
remarks on the connections between pride and "love of strife" are
perhaps relevant here.[19] God therefore, Herbert explains, quit His
"ancient claim" (that David's son "shall build an house for my name"—
II Samuel 7) and opted, in the present, for a different kind of building:

> now thy Architecture meets with sinne;
> For all thy frame and fabrick is within.[20]   [11–12]

The next stanza of "Sion" presents a remarkable scene. Instead of
enumerating the details of the inner frame and fabric, as in "The
Church-floore," Herbert drops the architectural analogy and develops
the implications of *"meets with* sinne." God is suddenly not an object
of worship but an intimate contender. The whole pace of the poem
changes. Instead of the rather stately mock meditative tone of stanza
1, and the rather dry, explanatory tone of lines 7–10, the tone is now

19. *Institutes*, III.vii.4. Herbert dramatized this connection in "Humilitie"; see Strier,
"Ironic Humanism," pp. 45–50.

20. Herbert's Latin poem on altars (*Lucus*, XXIX) is very close in both movement and
theme to stanza 2 of "Sion." It states that constructed altars, as opposed to the altars
that men *are*, "make for harm" (*nocent*). See Hutchinson, p. 417, and *The Latin Poetry
of George Herbert: A Bilingual Edition*, trans. Mark McCloskey and Paul R. Murphy
(Athens, Ohio, 1965), p. 107.

excited and dramatic (the final couplet mediates between the modes). "There thou art struggling with a peevish heart," says Herbert amazedly (line 13). This line can be read as either proceeding straight on from "There" to "struggling," so that this struggle is the focus of the line, or as having a caesura after "art" (perhaps reinforced by the internal rhyme), so that God's presence "there" as well as his willingness to struggle "with a peevish heart" is part of the amazement.

"Peevish" is a striking word. It presents sin, as Herbert so often does, not as grand but as petty. God condescends even to this. There is more, however. The "peevish heart . . . sometimes crosseth thee, thou sometimes it" (line 14). The two meanings of crossing nicely represent the difference between God and man, but Herbert keeps his emphasis on the equality of power between the two contestants— "The fight is hard on either part. / Great God doth fight, he doth submit" (lines 15–16). It is worth pausing for a moment over why Herbert wants this emphasis and, more particularly, why he does not here present God being "crossed" by the heart as a subject for lamentation. In "Decay," which occurs in the same section of "The Church," he presents God's decision to "immure and close" Himself in the heart as just such a mournful subject. The answer here is partly in the celebration of condescension—"Great God . . . doth submit"— and partly in the fact that what "Decay" laments the loss of—intimate personal contact with God ("thou didst lodge with Lot, / Struggle with Jacob, sit with Gideon")—"Sion" affirms. Under the New Dispensation, God internally struggles with the heart as truly as He literally struggled with Jacob.[21] In the couplet, Herbert explains why God enters this struggle. It has to do with His values. The "pomp and state" of the temple did not "affect" God (much) and "was not [His] aim"; we learn here what does affect God—and, presumably, something about His aim:

> All Solomons sea of brasse and world of stone
> Is not so deare to thee as one good grone.　　　[17–18]

Herbert tells us that God has this system of values, and the fact that He has them seems to account for His behavior, but Herbert has not yet provided a rationale for God's preferences. He has not told us why God places such value on "one good grone" that He is willing to go to the extraordinary lengths of "struggling with a peevish heart" to produce one. "Solomons sea of brasse and world of stone" can easily be seen as symbolic of irrelevant pomposity like the "half-acre

---

21. In "George Herbert and the Tradition of Jacob," *Cithara*, 18 (1978), 21, Garret Keizer connects the struggling in "Sion" with Jacob's wrestling and the relevant lines in "Decay." He does not deal with the contrasting tones of "Sion" and "Decay."

tombes" in Donne's "The Canonization," but Herbert has not yet made clear on what basis such things can be compared with a groan. Herbert has no problem providing the rationale. A moment's reflection seems to bring it to him; the final stanza begins:

> And truly brasse and stones are heavie things,
> Tombes for the dead, not temples fit for thee.   [19–20]

The contrast is no longer between the outer and the inner (or, as in Donne, between the large and gross and the small and fine) but between the animate and the inanimate. Herbert is relying on the Old Testament and Pauline stress on the *life* of God and man—as opposed, especially, to the deadness of idols—and he is locating this life primarily in the emotions.[22]

We return again to "quickness." What gives groans their privileged status is that they "are quick" (line 21); what does affect God is not "pomp and state" but sincerity, which has always been His aim. Groans are especially "quick" because they are spontaneous and genuine expressions of response. God can submit to being "crossed" by a peevish heart because He knows that in the regenerate this will stir up feelings of contrition and lead to "sighs and grones." The middle section of this stanza adopts God's perspective on groans; they are "quick"

> and full of wings
> And all their motions upward be;
> And ever as they mount, like larks they sing.   [21b–23]

Only in God's eyes (and ears) does a human groan, a barely articulate product of pain, "Like to the lark at break of day arising / From sullen earth" sing hymns at heaven's gate (see Shakespeare's Sonnet 29). The sincerity of groans makes them music in God's ears. However, in commenting on "Justice" (II) and "The Glance," we have already noted that Herbert prefers to end his poems on quiet rather than on ecstatic notes. The final line of "Sion" returns to sobriety; it integrates the ordinary perspective into the divine one:

> The note is sad, yet musick for a King.   [24]

The final phrase is important. It makes us realize that throughout the poem Herbert has been redefining both the nature of service to

---

22. For an extremely interesting treatment of this biblical theme, see Coolidge, *Pauline Renaissance*, chap. 2; see also Fish, *Living Temple*, chap. 2. Herbert's Latin poem on altars (*Lucus*, XXIX) is built on the contrast between living and dead earth. "Living earth" is man; dead earth, an altar (*Cespes vivus, Homo; mortuus, Ara fuit*). Through Christ, the two (man and altar) which, separated, make for harm, were brought together (*in unum / Conveniunt*), and man became God's living altar (*Homo viva fit Ara Dei*).

God—"with . . . glorie wast thou serv'd of old"—and the meaning of God's kingly state. In his conception of God, Milton is far more "royalist" then Herbert.[23] Like "Redemption" and "Prayer" (II), "Sion" emphasizes the difference between God's values and behavior and those of earthly lords. Like the petitioner in "Redemption" and the novice poet in "Jordan" (II), Solomon is presented as having assumed a continuity between earthly and heavenly conceptions of glory— "Nothing could seem too rich" for the temple (see "Jordan" [II], line 11). "Save expense" is the final phrase of "Jordan" (II). Herbert's God is never affected much by expense. "Prayer"(II), which follows "Jordan" (II) and precedes "Sion" by two poems, insists that God's "state," unlike that of earthly lords, "dislikes not easiness"—informality and spontaneity. Anyone familiar with the protocol of the Elizabethan and Stuart English court will realize how sharp the implied contrast here is.

Nothing more strongly distinguishes Herbert from a thinker like Richard Hooker than the latter's espousal of the analogy which Herbert systematically denied between earthly and heavenly glory. "Touching God himself," Hooker contemptuously asks, "hath he any where revealed that it is his delight to dwell beggarly?" Hooker takes this question to be purely rhetorical, and he sees no problem with Solomon's temple: "Even then was the Lord as acceptably honoured of his people as ever, when the stateliest places and things in the whole world were sought out to adorn his temple." In response to the typological argument against sumptuous buildings for worship ("this they will say was figurative, and served by God's appointment but for a time"), Hooker appeals to a "natural conveniency" which such bounteous expenditures have with "our cheerful affection which *thinketh nothing too dear* to be bestowed about the furniture of his service" and with the greatness of God, who ought to be served at least as well as "kings, his vicegerents in this world."[24]

Like Luther, Herbert denied the fundamental relevance to Christianity of the principle of "natural conveniency" to which Hooker appealed, the principle, that is, of decorum.[25] In "Gratefulnesse," Herbert presents a textbook case of indecorum, of gross impoliteness—"He makes thy gifts occasion more" (line 5)—as an image of the special privileges of the Christian. He also makes explicit the contrast between the God of devotion and the majestic and decorous

23. See (with caution) Malcolm MacKenzie Ross, *Milton's Royalism: A Study of the Conflict of Symbol and Idea in the Poems* (Ithaca, 1943), esp. chap. 3.

24. *Laws of Ecclesiastical Polity*, V.xv.3–4 (II, 48–50); emphasis mine. I do not mean to imply anything about the relation between Herbert's politics and Hooker's, only about their religious sensibilities. Politics in this context is a virtually independent variable.

25. See p. 57 above.

God of the philosophers and "common sense." He humorously imagines the encroachment of human need on a traditional picture of God as a great lord with a wonderful palace:

> Perpetuall knockings at thy doore,
> Tears sullying thy transparent rooms. [13–14]

Yet even though man behaves in this way—never satisfied, always demanding (and getting) "more" (lines 15–16)—Herbert notes that "thou wentst on, / And didst allow us all our noise" (lines 17–18). The idea of forbearance, however, is not strong enough. The God of this poem, as of "Sion," is stranger than that. "Nay," Herbert corrects himself,

> thou hast made a sigh and grone
>   Thy joyes. [19–20]

In the next stanza, as if recoiling from his "sullying" of the traditional image of heavenly harmonies, Herbert retreats a step. He acknowledges that he is aware of the traditional picture:

> Not that thou hast not still above
> Much better tunes, then grones can make. [21–22]

He now presents God as being whimsical in a way that many great lords are—compare the Duke in *Twelfth Night*—in having, that is, an oddly powerful penchant for pastoral:

> these countrey-aires thy love
>   Did take. [23–24]

The next stanza, however, does not develop this "balanced" conception of God as responding to both courtly and country tunes. It returns to the earlier images of importunity and noise by enacting them. The whole middle of the poem, meditating in general on the relations between God and man, has been preparation for a return to the personal mode of "Thou that hast giv'n so much to me, / Give one thing more, a gratefull heart" (lines 1–2). Having devoted practically the whole of the poem to a defense of human importunity, Herbert can, so to speak, turn up the volume:

> Wherefore I crie, and crie again;
> And in no quiet canst thou be,
> Till I a thankfull heart obtain
>   Of thee. [25–28]

Herbert returns to the God who is not serene and unapproachable in His dignity, who "could not / Encounter Moses strong complaints and mone, / [Whose] words were then, *Let me alone*" ("Decay," lines

3–5). God can be "in no quiet" until he grants Herbert's request. The joyous irony of the poem is that this request, phrased in the language of sinfulness and intense self-awareness, is for the gift of "a thankfull heart." "Gratefulnesse" links the tender conscience with the tender heart. Like "Sion," it shows that the life of the "tender" Christian is not one of anxiety but one of joy even in the face of the materials for anxiety.[26] The final stanza extends the self-analysis in the poem, but does so less to stimulate contrition than to reveal awareness of the magnitude of the gift for which it is asking, awareness of the way in which this gift could only be a product of grace. Herbert proceeds from the quiet, other-directed dimeter rather than from the noisy and humorous self-directed beginning of the previous stanza. He prays to be in the state which "Love unknown" sees God as working to put man in—"Each day, each houre, each moment of the week . . . new, tender, quick":

> Not thankfull, when it pleaseth me;
> As if thy blessings had spare dayes:
> But such a heart, whose pulse may be
>   Thy praise.   [29–32]

"Gratefulnesse" moves from a vision of the power of human desire to affect God to a vision of what it would mean for this desire to be entirely freed from human limitations, peevishness, and prudence ("*J'ai eu pitié des autres*," says Pound, "*probablement pas assez*, and at moments that / suited my own convenience").[27] Herbert returned to the theme of God's "vulnerability" to man in one other poem. Stein has rightly connected "Gratefulnesse" with "The Storm."[28] This latter poem, part of the sequence which moves from "The Bunch of Grapes" to "Paradise," provides the clearest vision in Herbert of the way in which God can be affected by human emotional need. Starting from the contemplation of, presumably, an actual storm, it proceeds to a striking "equation" of God's psychological situation in such circumstances with man's:

26. For joy even in the face of the materials for anxiety, see ch. 31 of *The Country Parson*, in which the Christian who finds "some emergent interruption in the day" curtailing or eliminating his normal devotions should not allow Satan to "inlarge [his] perplexity" over this, but ought to recall that "God knows the occasion as well as he [himself does]," and of this he is "so to assure himself, as to admit no scruple, but to go on *as cheerfully*, as if he had not been interrupted" ("The Parson in Liberty," *CP*, p. 272; emphasis mine).

27. Canto LXXVI, *The Pisan Cantos*, p. 38, in *The Cantos of Ezra Pound* (New York, 1956).

28. *Herbert's Lyrics*, p. 129; see also Keizer, "Herbert and the Tradition of Jacob," p. 21.

> If as the windes and waters here below
> > Do flie and flow,
> My sighs and tears as busie were above;
> > Sure they would move
> And much affect thee, as tempestuous times
> Amaze poore mortals, and object their crimes.   [1–6]

God can be as powerfully moved by the speaker's sighs and tears as men are moved by storms to thoughts of Judgment. Herbert's speaker is attempting to stimulate penitence in himself—to allow himself to be moved by the storm—by reminding himself of the extraordinary power of sighs and tears to affect God. The Reformation rejection of *apathia* as an ideal for either God or man is made explicit here (in the preface to his *Poetical Fragments*, Baxter not only defends passions and affections in man but attacks the conception of God as passionless, which he identified with "Cartesians and Cocceians").[29] Herbert is not afraid of the conception of God being "moved." He is not concerned with God's dignity. God is tender—and "quick."

The second stanza of "The Storm" elaborates on the opening analogy between the situations above and below. Beginning with an astronomical observation which denies that the literal heavens are static— "Starres have their storms, ev'n in a high degree, / As well as we"— it moves to contemplating one of the great mysteries of the spiritual cosmos, and provides the term which connects the "sighs and tears" of mortals to their "crimes":

> A throbbing conscience spurred by remorse
> > Hath a strange force.   [9–10]

"A throbbing conscience" is another image of "quickness"; it freely unifies the intellectual with the visceral. Baxter borrowed this tremendous phrase to describe the effect of his own spiritual awakening.[30] In the rest of the stanza, Herbert further specifies the "strange force" and boldness of "a throbbing conscience":

> It quits the earth, and mounting more and more
> Dares to assault thee, and besiege thy doore.   [11–12]

This is close to "Sion" and even more so to "Gratefulnesse," but the interesting feature of this vision of sighs and groans is that it does not present them as aesthetically pleasing. It does not present them as mounting like larks or as making any kind of music, even "coun-

---

29. *Poetical Fragments,* sig. A⁴v.
30. *Reliquiae Baxterianae,* I, 3. I believe this to be an actual though perhaps unconscious borrowing.

trey-aires." Like the poems on prayer, to which it is directly related, "The Storm" emphasizes the violence and imperiousness of human need—"how suddenly," as "Prayer" (II) puts it, "our requests [may] thine eare invade." To "assault thee and besiege thy doore" presents man's need for relief from a "throbbing conscience" as "Reversed thunder," an "Engine against th' Almightie," as Herbert says in "Prayer" [I]. Herbert insists on the "violence" here because he wants the contrast with traditional pictures of the harmony and tranquillity of heaven to be as sharp as possible. He develops further the most radical moment in "Gratefulnesse"—"Perpetuall knockings at thy doore":

> There it stands knocking, to thy musicks wrong,
> And drowns the song.   [13–14]

Keizer is certainly correct in suggesting that these lines build on the implications of "Knock, and it shall be opened to you" in Luke 11:9, and that in context this maxim means to praise importunity its force is "Knock, and keep knocking."[31] Herbert adds the contrast with the "normal" music of heaven in order to emphasize further the rudeness of the importunity. Essential to his entire theological framework is the belief that this rudeness is not an offense to God. In one of the most terrifying moments of *Grace Abounding*, Satan tells Bunyan God "hath been weary of you these several years . . . your bawlings in his ears hath been no pleasant voice to him" (par.117). The regenerate Christian cannot believe this.[32] Herbert presents God as putting aside all the concerns of His majesty in order to give the "throbbing conscience" what it needs:

> Glorie and honour are set by, till it
> An answer get.   [15–16]

Once again, even in their heavenly manifestations, "all this glorie, all this pomp and state" do not affect God much.

"The Storm" is the clearest statement in Herbert's poetry of the privileged indecorousness of genuine emotion. In *King Lear*, explaining his lack of "reverence," Kent claims that "anger hath a privilege"; Herbert's claim is closer to "Need has a privilege" (also present in *Lear*). In *The Country Parson*, Herbert argues that "evident miseries have a naturall priviledge, and exemption from all law" (p. 245). In relation to God, this "naturall priviledge" is available only to the

---

31. "Herbert and the Tradition of Jacob," pp. 20–21.

32. In the second part of *Pilgrim's Progress*, Mercy bangs at the Gate so hard that Christiana thought she "would a come in by violent hand, or a took the Kingdom by storm." To Mercy's question, "What said my Lord to my rudeness, was he not angry with me?" Christiana answers, "When he heard your lumbering noise, he gave a wonderful innocent smile" (p. 238).

regenerate. To have and exercise this privilege is part of what it means to be regenerate. The exact nature of the privilege becomes clearer if we compare the conception of "assaulting" God in "The Storm" with that presented in "Artillerie"—"Then we are shooters both." What "The Storm" presents is not a bargain but a need. The speaker does not argue that God *must* respond. He merely asserts that He will. The poem presents not a claim on God but an act of extraordinary trust in His responsiveness to need—however indecorously expressed.

We are now in a position to consider Herbert's attitude toward the value of poetry, toward the importance of art as opposed to "mere" sincerity. The framework that we have been examining makes it impossible to speak of "mere sincerity." Yet however unlikely it seems that the man who valued "one good grone" above the heavenly harmonies would rate earthly harmonies more highly, the question cannot be settled a priori. We must look at the texts themselves and at Herbert's own comments on sincerity and art. Before doing so, however, we must briefly consider a strain in Herbert's work which seems to run counter to the one we have been tracing, a strain which seems to place the highest value on inner neatness and order, and to denigrate rather than to privilege "noise." A great deal depends on whether one takes line 8 of "Conscience"—"My thoughts must work, but like a noiseless sphere"—as evoking "the quintessence of Herbert at his best," "the chief and distinctive direction of his poetry," or as another traditional attitude which Herbert in the main turns away from and which does not speak to his condition very fully.[33]

The poem which most explicitly develops the conception of "noiselessness" presented in "Conscience" is "The Familie." The speaker finds himself in the situation of "Longing," but instead of throwing himself into expression, he stands back to ask:

> What doth this noise of thoughts within my heart,
>   As if they had a part?
> What do these loud complaints and puling fears,
>   As if there were no rule or eares?   [1–4]

He turns to God, and says, quite sensibly:

> But, Lord, the house and familie are thine,
>   Though some of them repine.   [5–6]

The impulse of the poem, however, is not to accept this bittersweet state, but to pray for a state of perfection:

---

33. Vendler, *Poetry of Herbert*, p. 236; Martz, *Meditation*, p. 145; Stein, *Herbert's Lyrics*, p. 204.

> Turn out these wranglers, which defile thy seat:
> For where thou dwellest all is neat.   [7–8]

The next two stanzas are devoted to imagining this state of perfection; their language is abstract and allegorical and they do not deal with the problem of the emotions at all ("First Peace and Silence all disputes controll, / Then Order plaies the soul"). The penultimate stanza attempts to integrate the emotions into this vision. "Joyes oft are there," says Herbert, "and griefs as oft as joyes"—an unusually optimistic estimate, for Herbert—"But," he adds, "griefs *without a noise*" (lines 17–18; emphasis mine).

This should serve as a fully imagined answer to the opening desire for a "rule" for complaints and fears, but one of the most interesting features of the poem is that Herbert does not seem satisfied with its vision of noiselessness. He seems to be afraid that these noiseless griefs will be thought of as lukewarm or devotionally impotent, so he adds a paradox "Yet speak they louder then distemper'd fears"— and a surprisingly shrill rhetorical question, "What is so shrill as silent tears?" (lines 19–29). There is a strong sense of strain here; Herbert wants to give "Peace and Silence" all the power of privileged noise. He is attempting to recapture by paradox and rhetorical deftness the advantages of the framework his overt argument discredits. It is in fact difficult to know which framework is being invoked when the ultimate praise for silence is to be the most potent form of noise. "The Storm" seems to return through the back door.

Herbert ends, however, by ignoring the paradoxes of the penultimate stanza and harking back to the vision of an orderly household. He returns to the implications of God dwelling in the heart (line 8) rather than merely visiting there (compare the end of Jonson's "To Penshurst").

> This is thy house, with these it doth abound:
> And where these are not found,
> Perhaps thou com'st sometimes, and for a day;
> But not to make a constant stay.   [21–24]

The oddest thing about this ending is that it leaves the speaker's situation in doubt; by the criterion which the stanza establishes, the "house and familie" of Herbert's heart are not truly God's since "some of them repine." The poem is perhaps to be read as an attempt to regain some sense of equilibrium by creating a vision of equilibrium. Like "The Temper" (II) and "The Starre," "The Familie" is a poem of weariness with the paradoxes of being *simul justus et peccator*.[34] It

---

34. For *simul justus et peccator*, see p. 16 above.

presents a fantasy, not a philosophical or religious goal—or rather, not a philosophical or religious goal *for this life*. Most of "The Familie" must be read as being in the optative mood. When "Conscience," which shares the vision of "Harmonious peace," returns from vision to reality, it ends, as Vendler observes, on a triumphant but hardly peaceful note.[35]

Overestimating or misreading the place of order and neatness in Herbert's poetry has generated confusion about his attitude toward poetry. The central confusion is between poetic and religious success. When Mark Taylor states that Herbert's "ability to have [a poem] written through him [is] an unmistakable sign of grace,"[36] he is simply stating the critical consensus in rather reckless terms. The key text for the position is "Deniall." This poem seems to insist upon the equation of religious and poetic unsuccess—"When my devotions could not pierce / Thy silent eares; / Then was my heart broken, as was my verse"—and it enacts the disorder it describes by leaving the final short line of each stanza until the last unrhymed ("disorder" is the first of the unrhymed words). The major interpretive question is what to make of the restoration of order in the rhyme and prosody of the final stanza. "Enactment" becomes the crucial issue.

The reigning view is that "the form of the final prayer indicates that its request has already been answered"; the final lines enact the return of God's responsiveness to the poet.[37] Yet there is something odd about a prayer which implies that it has already received what it is requesting. The standard view obscures the optative force of the end of "Deniall":

> O cheer and tune my heartlesse breast,
> > Deferre no time;
> That so thy favours granting my request,
> > They and my minde may chime,
> > > And mend my ryme.   [26–30]

This is truly a prayer; it is truly presenting, as Vendler says, "a state of envisaged happiness."[38] The mending envisioned is in the future; the "may" of the penultimate line governs "mend" as well as "chime." What this means is that "my ryme" in the final line *cannot* refer to itself. The poet is asking that God do something to him analogous to

---

35. *Poetry of Herbert*, pp. 236–38.

36. *The Soul in Paraphrase: George Herbert's Poetics* (The Hague, 1974), p. 2.

37. Summers, *Herbert*, p. 136; and see Lewalski, *Protestant Poetics*, p. 299. Lewalski's adoption of this position is anomalous in the light of her dissent from critics who equate poetic and religious success in Edward Taylor (p. 502, n. 12), and her *denial* that Herbert and Taylor practice very different poetics (p. 502, n. 8).

38. *Poetry of Herbert*, p. 260.

what he has done in the poem—but not identical with it. "My ryme" in the final line is metaphorical and existential; it refers to a state of harmony ("chiming") between God's will and the poet's ("They and my minde"). The poet cannot, in this sense, mend his "rhyme" himself. He cannot mend his spiritual state by mending his representation of it. For Herbert truly to have thought he could would make the poem in effect a magical ritual working *ex opere operato;* for Herbert to have pretended to think this would make the poem the "piece of arbitrary wit" that Stein sees.[39] Only by taking "my ryme" *not* to refer to verbal rhyme can the poem be saved from these charges.

Seeing where the poem refers to itself and where it does not is equally important in reading "The Altar," one of Herbert's most puzzling poems. The best critics of "The Altar" have recognized that it does not in any way refer to the Eucharist; Summers correctly describes the poem as "artistically complex and religiously 'low.'"[40] We shall see that it is artistically complex *because* it is religiously "low." The special complexity of the poem lies in the relationship between its literal (typographical) shape and its conceptual content. As Fish says, "the first thing the poem does, even before we take in any of its words, is call attention to itself as something quite carefully made," and therefore to "the skill and ingenuity of the maker."[41] Fish is surely right in judging it unlikely that Herbert means to be praising his own ingenuity and in observing that instead of using the art that hides art, as he does elsewhere, Herbert here takes the more daring route of throwing "the fact of authorship and of 'wit' or 'invention' in the reader's face." One need not, however, follow Fish in taking the central issue of the poem as that of agency in general and of its own authorship in particular. The central issue of the poem can more properly be seen as the relationship between the art it displays and the art it discusses—the relationship, in other words, not between its authors but between its altars.

Fish assumes that (as he well puts it) "the altar in the poem and the altar that is the poem" are always being referred to simultaneously. This assumption is what enables him to conclude that Herbert ultimately means to ascribe the authorship of the poem to God. Yet the opening line, indeed the opening phrase, belies this. Fish's reading of "A broken Altar, Lord, thy servant reares" focuses exclusively on its syntax. He sees the suspension of the verb as momentarily creating a disturbing "surfeit of interpretative possibilities" by leaving us "uncertain of the relationship of the three noun phrases, altar, Lord,

---

39. *Herbert's Lyrics,* p. 16.

40. *Herbert,* p. 141; and see Rickey, *Utmost Art,* p. 16.

41. *Self-Consuming Artifacts,* p. 207. Fish's treatment of "The Altar" appears on pp. 207–215.

servant." "Words apart," however, as Herbert notes, are not a text "but a dictionary" (*CP*, p. 235). Fish speaks of noun phrases and then lists three nouns. Surely in the context of the developing sentence, the reader makes the linguistically natural assumption that the speaker-servant is addressing his Lord ("*thy* servant") and that the speaker is or was the performer of some action of which the altar is or was the object.[42] These natural assumptions about the syntax of the sentence prove to be correct. What makes the line problematic is not its syntax but its meaning. The opening phrase (the placement of which creates the suspended construction) is extremely puzzling. Why is the altar *broken*? As soon as we ask this question a disjunction opens up between the altar of the poem and the altar in it. The altar of the poem is not broken. It is, as Hutchinson, Rickey, and others have stated, a perfectly shaped classical altar.[43] The altar which the poem is here discussing, therefore, is *not* the altar which it is.

Seeing this distinction allows us to locate the mystery in the proper place—in the idea of a loyal servant rearing "a broken altar"—and to grasp the continuity of the whole first half of the poem. Fish insists on the "prideful claim" implicit in the grammatical status of "reares." His argument rests on the supposed logical and psychological properties of active verbs in general. He passes over the tone, stance, and content of the line—"A *broken* Altar, Lord, *thy servant* reares." The actual focus of the line is on the brokenness of the altar and the devotion involved in rearing it, not on the fact of the rearing. A reader who has responded to the content and tone of the line is not disturbed or surprised to find the next line beginning "Made of a heart." With even a minimal knowledge of the Bible, such a reader would have taken the puzzling opening phrase as, in Fish's words, a "direct and directing" reference to Psalm 51: "The sacrifices of God are a broken spirit: a broken and contrite heart, O God, thou wilt not despise" (verse 17). The "claim" the speaker is making is primarily embodied in the biblical implications of "broken," not in the logical status of "reares."

"Made of a heart, and cemented with teares" establishes the "altar" being described as purely internal and nonliteral. The next couplet insists on the disjunction between the perfectly shaped typographical altar, a product of human craft familiar as such (see Rickey's discussion

42. In a footnote to his discussion of line 1 (p. 209, n. 23), Fish rejects a theoretically possible reading of the line on the basis of the availability of a more "natural" reading (the quotation marks are his). I believe that he is correct in doing this, but I do not see that his framework allows it. His equivocation about "natural" acknowledges the problem.

43. Hutchinson, p. 484; Rickey, *Utmost Art*, pp. 10–16.

of other Renaissance and classical altar-poems), and the internal "broken altar,"

> Whose parts are as thy hand did frame;
> No workmans tool hath touch'd the same.   [3–4]

As in "Sion," the living God disdains dead matter and dead instruments. "Thy hand" is sharply contrasted with "workmans tool[s]." This is a direct and directing reference to one of the strongest anti-idolatry and antitechnology passages in the entire Bible: "If thou wilt make me an altar of stone, thou shalt not build it of hewn stone; for it thou lift up thy tool upon it, thou hast polluted it" (Exodus 20:25). In this rather terrifying context, filled, as Rudolf Otto would say, with a numinous dread of pollution,[44] Herbert could hardly be confusing or equating his art with God's. He is not being witty here; he is being sincere. He is claiming that he has not attempted to tamper with his religious emotions.[45] These lines exemplify rather than contradict the opening claim (Fish sees the "world pictures" projected by lines 1 and 3 as vastly different). Herbert is specifying the nature of the speaker's service, connecting the Mosaic rejection of tools to the psalmist's rejection of material offerings.

The next lines, the first of the dimeters which establish the poem as "shaped," extend the rejection of human art even further. Lines 3 and 4 seem to imply that the poet could have tampered with his emotional constitution if he had wanted to. The first two dimeter couplets reject this suggestion. They state the limits of human art and the special prerogative of God's:

> A *Heart* alone
> Is such a stone,
> As nothing but
> Thy pow'r doth cut.   [5–8]

God alone can "cut" and break the heart. The whole poem thus far has been an explication of the puzzling opening line, of what it means for the servant to rear "a broken altar."[46] Only at this point, when the

---

44. *Idea of the Holy*, chaps. 4, 10. See also Paul Ricoeur, *The Symbolism of Evil*, trans. Emerson Buchanan (1967; rpt. Boston, 1969), chaps. 1–2.

45. Compare Philip C. McGuire, "Private Prayer and English Poetry in the Early Seventeenth Century," *SEL*, 14 (1974), 76.

46. Lines 1–8 of "The Altar" can also be seen as conflating, in Reformation fashion, the categories that seemed so distinct in "Superliminare"—"holy, pure, and cleare, / Or that which groneth to be so." Contra Fish, *Living Temple*, p. 130, the *truly* profane have already been excluded from the mysterious and perilous world of "The Church." The grammar of "Superliminare" will not support Fish's construction, although he is right about the complicating effect of "at his perill." For the Reformation conflation of the holy and the "groaning," see p. 16 above.

full implications of the opening phrases are clear, does Herbert begin
to relate the altar in the poem to the altar that is the poem:

> Wherefore each part
> Of my hard heart
> Meets in this frame,
> To praise thy Name.   [9–12]

These lines truly, as Fish says, present God as "responsible . . . for
the poem's psychological occasion," but this does not make God the
"bestower" as well as the object of the praise. Herbert wants to pre-
sent the impulse toward praise as spontaneous and inspired ("each
part . . . *Meets in* this frame") while at the same time calling attention
to the specific human products and processes that result from the
impulse. "This frame" is the first piece of self-reference in the poem.
The repetition of "frame" from line 3 is surely intended both to relate
the poem to its occasion (the speaker's sense of God's hand upon
him) and to contrast the materials and effects of human and divine
art. If these lines, as Fish argues, equivocate on the matter of agency,
the next couplet clarifies the situation. It defines the utmost reach of
human art:

> if I chance to hold my peace,
> These stones to praise thee may not cease.   [13–14]

Herbert combines a profound recognition of his own sinfulness—"if
I chance to hold my peace"—with a modified version of the classical
and Renaissance claim for the immortality of poetry (no audience but
God is necessarily implied).

In terms of argument, the poem could end here. It has accounted
for its own existence without making any special claims for its maker's
spiritual state. The problem with this ending, however, is precisely
its lack of reference to the speaker's ultimate spiritual condition. The
final couplet is truly a *cri de coeur*. The speaker turns from the poem
to God. Although he is clearly one of the regenerate, he feels God's
hand upon him only in the negative sense, and in this situation "even
the deare children of God, who have received a great measure of
grace, while the hand of God is upon them, do doubt of his love and
favour."[47] Fish correctly notes that one "cannot ask for what one has
already been given" and we have seen how important this recognition
is for understanding the end of "Deniall," but one can coherently ask
for what one does not feel one has been given. The speaker is asking
to be assured or reassured of his regeneration, to feel God's hand
working upon him in a positive sense:

47. Downame, *Christian Warfare*, p. 94b.

> O let thy blessed *Sacrifice* be mine,
> And sanctifie this *Altar* to be thine   [15–16]

The poem assumes its shape as a perfect classical altar at a moment when the poet has turned away from all thought about the power of his art. He is speaking, as he was in the first half of the poem, about his spiritual state. The most extraordinary gesture of the poem occurs in the final line when, just as the poem is attaining completion, Herbert uses the phrase, "this *Altar*," to refer away from the poem and back to the internal "broken altar" of the opening. Herbert has already given human art credit for what it can do (establishing a context which, in a sense, perpetually speaks itself). He is here concerned with the "I" who may "chance to hold [his] peace," not with the "stones" of the poem-altar. The final line puts human art in its place by decisively turning away from it just as it attains its perfection. As we realize that "this *Altar*" refers to the heart rather than the poem, we recognize the relative importance of the two referents.

Herbert never presented his utmost art as being of ultimate value. The critics who quote the third stanza of "Praise" (II),

> Wherefore with my utmost art
>   I will sing thee,
> And the cream of all my heart
>   I will bring thee,   [9–12]

rarely take note of the coda:

> Small it is, in this poore sort
>   To enroll thee:
> Ev'n eternitie is too short
>   To extoll thee.[48]   [25–28]

In the same way, a critic who shares Walton's view of "My musick shall find thee, and ev'ry string / Shall have his attribute to sing" ("The Thanksgiving," lines 39–40) will not advert to the context of mistaken aspiration in which these lines occur.[49] Nor is such a critic likely to acknowledge that Herbert sometimes consciously mars poems

48. See Summers, *Herbert*, p. 113; Lewalski, *Protestant Poetics*, p. 228. Stein offers a fuller reading. He notes that "Praise" (II) is "a gesture offered while backing away" (*Herbert's Lyrics*, p. 132). The same movement occurs in the first part of "Easter." After Herbert exhorts his lute to celebrate Christ's rising "with all thy art," he ends by praying that the Spirit "make up our defects with his sweet art." Lewalski, who reads the first part of "Easter" as "probably the most complete statement of Herbert's poetics," downplays the significance of this shift (*Protestant Poetics*, p. 246).

49. Walton, *Life*, p. 317. Summers seems to endorse Walton's use of these lines (*Herbert*, p. 156). Again Stein demurs (*Herbert's Lyrics*, p. 112).

in order to assert his sincerity. At the end of "Home," he associates rhyme with reason and rejects both:

> Come dearest Lord, passe not this holy season,
>   My flesh and bones and joynts do pray:
> And ev'n my verse, when by the ryme and reason
>   The word is, *Stay,* sayes ever, *Come.*   [73–76]

At the end of "Grief," Herbert's speaker asserts that his grief, as opposed to that of lovers, does not allow him "musick and a ryme," and the poem ends with a naked, unrhymed, and syntactically disjunctive cry. When he writes these words, Herbert has given over "the poem."

Yet these are, as Stein says, minor examples.[50] The major statements on the matter are the "Jordan" poems, "A true Hymne," and "The Forerunners." These poems, especially the latter two, force the critics who believe in Herbert's high view of art into desperate maneuvers. The critics are constantly assuring us that in these poems Herbert cannot "really" be saying what he seems to be saying. Of "Jordan" (I), which does not bring poetry but only "fictions" into question, Stein notes that it "*seems to* take the severest Platonic line"; Lewalski hastens to assure us that the ideal of plainness the poem espouses is not that of William Perkins, the famous Puritan, though she fails to explain wherein the difference lies.[51] Regarding "Jordan" (II), Tuve cautions that "If we think we have found . . . a manifesto against fine style and over-subtlety," we should recall that "Herbert is quite as likely to berate himself because he is unable to 'write fine and wittie.' "[52] Yet the two examples of the latter phenomenon which she cites, "The Forerunners" and "Dulnesse," are not persuasive. "The Forerunners," as we shall see, does not defend "lovely enchanting language," and Stein has shown that in "Dulnesse" the ideal ex-

50. *Herbert's Lyrics*, p. 15.

51. Ibid., p. 11 (emphasis mine); *Protestant Poetics*, p. 227. Somewhat reluctantly, Lewalski does find *Traherne's* standard of plainness "analogous in some ways to that urged by Perkins" (p. 229; see also p. 355), but she ignores the direct allusion to "Jordan" (II) in Traherne's rejection of "curling Metaphors that gild the Sence" ("The Author to the Critical Peruser," line 11, in *Thomas Traherne: Poems, Centuries, and Three Thanksgivings,* ed. Ann Ridler [London, 1966]). Fish comments excellently on the "rigor" of "Jordan" (I) and connects it with Milton's "Platonic-Christian anti-aesthetic" in *Self-Consuming Artifacts,* pp. 194–95, and *Surprised by Sin,* p. 88, n. 1. Leah Sinanoglou Marcus attempts to distinguish an Anglican from a Puritan plain style in "George Herbert and the Anglican Plain Style," *"Too Rich to Clothe the Sunne,"* pp. 179–93, but does not convincingly locate Herbert in the context of churchliness for which she is arguing.

52. *A Reading of Herbert*, p. 192.

pressed "in the context of neo-Platonic ideas of the deity" is revealed to be misguided by the conclusion of the poem.[53]

In "Jordan" (II), Tuve argues, Herbert is criticizing "not subtlety of metaphor nor richness of style but his own intellectual pride," yet the thrust of the poem is to link these things. Tuve's treatment of "Jordan" (II) reflects her general anxiety that Herbert not be associated with "sincerity-is-enough sentimentality" and not be seen as preferring "the pious heart to the thinking mind."[54] But Herbert did prefer the pious heart to the thinking mind. "Jordan" (II) is part of the evidence for this. The movement of the poem is from brain-work ("Thousands of notions in my braine did runne") to the heart-work which is heaven-work. When the "friend" sets the bustling and eager poet to "copie out" what is "readie penn'd" in love, he is telling him, in effect, to "look in [his] heart and write," for this is where, as Herbert has made clear in many other poems, God primarily does His "penning." "Jordan" (II) shares the positive values as well as the critique of "Sion."

It is not clear, moreover, that the "copying out" which the end of "Jordan" (II), recommends refers to writing poetry at all, even plain style poetry. "Prayer" (II), which directly responds to the end of "Jordan" (II), is a poem in praise of the special power of confident and familiar prayer—above "Wealth, fame, endowments, vertues"— to affect God. This too is closer to "Sion" than may at first appear. Familiar and spontaneous prayer of the sort described must be sincere since only the regenerate, who have already felt God's love to them, can approach God with this "ease."[55] And this sort of prayer need not be verbal, let alone poetic—"If I but lift mine eyes, my suit is made"—just as the "grones" of "Sion" need not be psalmlike poems.[56] A great deal hangs on taking "grones" at the end of "Sion" as truly referring to groans, to spontaneous and untransformed expressions of emotion.

In "Herbert and *Caritas*," Tuve withdraws her reading of "Jordan" (II) as embodying "the Sidneian idea of poetry [in which] the 'erected wit' must contemplate universals" and then body them forth in "the great speaking images of poetry." She recognizes that "Jordan" (II) "turns out to be less about writing a poem than about living a life."[57] She does not, however, go on to see this movement from focusing

53. *Herbert's Lyrics*, pp. 98–100.

54. *A Reading of Herbert*, pp. 190, 194; "Herbert and *Caritas*," p. 172.

55. See Luther, "Preface to Romans," pp. 28–30; Calvin, *Institutes*, III.ii.15–16; Sibbes, *Commentary on II Corinthians I, Works*, III, 456–57.

56. Lewalski equates "grones" in "Sion" with psalmlike poems (*Protestant Poetics*, p. 315).

57. *A Reading of Herbert*, p. 193; "Herbert and *Caritas*," p. 176. Stein notes this shift in Tuve's views (*Herbert's Lyrics*, p. 22).

on poetry to focusing on "a life" as having any implications for Herbert's sense of the value of poetry. Yet the potentially anti-intellectualistic implications of "Jordan" (II) are confirmed by the other instance of the phrase "readie penn'd" in Herbert's writings. It occurs in the remarkable chapter of *The Country Parson* entitled "The Parson's Library" and exclusively devoted to the praise of experience. The chapter begins by asserting that "The Country Parson's Library is a holy Life," and does not mention a single book. In fact, it deprecates books. "Hee that considereth how to carry himselfe at table about his appetite, if he tell this to another, preacheth; and much more feelingly and judiciously, then he [that] writeth his rules of temperance out of bookes" (*CP*, p. 278). The phrase which links "The Parson's Library" to "Jordan" (II) occurs in the sentence continuing the argument that experience is itself an education; "So that the Parson having studied and mastered all his lusts and affections within, and the whole Army of Temptations without, hath ever so many sermons ready penn'd, as he hath victories."

"The Parson's Library" is the most radical chapter in *The Country Parson*, and although it makes Canon Hutchinson nervous, it is neither mistitled nor anomalous.[58] In his prose as in his poetry, Herbert always valued experience and feeling over learning and art. This is the link to Fox and Dell.[59] It could be argued that Herbert can speak as he does in "The Parson's Library" because he has already detailed "The Parson's Knowledge" in the fourth chapter of the manual. But this earlier chapter is itself complex. In explaining how the Parson is to

58. Hutchinson's note states that "the contents correspond so little with the title, *except for elaborating a paradox*, that the chapter is possibly misnamed" (p. 563; emphasis mine). This is an objection that answers itself and that looks even weaker in the face of "The Windows," "Church-lock and key," and other Herbertian titles. What truly disturbs Hutchinson is perhaps not the title but the paradox itself. He hastens to assure us that elsewhere "Herbert commends the reading of many books." I believe Hutchinson's nervousness to be justified. Annabel M. Endicott, (" 'The Soul in Paraphrase': George Herbert's 'Library,' " *Renaissance News*, 19 [1966], 14–16) has pointed out Donne's use of the same paradox in one of his sermons on Psalm 32 (*Sermons*, IX, 278). Donne does not dwell on the negative side of the paradox with quite Herbert's insistence.

59. In *The Tryal of Spirits Both in Teachers and Hearers* (1653), Dell asserted that "the word of God in the spirituall sense of it . . . is onely known by Temptation, Prayer, and God's own [inward] Teaching" (p. 62). In elaborating his praise of experience in "The Parson's Library," Herbert makes an analogy between ministers and physicians, using this commonplace to stress his preference for the physician/minister who "hath been sick . . . and knows what recovered him" over "he that is generally learned, and was never sick." He goes on to assert that "if the same person had been sick of all diseases, and were recovered of all by things that he knew; there were no such Physician as he, both for skill and tendernesse" (*CP*, p. 278). This ideal comes very close to Fox's picture of why he had been troubled with visions and apprehensions of sins to which he was never addicted; the Lord made him see "that it was needful I should have a sense of all conditions, how else should I speak to all conditions!" (*Journal*, p. 87).

go about understanding scripture, Herbert asserts that "the means he useth are first, a holy Life." This is a remarkable statement in a discussion of the means for *understanding* scripture, and Herbert fully commits himself to its implications. He quotes John 7:17 to the effect that "if any do God's will, he shall know of the doctrine," and he especially identifies a holy life with a life of feeling. The parson assures himself "that *wicked men, however learned, do not know the Scriptures, because they feel them not,* and because they are not understood but with the same spirit that writ them" (*CP*, p. 228; emphasis mine).[60]

The second "means" the parson uses is, as follows from the above, prayer for inspiration since in the world of religion, "the well is deep, and we have nothing of ourselves to draw with." Only the third "means" involves a term of human effort ("diligent Collation of Scripture with Scripture"); and finally, in fourth place, "are Commenters and Fathers, who have handled the places controverted." These, Herbert notes, the parson "by no means refuseth." This is a rather negative formulation to which Herbert immediately adds a reminder that the parson "doth not so study others, as to neglect the grace of God in himself." The next chapter, which *is* devoted to books, is entitled, "The Parsons Accessary Knowledges," and it too ends in praise of firsthand experience.[61]

As one would expect from "The Parson's Library," Herbert's emphasis on inspiration, experience, and feeling is equally evident in his chapters on prayer and on preaching. In praying, the parson is, above all, "hearty"—that is, sincere—so that, "being first affected himself, hee may affect also his people" (*CP*, p. 231). In preaching, the parson "is not witty, or learned, or eloquent, but Holy"—"A Character," Herbert adds, "that Hermogenes never dream'd of" (*CP*, p. 233).[62] Again we are in another world from that of "humane wis-

---

60. In *The Arte of Prophesying* (1607), Perkins asserted that "He that is not godly, howsoever he may understand the scriptures, yet doth not perceive the inward sense and experience of the word in the heart" (p. 137). Herbert's position is more radical in making *understanding* dependent upon "the inward sense and experience." Baxter denounces as a "desperate and destructive conceit" the idea that a man who has the Spirit "is therefore more able to expound Scripture, or teach it to the people . . . than learned men that have not the Spirit" (*Christ's Witness within Us: The Believer's Special Advantage against Temptations to Infidelity,* in *The Practical Works of Richard Baxter,* ed. Rev. William Orme [London, 1830], XX, 183).

61. The final sentence of "The Parsons Accessory Knowledge" begins, "Wherefore the Parson hath thoroughly canvassed al the particulars of humane actions." Stein (*Herbert's Lyrics,* pp. 23, 130) is perhaps correct to connect Herbert's emphasis on "particulars" with his admiration of and friendship with Bacon (see chap. 2, n.39).

62. Herbert is very close to Perkins here (see *Arte of Prophesying,* p. 132). In *Hermogenes and the Renaissance: Seven Ideas of Style* (Princeton, 1970), pp. 148–51, Annabel M. Patterson argues that Herbert thought of holiness as an "Idea of style" like Hermogenes' seven and that through this Idea Herbert sought in his poetry to reconcile Hermogenes'

dome" and eloquence.[63] The character of holiness is attained in a sermon through sincerity and passion—first, by choosing "moving and ravishing texts, whereof the Scriptures are full," and then by being moved and ravished by them, "dipping and seasoning all our words and sentences in our hearts, before they come into our mouths, truly affecting, and cordially expressing all that we say; so that the auditors may plainly perceive that every word is hart-deep" (*CP*, p. 233). The parson also turns often to God, asking for direct inspiration, as in "Aaron": "Oh my Master, on whose errand I come, let me hold my peace, and do thou speak thy selfe; for . . . when thou teachest, all are Scholers" (*CP*, p. 233).[64]

Herbert finds the prophets rich in these turnings to God, and he particularly admires Saint Paul for the intensity and range of his passions. "What an admirable Epistle is the second to the *Corinthians*? how full of affections? he joyes, and he is sorry, he grieves, and he gloryes." "Never," Herbert reflects, "was there such care of a flock expressed, save in the great shepherd of the fold, who first shed teares over *Jerusalem*." This care is to be learned in Paul and the gospels and manifested in the parson's sermons because the aim of preaching, as Herbert says in contrasting preaching with catechizing, is to "inflame or ravish" (*CP*, p. 257). This aim is much more important than that of informing.[65] Only at the very end of "The Parson Preaching," almost as an afterthought, does Herbert add a few remarks on the

---

Ideas of verity and beauty. Patterson's emphasis on reconciliation seems to me misguided (see the analysis of "The Forerunners" below). The exact implications of Herbert's reference to Hermogenes here remain unclear. Michael P. Gallagher suggests a different (more negative) point to the allusion in "Rhetoric, Style, and George Herbert," *ELH*, 37 (1970), 500.

63. Walton's account of Herbert's first sermon, delivered "after a most florid manner, both with great learning and eloquence" and then solemnly renounced, is probably a brilliant fiction, but it is certainly true that Herbert believed that sermons should be "plain and practical" and that "God does not mean to lead men to heaven by hard questions" (*Life*, p. 295). For a possible source in Augustine for Walton's acount, see Richard Douglas Jordan, "Herbert's First Sermon," *RES*, n.s., 27 (1976), 178–79. Another perhaps more probable source is the passage in *The Country Parson* just quoted (*CP*, p. 233).

64. Again Herbert is close to Perkins, who insists that the preacher must have "an inward feeling of the doctrine to be delivered" and "must be godly affected himself, [if he] would stir up godly affections in other men" (*Arte of Prophesying*, p. 140). Perkins's major argument for keeping all "humane learning" from being apparent in sermons is that "the hearers *ought not to ascribe their faith to the gifts of men* but to the power of the word" (*Arte of Prophesying*, p. 132; emphasis mine).

65. The special weight Herbert places on emotional apprehension makes the project of Fish's *The Living Temple*—to use Reformation catechisms and Herbert's remarks on catechizing as the basis for an account of the characteristic effects and aims of Herbert's poetry—seem bound to limited success at best. Catechizing remains in the intellectual realm.

parson's "Method in handling of a text," and these remarks them-
selves betray his strong anti-intellectualist bias.[66]

We are now in a position to approach "A true Hymne," Herbert's
most direct and extended treatment of the relative values of sincerity
and art. Stein suggests that the poem is ultimately less about writing
than about "something real in the experience of the religious life,"
though he never specifies what this "something" is.[67] The situation
which Herbert considers in "A true Hymne" is the opposite of that
of the learned wicked man who cannot feel; it is that of the man who
has been touched to the heart but cannot attain full or articulate
expression, let alone eloquence. The poem opens with Herbert pre-
senting himself as being in such a situation. He presents his heart,
independently of his other faculties, as having an impulse toward
praise and thanksgiving:

> My joy, my life, my crown!
> My heart was meaning all the day,
> Somewhat it fain would say:
> And still it runneth mutt'ring up and down
> With onely this, *My joy, my life, my crown.*   [1–5]

Fish sees this stanza as dramatizing an instance of self-centeredness
and misguided endeavor; he equates the impulse to "mean" with the
impulse to "observe the strict decree" in "The Holdfast" and to seek
out "quaint words" in "Jordan"(II).[68] But nothing in the poem justifies
this equation. The speaker's heart is not "threatening" anything (as
in "The Holdfast") or seeking out anything quaint or trim. It is merely,
in a striking intransitive usage, "meaning," seeking to "say" some-
thing, to do more than repeat to itself again and again the same
semiscriptural exclamation. The speaker never presents his heart as
being "self-moved"; he presents it as merely being moved, as being
in a state (that of "meaning") in which it powerfully desires expres-
sion. It seeks expression because it is in the state. The speaker presents
his heart as finding itself in this situation, not as putting itself into
it. Much of the humor of the presentation comes from the speaker's
sense of detachment from the rather ludicrous situation in which he
finds his heart.

66. As W. Fraser Mitchell and others have pointed out, Herbert's criticism of preach-
ers who "crumble" their texts is almost certainly a reference to Lancelot Andrewes
(see *English Pulpit Oratory from Andrewes to Tillotson* [1932; rpt. New York, 1962], p. 362;
and see Hutchinson, p. 557). Andrewes approached the emotions of his auditors
primarily through their intellects.
67. *Herbert's Lyrics*, p. 9; Stein's discussion of "A true Hymne" appears on pp. 6–10.
68. *Self-Consuming Artifacts*, p. 200; Fish's discussion appears on pp. 200–202.

"A true Hymne" does mean to educate its readers, but not through dramatizing a character making a mistake. In the rhetorical situation assumed by this poem, it is we who need to be educated, not the speaker or his heart. The presentation of the heart as childishly naive and silly—"still it runneth mutt'ring up and down"—is something of a trap for us. The poem works to defend this "ludicrous" behavior, not to attack or correct it. Herbert knows that he has led us into scorning the barely articulate, "muttering" heart of the first stanza. He turns and solemnly rebukes the attitude he knows he has created—"Yet slight not these few words," the second stanza begins. The mode of the poem changes from drama to exposition. Herbert wants us not merely not to slight the words his heart has been muttering "all the day," but to accord them the highest value (he knows how much *we* value art):

> If truly said, they may take part
>   Among the best in art.   [7–8]

Herbert is taking the offensive here. He is putting his claim for the value of the heart's few words in the form most outrageous to those who value eloquence and art. The point of the lines is not to raise the question of whether the few words have been "truly said," but to assert that if they have been, they have attained to the highest "art." Herbert is not raising doubts about the situation described but rather making an assertion about its implications. The words in question clearly have been truly said in the relevant sense, in the sense of being sincere. They are, after all, presented as coming from "the heart." More militantly than in "Jordan" (I), Herbert is insisting that there is beauty in truth, with truth here defined in terms of genuineness and conviction; the claim is that sincerity is beauty. This is a conception of beauty which, as Fish says of "Jordan" (I), "makes the standard of beauty as we are normally accustomed to apply it, irrelevant."[69]

The couplet of the stanza makes it clear that Herbert's claim is about the special status of devotional art rather than about art in general. Devotional art is not to be judged by aesthetic standards:

> The finenesse which a hymne or psalme affords,
>   Is, when the soul unto the lines accords.   [9–10]

This is the crucial sort of "fineness." Recalling "Deniall," this is the crucial "rhyme." Herbert has now defined with some precision the position he wants to defend, the position from which, to jump ahead slightly, the heart's few words constitute "a true hymne." The form

---

69. Ibid., p. 194.

"A (or The) true X" in the titles of seventeenth-century poems almost always signals a redefinition, often paradoxical, of the term in question, as in Herrick's 'To keep a true Lent," or Vaughan's "The true Christmas" (compare Herbert's "Thus are *true Aarons* drest"). "A true Hymne" is no exception. It redefines the true or beautiful or proper hymn. After the narrative opening, Herbert proceeds in a perfectly straightforward expository manner, although his critics have been remarkably unwilling to acknowledge this.

Stein admits that the couplet of stanza 2 "has an admirable ring," but insists that it "does not quite face the problems that have been raised" regarding how the "vital step" of "truly saying" is to be taken. But, as we have seen, the poem does not raise the "how" question; it presents the heart's sincerity as a fait accompli. Fish is even harder on the couplet. Sounding very much like Tuve, he deprecates it as "a traditionally pietistic resolution" and also as "complacent" and "premature." Both Stein and Fish agree that the stanza which follows this problematic couplet undercuts the stability the couplet seems to promise. Stein sees the stanza as purposely incoherent; Fish sees it as both incoherent and riddled with crippling ambiguities. Yet this stanza responds quite directly to a question which the couplet of stanza 2 obviously raises—"To whom does a hymn or psalm that is 'truly said' afford the sense of fineness in question?" The answer, of course, is "to God," and the second half of "A true Hymne" can be seen as explaining what it means for a hymn or psalm to be a literary work addressed *to God*. Like "Sion" and "Prayer" (II), "A true Hymne" expounds God's values.

The third stanza explains that if a hymn or psalm is to please God, it must respond to His known demands:

> He who craves all the minde,
> And all the soul, and strength, and time,
> If the words onely ryme,
> Justly complains, that somewhat is behinde
> To make his verse, or write a hymne in kinde.   [11–15]

Despite Stein's assumption that "He" is the poet, and Fish's insistence that the reference is profoundly ambiguous, the pronoun in line 11 unquestionably refers to God. As Summers pointed out, lines 11–12 are a direct and directing reference to Luke 10:27: "Thou must love the Lord thy God with all thy heart, and with all thy soul, and with all thy strength, and with all thy mind."[70] What God demands from man in any work directed toward Him, including a poetic one ("*his*

---

70. *Herbert*, chap. 5, n. 34 (p. 233).

verse"), is love. He is not affected much by technical proficiency any more than by pomp and state.

Again, what does affect God is sincerity. In "The Parson's Library" Herbert affirms that "the chiefe thing which God in Scriptures requires, is the heart." Discussing the relation between weeping and penitence in this light, Herbert concludes that since repentance is an act of the mind and heart, not the body, if a Christian *"endeavour to weep, and cannot . . . this sufficeth"* (emphases mine). "A true Hymne" discusses skillful versifying in this same light. God "justly complains" if He is offered mere art,

> Whereas if th' heart be moved,
> Although the verse be somewhat scant,
> God doth supplie the want.   [16–18]

The greatest confusion that exists about "A true Hymne" has been caused by line 18, the central short line of the final stanza. Every critic writing on the poem has taken "supplie the want" literally, as asserting that whenever Herbert felt himself "moved" but incapable of artistic expression, he could rely on God to provide the inspiration that would lead him to artistic success.[71] But the whole point of the poem has been that religious success—God finding an utterance "fine"—is independent of artistic success. Either the poem has truly become incoherent at this point and means to praise not the "few words" of the heart but a perfectly formed, inspired work, or some other way must be found to read line 18.

Luckily, Herbert himself has supplied the answer. "Supplie the want" is a joke. This is made clear by the example that Herbert provides; it is an oddly paradoxical case:

> As when th' heart sayes (sighing to be approved)
> *O, could I love!* and stops: God writeth, *Loved.*   [19–20]

In the example of God supplying the want, God does *not* supply the heart with what it wants and lacks. He does not give the heart the ability to love, to fulfill the commandment paraphrased in stanza 3. Instead, as Vendler notes, He "changes the soul from subject to object and writes 'Loved.' "[72] Fish protests the illogic of this. He agrees that "at first we tend to read 'Loved' as 'you are loved by me,' " but insists that "the immediate context ('O, could I love!') demands an alternative reading: 'I decree that I am loved by you.' " But this overlooks a key element in "the immediate context," the parenthesis which explains

---

71. See Stein, *Herbert's Lyrics,* p. 8; Lewalski, *Protestant Poetics,* p. 299; Taylor, *Soul in Paraphrase,* p. 41; Fish, *Self-Consuming Artifacts,* p. 202.

72. *Poetry of Herbert,* p. 28.

why the heart desires to love. It wants to love God perfectly because it assumes that it could only be loved ("approved") by God if it does so, if it fulfills the commandment. God, on the other hand, grants the heart what it wants without supplying what it lacks. He takes the will for the deed.

What Herbert is ultimately criticizing in "A true Hymne" is the kind of mentality that can think only in terms of accomplishment. The idea that only the most accomplished works of art could be pleasing to God is another form of the demand for actual righteousness which the reformers saw as tyrannical and misleading. The doctrine of imputation opposed the demand for perfection. To be regenerate was to *desire* to love God perfectly (a want which God supplies) and to have this desire accepted for the deed. "Under this gracious covenant," as Sibbes said, "sincerity is perfection."[73] Christ, said Downame, "respecteth not so much our actions as our affections; nor our workes as our desires and endeavors."[74] God does not complete or perfect the heart's "poem"; He merely accepts it as "a true hymne." God's "writing" *Loved* has nothing to do with poetry. Herbert is not in any way claiming that God actually wrote the final word of his poem.[75]

The emphasis on sincerity and imputation was part of the anti-elitism of the doctrine of faith alone. The defense of the childish and silly heart is fully serious. The reformers never insisted on eloquence or even articulateness as a mark of faith. Baxter affirmed that "thousands believe savingly, that have not wit enough to tell you truly what believing is; and many thousands have the Spirit that know not what the Spirit is."[76] Bunyan, as one might expect, put the point even more passionately.[77] Prayer was an activity that was particularly singled out as independent of verbal skill or capacity. Richard Hollinworth explained that believers often find "their affections . . . too big for their expressions," but this is not a problem since believers have the spirit of adoption and "the Father hath compassion on his sick Child, though

---

73. *The Bruised Reed and Smoking Flax, Works,* I, 59.

74. *The Christian Warfare,* p. 57a.

75. It should also be noted that the poem "A true Hymne" is not itself being put forth as a "true hymne" but rather as a piece defining the term. The heart's few words are the true hymn in the poem.

76. *Christ's Witness within Us,* p. 189. It must be recalled, however, that Baxter begins this section with the caveat quoted in n. 60 above.

77. *Grace Abounding,* par. 300 (in "A Brief Account of the Author's Call to the Work of the Ministry"): "I am fully convinced of it, that it is possible for a soul that can scarce give a man an answer, but with great confusion as to method, I say it is possible for them to have a thousand times more grace, and so to be more in the love and favour of the Lord than some who, by virtue of the gift of knowledge, can deliver themselves like angels."

it cannot speak articulately, nor speak at all, but only sighs, groans, looks upon his Father."[78] William Dewsbury comes even closer to "A true Hymne" when he addresses the weak believer thus: "And thou faithful Babe, though thou stutter and stammer forth a few words in the dread of the Lord, they are accepted."[79] In "A true Hymne," Herbert is applying the standard Protestant teachings on prayer to the matter of devotional verse. Fish correctly sees Romans 8:26, "for we know not what we should pray for as we ought: but the Spirit itself maketh intercession for us with groanings that cannot be uttered," as relevant to "A true Hymne," but the pressures of his argument force him to see humiliation even in this most comfortable of texts.

That Herbert fully endorsed the anti-elitism of the doctrine of imputation is confirmed by two poems that treat the doctrine, "Faith" and "The Elixir." Both of these poems are deeply relevant to "A true Hymne." "Faith" is another defence of "naive" perception and behavior. Like "Prayer" (II), it emphasizes God's regard for man's "ease" in the doctrine of faith alone. It presents faith alone as the most straightforward kind of wish-fulfillment:

> Hungrie I was, and had no meat:
> I did conceit a most delicious feast;
> I had it straight, and did as truly eat,
> As ever did a welcome guest. [5–8]

The emphasis here is on as truly eating by means of a "conceit" as through actually receiving food. Later in the poem, this emphasis on the equivalence of "as if" and "actually" approaches more closely to theological formulation (see especially stanza 4). The naive or mock-naive tone persists until suddenly, at line 25, Herbert shifts from personal affirmation to theological reflection. The naiveté of the earlier stanzas was not accidental; it illustrates a central truth. Fairy tale merges with theology:

> If blisse had lien in art or strength,
> None but the wise or strong had gained it:
> Where now by Faith all arms of a length;
> One size doth all conditions fit. [25–28]

The moral is this:

> A peasant may beleeve as much
> As a great Clerk, and reach the highest stature.

---

78. *The Holy Ghost on the Bench* (1656), p. 54 (quoted in Nuttall, *Holy Spirit*, pp. 65–66).

79. Quoted in Nuttall, *Holy Spirit*, p. 86.

Thus dost thou make proud knowledge bend & crouch,
    While grace fills up uneven nature.[80]   [29–32]

The anti-elitism of faith alone could hardly be more clearly expressed. The next stanza directly refers to imputation:

When creatures had no reall light
Inherent in them, thou didst make the sunne,
Impute a lustre, and allow them bright;
    And in this shew, what Christ hath done.[81]   [33–36]

This is the essential contrast—between real or inherent qualities and imputed ones, between *being* "bright" and being counted such through getting credit for brightness reflected from elsewhere. "The Elixir" develops this theme. It explains how things, in its case actions, grow "bright and clean" through imputation. Like "Faith," "The Elixir" also humorously adopts some magical thinking, but the elixir which "turneth all to gold" turns out to be not a substance but an attitude ("Grace is not medicine, but favor").[82] Like "Faith," "The Elixir" is about the power of "conceit." "The Elixir" is not, as it looks as if it were going to be, a poem about visionary ascent; nor is it, as it once was, a poem about actually doing things well.[83] Rather, it is about the transforming power of a fiction—or, more accurately, of an attitude:

Teach me, my God and King,
In all things thee to see,
And what I do in any thing,
    To do it as for thee.   [1–4]

Doing things "as for" God turns out to be the "tincture" through which even the meanest activity can "grow bright and clean" (lines 11–16). But these actions—like sweeping a room, in the example Herbert gives (line 19)—are not changed in their nature. God does not

---

80. Halewood's reading of line 32 of "Faith" as a denial of predestination and limited atonement is entirely noncontextual (*Poetry of Grace*, p. 104). The line does not treat these issues. Herbert is not "liberalizing" Reformation doctrine here; he is expressing it.

81. In a striking departure from his stated editorial policy (see p. lxxv), Hutchinson follows "W" rather than *both* "B" and "1633" in omitting the comma after line 34 here. To omit this comma blurs the distinction between imputed and actual "lustre." It makes "the sunne" rather than God the agent of the verbs of line 35. The textual sleight-of-hand here might be doctrinally motivated.

82. See p. 120 above.

83. On "The Elixir" seeming to prepare for a visionary ascent, see Stein, *Herbert's Lyrics*, pp. 202–3; on the original version of the poem (entitled "Perfection"), see Stein, pp. 139–41, and Helen C. White, *The Metaphysical Poets: A Study in Religious Experience* (1936; rpt. New York, 1962), pp. 178–82. On pp. 174–75, White uses "The Elixir" to speak of "the sacramental principle" in what seems to me an overly ontological way.

"supplie [their] want" by adding anything to them but by acknowl-
edging and accepting the frame of mind (or heart) in which they are
done.

In the final stanza of "The Elixir," Herbert first reasserts the out-
landish claim that "this clause" ("as for thee") is the tincture, the
famous philosopher's stone, and then, as always in contexts like this,
seriously defends the claim:

> For that which God doth touch and own
> Cannot for lesse be told.   [23–24]

Any action done, as Tyndale puts it, "within the law of God, in faith,
and with thanksgiving to God"—any action in which the agent
"touches and owns" God (makes Him as "The Elixir" says "prepos-
sest")—is touched and owned by God.[84] God's acceptance of these
actions makes them "gold, and much more, just."[85] And this accep-
tance, as we have seen, is not based on the inherent greatness of the
acts or the perfection with which they are done. God's favor, as
Herbert says elsewhere, gives them savor ("An Offering," lines 37–
42). Again, a servant or a peasant can "reach the highest stature."
When Sibbes was explaining how common actions performed "with
an eye to God" are all *religious* actions, he came very close to Herbert's
poem: "For the grace of God is a blessed Alcumist; where it touches
it makes good and religious."[86]

Our treatment of the value which Herbert placed on poetry must
end with a consideration of "The Forerunners," Herbert's most com-
prehensive poem on the subject. Like Yeats's "The Circus Animals'
Desertion," "The Forerunners" is a great poem about feeling unable,
through old age, to write great poems.[87] "The Forerunners" presents
the whole range of attitudes toward poetry which Herbert has pre-
viously expressed or represented. It dramatizes Herbert's struggle to
face up to the radical devaluations of poetry implicit in "Jordan" (II)
and "The Altar" and explicit in "A true Hymne." Autobiography in

84. *The Parable of the Wicked Mammon, Doctrinal Treatises,* p. 100. Compare Luther,
"Preface to Romans," p. 26; *Babylonian Captivity (Pagan Servitude),* p. 311; *That These
Words . . . Still Stand Firm against the Fanatics, LW,* XXXVII, 92.

85. "Easter," part 1, lines 5–6. As Breiner, ("Herbert's Cockatrice," p. 13) points out,
Herbert here, as in "The Elixir," mocks the literal conception of alchemy and of Christ
as "the Stone." In "An Offering," Herbert mocks the idea of a literal panacea (the elixir
was supposed to cure all diseases).

86. *Commentary on II Corinthians I, Works,* III, 257. Compare Calvin, *Institutes,* III.x.6.

87. Although Joseph E. Duncan in *The Revival of Metaphysical Poetry: The History of a
Style, 1800 to the Present* (Minneapolis, 1959), pp. 135–36, points out a number of echoes
of Herbert in Yeats (especially of "Vertue" in "A Friend's Illness" and of "The Collar"
in "Father and Child"), I am not claiming that "The Circus Animals' Desertion" was
directly influenced by "The Forerunners." The possibility, however, is intriguing.

this poem is not stylized into comedy. Like "The Crosse," "The Fore-runners" emphasizes the human cost of attitudes which Herbert else-where expressed with great serenity. And, like "The Crosse," it shows Herbert willing to pay the price.

The poem begins bluntly with a plain but cryptic statement which it then excitedly elaborates. "The Forerunners" is clearly going to be a poem of vigorous dramatic speech rather than of calm or polished lyricism; it is going to use its mainly pentameter stanzas the way the dramatists used blank verse:

> The harbingers are come. See, see their mark;
> White is their colour, and behold my head.   [1–2]

The first half of line 1 is calm and factual; the second half is almost overemphatic. The speaker seems to have an extraordinary invest-ment in his point. The second line ends on the self-satisfied note of a magician unveiling a trick or a logician concluding a proof. But just as we, with the viewer-auditor, grasp the harbinger–white hair con-ceit, the verse becomes animated again and we realize that the em-phatic quality of the opening expresses bitterness, not merely insistence on a point. This whole stanza takes on the speed of "See, see their mark" as the speaker bursts resentfully into a flurry of questions:

> But must they have my brain? must they dispark
> Those sparkling notions, which therein were bred?
>   Must dulnesse turn me to a clod?   [3–5]

This speaker identifies strongly with his "brain" and the "sparkling notions which therein were bred." His "brain" is him ("Must dulnesse turn me to a clod?"), and he has only disdain for "clods" (country people?). His complaint is poignant and immediately intelligible, but in the light of many poems which precede "The Forerunners" in Herbert's volume, it is difficult to have unqualified sympathy with the terms in which this speaker phrases his distress. We may recall the "clod" in "Divinitie," who bears comparison with the brainy folk of that poem rather well. More directly, we recall the misguided earlier self of "Jordan" (II) who also spoke prominently of his "brain" and who was also fertile in "notions" and much taken with "lustre." We have learned from these poems, as from "Sinnes Round," to be dis-trustful of "sparkling notions" bred in the brain. Yet even within the lines we have reason for distrust. There is something almost desper-ately witty about them. They seem to be a case of sound taking precedence over sense. The "disparking" of "sparkling notions" is a dazzling figure of sound but difficult to unpack as a figure of sense. We are almost relieved when we arrive at the plain statement on which the stanza ends:

> Yet have they left me, *Thou art still my God.*   [6]

The tone here is very close to Yeats's "Maybe at last, being but a broken man, / I must be satisfied with my heart" ("Circus Animals," lines 3–4). The speaker has not chosen what remains to him; he merely finds that he has been left something. In the next stanza, Herbert's speaker tries to make a virtue of necessity. "Good men ye be," he says rather stiffly, "to leave me my best room" (line 7). In explicating his metaphor, the speaker's language begins to take on some real warmth of affirmation—"Ev'n all my heart" (line 8a). Herbert does not seem to have quite Yeats's feeling of *merely* my heart. Yet the rest of line 8, "and what is lodged there," is extremely abstractly phrased, and the lines which follow are a model of protesting too much or whistling in the dark:

> I passe not, I, what of the rest become,
> So *Thou art still my God,* be out of fear.   [9–10]

"I passe not, I, what of the rest become" sounds like Astrophil in some of his most comically and obviously self-deceived moments ("I may, I must, I can, I will, I do").[88] The speaker of "The Forerunners" has not earned his right to speak so cavalierly of "the rest," including, of course, his precious "brain." He is making his affirmation, but with, as Guildenstern says of Hamlet's gentlemanlike welcome, "much forcing of his disposition."

The feeling of someone making an official rather than a "hart-deep" affirmation culminates in the final lines of the stanza (used as if they were a full couplet). Of *"Thou art still my God,"* the speaker asserts:

> He will be pleased with that dittie;
> And if I please him, I write fine and wittie.   [11–12]

This refers directly to the position of "A true Hymne." What makes this formulation of the position problematic is not that the lines are themselves "egregiously witty,"[89] but that the speaker's stress is entirely on what God will be pleased with. The speaker is appealing to God's will and His standards, but not accepting this will as his own. He is putting aside—in a way that the speaker of "A true Hymne" does not—the whole question of his own pleasure.

To emphasize pleasing God regardless of the emotional price of doing so is a perfectly intelligible religious position, and one with

---

88. *Astrophil and Stella,* sonnet 47. It seems reasonable to suppose that Herbert, like Donne, learned this technique of comic first-person dramatization from Sidney.

89. *Self-Consuming Artifacts,* p. 218. Fish's analysis of "The Forerunners" appears on pp. 216–23.

which, as we know from "To all Angels and Saints," Herbert was fully familiar. Yet it is not a position characteristic of Herbert. His view of the religious life is not normally so dour.[90] Yet thematically "The Forerunners" could end here. The speaker has articulated a point of view from which the fineness that he feared to lose is seen to be religiously irrelevant. Fineness and wit, however, have not been shown to be personally irrelevant. The poem has attained closure only thematically, not emotionally and psychologically. The content of the poet's impending loss has been dealt with, but the "affect" of it, so strong in stanza 1, has not been. Herbert demonstrates his awareness of this by dramatizing an act of ineffective closure. The speaker attempts to take his situation in hand, to bid a calm and tender farewell to the products of his poetic abilities. He tries to sound as if he were leaving them, or as if he can watch them depart with emotion but without panic:

> Farewell sweet phrases, lovely metaphors.   [13]

This line is the beginning of the third stanza, and as soon as it is said, the poem opens up again rather than gracefully and elegiacally closing. When the speaker actually begins thinking about the "sweet phrases" and "lovely metaphors," the anger and resentment of the opening resurfaces. "But will ye leave me thus?" (line 14a) echoes the tone and phrasing of "But must they have my brain?" (line 3a) as if the intervening stanza of reflection and resolution had never existed. Like Yeats, Herbert is led to review his poetic career by the prospect of losing his poetic abilities. Continuing to address the sweet phrases and lovely metaphors directly, Herbert recounts what he has done for them:

> when ye before
> Of stews and brothels onely knew the doores,
> Then did I wash you with my tears, and more,
>   Brought you to Church well drest and clad.   [14b–17]

The line in which Herbert summarizes his motives for having done all this is phrased partly in the present and partly in the past:

> My God must have my best, ev'n all I had.   [18]

A major difference now emerges between Herbert's poem and Yeats's. Whereas Yeats surveys his whole poetic career with a certain detachment and irony throughout ("Lion and woman *and the Lord knows what* . . . Themes of the embittered heart, *or so it seems*"), Herbert presents himself as harking back only to the beginning of his

90. See Strier, " 'To all Angels and Saints': Herbert's Puritan Poem," pp. 132–45.

poetic career and doing so without, from the dramatized point of view, any irony. Herbert, presumably, is conscious of the different and even opposed meanings of "my best" in "My God must have my best" and "to leave me my best room" but the speaker of "The Forerunners" is not. Herbert wants, as Yeats does not, to recreate his actual state of mind as a younger poet. We can now see the psychological and dramatic point of the echoes of "Jordan" (II). Herbert presents his panic at losing his poetic powers as returning him to his state of mind "When first [his] lines of heav'nly joyes made mention." Line 18 of "The Forerunners," "My God must have my best, ev'n all I had," exactly restates the attitude of "Nothing could seem too rich to clothe the sunne" ("Jordan" [II], line 11).

Again the poem seems to come to a full stop. The third stanza, like the second, has ended with a generalized assertion of the poet's proper relationship to God, although the two formulations are radically opposed. The fourth stanza opens up again in the same way the third did. Again, the energies released in the body of a stanza have not been fully resolved by its final assertion. Stanza 3 ended by reasserting the transcended position dramatized in "Jordan"(II), but the body of the stanza evokes a state of mind even earlier in Herbert's development. The language of redeeming poetry from "stews and brothels" recalls "Love" (I) and (II) and, behind them, the earliest poems we have of Herbert's, the sonnets to his mother preserved in Walton's *Life*.[91] The contrast between "Venus' livery" (conceived of as whorish) and God's is precisely the terminology of the first juvenile sonnet. The concern of these sonnets, and of "Love" (I) and (II), with sublimating and redirecting eroticism is strongly present in the third stanza of "The Forerunners."

Like Yeats, Herbert is intensely aware of the erotic component in his earliest relation to poetry, but unlike Yeats, he wants to give this component nondetached expression (Yeats mocks his earliest poetic self for being "starved for the bosom of [Oisin's] faery bride"). In the fourth stanza Herbert gives up the coolness and control he momentarily attained in "Farewell sweet phrases, lovely metaphors" for an attempt at metaphorically evoking the sweetness of the metaphors and phrases. In this stanza, contemplation of the pleasures of poetry produces a kind of ecstasy which, in its turn, produces panic and something like jealousy. Where the first stanza emphasized the "spar-

91. Walton, *Life*, p. 268. Walton says Herbert sent the sonnets to his mother "for a New-yeare gift" in "the first year of his going to Cambridge" (p. 267). Herbert matriculated on December 18, 1609 (see Hutchinson, p. xxv; Amy M. Charles, *A Life of George Herbert* [Ithaca, 1977], p. 66). He was sixteen. On the relation between the Walton sonnets and "Love" (I) and (II), see Tuve, *A Reading*, p. 192; Stein, *Herbert's Lyrics*, pp. 2–4; Fish, *Self-Consuming Artifacts*, pp. 191–93.

kling" quality of poetry, its wit and "invention," the fourth stanza develops the erotic content that has now been introduced, emphasizing sensual qualities:

> Lovely enchanting language, sugar-cane,
> Honey of roses, whither wilt thou flie?
> Hath some fond lover tic'd thee to thy bane?
> And wilt thou leave the Church, and love a stie?   [19–22]

The end of the stanza develops the idea expressed in "tic'd thee *to thy bane.*" The speaker's concern is not for his own state, but for poetry itself and for poets:

> Fie, thou wilt soil thy broider'd coat,
> And hurt thy self, and him that sings the note.   [23–24]

Although these lines begin with an expletive which is intensified by picking up the rhyme from the previous line, they grow calmer and less abrupt as they proceed. Together with the contrast to "fond" lovers, the element of "other-directed" concern serves to stabilize somewhat the emotional state Herbert is dramatizing. In the next stanza Herbert presents the voice of his earliest poetic self at its most assured and, as Fish says, philosophically respectable. This voice is concerned entirely with the proper use of poetry, which it conceives as synonymous with eloquence. In the third stanza, the departure of poetry from the speaker was unfair *to him* ("But will ye leave me thus?"); in the fourth, it was harmful to itself ("thou wilt soil thy broider'd coat"); in the fifth, it violates fundamental principles. Herbert's voice is now authoritative:

> Let foolish lovers, if they will love dung,
> With canvas, not with arras, clothe their shame:
> Let follie speak in her own native tongue.   [25–27]

Herbert approaches the hysteria of the Walton sonnets in "if they will love dung" but attains clarity and evenness at "Let follie speak in her own native tongue" (line 27). This line is a corollary of the Ciceronian or Isocratean view that eloquence is the "native tongue" of wisdom.[92] The rest of the stanza presents itself as elaborating this position. It makes what has rightly been called a handsome statement, but one

---

92. "Eloquence," said Cicero, "is nothing other than wisdom speaking fully" (*Nihil enim est aliud eloquentia nisi copiose loquens sapientia*), *De partitione oratoria*, trans. Henry Rackham (Cambridge, Mass., 1942), p. 368 (translation slightly amended). For the centrality of this view to Renaissance humanism, see Hanna H. Gray, "Renaissance Humanism: The Pursuit of Eloquence," in *Renaissance Essays*, ed. Paul Oskar Kristeller and Philip Wiener (New York, 1968), pp. 199–216.

which, when examined, raises more problems than it solves.⁹³ The
exposition is disposed into separate assertions in a manner that seems
virtually syllogistic:

> True beautie dwells on high: ours is a flame
> But borrow'd thence to light us thither.
> Beautie and beauteous words should go together.   [28–30]

The main problem with this conclusion is that it does not seem to
follow from its premises. If beauty is taken as standing in for wisdom
as the opposite of "follie," line 30 would follow better from line 27
than it does from 28–29. These latter lines point to what Stein calls
the "Platonic division" rather than to the "Platonic solution"; they
suggest, in Herschel Baker's terms, *echt* Platonism rather than Neo-
platonism.⁹⁴ Rather than dignifying our earthly beauty they seem to
accord it only, as Lovejoy paraphrasing *The Symposium* puts it, "the
use that belongs to steps."⁹⁵ Our beauty exists only "to light us thither";
"true beautie" is sharply distinct from "ours." In this context, line 30
is intellectually puzzling and rhetorically weak ("*should* go together").
The beauty to which the line refers is obviously meant to be "true
beautie," but the thrust of the previous lines is that when we arrive
at *that* beauty we shall have no more need of "ours"—including,
presumably, "beauteous words." The transcendentalism of lines 28–
29 undermines the harmony posited in line 30. The top of the Platonic
ladder is nonverbal.

The impulse to celebrate and purify the beauties and pleasures of
poetic language has been allowed to run its full course and to attain
its own kind of dignity. Herbert has located the attitudes expressed
in stanzas 1 and 3–5 of "The Forerunners" in a fully dramatized
moment of psychological stress and has related these attitudes to
positions and gestures criticized or abandoned earlier in "The Church."
He has allowed the atavistic impulse which broke out in the first
stanza to "speak in her own native tongue," and he has done so
without explicitly presenting the impulse as "follie." The pressures
which an official resolution would have had to suppress have been
allowed to run themselves into the ground and reveal their own
inherent contradictions. Herbert can now return in a calmer way to
the resolution which the second stanza prematurely attempted. Again

93. See Stein, *Herbert's Lyrics*, p. 17. Stein's discussion of "The Forerunners" appears
on pp. 17–19.
94. Ibid., for the first distinction; for the second, see Herschel Baker, *The Image of
Man: A Study of the Idea of Human Dignity in Classical Antiquity, the Middle Ages, and the
Renaissance* (1947; rpt. New York, 1961), p. 248 (originally published as *The Dignity of
Man*).
95. *The Great Chain of Being*, p. 90, paraphrasing *Symposium*, 211C.

directly addressing the phrases, metaphors, and notions of poetry, he opens the final stanza with a serene declaration: "Yet if you go, I passe not; take your way" (line 31).

This line truly has a double motion in "The Forerunners." On the one hand it throws us back to line 9 ("I passe not, I, what of the rest become") which it both duplicates and rewrites, and on the other hand it exercises, as Fish has observed, a remarkable retroactive effect on the end of the previous stanza. It alters its entire meaning. The word "go" in "Beautie and beauteous words should go together" (line 30) seems to function in this poem the way "forlorn" does in the "Ode to a Nightingale"—it "tolls" the poet back to his initial situation. Once line 31 is read, "Beautie" in line 30 becomes earthly rather than "true," and the line becomes a renunciation of both "Beautie and beauteous words" ("go" as "depart" rather than "keep company"). In this final stanza, Herbert makes his gesture of resignation more calmly than he did in stanza 2, and also offers a discursive explanation rather than merely a series of logically related but syntactically disjunct assertions. He even grants something to the sweet phrases and lovely metaphors:

> Yet if you go, I passe not; take your way:
> For, *Thou art still my God*, is all that ye
> Perhaps with more embellishment can say.   [31–33]

A great deal of weight has been placed on this "Perhaps." Stein finds it "a little disappointing" that words are dismissed here "as if they were no more than a conventional garment of style," but he adds rather ruefully that Herbert "does at least say 'perhaps' "; Martz, committed to the view of Herbert as a "devout humanist," saw "a world of reservation [in] that one word, so emphatically placed."[96] But is this "perhaps" emphatically placed? Since it follows a nonendstopped line and is part of a qualifying phrase which functions as a single unit, we tend to read right through it. The qualifying phrase is not a "world of reservation" but a small concession. Witty and lovely phrases can do *something*—they can provide embellishment for "the sense," the "plain intention."[97] Herbert returns from the immaturities of his critique of love poetry to the sobriety of his critique of the importance of verbal fineness to sincere religious expression. He is not conceding very much.

From a structural point of view, the final stanza of "The Forerunners" is very close to the previous one. Against the "sweet phrases,

---

96. Stein, *Herbert's Lyrics*, p. 17; Martz, *Meditation*, p. 314.

97. This is the Ramist attitude toward rhetoric (see Miller, *New England Mind*, chap. 11). Herbert's relation to Ramism remains to be explored.

[and] lovely metaphors" of religious poetry, Herbert uses the structure which his earlier voice had used against secular poetry and poets. Like Yeats in "A Coat," though for different reasons, Herbert realizes that there can be "more enterprise" in "walking naked." He dismisses the phrases and metaphors with a final metaphor: "Go birds of spring" (line 34a). Fish sees this metaphor as again showing the speaker "caressing what he is relinquishing." But this phrase, like the title image of "The Rose," which immediately follows "The Forerunners," allows Herbert to make a concession to beauty while still suggesting its basic unreliability. In the second half of the line and in the short line which follows, the poem begins to sound rather grim—"let winter have his fee; / Let a bleak paleness chalk the doore" (lines 34b–35). The attitude truly seems, as Vendler says, to be Stoic.[98] Herbert seems to be merely acceding to the inevitable; these "Let's" are different from the commanding ones of the previous stanza. The final line, however, changes all this. The concessive "Let's" are merely part of a conditional construction. The imagery of winter turns out to be unexpectedly positive:

> So all within be livelier than before.   [36]

The seasonal imagery yields something like the contrast between outdoor cold and indoor coziness of the winter song at the end of *Love's Labours Lost*. The poem comes to a positive conclusion when it shifts to conceiving of the heart rather than the brain as what is "within." The liveliness that matters is not that of "sparkling notions" but, as in "A true Hymne," of the heart feeling more and more "loved." The speaker does not have to rest in the cold comfort of "if I please him, I write fine and wittie." He expects to receive something himself, an inner liveliness for which he is completely willing to renounce the pleasures of wit and versing. And he expects to receive this feeling, this inner "quickness," in the present or the immediate future. The poem does not, as Fish argues, offer hope only after death. It does not consider the afterlife at all. What ultimately distinguishes "The Forerunners" most sharply from "The Circus Animals' Desertion" is the strongly positive quality of Herbert's ending. Like Herbert, Yeats is able, in his final stanza, to remake more successfully a renunciatory gesture which he had tried to make earlier—"Maybe . . . I must be satisfied" becomes "I must lie down"—and, like Herbert, Yeats finds that he will be left, finally, with only his heart "and what is lodged there," but for Yeats the problem is that what he finds there is not an assertion of confidence in God but "the foul rag-and-bone shop" out of which all human aspirations and ideals must initially emerge.

98. *Poetry of Herbert*, p. 124.

Even if Yeats's ending is seen as embodying some form of tragic joy, Herbert's is more positive.

"The Forerunners" is Herbert's final statement on the relative value of emotion and art. Like "A true Hymne," it reveals the relation between the rejection of the value of poetry and the impulses which impelled the Spiritualists and radicals of the Reformation and English revolution. The radicals were those who truly wanted to "walk naked" from a liturgical point of view and to rely *solely* on the vitality of the Holy Spirit "lodged" in the heart.[99] In a comment that reveals how easily aesthetic issues slip into religious ones in the criticism of Herbert's poetry, Stein proposes what can rightly be described as an Anglican reading of "The Forerunners": "As the Visible Church stands truly, beautifully, but imperfectly for the Invisible Church, so the 'sweet phrases, lovely metaphors' express imperfectly the 'True beautie' on high." This blurs the contrast that Herbert keeps sharp. "The Forerunners" and "A true Hymne" should serve to show us that despite his undoubted personal loyalty to the fitly (but *not* finely) dressed British Church, Herbert's ultimate commitment was to the Spirit and to "feeling." At the crucial moments, Herbert never forgot that "the chiefe thing which God in Scriptures requires, is the heart, and the spirit, and to worship him in truth, and in spirit" (*CP*, p. 279). In relation to this, all other matters, however sweet, beautiful, or even fit, are merely "the rest." Herbert never held that anything intellectual, visible, or external was essential to salvation. What was essential was conative and "within," a matter of the heart.

99. For the relation between the radicals and the orthodox or magisterial reformers, see pp. 145–46 above.

8

The Limits of Experience

Herbert's extraordinary respect for emotion and for personal experience should by now be clear. What remains to be explored is whether there are limits to Herbert's commitment to experience and "feeling." "The Forerunners" helps to point us to these limits. It shows Herbert's respect for emotion in the priority it gives to the heart "and what is lodged there," and in its willingness to allow the emotions, even when clearly misguided, to speak in their "own native tongue." The poem both allows the emotions full expression and places the contents of their expression. This double commitment to both expression and judgment produces some of Herbert's most complex poetry. It exemplifies Eliot's definition of true wit—"a constant inspection and criticism of experience," a recognition, implicit in the expression of experience, of other kinds of experience which are possible.[1]

In Herbert, there is a theological basis for this double commitment. The fact that faith was an experience accounts for one half of it. The fact that faith was not merely an experience accounts for the other. "If you had experience," Cardinal Newman is quoted as remarking, "how would it be faith?"[2] This is a shrewd question and shows a much more profound grasp of historical Protestantism than is present in talk of "dryness," but it does not reveal a problem of which the reformers were unaware. Although faith was an experience, it was not a continuous one. As many—perhaps most—poems in *The Temple* show, the life of the regenerate was not a continuous ecstasy. The

1. "Andrew Marvell," *Selected Essays*, p. 262.
2. Wilfrid Ward, *The Life of John Henry Cardinal Newman* (London, 1912), II, 277 (quoted in Nuttall, *Holy Spirit*, p. 92 n.).

"sense of Heav'ns desertion" was a familiar experience to them. Luther argues that God often "hides His grace" to teach us to think of Him not "according to our own feelings and reactions" but rather "according to His word."[3] Faith both produces and is contradicted by experience. In moments of negative feeling, faith relies on the evidence of something not seen or (immediately) felt.[4] "The promises of the gospel," Downame explained, "are not restrained to those who [always] feel their faith, but to those that have faith."[5]

The Christian who is feeling deserted by heaven has, as we have seen, the right to complain.[6] What he cannot properly do is draw conclusions on the basis of his feelings. Downame notes in this context, as does Sibbes, that "arguments drawn out of sense and feeling often fail."[7] Luther stated that in times of spiritual temptation, "the devil can so aggravate sin, that during the conflict [the Christian] thinketh himself to be utterly overthrown, and feeleth nothing else but the wrath of God and desperation"; Luther warned that "here in any wise let [the Christian] not follow his own feeling."[8] There is a major difference between complaining and concluding. This distinction brings into focus the structure and much of the meaning of "The Collar," Herbert's most famous "complaint." The significance of the structure of this poem has not been sufficiently noted.

"The Collar" begins in an unusually straightforward and dramatic way. It describes an action rather than a situation, and it describes this action in a naturalistic, mainly noncomic manner. "I struck the board, and cry'd" contrasts, for instance, with "I threatened to observe the strict decree." We are presented with a figure first physically signifying and then stating that he has made a decision; he cried, "No more. / I will abroad" (lines 1b–2). "The Collar" begins where "Hope" ended—"I'le *no more, no more* I'le bring" (or in this case, endure). We would expect that the next lines, perhaps the rest of the poem, would narrate what the speaker did and encountered "abroad," producing a poem like "The Pilgrimage." But instead of presenting the results of his decision, the speaker presents a justification of it. Shakespeare used this technique to dramatize ambivalent or inau-

---

3. *Luther's Church Postil, Second Sunday in Lent*, Sermon on Matthew 15:21–28, in *The Precious and Sacred Writings of Martin Luther*, tr. John Nicholas Lenker (Minneapolis, 1906), XI, 152 (slightly amended); *WA*, XVII^ii, 203.

4. See Luther, "Commentary on Psalm 68," *LW*, XIII, 22 ff.; *Bondage of the Will*, p. 101; *Commentary on Galatians*, ed. Watson, pp. 509–10.

5. *Christian Warfare*, p. 257a; see also 106a.

6. See pp. 176–79 above.

7. *Christian Warfare*, p. 251b; Sibbes, *The Bruised Reed and Smoking Flax, Works*, I, 58.

8. *Commentary on Galatians*, p. 509. See also Calvin, *Commentary on the Psalms*, I, 182.

thentic decisions.[9] We realize that the poem is dramatizing a state of mind rather than a decision. By the third line we could already guess that the speaker did not, in fact, go anywhere. His firm assertions immediately yield to a question: "What? shall I ever sigh and pine?" (line 3).

We have heard questions and statements like this before. Just two poems earlier, we heard "No end?" and many other such questions in "Longing"; in "Complaining," we heard "Am I all throat or eye, / To weep or crie? / Have I no parts but those of grief?"; in "Deniall," the speaker's "thoughts" said "as good go any where" ("abroad" in line 2 of "The Collar" is notably unspecified). "The Collar" seems to be another legitimate and allowed expression of need, of the heart's frustration at God's apparent indifference. "The Collar" is somewhat different from the poems we have cited, however, in the orientation of its opening assertion and in its lack of an explicitly dialogal framework. This voice is speaking to itself, not to God. Consciously at least, it is not depositing its groans in God's bosom. The next lines seem unequivocally self-directed; the speaker makes an assertion and then attempts to convince himself of it:

> My lines and life are free; free as the rode;
> Loose as the winde, as large as store. [4–5]

The reader hears a rather pathetic "Aren't they?" under these apparently bold assertions. The analogies are either hackneyed or almost tautological ("large as store"). These lines do not seem to express any definite or considered conception of freedom, and their claim to be "free" is undercut by their providing the first two rhymes in the poem. Duplicating the movement from lines 1 and 2 to line 3, the speaker turns from a failed attempt at convincing assertion to a mode in which he cannot fail of authenticity, that of the complaining question:

> Shall I be still in suit?
> Have I no harvest but a thorn
> To let me bloud, and not restore
> What I have lost with cordiall fruit? [6–9]

Herbert seems to be doing all he can here to lead us to perceive this speaker, like his impatient cousin in "Hope," as another beneficiary of "love unknown." Many critics have noted the references,

9. The clearest example is probably Brutus's soliloquy in *Julius Caesar*, II.i.10–34; see also Iago's soliloquies in *Othello*, I.iii.380–98, II.i.285–306.

unintended by the speaker, to the Crucifixion and the Eucharist here.[10] The speaker, like every regenerate Christian, is feeling Christ's experience psychologically duplicated in himself, yet he does not take any comfort in, or apparently even perceive, this continuity. Like the equally unhappy but much more theologically aware speaker of "The Bunch of Grapes," this speaker is experiencing all the painfulness of biblical experience without any of its joys. The way in which the speaker of "The Collar" sees himself—as a man pining for absent fruit—is exactly the way Herbert presents "The Jews" in the poem immediately preceding "The Collar." This juxtaposition implicitly establishes the correlations which "The Bunch of Grapes" explicitly builds upon. The complaining voice of "The Collar," however, never even intellectually realizes that he has "their [the Jews'] fruit and more" ("The Bunch of Grapes," line 23).[11]

The speaker of this section of "The Collar" is also unclear about the sort of "fruit" he wants. He seems to think he wants a literal cordial. He seems to ignore *both* the physicality and the significance of the Eucharistic elements. He ventures another set of assertions with results even more ludicrous than in his previous attempts. He reminds himself that the physical world does exist—or used to:

> Sure there was wine
> Before my sighs did drie it: there was corn
> Before my tears did drown it.   [10–12]

There is no doubt what the speaker means here, but it is equally clear that he is not quite saying it. He is not rhetorically sophisticated enough to master hyperbole or mock-hyperbole, but when he returns to the questioning mode he expresses himself with precision:

10. See especially Jeffrey Hart, "Herbert's 'The Collar' Re-read," in W. R. Keast, ed., *Seventeenth-Century Poetry: Modern Essays in Criticism*, rev. ed. (New York, 1971), pp. 249–56. Hart, however, too easily assumes that because the natural imagery of the poem "is also the imagery traditionally associated with the Eucharist," the *solution* of the poem must also, therefore, be sacramental (p. 249). Moreover, Hart seems to attribute to Herbert views of the Eucharist and the priesthood that he certainly did not hold. Hart speaks of transubstantiation (p. 254) and suggests that Herbert believed "the priest who administers the Eucharist" to be a "child of God" in some special sense that does not include all other regenerate Christians (p. 256).

11. In *The Living Temple*, pp. 140–42, Fish suggests some general reasons why "The Jews" was included in *The Temple*, but does not attempt to account for its specific position. His reading of "The Jews" ignores its apocalyptic-millennial content and obscures the contrast (being missed by the dramatized speaker of "The Collar") between the historical situation of the Jews and that of the regenerate Christian. The latter do not have to wait for the apocalypse to feel the "sweet sap" of grace.

Is the yeare onely lost to me?   [13]

This is powerful and surprisingly carefully expressed; the next lines
of the poem elaborate:

Have I no bayes to crown it?
No flowers, no garlands gay? all blasted?
All wasted?   [14–16]

The speaker feels "dried up," incapable of any kind of responsive-
ness. Everywhere around him he finds natural fruition and "natural"
responses to it ("bayes to crown" the season). The speaker's complaint
becomes more poignant and his dramatic situation more definite if
we view "The Collar" as written or imagined at the harvest season.
If we recall that Herbert's parson celebrates communion both "afore
and after Harvest," and if we also recall how large a percentage of
his yearly communions this is,[12] both the presence of Eucharistic im-
agery in the poem and the problem of the speaker's lack of a strong
response to this imagery become more intelligible. The complaining
speaker seems to want to participate, Herrick-like, in actually or po-
etically decking the hock-cart. His questions are not merely rhetorical.
He is truly not sure whether he is capable of the response he would
like to imagine. This lack of certainty is what undermines his "bold"
assertions. "No flowers, no garlands gay" seems, in fact, to call for
a "yes" rather than a "no" answer.

The key to much of the meaning of "The Collar" lies in a shift which
takes place after the questions of lines 13–16. The "blasted . . . wasted"
rhyme in lines 15 and 16 brings the cry recollected in the poem to a
full stop. After line 16, there are no more questions. The rhetorical
mode of the poem becomes hortatory and genuinely assertive; the
grammatical mode changes from first to second person. According to
Summers, the voice of the poem shifts from being that of the heart
to being that of the will here.[13] There can be no doubt that the speaker
of lines 1b–16 is identified with the heart—"Not so, my heart" is the
first utterance of the second narrated voice—but this second voice
should not be identified with the will. Helen White notes that the
line of argument in the poem "falls from the humanist to the mate-
rialist and opportunist." She confuses the issue, however, by speaking
of the "dikes of reason" being swept away as the poem proceeds.[14]
The striking feature of the second narrated voice in "The Collar" (lines
17–32) is its commitment not to passion but to reason. This voice is

12. See "The Parson in Sacraments" (*CP*, p. 259): "touching the frequency of the
Communion, the Parson celebrates it, if not duly once a month, yet at least five or six
times in the year."
13. *Herbert*, p. 91; adopted by Hart, "Herbert's 'The Collar' Re-read," *passim*.
14. *The Metaphysical Poets*, pp. 172–73.

much calmer and more even in tone than the previous one, and much more intellectual. It even begins to establish a more ordered prosody. No line in this section is unrhymed, no rhyme in this section is delayed more than three lines, no feminine endings occur, and the separated rhymes are used in such as way as to approach framing couplets or cross rhymes.[15]

We recall that Herbert presented sin primarily as intellectual. What he is dramatizing in the body of "The Collar" is the way in which reason can attempt to corrupt the heart by building upon its perfectly intelligible and "natural" frustrations and desires. Natural desire is not what frightens Herbert; natural reason is. The best gloss on "The Collar" is "Nature," the first lines of which present the major meaning of "the flesh" for Herbert: "Full of rebellion, I would die, / Or fight, or travell." The next item in this list is the most sinister; it involves an intellectual claim rather than an erratic impulse—"or denie / That thou has ought to do with me." The second stanza continues, "if thou shalt let this venome lurk / And in suggestions fume and work, / My soul will turn to bubbles straight" (lines 7–9). The venom of nature is at its most truly destructive when it works "in suggestions." We recall the language of wit and poison in the first stanza of "Assurance."

Herbert means us to shudder when the second narrated voice of "The Collar" answers the heart's frustrated and baffled questions with a perfectly reasonable assertion:

> Not so, my heart: but there is fruit,
>   And thou hast hands.   [17–18]

This is cool and deliberate speech, although its association with the Fall of man is unmistakable. Suddenly the unconscious allusions of the language are damning rather than redemptive. The supervention of this voice on the previous one recalls a passage that Owen Watkins characterizes as "one of the most effective moments in Puritan literature," the moment when Satan, as Watkins puts it, "makes his first appearance as an active participant" in *Grace Abounding:*

> Therefore, this would still stick with me, How can you tell that you are elected? And what if you should not? How then? O Lord, thought I, what if I should not, indeed? It may be you are not, said the tempter; it may be so, indeed, thought I. Why, then, said Satan, you had a good leave off, and strive no further.[16]

---

15. Hart sees the line endings beginning to "reflect a gathering of order" as the poem proceeds, but only beginning with line 27 ("Herbert's 'The Collar' Re-read," p. 255).

16. *The Puritan Experience*, p. 111; *Grace Abounding*, par. 59–60.

As in "The Collar" the Satanic voice enters at precisely the moment when questions turn into assertions and, especially, into conclusions.

Where the heart had cried out for refreshment and some modicum of responsiveness, the reasoning voice, working "in suggestions," puts forth a much grander and more specific project:

> Recover all thy sigh-blown age
> On double pleasures   [19–20a]

What C. S. Lewis calls the "doom of nonsense" is beginning to fall on this voice as it did, much more transparently, on that of lines 4–5.[17] After this brief appeal to "double pleasures," however, the reasoning voice concentrates on negative characterizations of the heart's habitual state rather than on positive evocations of the alternatives to it. As if realizing that it can appeal more effectively to the heart's discomfort than to its capacity for fantasy, this voice characterizes the religious life as not merely one of constant longing ("still in suit") but as one of tiresome overscrupulousness. It brilliantly shifts from offering pleasure to parodying conscience—"leave thy cold dispute / Of what is fit, and not" (lines 20b–21a). In this mode the reasoning voice, which is "nothing if not critical," is at its most effective. The next injunction is its masterpiece. Where its previous remarks had been abrupt and paratactic, this one moves from an opening injunction to an elaborately subordinated and coordinated description:

> Forsake thy cage,
> Thy rope of sands
> Which pettie thoughts have made, and made to thee
> Good cable, to enforce and draw,
> And be thy law,
> While thou didst wink and wouldst not see.   [21b–26]

This is sophisticated indeed. Its imagery and argument are as elaborate as its syntax. Where the heart had longed for the simple goods of nature, this voice offers a complex analysis of the heart's situation. The difference between the voices is underscored by the rhyme connecting them. "Is the yeare onely lost to me?" expressed the heart's sense of isolation; the other voice's complementary "to thee" stresses the heart's subjectivity. This voice is making a point, not expressing a feeling. The difference is between a generalized longing to be in touch with nature and a *doctrine* of naturalism. The voice recreated in this address is that of Renaissance libertinism. We would call it a

---

17. *A Preface to Paradise Lost* (1942; rpt. New York, 1961), p. 97 (on Satan).

Nietzschean voice. It presents, in individual terms, a genealogy of morals.[18]

The essential strategy of this voice is to present the heart's situation as both unnatural and self-created. Only under very special circumstances can a "rope of sands" function effectively as a cage. The two elements of this conceit allow the persuading voice to acknowledge the subjective reality while denying the objective necessity of the heart's situation. The rest of the sentence explicates the conceit; "Pettie thoughts" is particularly effective, implying both triviality and meanness. These thoughts are presented as an external force which the heart has allowed to domineer over it through cowardice and half-conscious collusion ("While thou didst wink and wouldst not see"). The reasoning here is, of course, a tissue of fallacies—the heart is being bullied in the name of freedom; "thoughts" are seen has having no relation to the agent who thought them—but the important point, for the structure of the poem, is the fineness and intellectuality of the tissue.

At this moment, having presented its most subtle critique of the heart's situation, the reasoning voice exhorts the heart to act (having now a more solid basis for action) and appropriates the heart's initial cry as its own:

> Away; take heed:
> I will abroad. [27–28]

This is still the reasoning voice; the line which follows the repetition of "I will abroad" is "Call in thy deaths head there: tie up thy fears" (line 29), the last exhortation in the poem. This voice was perhaps mistaken to mention death at all, but it immediately proceeds to a mode even more congenial to it than exhortation:

> He that forbears
> To suit and serve his need,
> Deserves his load. [30–32]

The generalized prudential maxim is the perfect medium for this voice. This maxim at once puts forth its wisdom and absolves itself of any responsibility for those who fail to follow it (compare "Who say, I care not, those I give for lost" in "The Church-porch").[19] These lines, as Stein says, voice "a new law of reason," and the doom of nonsense falls heavily upon them.

---

18. Compare Stein, *Herbert's Lyrics*, p. 124 (citations of Stein on "The Collar" are all to this page); for background, see Louis I. Bredvold, "The Naturalism of Donne in Relation to Some Renaissance Traditions," *JEGP,* 22 (1923), 471–502.

19. Line 347; see Strier, "Herbert and the World," 227–29.

The final maxim of the reasoning voice virtually deconstructs itself. It reveals the conception of freedom which the libertine voice is offering as merely another form of bondage. We recognize Caliban's conception of freedom—being a new man through getting a new master. The repetition of "suit" makes the point. In place of being "still in suit" to an apparently indifferent master, the heart is offered the possibility of being in suit and service to its own need. The conception of freedom implied here involves not merely changing one form of service for another but changing one form for a more degraded one (again the example of Caliban is relevant). To spend one's life suiting and serving one's (physical) needs seems like bondage indeed. Were the heart to take this option, it would put itself in the position to say, with Marlowe's Faustus, "The God thou servest is thine own appetite."

The poem seems truly to have come, as Stein says, to "a monumental dead end." There seems to be no conception of freedom at all in it, merely of two kinds of service, one fruitless, the other degrading, both self-destructive. We seem to be viewing an impasse like that of "Affliction" (I), where the agonized and baffled speaker, thinking that he wishes to "change the service," can neither "go away, nor persevere." The reasoning voice's final maxim in "The Collar" implies an awareness that the heart might well not take its advice. The reasoner is covering itself, washing its hands of the matter, reconciling itself to its own failure. Oddly, there is a certain pathos in this voice here, in spite of its contemptuous tone. It seems to be acknowledging the limits of its power. We recall that the speaker is still, after all, standing at "the board."[20]

The coda of the poem restores the wholeness of the narrator's personality by including both voices in the "I" who "rav'd and grew more fierce and wilde," and it restores the narrator's sense of not living in a vacuum, of being in a relationship. Whether the call to which Herbert presents himself as responding is objective or subjective does not matter ("Me thoughts" necessarily raises the question).[21] What does matter is the presentation of the immediacy of his response to this call:

> Me thoughts I heard one calling, *Child!*
> And I reply'd, *My Lord.* [35–36]

20. A modern reader is inevitably reminded of " 'Well, shall we go? Yes, let's go.' *They do not move*" (the final words of both acts of *Waiting for Godot*). In "The Collar," however, Godot comes.

21. Barbara Leah Harman, "The Fiction of Coherence: George Herbert's 'The Collar,' " *PMLA*, 93 (1978), 875, uses this ambiguity to destabilize the ending of "The Collar."

Although the call is characterized as having been coextensive with all the "raving," it is dramatized as having been responded to as soon as it was clearly perceived. What makes this ending so satisfying is not merely the love implied in God's rebuke but the simplicity and "naturalness" of the human speaker's response. Just as it is natural for the speaker to complain and even "in suggestions fume and work," it is also natural for him to respond to his sense of God's love with his own love and with a readiness to serve.[22] He does not have to think to give his reply. It is spontaneous. This spontaneity is the true vision of freedom in the poem. It is what Luther called the freedom of a Christian, the capacity to serve God without a feeling of constraint and without having to worry about "fruit";[23] it is the capacity to have "Such a Heart, as joyes in love."[24]

"The Collar" is unusual among Herbert's poems in its lack of address to God, in its concern with *natural* pleasures, and in the especially sinister and sophistical way that the voice of reason builds upon the heart's complaints. Normally, as in "The Glimpse," which immediately follows "The Collar," Herbert's complaints have to do with the lack of specifically religious delight and comfort, or with the brevity and intermittency of such moments:

> For many weeks of lingring pain and smart
> But one half houre of comfort to my heart?
>
> [The Glimpse," lines 4–5]

Herbert sees natural reason building on the experiences of desolation and unevenness in various ways, all of them misguided but not all of them equally sinister. The first of the poems entitled "The Temper" embodies a critique of a certain very "natural," almost inevitable way of conceptualizing spiritual experiences.

The poem opens as if it were going to enact a fairly obvious form of folly, as if it were going to attempt to bribe God with the prospect of ungrudging and assiduous poetic praise. As the first stanza con-

22. "The Collar" is perhaps best read as a dramatization and exploration of what is "natural" to a regenerate Christian. Compare Vendler, *Poetry of Herbert*, p. 135, though I believe she misdescribes the paradoxes of the "natural" in the poem by putting them into the language of developmental psychology (building on Huxley, *Texts and Pretexts*, p. 90).

23. See *The Freedom of a Christian*, Dillenberger, p. 53: "Love by its very nature is ready to serve." See also *Freedom*, pp. 67–69, 74–76; "Preface to Romans," pp. 21–22, 30.

24. Herbert's "The Call," line 12. See Vendler's excellent comments on this line (*Poetry of Herbert*, p. 208), and Stein, *Herbert's Lyrics*, p. 146. The placement of "The Call" perhaps serves as a retroactive reminder that the heart as well as God is a "caller" in "The Collar." There is perhaps a sequence in the movement from "The Collar" through "The Glimpse" and "Assurance" to "The Call."

tinues, however, the speaker shifts from attempting to make his offer maximally desirable to contemplating the situation which leads him to make the offer in the first place. Address gives way to contemplation:

> How should I praise thee, Lord! how should my rymes
> Gladly engrave thy love in steel,
> If what my soul doth feel sometimes,
> My soul might ever feel!   [1–4]

The final tone here is wistful rather than assertive. The focus is less on what the speaker wants than on why he wants it. "What my soul doth feel sometimes" dominates the stanza. It is the only phrase in the indicative in the stanza, and, syntactically, the other lines lead to and from it. The sense of the speaker referring to something with which he is intimately familiar—a sense that is reinforced by the elliptical construction and the use of the historical (and psychological) present—gives the extrapolation from the known ("sometimes") to the unknown ("ever") the quality of fantasy rather than of demand. The poem is going to focus less on the speaker's attempt to bribe God than on his relation to the paradoxes of his own emotional experience.

The second stanza describes this experience. Whereas the first stanza contrasted "sometimes" with "ever," the second contrasts the wonderful moments of immediately feeling God's love with other moments in the speaker's experience. "Sometimes" becomes the key word. The odd thing about this stanza, however, is that it translates times into places. It correlates emotions with cosmological locations:

> Although there were some fourtie heav'ns, or more,
> Sometimes I peere above them all;
> Sometimes I hardly reach a score,
> Sometimes to hell I fall.   [5–8]

The device, familiar from Donne, of simultaneously using and mocking a particular framework always creates problems of tone.[25] Here the speaker's awareness of the absurdity of the framework he is using has the effect of making the first two lines seem either playful or consciously ingenuous, but his continuing commitment to the framework becomes more problematic. The absurdity of the framework does not seem to outweigh its usefulness as a way of characterizing and dramatizing the unevenness of his emotional experience. The vocabulary of "highs and lows" is almost inevitable in a phenomenological context, and, when the content of the emotions is religious,

25. See, for instance, "The Phoenix ridle hath more wit / By us" in "The Canonization," and the Holy Sonnet beginning, "At the round earths imagin'd corners, blow / Your trumpets, Angells." On the problems of tone this device creates, see Sanders, *Donne's Poetry*, pp. 21–22, 132.

the possibility arises of taking this vocabulary seriously in terms of mystical or visionary ascent. Perhaps there is meant to be humor in "I *peere* above them all," and perhaps "Sometimes I hardly reach a score" is mock rather than actual precision, but there is no mistaking the potential seriousness of "Sometimes to hell I fall."[26]

Still, this could all be playful. The speaker could be writing from within the experience or memory of one of the "highs." The immediate effect of the introduction of the spatial vocabulary into the poem, however, is to make explicit the element of protest implicit in the opening stanza. Conceptualization, in stanza 2, remains close to phenomenology; stanza 3 builds on it rationalistically. Wit enters the poem as the speaker turns back from contemplating his spiritual experience to addressing God. The spatial terms prove remarkably adaptable to the purpose of protest; the more literally they are taken the better. Referring back to the "cosmology" of the second stanza, the speaker cries:

> O rack me not to such a vast extent;
>> Those distances belong to thee:
>> The world's too little for thy tent
>> A grave too big for me. [9–12]

The fourth stanza continues in this mode, moving from plea and assertion to open questioning:

> Wilt thou meet arms with man, that thou dost stretch
>> A crumme of dust from heav'n to hell?
>> Will great God measure with a wretch?
>> Shall he thy stature spell? [13–16]

These stanzas are probably the most sustained example in Herbert of an aggressive, even militant, humility. All the praise of "great God" and dispraise of man is in the service of accusing God of unfairness—"Shall he thy stature spell?" We are certainly far from the opening vision of gladly engraving God's love in steel. The God of these stanzas does not seem in any way lovable. He seems a tyrant and a bully, making impossible demands. It would seem that at this point, having once again let folly speak "in her own native tongue," Herbert would have his speaker pull back, making a characteristic gesture of renunciation and real humility. One of the many interesting features of "The Temper" (I) is that it holds off before doing so. To the protest of "O rack me not," Herbert adds a positive entreaty. He makes new

26. The analogue in Vaughan to "Sometimes I peere above them all" does not help settle the matter of tone. In "They are all gone into the world of light," Vaughan speaks with complete seriousness of "strange thoughts" which "transcend our wonted theams" and "into glory peep" (lines 27–28).

use of the cosmology of the second stanza and the humility of the third and fourth. He returns to the barter framework of the opening stanza, although what he "offers" God here is merely a double negative. He frees the pathos from the aggression of the previous stanzas:

> O let me, when thy roof my soul hath hid,
>   O let me roost and nestle there:
>   Then of a sinner thou art rid,
>   And I of hope and fear.   [17–20]

The key to this stanza lies in its shift from emphasizing ascent to emphasizing enclosure. The speaker redescribes his "peak" moments in terms of the swallow of Psalm 84 rather than in terms of the exalted flight of lines 5 and 6 ("Sometimes I peere above them all"). God's "roof" is conceived of in cottage rather than cosmological terms. And something has begun to happen to the spatial vocabulary. Despite the persistence of this language, "there" in line 18 seems to be less a place than a state of mind or soul, an imagined state of complete security and protectedness. Hutchinson suggests that Herbert had a Pascalian fear of unlimited space,[27] but the second half of the stanza, with its focus on named emotions, reminds us that the actual context of the poem is psychological rather than ontological. What the speaker wishes to escape from is not life in space but life in time. Hope and fear are both future-oriented emotions and they are both responses to the possibility of change. This stanza clarifies the previous ones by showing that the speaker wants to be freed not merely from having to be God—the argument of the previous stanzas—but from having to be man, a sinner, living with "hope and fear."[28]

This stanza of "The Temper" (I) is an excellent example of how an entirely understandable cry of the heart can begin to turn into something perverse when it ceases to be a fantasy and becomes the basis

27. Note on "The Temper" (I), p. 494. See also Valentina Poggi, *George Herbert* (Bologna, 1967), p. 174. For Pascal, see *Pensées*, intro. T. S. Eliot (New York, 1958), No. 206 (p. 61).

28. If Tuve (*A Reading of Herbert*, p. 142) is right that there is an inverted reference to "Lord, I am not worthy that thou shouldest come under my roof" (Matthew 8:8) in "When thy roof my soul hath hid," the implication of the allusion would be the speaker's refusal to acknowledge the Incarnation, *God's* endurance of the human condition. The Gnostics who elaborated "fourtie heav'ns, or more" were notably unwilling to accept the reality of the Incarnation (see Jonas, *The Gnostic Religion*, chaps. 6, 8, 9; Elaine Pagels, *The Gnostic Gospels* [New York, 1979], chaps. 1, 4). All this, however, is in the realm of what Christopher Ricks calls "enhancing suggestions" (*Milton's Grand Style* [Oxford, 1963], p. 78, citing Walter Bagehot) rather than of definite meanings. Tuve's insistence on a Eucharistic reference here is entirely noncontextual, as is the overtly associational process by which Fredson Bowers ("Herbert's Sequential Imagery: 'The Temper,' " *MP*, 59 [1962], 209 ff.) imports such meaning into the poem even while acknowledging its (literal) nonexistence there.

for an argument, a rational proposal—"Then of a sinner thou art rid."
The proposal implies that God wishes to be "rid" of sinners and that
He wishes those to whom He shows His love to be rid of hope and
fear. Here, as in the previous stanzas, Herbert's speaker is telling God
what to do (and not to do), telling Him what would be best. That this
stanza is free of aggression does not mean that it is free of willfulness.[29]
And as always, Herbert is sensitive to willfulness, however "minimal"
its demands. In the sixth stanza, he has his speaker recoil from pro-
posing a course to God:

> Yet take thy way; for sure thy way is best:
>   Stretch or contract me, thy poore debter:
>   This is but tuning of my breast,
>   To make the musick better.   [21–24]

This is, in many ways, a brilliant resolution. It responds, however,
more fully to stanzas 3 and 4 than to stanza 5. It is close in structure
to stanza 3 (both have full stops after each of their first two lines) and
it responds directly to the image of the rack, making it fully Procrus-
tean by including contracting as well as stretching. God's actions as
torturer are ascribed to His role as temperer (thereby explaining the
title). The musical image responds to the problem of praise by sug-
gesting a less restrictive conception of religious poetry than that on
which the opening relied. The image also, as Tuve and Bowers argue,
perhaps serves to associate the speaker's pain with Christ's ("His
stretched sinews taught all strings, what key / Is best to celebrate this
most high day").[30]
Yet there is something forced about this stanza and also something
pat. The musical metaphor works almost too well; it is too palpably
(however traditional) a stroke of wit. There is still an element of
grudgingness, of merely formal assent in "Yet take thy way; *for sure
thy way is best*," and there is an element of dutifulness, of merely
declaring that it is so, in "This is but tuning of my breast." This stanza
does not escape the self-pity that has come to pervade the poem—
"Stretch or contract me, *thy poore debter*"—and it succeeds in rede-
scribing but not in reconstituting the self. Part of what gives this stanza
its "official" and dutiful feeling is that it views the self from the
outside, as an object, rather than speaking from within it, as a subject.
There is no "I" here, another feature that connects this stanza to 3
and 4 and distinguishes it from stanza 5.

29. Stein (*Herbert's Lyrics*, p. 125) observes: "That the essential motive is willful and
assertive is indicated by the prominent intellectuality of the proposal."
30. "Easter," part 1, lines 11–12; Tuve, *A Reading of Herbert*, p. 145; Bowers, "Se-
quential Imagery," 206–7.

All the best commentators on "The Temper" (I) have located its deepest meaning in its final stanza. Stein, with characteristic perceptiveness and characteristic unwillingness to treat ideas directly, has suggested that the difference between the penultimate sixth and the final seventh stanza *"resembles* that between intellectual acceptance and complete resignation."[31] Vendler provides a more internal account. She recognizes that the sixth stanza transforms but does not transcend the schematization of experience introduced in stanza 2 and built upon in stanzas 3 and 4. She notes that the image of tuning still adheres "to the poem's original primitive and anthropocentric notion of being stretched, of being first lifted by God to heaven and then dashed to earth."[32] In response to this, as she says, Herbert "invents a brilliant coda to the poem, expunging all its former terms of spatial reference":

> Whether I flie with angels, fall with dust,
> > Thy hands made both, and I am there:
> > Thy power and love, my love and trust
> > Make one place ev'ry where.   [25–28]

Vendler does not offer a very clear account of why Herbert would want to expunge all terms of spatial reference from the poem. She states that this stanza represents "a more celestial point of view" from which "heaven and earth are equally in God's presence and of his making." This is where Fish comes in. He points out that the alliteration of "flie" and "fall" serves to associate rather than to distinguish the terms and that "the precisely ambiguous 'there' " in line 26 "refers neither to the earth ('dust') nor to the ('fortie') heavens, but to God's hands."[33] He sees the reader of lines 25–26 as passing "from a (syntactical) world where everything is in its time and place to a world where specification of either is impossible, to a *uni*verse." But surely Herbert's point is not that specification of places is impossible but that it is misleading and, even if it were true, irrelevant. The point is not a general one about language but a specific one about the dangers of conceptualizing spiritual experience in certain abstract, spatial, and cosmological ways.

An important feature of this final stanza is that it does not merely expunge a set of terms; it also substitutes another set for them. It replaces the spatial terms of flying and falling and the whole vocab-

31. *Herbert's Lyrics*, p. 31 (emphasis mine).
32. *Poetry of Herbert*, p. 40. There are some small inaccuracies in this account. The "original" position of the poem (stanza 1) is *not* the "primitive and anthropocentric notion" that emerges in stanzas 2–4, and it is not earth but *hell* that is the opposite pole from heaven in the poem (lines 8 and 14).
33. *Self-Consuming Artifacts*, p. 161.

ulary of places with terms denoting qualities of personal relationship—love and trust. Stanza 7 responds to stanza 5; "there" appears in the same position in both. The final paradoxical use of the term answers the earlier prayer ("O let me roost and nestle there") by freeing the idea of security from any connection with times or places. The realities to which this final stanza points are independent of times and places. They are also, to return to the preconceptualized terms of the poem, independent of "feelings" in the sense of responses to immediate stimuli—sensations. "Love and trust" are neither objective and cosmological nor "merely" subjective matters of how one is feeling at the moment. They are distinguished in the poem from "what my soul doth feel sometimes." The final equilibrium of the poem, the "Christian temper" which it finally attains, is precisely "that firm and steadfast constancy of heart which is the chief part of faith" (*Institutes*, III.ii.33). The dust-trust rhyme was nearly always an affirmation of faith for Herbert.[34] Faith too, as we have seen, is neither merely an experience nor merely a fact. It is the principal work of the Spirit in man (*Institutes*, III.i.4). Stein has noted that "God's power and man's love are prominently balanced" in the penultimate line of "The Temper" (I).[35] But it is not clear whether "power" is meant to balance "love" or "trust," or which nouns govern the final verb. "Thy hands made both," however, would strongly point to God again doing the "making." Part of the point of the final stanza is that God's power and love produce man's love and trust—or rather, they are it. These four terms themselves "make one place."[36]

The final stanza of "The Temper" (I) replaces ontological and spatial terms with personalistic and qualitative ones. This movement is parallel to that by which Herbert replaces the material "elixir" with an attitude in "The Elixir" and replaces an "infusion" with a glance in "The Glance." All of these redefinitions and replacements flow from the central Reformation emphasis on conceiving of the religious life in terms of a relationship between persons, an "I-thou" relationship. Herbert knew, however, that just as it was almost impossible to keep from conceiving of the religious life in terms of decorum and merit, it was also difficult, though not perhaps impossible, to keep from

34. See the final stanza of "Faith," which precedes "The Temper" (I), and the final stanza of "Death," which echoes that of "Faith."

35. *Herbert's Lyrics*, p. 82; adopted by Vendler, *Poetry of Herbert*, p. 41.

36. It is interesting to compare the end of "The Temper" (I) with the vision of the power of love to make "one little roome, an every where" in "The good-morrow." The lines work in opposite directions: Donne's to include everything in one place; Herbert's to eliminate the significance of places by making them all functionally the same. "One place" in Herbert means "the same place," that is, not in a "place" at all. Compare Earl Miner, *The Metaphysical Mode from Donne to Cowley* (Princeton, 1969), p. 105.

thinking about God in spatial terms. He knew how "natural" the impulse toward such thinking is. As "The Temper" (I) shows, the problem of the relation between faith and immediate experience is related to the problem of spatial thinking through the tendency to talk of the "ups and downs" of immediate experience. "The Search" concerns another such utterly natural way of perversely conceptualizing the God-man relationship on the basis of immediate experience.

"The Search" is entirely built upon its title conceit, the idea of a "search" for God. The speaker's "sense of Heav'ns desertion" is here phrased in terms of a sustained and fruitless search for the place to which God has fled:

> Whither, O, whither art thou fled,
>> My Lord, my Love?
> My searches are my daily bread;
>> Yet never prove.   [1–4]

This poem is clearly not going to be what Stein calls "pure lament";[37] it will not only be expressing a feeling but exploring a typical way of conceptualizing it. The extreme regularity and compactness of the stanza form—as contrasted, for example, with the stanza of "Longing"—perhaps itself suggests this. The speaker's characterizations of his situation are going to be stylized and witty as well as poignant. The play on "my daily bread" calls attention to its wit.

In the second stanza, Herbert presents his daily searches, his prayers, as powerful tools for penetrating the elements. He is like the astronomer and the diver in "Vanitie" (I):

> My knees pierce th' earth, mine eies the skie;
>> And yet the sphere
> And centre both to me denie
>> That thou art there.   [5–8]

The sense in which "the sphere / And centre . . . denie" to Herbert that God is "there," in either place, is an extremely important matter in "The Search." This would seem to mean that Herbert is unable to find any traces, *vestigia*, or "footprints" of God in these places. It turns out, however, that this is not the case, since the next two stanzas expressly deny this conclusion (treating "the sphere / And centre" in reverse order):

> Yet can I mark how herbs below
>> Grow green and gay,
> As if to meet thee they did know,
>> While I decay.

37. *Herbert's Lyrics*, pp. 89–91.

> Yet can I mark how starres above
> > Simper and shine,
> As having keyes unto thy love,
> > While poore I pine. [9–16]

Herbert is unable to find God "there" in the creation even in the face of the very evidence for the view that the created things he is contemplating are in touch with God—or that God is "in" them. Herbert leaves the question open as to whether or not these things are "in touch" with God. The "as if" and "as" here seem to be genuinely neutral rather than skeptical. The important point, however, is that it does not matter whether or not God is there, in the ontological sense, in the herbs and stars. God is not "there" *for the speaker* in these things even if He is literally there. The "sphere / And centre both to me denie / That thou art there" by not providing any comfort, any sense of being loved, to the speaker—not by not (conceivably) manifesting God's presence. Luther expressed this distinction very clearly. In a context of insisting on God's omnipresence "in every single creature in its innermost and outermost being," he warns against thinking that this means that God is to be sought in the creatures. "It is one thing for God to be present," Luther notes, "it is another for Him to be present for you." To grasp this distinction is crucial, for "otherwise you will run back and forth throughout all creation, groping here and groping there, yet never finding [God], even though God is actually there, for He is not there for you."[38]

After stanzas 3 and 4 of "The Search," Herbert could drop the title metaphor, but he wants to develop some of its implications further: first, its pathos (the speaker sends "a sigh to seek [God] out . . . Wing'd like an arrow"); and second, its potential for irreverence. After the stanzas on sighs and groans (5–6), the speaker addresses God with a cosmological speculation similar to "Has thou left all things to their course, / And laid the reins / Upon the horse?" in "Longing," but bolder and more imaginative:

> Lord, dost thou some new fabrick mould,
> > Which favour winnes,
> And keeps thee present, leaving th' old
> > Unto their sinnes? [25–28]

Herbert seems to have seen spatial thinking about God as leading to potentially heretical absurdities (compare "some fourtie heav'ns, or more"). This is exactly the kind of speculative and unscriptural di-

---

38. *That These Words of Christ, 'This is my Body,' Still Stand Firm against the Fanatics,* LW, XXXVII, 58, 68, 69.

vinity that Luther and Calvin warned against.[39] From the point of view of natural reason, however, it is a perfectly plausible explanation of the phenomenon at hand.

Following this stanza, the poem seems to return to its opening question with renewed intensity. Putting aside the fanciful cosmology of stanza 7, the speaker asks:

> Where is my God? what hidden place
> Conceals thee still?
> What covert dare eclipse thy face?   [29–31]

Again, however, as the speaker tries to specify his sense of the problem—"what hidden place . . . What covert . . . ?"—the doom of nonsense begins to fall. In the concluding dimeter of the stanza, the thought that the speaker has been evading ever since his discussion of God's being or not being in the "sphere / And centre" bursts into the poem:

> Is it thy will?   [32]

Suddenly all the speculation about where God is or has "fled" to falls away. The speaker is conceiving of this situation in terms of God's disposition, not His location. In the cosmological stanza, the two are confused—"some new fabrick . . . *favour* winnes." Here, cosmology is irrelevant. The relevant framework is of an entirely different sort. In warning against seeking God merely where He is, Luther was stressing the importance of seeking God where He has indicated that He wishes to be sought, where He has indicated His will.[40] When Luther (or Augustine) emphasizes the omnipresence of God in the cosmos, the point is not solely the attack on spatial thinking. The main point is the importance of revelation.[41]

With line 32 of "The Search," the whole framework which the poem has been employing is recognized to be an evasion. The idea that the speaker's desolation results from God's will is much more terrifying than the idea of any physical barrier. Continuing the language of "coverts," the speaker cries:

39. See chap. 1, n. 45 above. I believe that Herbert would have found Vendler's praise of his "metaphysical daring" (*Poetry of Herbert*, p. 114) quite puzzling. Hutchinson (p. 534) is probably correct in identifying the "new fabrick" of line 25 of "The Search" as a new world (Vendler argues for a new species). The assertion of "other worlds" was a famous piece of metaphysical daring in the period, as, for instance, in Bruno. To read the phrase in this way keeps the focus of the poem spatial. As Vendler notes, however, there is some grammatical awkwardness in the stanza.

40. *That These Words . . . Still Stand Firm*, p. 66.

41. The sentence which Fish twice (*Self-Consuming Artifacts*, pp. 41, 160) cites from Augustine, "He came to a place where He was already," is part of Augustine's discussion of the necessity of the Incarnation (*Christian Doctrine*, p. 14).

> O let not that of any thing;
>> Let rather brasse,
> Or steel, or mountains be thy ring,
>> And I will passe.   [33–36]

This is the speaker's last burst of nonsense. The specifying of his own resolution and the claim to hyperbolical abilities bring him back to the topic he can no longer evade—that of "Thy will":

> Thy will such an intrenching is
>> As passeth thought:
> To it all strength, all subtilties
>> Are things of nought.   [37–40]

At this point, having deprived himself of "all strength, all subtilties," there is nothing for the speaker to do but contemplate the mystery. He retains the rather formal meditative structure of the previous stanza in emphasizing the way in which God's will "passeth thought," especially spatial thought:

> Thy will such a strange distance is
>> As that to it
> East and West touch, the poles do kisse,
>> And parallels meet.   [41–44]

This distance is so strange as not to be thinkable as distance. Instead of dropping this vocabulary, however, Herbert continues using it, but now in full awareness of its ironic status.[42] All the spatial terms in his new self-description are present, so to speak, in spite of themselves, in implied quotation marks:

> Since then my grief must be as large,
>> As is thy space,
> Thy distance from me; see my charge,
>> Lord, see my case.   [45–48]

The speaker prays for God to be not "Against, but for" him (line 52), but continues to conceive of these terms as spatial. God being "for" him is God being *near* him. After a stanza describing how close God can be if He will "be neare" (lines 53–56), the poem concludes:

> For as thy absence doth excell
>> All distance known:
> So doth thy nearenesse bear the bell,
>> Making two one.   [57–60]

---

42. Compare Vendler, *Poetry of Herbert*, p. 115.

We are clearly in another world here from that to which spatial and quantitative terms apply. The relevant conceptions of distance and closeness are emotional, not physical. Absence and nearness are themselves only inadequate and potentially misleading metaphors. The "search" is misguided from the beginning. The poem as a whole has been a critique and a *reductio* of its title conceit.[43] The proper way of dealing with the sense of heaven's desertion is not through "the search" but through "the method"—the assumption that if God "refuseth still, / There is some rub, some discontent" with oneself "which cools his will" ("The Method," lines 1–4). To think about God's distance as literal is to miss the essential religious point. Sin, not space, is what keeps man from God. Mercy, not physical closeness, is what brings God "near." One must not give in to the temptations implicit in ordinary language. Natural reason is only too ready to build systems and cosmologies upon these hints and thereby to keep man from the "two vast, spacious things, / The which to measure it doth more behove" ("The Agonie," lines 5–6).

The goal, for Herbert, is to contemplate the fluctuations of immediate emotional experience without attempting to "map" this experience in an ontological or cosmological way. Even "The Temper" (II), which distinguishes sharply between "the grosser world" of physical nature and the "diviner world of grace," phrases its final prayer for God to keep the speaker from the irreverence of his own "powers" in terms of God coming and going from the heart or soul. Even there, despite the profundity of the speaker's self-knowledge, he is still, albeit implicitly, thinking of God "according to [his] own feelings and reactions" rather than according to the Word. "A Parodie" provides the final critique that "The Temper" (II) lacks. In "A Parodie," Herbert confronts not the extravagant fantasies of "The Search," but the ordinary and almost unconscious ways we make assertions about God's "location" on the basis of our immediate feelings. If, like "Assurance," "A Parodie" is perhaps too expository a piece to rank among Herbert's finest lyric achievements, it certainly does rank among his finest moments of theological clarity.

43. The thoroughness of Herbert's devaluation of "the search" idea emerges very clearly in the contrast between his poem and Vaughan's "The Search." As Lewalski has shown (*Protestant Poetics*, p. 335), Vaughan's poem is a critique of the Catholic, especially the Ignatian, conception of meditation (perhaps also of pilgrimage). When the speaker finds mental travel to various sites in the life of Christ fruitless, he turns with greater optimism to "the Wilderness," but is rebuked, Herbert-style, by an authoritative voice which tells him to give up focusing on "The skinne, and shell of things" and instead to "search well another world." The point of the advice is to reorient "the search," to direct it upward and inward, not to undermine the entire "search" idea. The "other world" for Vaughan is conceived of epistemologically and metaphysically.

The title of "A Parodie" refers to its relation to a secular love poem, a song probably by William Herbert, third earl of Pembroke, Herbert's cousin. As Tuve has shown, Herbert's poem is intended to "parody" the earl's only in a specific musical sense; it is not meant to comment on the content of Pembroke's poem.[44] In the central conceit of the song, Herbert found a theme in which he himself was deeply interested. Pembroke's poem was literally a point of departure for Herbert. "A Parodie" appears in "The Church" immediately after "The Posie," a poem which rejects secular poetry and especially wit. Herbert did not, I think, intend "A Parodie" to be witty. It is an extremely serious piece.

Pembroke's poem is a valediction forbidding mourning. Its entire first half is a single sentence:

> Soules joy, when I am gone,
> And you alone,
> (Which cannot be,
> Since I must leave my selfe with thee,
> And carry thee with me)
>
> Yet when unto our eyes
> Absence denyes
> Each others sight,
> And makes to us a constant night,
> When others change to light:
>
> O give no way to griefe,
> But let beliefe
> Of mutuall love,
> This wonder to the vulgar prove
> Our Bodyes, not wee move.[45]   [1–15]

The second half continues the argument. The fourth stanza begins, "Let not thy wit beweepe / Wounds but sense deepe"; the fifth amplifies the contrast with "the vulgar" ("Fooles have no meanes to meet / But by their feet"); and the poem ends with a repeat of stanza 3 ("O give no way to griefe," etc.).

What seems to have interested Herbert in Pembroke's poem was its initial conceit, the turn in the middle of the first stanza in which the speaker retracts the description of his situation that he has just

---

44. "Sacred 'Parody' of Love Poetry, and Herbert," in *Essays by Tuve*, ed. Roche, pp. 207–49. On the authorship of the "Song," see also Sir Herbert J. C. Grierson, *The Poems of John Donne* (Oxford, 1912), II, cxxv–cxxxvi.

45. Text and lineation from Tuve, "Sacred 'Parody,'" pp. 239–40, except that I have used the "Lansdowne MS" opening line (see Hutchinson, p. 541), substituting "when" for "now."

offered. *Metanoia* or *correctio*, the figure which Puttenham, "following the Greeke," calls "the penitent or repentant," is one of Herbert's favorite devices.[46] Apart from reversing the pronouns, he echoes Pembroke's opening lines exactly (Tuve notes that this is normal in the musical practice):

> Souls joy, when thou art gone,
> And I alone,
> Which cannot be . . .   [1–3]

Like Pembroke's, Herbert's poem is going to explain why an apparent separation cannot truly be one. Herbert's first departure from Pembroke occurs in the first explanation of why the situation initially described "cannot be": "Because thou dost abide with me / And I depend on thee" (lines 4–5). The mention of dependence introduces a new element, substituting an emotional and psychological term for the pseudo-physical conception in the equivalent lines of the song. Herbert's poem is going to be about what it means *to depend* on God. The shift in the pronouns in the opening lines already suggests this. Herbert is speaking from the point of view of the one who is left rather than of the one who is leaving. He is the passive partner.

Herbert follows Pembroke in making the second stanza continuous with the first (departing from his usual practice), and in devoting the stanza to explaining the circumstances which provoked the initial misdescription. He retains the opening "Yet when" of Pembroke's stanza and its general structure (its punctuation and its beginning of the fourth line with "And"), but he fills in the content entirely differently. In place of the self-consciously witty play on "constant night" versus "lightness" (a very shopworn pun), Herbert offers a remarkably complex and precise analysis of how it is possible for a man with whom God "dost abide" to have the impression that he is alone:

> thou dost suppresse
> The cheerfulnesse
> Of thy abode,
> And in my powers not stirre abroad,
> But leave me to my load.   [6–10]

And in place of the rather jaunty exhortation which begins the third stanza and main clause of the sentence in Pembroke's poem ("O give no way to griefe"), Herbert provides a poignant evocation of grief: "O what a dampe and shade / Doth me invade!" (lines 11–12). This is where the "plot" of Herbert's poem begins to diverge sharply from

---

46. See p. 11 above. "A Parodie" is unusual in that Herbert tends to employ *metanoia* at the end rather than the beginning of poems.

that of Pembroke's. Where Pembroke's poem is devoted primarily to the solution to the apparent dilemma of the opening, Herbert's is devoted primarily to evoking and analyzing the dilemma.

The great advantage Herbert has over Pembroke in making use of the you or I "cannot be alone" conceit is that Herbert is able actually to mean what he says. He does not have to be witty. When Herbert calls the other his "souls joy" and speaks of this other as continuously "with" and "in" him, he is not speaking hyperbolically or meta-phorically. He is not even speaking paradoxically. One of the most striking features of Herbert's presentation of the dilemma (and the solution) in his poem is that he does not have to resort to paradox— "Here but not here." The too easy resort to paradox ("Our Bodyes, not wee") generates the hint of overfacility that vitiates the resonance if not the beauty of Pembroke's song. The relation between Pem-broke's poem and Herbert's is very much like that which Yvor Winters saw between Sidney's lyrics and those of the greatest masters of the English Renaissance—Pembroke's poem offers formal possibilities for a mode of perception more complex than it attains.[47]

What allows Herbert to avoid the "here but not here" paradox is his refusal of the spatial framework. The precision of the second stanza is necessary for the delineation of the alternative. God does not "leave" the regenerate soul, but at times, in Herbert's wonderfully careful formulation, "suppresse[s] / The cheerfulnesse / Of [His] abode." God wills that the Christian at times not feel His presence and His love. He wills to leave the regenerate soul only aware of nature within it—"in my powers not stirre abroad, / But *leave me to my load*." Herbert's effort in this stanza is to express his understanding of God's actions with maximal precision. The third stanza begins, as we have seen, by evoking the experience of spiritual desolation. The triple rhyme comments on the special horror of this experience. We are back to Luther's *Anfechtungen*:[48]

> No stormie night
> Can so afflict or so affright
> As thy eclipsed light.   [13–15]

The image of "eclipsed light" is a precise imagistic version of the analysis of presence without affect developed in stanza 2. Stanza 4 introduces a new element. Like the equivalent stanza in Pembroke, it is in the mode of negative exhortation ("Let not thy wit beweepe / Wounds but sense deepe"), but, in making its plea, Herbert's stanza

47. "The Sixteenth Century Lyric in England: A Critical and Historical Reinterpre-tation," in Paul Alpers, ed., *Elizabethan Poetry: Modern Essays in Criticism* (New York, 1967), p. 105.
48. See pp. 107–8 above.

mentions and then dramatizes a response to God's suppression of
the feeling of His presence more uncanny than mere terror. Losing
the sense of God's presence is not merely a loss, a deprivation; it
creates a vacuum in which another force, equally independent of the
will, becomes active. The "load" to which Herbert is left is not merely
an inert burden. As in "The Temper" (II), Herbert's "powers," left to
act purely naturally, cannot "fix their reverence":

> Ah Lord! do not withdraw,
> > Lest want of aw
> > Make Sinne appeare;
> And when thou dost but shine lesse cleare,
> Say, that thou art not here.   [16–20]

When Sin "appears" in the poem and in Herbert's psyche ("here"),
it comes, as we would now expect, not in the form of a fleshly impulse
but in that of an intellectual hypothesis. Again the proper gloss is
"Nature": "Full of rebellion, I would die, / Or fight, or travell, *or
denie / That thou hast ought to do with me*" (emphasis mine). Sin draws
a "natural" conclusion on the basis of immediate experience. As in
"Nature," Herbert describes the way in which the "venom" of sin's
suggestions could "fume and work" in the soul, though here Herbert
subtly shifts from a hypothetical to a narrative mode:

> And then what life I have,
> > While Sinne doth rave,
> > And falsely boast,
> That I may seek, but thou art lost;
> Thou and alone thou know'st.   [21–25]

We are back here to the calmly rational "bitterly spitefull" thought of
stanza 2 of "Assurance" and to the equally calm Satanic voice which
"raves" in the assertive section of "The Collar." "I may seek, but thou
art lost" has exactly the same tone of lofty contempt built upon su-
perior moral and intellectual penetration as "thou didst wink and
wouldst not see" in "The Collar" and "all was not so fair, as I con-
ceiv'd, / Betwixt my God and me" in "Assurance."

In "A Parodie," Herbert's emphasis is strongly on the Christian's
lack of experiential confirmation of his regenerate state in a moment
like that evoked in stanzas 2–5 of the poem—"And then what life I
have . . . Thou and alone thou know'st." In such a moment the in-
dividual cannot "know" that he is saved. Everything in his experi-
ence—and especially his consciousness of sin—suggests the opposite.
This is the worst temptation, the temptation to despair of God's mercy.
We have seen, however, that the reformers held that even this temp-
tation is characteristic of the regenerate, and that "our Saviour Christ

himselfe, who could not sinne through infidelitie, *in respect of his present sense and feeling* complaineth that God hath forsaken him."[49] In the final stanza of "A Parodie," Herbert dramatizes precisely how far toward desperation God will allow the regenerate to fall. Following the structure of Pembroke's "Song," which ends by repeating its third stanza, Herbert returns to the exclamatory and phenomenological mode of his third stanza, echoing its opening words ("O what a damp and shade"). In contemplating the effects of God's suppression of the sense of His presence, the speaker begins to feel these effects. The poem lurches startlingly into the present only to be resolved when this present becomes part of the continuing narrative:

> O what a deadly cold
> > Doth me infold!
> > I half beleeve
> That Sinne sayes true: but while I grieve,
> Thou com'st and dost relieve.   [26–30]

In a sense, the speaker *can* trust his experience, but only the whole pattern of it. He cannot trust particular moments, especially those of grief and temptation. God will always "come" to relieve the regenerate individual, though He has not "gone" anywhere (Herbert can relapse into the vernacular here, confident that he will not be misunderstood). It is inevitable that God will behave in this way—the final line is in a historical present that implies a repeated process— just as it is inevitable that the speaker will be tempted to doubt of his salvation when God "suppresse[s] / The cheerfulnesse" of His abode in him. As Calvin notes, "when we do not perceive any sign of divine aid, this thought unavoidably forces itself upon us, that God has forgotten us."[50] Herbert is at pains to make clear the exact extent of this doubt—"I *half beleeve*, / That Sinne sayes true." Only God *knows*, in the moments when Herbert is being assailed by temptation, that Herbert is elect, but Herbert only "half beleeve[s]" that he is not, even at these moments.[51] He emphasizes the inevitability of both his fall and God's relief. "A Parodie" might well be called "Comfort's Round."

Herbert most fully dramatizes his "constant inspection and criticism of experience" in "The Flower," one of his greatest lyrics, a poem that includes virtually all the insights into the dangers of conceptualizing on the basis of immediate experience we have examined in "The Temper" (I), "The Search," and "A Parodie." What makes "The Flower"

49. Downame, *Christian Warfare*, p. 256b (emphasis mine); see pp. 177–78 above.
50. *Commentary on the Psalms*, I, 182.
51. See Calvin's discussion of the weakness and strength of faith in *Institutes*, III.ii.17–21.

remarkable is not only the vividness with which it evokes immediate experience but the fact that the misleading experience on which it mainly focuses is positive rather than negative. "The Flower" is the poem in *The Temple* in which Herbert subjects the widest range of fully represented immediate experience to the most intense objective scrutiny. It is Herbert's greatest triumph of placing immediate experience without undermining it with irony.

The poem begins as a rapturous general meditation on the type of experience to which the endings of "The Search" and "A Parodie" allude and that of "The Collar" dramatizes. The speaker seems to have a perspective on these experiences which allows him to correlate the delight they provide with the pain they relieve. The natural image announced in the title is the key to this correlation:

> How fresh, O Lord, how sweet and clean
> Are thy returns! ev'n as the flowers in spring;
>   To which, besides their own demean,
> The late-past frosts tributes of pleasure bring.   [1–4]

The explanatory mode, syntactic complexity, and elevated diction of the second half of this quatrain are almost a shock after the ingenuous and exclamatory mode of the opening.[52] The natural image, introduced with an almost extreme casualness, provides the transition, allowing the speaker to relate the special pleasure of God's "returns" to the (implied) pain of His "absences." Pain does not seem to be a problem here at all. It merely serves to provide "tributes" to pleasure. Everything seems beautifully integrated and under control, the darkness complementing the light.

In the second part of the stanza, however, something odd happens. In extending the seasonal analogy, Herbert seems to contradict himself. The dynamics of the analogy work against the use to which he has put it. The memory of pain may intensify pleasure, but winter does not linger on as a presence in spring. The more closely Herbert identifies the psychological with the seasonal situation—which he does most fully in the short lines beginning the lyrical coda of the stanza—the less is he able to argue for the tribute of pain to pleasure. The continuation of the analogy produces a shift and a fissure in the psychology. Winter disappears; it does not linger on in a tributary role:

---

52. For a closely analogous moment, see the movement from the lyrical exclamation that opens stanza 2 of "The good-morrow" ("And now good morrow to our waking souls") to the explanatory lines that follow ("Which watch not one another out of fear, / For love . . .").

> Grief melts away
> Like snow in May,
> As if there were no such cold thing.   [5–7]

The remarkable final line of the stanza attempts a compromise be-
tween the explanatory and evocative modes; it acknowledges without
in any way diminishing the hyperbole of which it is part. The rhyme
with line 4 only serves to intensify how far we have come from the
equilibrium of the quatrain.

And yet the stanza does not *feel* contradictory. Vendler sees Herbert
as purposely saying something which he knows to be false in the
coda of this stanza—"in the first flush of reconciliation, Herbert gen-
erously says that God has obliterated all past grief in the soul."[53] But
surely this misses the tone of these lines. They do not have this quality
of half-meant concession and half-conscious bad faith. They are stated
as a fact, not as a concession. They hark back to and recapture the
ingenuous quality of the opening. The philosophical perspective of
lines 3 and 4 has not been able to master and assimilate the energy
present in the initial exclamation. The idea of pain as complementing
pleasure is a product of reflection; the opening exclamation and final
assertion are not reflecting on experience, they are recounting it.

Earl Miner has suggested that we feel "a greater weight than is at
once measurable" in the opening exclamation and that the source of
this "greater weight" is revealed at the beginning of the second stanza
with, as he finely puts it, "its almost supererogatory felicity in im-
agery."[54] What has been missing, though implied, in the opening
stanza is the note of personal testimony. At the beginning of the
second stanza, Herbert identifies the immediate experience out of
which the meditations of the first stanza emerged. The springtime of
God's return is suddenly internalized and made particular. Herbert
focuses not on the sweetness or the beauty of the spring foliage, but
on its life. That is the miracle. The idea of "freshness" in the opening
exclamation is given great depth:

> Who would have thought my shrivel'd heart
> Could have recover'd greennesse?   [8–9a]

This question, is, of course, meant to be rhetorical—no one "would
have thought" it. The experience of grief is subjectively absolute in
just the same way the experience of joy is. As the stanza continues,
however, the implied answer to the opening question changes from

---

53. *Poetry of Herbert*, p. 49. Vendler's discussion of "The Flower" appears on pp. 48–
54.

54. *The Metaphysical Mode*, p. 244.

"no one" to "anyone who has considered the matter." In the first stanza, the pressure of a phenomenological account undermined the attempt at perspective; here, the emergence in imagistic form of a fully developed theological perspective undermines the cognitive content of the opening question. Herbert seems to want to continue the opening point of view, but every time he attempts to do so the progress of the verse denies the closure necessary to maintain the initial sharp "before and after" contrast. Although line 9 concludes that the speaker's heart "was gone," the continuation of the sentence in line 10a—"Quite under ground"—weakens the initial absoluteness. The effect is even more striking in the enjambment between lines 10b and 11a. "As flowers depart" (10b) is continued by "To see their mother-root." Suddenly in place of going or shriveling we have an image of purposive movement to a comforting situation, and the imagery of domestic comfort comes to dominate the stanza.[55] Herbert does not end the sentence with the end of the quatrain, but rather allows the sentence to continue on, describing the existence of the flowers with "their mother-root,"

> Where they together
> All the hard weather,
> Dead to the world, keep house unknown.   [12–14]

We are miles away from the phenomenological perspective here, the perspective from which the speaker's heart felt "shrivel'd" and then miraculously reborn. The new perspective is that of faith, of the belief so precisely expressed in "A Parodie" that God is present to the redeemed individual even when the individual is unaware of His presence. The cozy snugness of the image is entirely a matter of faith; it is not directly experienced.[56] In terms of immediate experience, the

55. Hutchinson (p. 535) is surely correct that Herbert is borrowing from Donne's "A Hymne to Christ, at the Authors last going into Germany" (lines 12–14) both the image and the sense of purposiveness here, but Herbert's image is both more fanciful and more reassuring through being less naturalistically precise. In Donne, "the trees sap doth seeke the root below / In winter"; in Herbert, the actual flowers "see their mother-root."

56. In "I walkt the other day," Vaughan presents coziness like this as empirical ("I saw the warm Recluse alone to lie / Where fresh and green / He lived of us unseen"), and uses it in traditional emblematic fashion as one of those "prolusions and strong proofs of our restoration laid out in nature" (*Man in Darkness, or A Discourse of Death,* in *Works,* p. 177). Thomas Hooker's use of the image is closer to Herbert's. Just as the graces of God in the soul have their springtime, says Hooker, "so have they their winter, wherein the sap retireth to the root, the branches seeme to be withered, as if they were not the same, no life in them . . . and as we must not call in question the vegetative power and life that is in plants and hearbs, by reason of the little appearance thereof in the dead time of the yeere; no more must wee make question of the truth of grace in our hearts" (*The Christians Two Cheife Lessons, Selfe-Deniall, and Selfe-Tryall,* in *The Works of the Rev. Thomas Hooker* [1640], IV, 210–11).

speaker himself is one of those to whom the flower-heart was "dead" and "unknown." The point is not, as Vendler says, that Herbert is here throwing a "cloak of palliation" over the truth but rather that the perspective of experience and the perspective of reflection have once again neither been properly distinguished nor properly brought into relationship. What makes the stanza particularly unsettling is that it nowhere acknowledges that it has ended in a realm entirely "unknown" to its beginning.

The third stanza opens with a general reflection ("These are thy wonders") that recalls the first lines of the poem but does not specify *which* wonders it is celebrating—those of resurrection or those of continuity. The epithet with which it addresses God and the characterization of God's activities that follows suggest the former, recalling the unmediated wonder of the opening of stanza 2 rather than the calmer, less astonished perspective of its end:

> These are thy wonders, Lord of power,
> Killing and quickning, bringing down to hell
> And up to heaven in an houre; [15–17]

The seasonal metaphor is dropped here as not providing an adequate analogy for God's power. "Killing and quickning" can be seen as continuing the natural analogy—though "killing" seems a bit brutal—but hell and heaven bring us out of nature, and "in an houre" makes the analogy seem hopelessly misleading. We are back to the "suddenness" which led Herbert to distinguish the "world of grace" from that of nature in "The Temper" (II).[57]

The line that closes the quatrain of the third stanza contains another of what Stein calls the "imperious gerunds of power,"[58] yet is quite different from the previous two lines. Instead of showing God acting directly on the human emotions—heaven and hell are states of feeling here, as in "The Temper" (I)—it shows God acting on the emotions through the intellect and the perceptions. In line 18, "Making a chiming of a passing-bell," God brings man from hell to heaven by transforming his perceptions, enabling him to perceive harmony and beauty in a phenomenon that would normally terrify or depress him. The difference between being in hell and heaven seems to be entirely a matter of perception. Rightly perceived, there seems only to be heaven—as in the view of "death" presented in stanza 2.

The coda of the stanza develops this suggestion. For the first time in the poem, Herbert uses the coda as a genuinely independent unit,

---

57. In "The Temper" (II), Herbert contrasts "The grosser world" which "stands to" God's "word and art" with God's "diviner world of grace" that He "suddenly doth raise and race" (lines 5–7).

58. *Herbert's Lyrics*, p. 198. Stein's discussion of "The Flower" appears on pp. 197–200.

giving it formal as well as substantive authority (the stop after the quatrain in the first stanza was a weak one). Herbert both explains and dismisses the fluctuations in human emotional experience:

> We say amisse,
> This or that is:
> Thy word is all, if we could spell.   [19–21]

Everything that happens, whether in the inner or the outer world, is a direct result of a specific—and benevolent—act of divine decision. The proper gloss on these lines is the chapter on providence in *The Country Parson* in which Herbert presents the parson laboring to make his parishioners "see Gods hand in all things" (*CP,* p. 270).[59] Vendler sees these lines as filled with resentment, as uttered by "the rebellious soul, bent on calling God's actions arbitrary." But the lines are strikingly calm and even in their tone, and they are saying the opposite of "God's actions are arbitrary." The word-spelling conceit seems to function as a guarantee of ultimate intelligibility and, perhaps, of benevolence.

Vendler rightly reminds us, however, that a full reading of "The Flower" must confront the fact that the poem does not end here, at what would seem to be a powerful conclusion. The problem with this coda as conclusion is not that it seems overly pat, like the penultimate stanza of "The Temper" (I), or even that, like stanza 2 of "The Forerunners," it seems merely official and uttered through clenched teeth. "The Flower" moves in an even less linear fashion than those poems do. The problem in "The Flower" is that the two voices in the poem— that which responds to the immediacies of personal experience and that which enunciates the perspective of faith—do not respond to one another at all. They are *simply* at cross-purposes. The gap between what "we say" and what "Thy word" says seems absolute. The third stanza's coda diagnoses our condition of saying "amisse," but does not respond any more fully than the end of the second to *the particular things* that "we say." This lack of specific response is what leads to the peculiar "zigzag" progression of the poem.[60] The fourth stanza opens with an emotional exclamation just as the second stanza did. The voice of meditation on personal experience responds only to the third stanza's presentation of experience, the vision, however misleading, of God "Killing and quickning, bringing down to hell / And up to heaven in an houre." The intervening reflective lines, from "Making a chiming" to "if we could spell" (18–21), do not exist for it:

59. For the strongly Calvinist orientation of this chapter, see Strier, " 'To all Angels and Saints,' " p. 138.

60. Freer, *Music for a King,* p. 218.

> O that I once past changing were,
> Fast in thy Paradise, where no flower can wither! [22–23]

We are back to stanza 5 of "The Temper" (I): "O let me, when thy
roof my soul hath hid, / O let me roost and nestle there." The voice
of these prayers can conceive of steadfastness and comfort only on-
tologically, in terms of being in a different state or place, rather than
functionally, through seeing or "spelling" differently. A way in which
the perspective of faith might be brought to bear more responsively
on that of experience begins to suggest itself. By allowing the voice
which responds to experience to make its most unguarded gesture,
Herbert seems to be clarifying the relation between the voices, sep-
arating them out in order to create the possibility of a dialectic. In the
fourth stanza, as in the second, the opening burst of emotion leads
into a narrative, but here the voice of empirical meditation is entirely
in control. The speaker of "Love unknown" resurfaces, a man with
a story to tell. The flower becomes an image of aspiration and yearning
rather than of appreciation and response:

> Many a spring I shoot up fair,
> Offring at heav'n, growing and groning thither:
> Nor doth my flower
> Want a spring-showre,
> My sinnes and I joining together. [24–28]

Stein sees this narrative as gently self-mocking, but the zigzag
movement of the poem and the similarities to "Love unknown" sug-
gest that the voice dramatized in these lines is entirely in earnest.
This voice is obsessed with its own effort and longing, and seems
unaware of the almost cavalier quality with which, in Luther's phrase,
it confides in its own contrition ("Nor doth my flower / Want a spring-
showre").[61] The proof of this lack of self- and theological awareness
is provided by the next stanza, which continues the story. The speaker
finds his experience unintelligible:

> But while I grow in a straight line,
> Still upwards bent, as if heav'n were mine own,
> Thy anger comes, and I decline:
> What frost to that? what pole is not the zone,
> Where all things burn,
> And thou dost turn,
> And the least frown of thine is shown? [29–35]

61. *Babylonian Captivity (Pagan Servitude)*, Dillenberger, p. 318.

"Thy anger comes, and I decline"—this speaker sees no relation between his upward bending and God's anger. The speaker's main concern, however, is less to build a case against God than to evoke the horror and unimaginableness of God's anger when it mysteriously "comes." We return to the "Lord of power."

A remarkable structural feature of "The Flower" is that it does not proceed directly from stanza 5 to its conclusion. The poem would be perfectly symmetrical if it did so, each of its halves consisting of two stanzas describing experience followed by an address to God beginning, "These are thy wonders." One would also think that, after the mock-tragic narrative of stanzas 4 and 5, we are in a position to understand the relation between God's anger and His benevolence. What is perceived as punishment is actually correction ("the godly," Herbert explained in his notes on Valdes, "are chastized but not punished" [p. 311]). However, as the focus of the fifth stanza on evocation of the experience of God's anger suggests, the main concern of "The Flower" is not the rationalization of affliction. The sixth stanza returns to the more general problem of how to think about immediate experience. The stanza begins as if to continue the narrative of stanzas 4 and 5, but shifts suddenly from the historical into the actual present. The joy that animated the first stanza and burst out at the beginning of the second returns; the persona turns back into a person. Herbert continues the metaphor which informed the narrative, but eliminates the element of aspiration from it and introduces a number of insistently naturalistic and literalizing details:

> And now in age I bud again,
> After so many deaths I live and write;
> I once more smell the dew and rain,
> And relish versing. [36–39a]

Herbert seems to have attained here the balance he was seeking in stanza 1—the appreciation of the present is intensified by the recollection of the past. And yet the miracle and the cunning of the "versing" here is to present the experience of joy and "relish" so vividly and with such particularity that it tends to fall out of history, to feel like something unique, sui generis. The "again's" and "once more's" tend to fall away as the present overwhelms the past. That this effect is intended is confirmed by the second half of the stanza. The coda begins within the last line of the quatrain. Herbert turns to God and exclaims:

> O my onely light,
> It cannot be
> That I am he
> On whom thy tempests fell all night. [39b–42]

We are back to "As if there were no such cold thing" (line 7). From within the immediate experience, the sense of continuity cannot be maintained. In the coda of stanza 1, Herbert could not truly acknowledge the reality of past grief; here, when the memory of grief has been fully awakened by the previous stanza, he cannot imagine that it could truly be he who lived through an experience so contrary to that of the present. Experience still seems irrevocably at odds with reality, with what "is."

We strongly feel the need for some unifying perspective, for a perspective that will relate the fluctuations and special pressures of immediate experience to the continuity of divine intentions toward the regenerate. The quatrain of the final stanza—well-defined again, as in the third—does just this. It reveals power as love by providing a motive for God's behavior, by presenting God as using the immediacies of experience to teach man to "spell." It provides the missing dialectic between "Thy word" and our sayings. Herbert drops the catalogue structure of stanza 3 for a teleological construction that combines the unassimilated perspective of "*To see* their mother-root" with that of "*Making* a chiming of a passing-bell" in an explanatory mode similar to that of lines 3 and 4, but less abrupt:

> These are thy wonders, Lord of love,
> To make us see we are but flowers that glide:
> Which when we once can finde and prove,
> Thou hast a garden for us, where to bide.   [43–46]

"To make us see we are but flowers that glide" must mean more here than "to make us see that we are transitory." It must mean "to make us see we are but flowers that glide *through cycles.*" God puts man through the fluctuations and pressures of immediate emotional experience in order to provide him with the possibility of attaining a perspective on this experience, of not being at the mercy of its phenomenological absoluteness. Possibly "glide" cannot quite bear the weight of meaning it has to carry—I do not share Stein's confidence that it offers "a precise answer to the full display of flower movements in the poem"—but the intended meaning is clear. The garden referred to in line 46 replaces the atemporal paradise of line 23 and is certainly a "paradise within," a state of mind which attains stability and comfort through accepting what the "natural" consciousness would flee from. In this sense, then, "The Flower" connects closely with "The Crosse," the poem that precedes it, which ends, "Thy will be done." The fullest gloss on the state of mind of those who bide in God's garden is provided not by "Heaven," Herbert's poem on the afterlife, but by "Paradise," his poem about this life in which Herbert blesses God for cutting him as well as for giving him fruit.

This still leaves the coda unmentioned. The final lines of "The Flower" are unexpectedly grim and unexpectedly moralistic. Instead of elaborating on the garden-state of those who have fully proved upon their pulses—"from the very bone"—the lessons which the fluctuations and intensities of the "world of grace" teach, Herbert turns to the alternative:

> Who would be more,
> Swelling through store,
> Forfeit their Paradise by their pride.   [47–49]

Again, I think, the paradise in question here is the paradise within, but the problem of the sudden grimness remains. The solution to this problem (and perhaps to many such problems) is found by returning to the implied dramatic situation of the poem. We have already seen that stanza 6, "And now in age I bud again," seems both to continue and to escape from the history of stanzas 4 and 5. We do not know whether to connect the budding of stanza 6 with the shooting up-wards of stanza 4 or the proud swelling of the ending.[62] The final negative image has a powerfully sexual charge ("pride" can mean lust) but "I bud again" seems curiously innocent and gentle.[63] The delighted stanza is surely not sinister, and yet it does, as we have seen, lead to a retreat from reality. What Herbert seems to be doing in the grim final lines is reminding himself not to build any conclu-sions about his future (or past) on the sense of resurrection which he cannot but experience as absolute. In the chapter on providence in *The Country Parson*, Herbert insisted that men should "depend, and fear continually," regardless of "how faire soever the opportunities present themselves" at any particular moment (*CP*, p. 271). The si-multaneous respect for and criticism of experience which Eliot called wit, Herbert would have called faith, the Christian temper.

62. Compare Vendler, *Poetry of Herbert*, p. 51.
63. For the sexual sense, see *OED*, "pride," sb. 11. For a particularly clear (and phallic) Shakespearean example, see sonnet 151, line 10. For a close analogue, also in a po-tentially phallic context, to the innocent budding of stanza 6, see Donne's spring-after-winter poem, "Loves growth," lines 19–20: "Gentle love deeds, as blossomes on a bough, / From loves awaken'd root do bud out now." As Barbara Hardy says, "the phallic feeling in 'loves awaken'd root' is astonishingly gentle" ("Thinking and Feeling in the Songs and Sonnets," in A. J. Smith, ed., *John Donne: Essays in Celebration* [London, 1972], p. 78). For a Herbertian use of "store" in an at least implicitly sexual context, see "The Pearl," line 26 (and chap. 4, n. 16 above).

Afterword

I have tried to show how rich and fruitful a context the main positions and emphases of Reformation theology provide for Herbert's poetry. I hope also to have suggested how potentially rich in psychological insight this tradition itself is. It might be well to try to specify some of the psychological insights the theology expresses and enables in the poetry. Most prominent would be an awareness of the subtle, seemingly innocent, and even laudable forms that egotism, ungratefulness, and self-assertion can take. Correlative with this would be a deeper sense of what trust means and of how difficult it is to attain— of what it means to believe that one is loved in spite of evidence to the contrary and the most penetrating and humbling self-awareness. The perception of the "givenness" of love is surely a major and potentially liberating insight. The theological formulations of these insights can perhaps help us with the secular formulation of them, especially when the theological formulations are as fully and skillfully realized in a human context as they are in Herbert's lyrics.

Much else, of course, remains to be done. Psychoanalysis, delicately applied, could probably provide further insight into the conceptions of love and trust at work in Herbert's poetry. Many formal and historical tasks remain. The resources of "plain-style" poetry can still be further explored. Comparisons need to be reopened or newly undertaken: with Donne and Vaughan, with Andrewes, Sibbes, and Baxter. Many doctrinal points remain to be explored. I hope that my study will encourage students of seventeenth-century literature to move more freely within the Protestant tradition and to conceive of this tradition in a richer and less presupposition-laden way, not worrying too deeply, or at least too quickly, about who is an "Anglican," who a "Puritan," who a "radical." I hope that greater rapprochement will be encouraged between students of sixteenth- and students of seventeenth-century religion, between religious and general historical scholarship, and between students of English and students of American literature and religion in the seventeenth century. Surely Perry Miller should not be the property only of "Americanists," nor Anders Nygren only of Luther scholars.

I hope, too, that the claims I have made about Herbert's attitudes toward and presentations of experience, sincerity, and art will encourage fresh investigations of the relations between seventeenth- and nineteenth-century treatments and conceptions of these matters. Controlled comparisons of particular seventeenth-century and particular nineteenth-century lyrics need to be undertaken—again without deciding in advance what the relationship *must* be. Some important and historically significant continuities might be established, and our sense of the nature and degree of the contrasts might be usefully sharpened. Perhaps Herbert and Vaughan wrote the first "conversation poems." Certainly the relation between Herbert and Dickinson needs to be further investigated. I have tried to do some "nailing down" in this study, but I hope to have provided a floor or a road rather than a wall.

Bibliography

Primary Works

Anonymous. "Answer to the Archbishop's Articles (1584)." In *The Second Parte of a Register,* ed. Albert Peel, I, 174–85. Cambridge: Cambridge University Press, 1915.

Aquinas, St. Thomas. *Nature and Grace: Selections from the Summa Theologica of Thomas Aquinas.* Ed. and trans. A. M. Fairweather. Philadelphia: Westminster Press, 1954.

Aratus Solensis. *Phaenomena.* Ed. and trans. G. H. Mair. In *Callimachus, Lycophron, Aratus.* Loeb Classical Library. Cambridge, Mass.: Harvard University Press, 1955.

Aristotle. *Nicomachean Ethics.* In *Introduction to Aristotle,* ed. Richard McKeon, pp. 308–543. New York: Modern Library, 1947.

Arminius, James. *The Works of James Arminius.* Trans. James Nichols. London: Longman, Hurst, Rees, Orme, Brown & Green, 1825.

Athanasius, St. *Athanasius: The Life of Antony and the Letter to Marcellinus.* Trans. Robert C. Gregg. New York: Paulist Press, 1980.

Augustine, St. *On Christian Doctrine.* Trans. D. W. Robertson, Jr. Indianapolis: Bobbs-Merrill, 1958.

———. *On the Spirit and the Letter.* In *St. Augustine's Anti-Pelagian Works,* trans. Peter Holmes and Robert Ernest Wallis, rev. Benjamin Warfield, pp. 80–114. Vol. V of *A Select Library of the Nicene and Post-Nicene Fathers.* Ed. Philip Schaff. 1887; rpt. Grand Rapids: Eerdmans, 1971.

Bacon, Francis. *The Advancement of Learning.* In *Selected Writings of Francis Bacon,* ed. Hugh G. Dick, pp. 157–392. New York: Modern Library, 1955.

Baxter, Richard. *Christ's Witness Within Us*. In *The Practical Works of Richard Baxter*. Ed. William Orme, XX, 131–202. London: J. Duncan, 1830.

———. *One Sheet against the Quakers*. London, 1657.

———. *Plain Scripture Proof of Infants Church-membership and Baptism*. 3d ed. London, 1653.

———. *Poetical Fragments*. London, 1681. Facs. with note by V. de Sola Pinto. Westmead: Gregg International Publishers, 1971.

———. *The Quakers Catechism*. London, 1655.

———. *Reliquiae Baxterianae: or, Mr. Richard Baxter's Narrative of the most Memorable Passages of His Life and Times*. London, 1696.

———. *The Saints Everlasting Rest*. 7th ed., rev. London, 1658.

Blake, Thomas. *Vindiciae Foederis; or, a Treatise of the Covenant of God Entered with Man-kinde*. London, 1653.

Browne, Sir Thomas. *Sir Thomas Browne: Selected Writings*. Ed. Sir Geoffrey Keynes. Chicago: University of Chicago Press, 1968.

Bunyan, John. *Grace Abounding to the Chief of Sinners*. Intro. G. B. Harrison. Rpt. New York: Everyman's Library, 1969.

———. *The Pilgrim's Progress*. Ed. Roger Sharrock. Baltimore: Penguin Books, 1965.

Calvin, John. *Commentary on Genesis*. Trans. John King. Edinburgh: Printed for the Calvin Translation Society, 1847.

———. *Commentary on the Psalms*. Trans. James Anderson. Edinburgh: Calvin Translation Society, 1845.

———. *Concerning Scandals*. Trans. John W. Fraser. Grand Rapids: Eerdmans, 1978.

———. *Institutes of the Christian Religion*. Trans. Ford Lewis Battles. Ed. John T. McNeill, Philadelphia: Westminster Press, 1960.

———. *Joannis Calvini Opera Selecta*. Ed. P. Barth and D. Scheuner. Munich: C. Kaiser, 1952.

Cicero, Marcus Tullius. *De Officiis*. Trans. Walter Miller. Loeb Classical Library. Cambridge, Mass.: Harvard University Press, 1913.

———. *De Partitione Oratoria*. Trans. Henry Rackham. Loeb Classical Library. Cambridge, Mass.: Harvard University Press, 1942.

Confession of Faith, Church of Scotland. Edinburgh: Printed by D. M. Blair & J. Bruce, 1815.

Cotton, John. *Gospel Conversion*. London, 1646.

———. *The Grounds and Ends of the Baptisme of the Children of the Faithfull*. London, 1647.

———. *The New Covenant*. London, 1654.

Dell, William. *A Plain and Necessary Confutation of . . . Sir Sydrach Simpson*. London, 1654.

———. *The Tryal of Spirits Both in Teachers and Hearers*. London, 1653.

Donne, John. *Biathanatos*. Facs. New York: The Facsimile Text Society, 1930.

———. *Devotions upon Emergent Occasions*. Ann Arbor: University of Michigan Press, 1959.

———. *The Sermons of John Donne*. Ed. Evelyn Simpson and G. F. Potter. Berkeley and Los Angeles: University of California Press, 1954.

Downame, John. *The Christian Warfare against the Devill, World, and Flesh*. London, 1634.

Downame, George. *The Covenant of Grace*. Dublin, 1651.

Fox, George. *The Journal*. Ed. Rufus M. Jones. 1904; rpt. New York: Capricorn Books, 1963.

Goodwin, Thomas. *Memoir of Thomas Goodwin*. In *The Works of Thomas Goodwin, II*. Edinburgh, 1861.

Herbert, George. *The Latin Poetry of George Herbert: A Bilingual Edition*. Trans. Mark McCloskey and Paul R. Murphy. Athens: Ohio University Press, 1965.

———. *The Williams Manuscript of George Herbert's Poems*. Fasc. Intro. Amy N. Charles. Delmar, N.Y.: Scholars' Facsimiles & Reprints, 1972.

———. *The Works of George Herbert*. Ed. F. E. Hutchinson. Corr. ed. Oxford: Oxford University Press, 1945.

Hollinworth, Richard. *The Holy Ghost on the Bench*. London, 1656.

Hooker, Richard. *Of the Laws of Ecclesiastical Polity*. Intro. Christopher Morris. Rpt. New York: E. P. Dutton, 1965.

Hooker, Thomas. *The Application of Redemption by the Effectual Work of the Word, Books One through Eight*. London, 1657.

———. *The Application of Redemption by the Effectual Work of the Word, The Ninth and Tenth Books*. 2d ed. London, 1659.

———. *The Works of the Rev. Thomas Hooker*. London, 1640.

Hooper, John. *A Declaration of the Ten Holy Commandments*. In *The Early Writings of John Hooper*, ed. Samuel Carr, pp. 249–430. Cambridge: University Press, 1843.

Keble, John. *The Christian Year: Thoughts in Verse for the Sundays and Holydays*. London, 1827.

Lactantius, Lucius Caecilius Firmianus. *The Wrath of God (De Ira Dei)*. In *Lactantius: The Minor Works*, trans. Sister Mary Francis Mac-Donald, pp. 59–116. Washington, D.C.: Catholic University of America Press, 1965.

Loyola, St. Ignatius. *The Spiritual Exercises of St. Ignatius*. Trans. Anthony Mottola. New York: Doubleday, 1964.

Lucretius. *De Rerum Natura*. Trans. W. H. D. Rouse. Loeb Classical Library. London: W. Heineman, 1924.

Luther, Martin. *A Commentary on St. Paul's Epistle to the Galatians: A Revised and Completed Translation of the "Middleton" Edition of the English Version of 1575.* Ed. Philip S. Watson. London: J. Clarke, 1953.

――――. *D. Martin Luthers Werke Kritische Gesamtausgabe.* Ed. J. C. F. Knaake, et al. Weimar: Bohlau, 1883.

――――. *Luther's Church Postil.* Trans. John Nicholas Lenker. Minneapolis: Lutherans in All Lands Co., 1905.

――――. *Luther's Commentary on Genesis.* Trans. J. Theodore Mueller. Grand Rapids: Zondervan Publishing House, 1958.

――――. *Luther's Lectures on Romans.* Trans. Wilhelm Pauck. Philadelphia: Westminster Press, 1961.

――――. *Luther's Works.* Ed. Jaroslav Pelikan and Helmut Lehman. St. Louis: Concordia Publishing House, 1958.

――――. *Martin Luther: Selections from His Writings.* Ed. John Dillenberger. Garden City, N.Y.: Doubleday, 1961.

――――. *The Bondage of the Will.* Trans. J. I. Packer and O. R. Johnston. Westwood, N.J.: Revell, 1957.

Melanchthon, Philip. *Loci Communes.* 1521. In *Melanchthons Werke,* ed. Hans Engelland, et al., II, 1–163. Gutersloh: C. Bertelsmann, 1952.

Milton, John. *The Reason of Church Government Urged against Prelaty.* In *John Milton: Complete Poems, Major Prose.* Ed. Merritt Y. Hughes, pp. 640–89. Indianapolis: Odyssey Press, 1957.

More, St. Thomas. *The Confutation of Tyndale's Answer.* Ed. Louis A. Schuster, et al. New Haven, Conn.: Yale University Press, 1973.

Pennington, Isaac. *Babylon the Great Described.* London, 1659.

Perkins, William. *The Arte of Prophesying.* London, 1607.

――――. *The Workes of . . . William Perkins.* London, 1626.

Preston, John. *The New Covenant, or the Saints Portion.* 4th ed., corr. London, 1630.

――――. *The New Creature: Or a Treatise of Sanctification.* London, 1633.

Puttenham, George. *The Arte of English Poesie.* Ed. Gladys Doidge Willcock and Alice Walker. Cambridge: University Press, 1936.

Rogers, John. *Ohel or Beth-shemesh, a Tabernacle for the Sun . . . An idea of Church-Discipline, In the Theorick and Practick Parts.* London, 1653.

Shepard, Thomas. *The Parable of the Ten Virgins Opened and Applied.* In *The Works,* II, 1–203. London, 1659; rpt. Boston: Doctrinal Tract & Book Society, 1853.

Sibbes, Richard. *The Complete Works of Richard Sibbes.* Ed. Alexander Grosart. Edinburgh: J. Nichol, 1862.

Sidney, Sir Philip. *An Apology for Poetry.* Ed. Geoffrey Shepherd. London: Nelson, 1965.

Tertullianus, Quintus Septimius. *Adversus Marcionem.* Ed. and trans. Ernest Evans. Oxford: Clarendon Press, 1972.

Traherne, Thomas. *Thomas Traherne: Poems, Centuries, and Three Thanksgivings.* Ed. Anne Ridler. London: Oxford University Press, 1966.

Tyndale, William. *An Answer to Sir Thomas More's Dialogue.* Ed. Rev. Henry Walter. Cambridge: University Press, 1850.

————. *Doctrinal Treatises and Introductions to Different Portions of the Holy Scriptures by William Tyndale.* Ed. Rev. Henry Walter. Cambridge: University Press, 1848.

Vaughan, Henry. *The Works of Henry Vaughan.* Ed. L. C. Martin. 2d ed. Oxford: Oxford University Press, 1957.

Willard, Samuel. *The Doctrine of the Covenant of Redemption.* Boston: Printed by Benj. Harris. 1693.

Williams, Roger. *George Fox Digg'd Out of His Burrowes.* 1676. In *Publications of the Narragansett Club,* V, 1–503. Providence, R.I., 1872.

Wilson, Thomas. *The Arte of Rhetorique.* Intro. George Herbert Mair. Oxford: Clarendon Press, 1909.

Winstanley, Gerrard. *Truth Lifting up Its Head above Scandals.* In *The Works of Gerrard Winstanley.* Ed. George H. Sabine. Ithaca, N.Y.: Cornell University Press, 1941.

Secondary Works

Allen, Don Cameron. "George Herbert's 'Sycomore.' " *MLN*, 59 (1944), 493–95.

Asals, Heather. "The Voice of George Herbert's 'The Church.' " *ELH*, 36 (1969), 511–28.

Auerbach, Erich. *Mimesis.* Trans. Willard R. Trask. Princeton, N.J.: Princeton University Press, 1953.

————. "Sermo Humilis." In *Literary Language and Its Public in Late Latin Antiquity and in the Middle Ages,* trans. Ralph Manheim, pp. 27–66. New York: Pantheon Books, 1965.

Bainton, Roland H. *Erasmus of Christendom.* New York: Scribner, 1969.

————. *Here I Stand: A Life of Martin Luther.* New York: Mentor, 1950.

Baker, Herschel C. *The Dignity of Man: A Study of the Idea of Human Dignity in Classical Antiquity, the Middle Ages, and the Renaissance.* 1947; rpt. as *The Image of Man.* New York: Harper Torch Books, 1961.

Bald, R. C. *John Donne: A Life.* Oxford: Oxford University Press, 1970.

Bell, Ilona. " 'Setting Foot into Divinity': George Herbert and the English Reformation." *MLQ*, 38 (1977), 219–41.

Bercovitch, Sacvan. *The Puritan Origins of the American Self.* New Haven, Conn.: Yale University Press, 1975.

————. "Typology in Puritan New England: The Williams-Cotton Controversy Reassessed." *AQ*, 19 (1967), 166–91.

Bercovitch, Sacvan, ed. *Typology and Early American Literature*. Amherst: University of Massachusetts Press, 1972.

Billing, Einar. *Our Calling*. Trans. Conrad Bergendoff. Philadelphia: Fortress Press, 1964.

Bloch, Chana. "George Herbert and the Bible: A Reading of 'Love' (III)." *ELR*, 8 (1978), 329–40.

Bornkamm, Heinrich. *Luther's World of Thought*. Trans. M. H. Bertram. St. Louis: Concordia Publishing House, 1958.

Bowers, Fredson. "Herbert's Sequential Imagery: 'The Temper.' " *MP*, 59 (1962), 202–13.

Bredvold, Louis I. "The Naturalism of Donne in Relation to Some Renaissance Traditions." *JEGP*, 22 (1923), 471–502.

Breiner, Lawrence A. "Herbert's Cockatrice." *MP*, 77 (1979), 10–17.

Brilioth, Yngve. *Eucharistic Faith and Practice, Evangelical and Catholic*. Trans. A. G. Hebert. London: Society for Promoting Christian Knowledge, 1934.

Brinkley, Roberta F., ed. *Coleridge on the Seventeenth Century*. Durham, N.C.: Duke University Press, 1955.

Brooks, Peter. *Thomas Cranmer's Doctrine of the Eucharist*. New York: Seabury Press, 1965.

Bullough, Geoffrey. "Fulke Greville, First Lord Brooke." *MLR*, 28 (1933), 1–20.

Bush, Sargent, Jr. *The Writings of Thomas Hooker: Spiritual Adventure in Two Worlds*. Madison: University of Wisconsin Press, 1980.

Cavell, Stanley. *Pursuits of Happiness: The Hollywood Comedy of Remarriage*. Cambridge, Mass.: Harvard University Press, 1981.

———. "The Avoidance of Love: A Reading of *King Lear*." In *Must We Mean What We Say?* pp. 267–353. New York: Scribner, 1969.

Charles, Amy M. *A Life of George Herbert*. Ithaca, N.Y.: Cornell University Press, 1977.

Clark, Ira. " 'Lord, in Thee the *Beauty* Lies in the *Discovery*': 'Love Unknown' and Reading Herbert." *ELH*, 39 (1972), 560–84.

Clebsch, William A. "The Elizabethans on Luther." In *Interpreters of Luther: Essays in Honor of William Pauck*, ed. Jaroslav Pelikan, pp. 97–120. Philadelphia: Fortress Press, 1968.

Clements, A. L. "Theme, Tone, and Tradition in Herbert's Poetry." *ELR*, 3 (1973), 264–83.

Collinson, Patrick. *The Elizabethan Puritan Movement*. Berkeley and Los Angeles: University of California Press, 1967.

Coolidge, John S. *The Pauline Renaissance in England: Puritanism and the Bible*. Oxford: Clarendon, 1970.

Cope, Jackson I. "Seventeenth-Century Quaker Style." In *Seventeenth-Century Prose: Modern Essays in Criticism*, ed. Stanley E. Fish, pp. 200–235. New York: Oxford University Press, 1971.

Croll, Morris W. *Style, Rhetoric, and Rhythm: Essays by Morris W. Croll.* Ed. J. Max Patrick, et al. Princeton, N. J.: Princeton University Press, 1966.

Curtius, E. R. *European Literature and the Latin Middle Ages.* Trans. Willard Trask. 1953; rpt. New York: Harper & Row, 1963.

Davies, Godfrey. "Arminianism vs. Puritanism in England, ca. 1620–1640." *HLB,* 5 (1934), 157–79.

Davies, Horton. *The Worship of the English Puritans.* London: Dacre Press, 1948.

Delany, Paul. *British Autobiography in the Seventeenth Century.* New York: Columbia University Press, 1969.

Dickens, A. G. *The English Reformation.* New York: Schocken Books, 1964.

Duncan, Joseph E. *The Revival of Metaphysical Poetry: The History of a Style, 1800 to the Present.* Minneapolis: University of Minnesota Press, 1959.

Eliot, T. S. "Andrew Marvell." In *Selected Essays,* pp. 251–63. New York: Harcourt, Brace, & World, 1932.

———. "Shakespeare and the Stoicism of Seneca." In *Selected Essays,* pp. 107–20. New York: Harcourt, Brace, & World, 1932.

Ellrodt, Robert. *L'Inspiration personnelle et l'esprit du temps chez les poetes metaphysiques anglais.* Paris: Librairie J. Corti, 1973.

Emerson, Everett H. "Calvin and Covenant Theology." *Church History,* 25 (1956), 136–44.

Empson, William. "George Herbert and Miss Tuve." *KR,* 12 (1950), 735–38.

———. *Seven Types of Ambiguity.* 3d ed. New York: New Directions, 1955.

Endicott, Annabel M. (Patteroon). " 'The Soul in Paraphrase'. George Herbert's 'Library.' " *Renaissance News,* 19 (1966), 14–16.

Erdt, Terrence. "The Calvinist Psychology of the Heart and the 'Sense' of Jonathan Edwards." *Early American Literature,* 13 (1978), 165–80.

Fish, Stanley E. "Catechizing the Reader: Herbert's Socratean Rhetoric." In *The Rhetoric of Renaissance Poetry,* ed. Thomas O. Sloan and Raymond B. Waddington, pp. 174–88. Berkeley and Los Angeles: University of California Press, 1974.

———. "Letting Go: The Reader in Herbert's Poetry." *ELH,* 37 (1970), 495–516.

———. *The Living Temple: George Herbert and Catechizing.* Berkeley and Los Angeles: University of California Press, 1978.

———. *Self-Consuming Artifacts: The Experience of Seventeenth-Century Literature.* Berkeley and Los Angeles: University of California Press, 1972.

————. *Surprised by Sin: The Reader in "Paradise Lost."* New York: St. Martin's Press, 1967.

Freeman, Rosemary. *English Emblem Books.* London: Chatto & Windus, 1948.

Freer, Coburn. *Music for a King: George Herbert's Style and the Metrical Psalms.* Baltimore: Johns Hopkins Press, 1972.

Gallagher, Michael P. "Rhetoric, Style, and George Herbert." *ELH,* 37 (1970), 495–516.

Gardner, Helen, ed. Introduction. *The Divine Poems of John Donne,* pp. xv–lv. Oxford: Clarendon Press, 1952.

George, Charles H., and Katherine George. *The Protestant Mind of the English Reformation, 1570–1640.* Princeton, N.J.: Princeton University Press, 1961.

Gerrish, B. A. *Grace and Reason: A Study in the Theology of Luther.* Oxford: Clarendon Press, 1962.

————. "John Calvin on Luther." In *Interpreters of Luther: Essays in Honor of William Pauck,* ed. Jaroslav Pelikan, pp. 67–96. Philadelphia: Fortress Press, 1968.

Gerrish, B. A., ed. *The Faith of Christendom: A Sourcebook of Creeds and Confessions.* Cleveland: World Publishing Co., 1963.

Gilman, Ernest B. "Word and Image in Quarles' *Emblemes.*" *Critical Inquiry,* 6 (1980), 385–410.

Grabo, Norman S. "The Art of Puritan Meditation." *SCN,* 26 (1968), 7–9.

Grant, Patrick. *The Transformation of Sin: Studies in Donne, Herbert, Vaughan, and Traherne.* Amherst: University of Massachusetts Press, 1974.

Gray, Hanna H. "Renaissance Humanism: The Pursuit of Eloquence." In *Renaissance Essays,* ed. Paul Oskar Kristeller and Philip Wiener, pp. 199–216. New York: Harper & Row, 1968.

Gunn, George S. *God in the Psalms.* Edinburgh: Saint Andrew Press, 1956.

Halewood, William. *The Poetry of Grace: Reformation Themes and Structures in English Seventeenth-Century Poetry.* New Haven, Conn.: Yale University Press, 1970.

Hall, David C. *The Antinomian Controversy, 1636–1638: A Documentary History.* Middletown, Conn.: Wesleyan University Press, 1968.

Haller, William. *The Rise of Puritanism.* 1938; rpt. New York: Columbia University Press, 1957.

Hanson, R. P. *Allegory and Event: A Study of the Sources and Significance of Origen's Interpretation of Scripture.* Richmond: John Knox Press, 1959.

Harbison, E. Harris. *The Christian Scholar in the Age of the Reformation.* New York: Scribner, 1956.

Hardy, Barbara. "Thinking and Feeling in the Songs and Sonnets." In *John Donne: Essays in Celebration*, ed. A. J. Smith, pp. 73–88. London: Methuen, 1972.

Harman, Barbara Leah. "George Herbert's 'Affliction' (I): The Limits of Representation." *ELH*, 44 (1977), 267–85.

———. "The Fiction of Coherence: George Herbert's 'The Collar.' " *PMLA*, 93 (1978), 865–79.

Hart, Jeffrey. "Herbert's 'The Collar' Re-read." In *Seventeenth-Century Poetry: Modern Essays in Criticism*, ed. W. R. Keast, pp. 248–56. Rev. ed. New York: Oxford University Press, 1971.

Hartshorne, Charles. *Man's Vision of God and the Logic of Theism*. New York: Willet, Clark & Co., 1940.

Heissler, John Martin, ed. "George Ryley, *Mr. Herbert's Temple & Church Militant Explained & Improved*." Ph.D. diss., University of Illinois, 1960.

Hill, Christopher. *Puritanism and Revolution: Studies in Interpretation of the English Revolution of the Seventeenth Century*. 1958: rpt. New York: Schocken, 1964.

Hoffman, Bengt R. *Luther and the Mystics: A Re-examination of Luther's Spiritual Experience and His Relationship to the Mystics*. Minneapolis: Augsburg Publishing House, 1976.

Holifield, E. Brooks. *The Covenant Sealed: The Development of Puritan Sacramental Theology in Old and New England, 1570–1720*. New Haven, Conn.: Yale University Press, 1974.

Howell, A. C. "Res et Verba: Words and Things." *ELH*, 13 (1946), 131–42.

Hubler, Edward. *The Sense of Shakespeare's Sonnets*. 1952; rpt. New York: McGraw-Hill, 1959.

Hunt, Clay. *Donne's Poetry: Essays in Literary Analysis*. New Haven, Conn.: Yale University Press, 1954.

Hunter, Jeanne Clayton. " 'With Wings of Faith': Herbert's Communion Poems," *Journal of Religion*, 62 (1982), 57–71.

Huntley, Frank Livingstone. "Joseph Hall and Protestant Meditation." *Studies in the Literary Imagination*, 10 (1977), 57–71.

Huxley, Aldous. *Texts and Pretexts: An Anthology with Commentaries*. New York: Harper, 1933.

Hyma, Albert. *The Christian Renaissance: A History of the "Devotio Moderna."* New York: Century Co., 1924.

———. *The Youth of Erasmus*. Ann Arbor: University of Michigan Press, 1930.

Jonas, Hans. *The Gnostic Religion: The Message of the Alien God and the Beginning of Christianity*. 2d ed., rev. Boston: Beacon Press, 1963.

Jones, Rufus M. *Spiritual Reformers in the Sixteenth and Seventeenth Centuries*. 1914; rpt. Boston: Beacon Press, 1959.

Jordan, Richard Douglas. "Herbert's First Sermon." *RES*, n.s., 27 (1976), 178–79.

Kaufman, U. Milo. *"The Pilgrim's Progress" and Traditions in Puritan Meditation*. New Haven, Conn.: Yale University Press, 1966.

Keizer, Garret. "George Herbert and the Tradition of Jacob." *Cithara*, 18 (1978), 18–26.

Kelley, Maurice, and Samuel D. Atkins. "Milton's Annotations of Aratus." *PMLA*, 70 (1955), 1090–1106.

Kermode, Frank. Review of *The Poetry of George Herbert*, by Helen Vendler. *New York Times Book Review*, 6 July 1975, p. 13.

Knieger, Bernard. "The Purchase-Sale: Patterns of Business Imagery in the Poetry of George Herbert." *SEL*, 6 (1966), 111–24.

Koppl, Sebastian. *Die Rezeption George Herberts im 17. um 18. Jahrhundert*. Anglistische Forschungen, Heft 129. Heidelberg, 1978.

Leach, Elsie A. "John Wesley's Use of George Herbert." *HLQ*, 16 (1953), 183–202.

Lein, Clayton D. "Art and Structure in Walton's *Life of Mr. George Herbert*." *UTQ*, 46 (1976–77), 162–76.

Levin, Richard. "Refuting Shakespeare's Endings." *MP*, 72 (1975), 337–49.

Lewalski, Barbara Kiefer. *Donne's "Anniversaries" and the Poetry of Praise: The Creation of a Symbolic Mode*. Princeton, N.J.: Princeton University Press, 1973.

———. *Protestant Poetics and the Seventeenth-Century English Lyric*. Princeton, N.J.: Princeton University Press, 1979.

———. "Samson Agonistes and the 'Tragedy' of the Apocalypse." *PMLA*, 85 (1970), 1050–61.

———. "Typology and Poetry: A Consideration of Herbert, Vaughan, and Marvell." In *Illustrious Evidence: Approaches to English Literature of the Early Seventeenth Century*, ed. Earl Miner, pp. 41–69. Berkeley and Los Angeles: University of California Press, 1975.

Lewis, C. S. *A Preface to Paradise Lost*. 1942; rpt. New York: Oxford University Press, 1961.

———. "Donne and Love Poetry in the Seventeenth Century." In *Seventeenth Century Studies Presented to Sir Herbert Grierson*, pp. 64–84. Oxford: Clarendon Press, 1938.

———. *English Literature in the Sixteenth Century, Excluding Drama*. Oxford: Clarendon Press, 1954.

Lovejoy, Arthur O. *The Great Chain of Being: A Study of the History of an Idea*. 1936; rpt. New York: Harper, 1960.

MacIntyre, Alasdair C. *A Short History of Ethics*. New York: Macmillan, 1966.

McCanles, Michael. *Dialectical Criticism and Renaissance Literature*. Berkeley and Los Angeles: University of California Press, 1975.

McDonnell, Killian. *John Calvin, the Church, and the Eucharist.* Princeton, N.J.: Princeton University Press, 1967.

McGiffert, A. C. *Protestant Thought before Kant.* New York: C. Scribners Sons, 1919.

McGiffert, Michael. "American Puritan Studies in the 1960's." *William and Mary Quarterly,* 27 (1970), 37–67.

McGuire, Philip C. "Private Prayer and English Poetry in the Early Seventeenth Century." *SEL,* 14 (1974), 63–77.

Madsen, William G. *From Shadowy Types to Truth: Studies in Milton's Symbolism.* New Haven, Conn.: Yale University Press, 1968.

Mahood, M. M. *Poetry and Humanism.* 1950; rpt. New York: Norton, 1970.

Marcus, Leah Sinanoglou. "George Herbert and the Anglican Plain Style." In *"Too Rich to Clothe the Sunne": Essays on George Herbert,* ed. Claude J. Summers and Ted-Larry Pebworth, pp. 179–93. Pittsburgh: University of Pittsburgh Press, 1980.

Martz, Louis L. *The Poetry of Meditation: A Study of English Religious Literature of the Seventeenth Century.* Rev. ed. New Haven, Conn.: Yale University Press, 1962.

Mazzeo, Joseph A. "St. Augustine's Rhetoric of Silence." In *Renaissance and Seventeenth-Century Studies,* pp. 1–28. New York: Columbia University Press, 1964.

Mergal, Angel M. "Evangelical Catholicism as Represented by Juan de Valdes." In *Spiritual and Anabaptist Writers,* ed. George Huntson Williams and Angel M. Mergal, pp. 297–394. Library of Christian Classics. Philadelphia: Westminster Press, 1957.

Miller, Perry. "The Marrow of Puritan Divinity." In *Errand into the Wilderness,* pp. 48–98. 1956; rpt. New York: Harper & Row, 1964.

———. *The New England Mind: The Seventeenth Century.* 1939; rpt. Boston: Beacon Press, 1961.

———. " 'Preparation for Salvation' in Seventeenth-Century New England." In *Nature's Nation,* pp. 50–77. Cambridge, Mass.: Belknap Press of Harvard University Press, 1967.

Miner, Earl. *The Metaphysical Mode from Donne to Cowley.* Princeton, N.J.: Princeton University Press, 1969.

Mitchell, W. Fraser. *English Pulpit Oratory from Andrewes to Tillotson.* 1932; rpt. New York: Russell & Russell, 1962.

Møller, Jens G. "The Beginnings of Puritan Covenant Theology." *Journal of Ecclesiastical History,* 14 (1963), 46–67.

Montgomery, Robert L., Jr. "The Province of Allegory in George Herbert's Verse." *TSLL,* 1 (1960), 457–72.

Morgan, Edmund S. *Visible Saints: The History of a Puritan Idea.* New York: New York University Press, 1963.

Nestrick, William V. " 'Mine and Thine' in *The Temple*." In *"Too Rich to Clothe the Sunne": Essays on George Herbert*, ed. Claude J. Summers and Ted-Larry Pebworth, pp. 115–27. Pittsburgh: University of Pittsburgh Press, 1980.

Nuttall, Geoffrey F. *The Holy Spirit in Puritan Faith and Experience*. 2d ed. Oxford: B. Blackwell, 1947.

Nygren, Anders. *Agape and Eros*. Trans. Philip S. Watson. 1953; rpt. New York: Harper, 1969.

Oberman, Heiko A. *The Harvest of Medieval Theology: Gabriel Biel and Late Medieval Nominalism*. Rev. ed. Grand Rapids: W. B. Eerdmans Publishing Co., 1967.

———. *"Simul Gemitus et Raptus:* Luther and Mysticism." In *The Reformation in Medieval Perspective*, ed. Steven E. Ozment, pp. 220–51. Chicago: Quadrangle Books, 1971.

Otto, Rudolph. *The Idea of the Holy*. Trans. John W. Harvey. 2d ed., 1950; rpt. New York: Oxford University Press, 1958.

———. *Mysticism East and West*. Trans. Bertha L. Bracey and Richenda C. Payne. New York: Macmillan Co., 1932.

Ozment, Steven E. *"Homo Spiritualis": A Comparative Study of the Anthropology of Johannes Tauler, Jean Gerson, and Martin Luther (1509–16)*. Leiden: E. J. Brill, 1969.

Pagels, Elaine. *The Gnostic Gospels: A New Account of the Origins of Christianity*. New York: Random House, 1979.

Partridge, Eric. *Shakespeare's Bawdy*. Rev. ed. New York: E. P. Dutton & Co., 1948.

Patterson, Annabel M. *Hermogenes and the Renaissance: Seven Ideas of Style*. Princeton, N.J.: Princeton University Press, 1970.

Pettit, Norman. *The Heart Prepared: Grace and Conversion in Puritan Spiritual Life*. New Haven, Conn.: Yale University Press, 1966.

Pinomaa, Lennart. *Der Zorn Gottes in der Theologie Luthers*. Helsinki: Druckerei-A.G. der Finnischen Literaturgesellschaft, 1938.

Poggi, Valentina. *George Herbert*. Bologna: Casa Editrice Prof. Riccardo Patron, 1967.

Prenter, Regin. *Spiritus Creator: Luther's Concept of the Holy Spirit*. Trans. John M. Jensen. Philadelphia: Muhlenberg Press, 1953.

Preus, James Samuel. *From Shadow to Promise: Old Testament Interpretation from Augustine to the Young Luther*. Cambridge, Mass.: Belknap Press of Harvard University, 1969.

Quanbeck, Warren A. "Luther's Early Exegesis." In *Luther Today*, pp. 37–103. Decorah, Iowa: Luther College Press, 1957.

Ray, Robert. "George Herbert in the Seventeenth Century: Allusions to Him, Collected and Annotated." Ph.D. diss., University of Texas at Austin, 1967.

Rickey, Mary Ellen. *Utmost Art: Complexity in the Verse of George Herbert.* Lexington: University of Kentucky Press, 1966.

Ricks, Christopher. *Milton's Grand Style.* Oxford University Press, 1963.

Ricoeur, Paul. *The Symbolism of Evil.* Trans. Emerson Buchanan. 1967; rpt. Boston: Beacon Press, 1969.

Ross, Malcolm MacKenzie. *Milton's Royalism: A Study of the Conflict of Symbol and Idea in the Poems.* Ithaca, N.Y.: Cornell University Press, 1943.

————. *Poetry and Dogma: The Transformation of Eucharistic Symbols in Seventeenth-Century Poetry.* New Brunswick, N.J.: Rutgers University Press, 1954.

Roston, Murray. *Biblical Drama in England from the Middle Ages to the Present Day.* London: Faber, 1968.

Rudenstine, Neil. *Sidney's Poetic Development.* Cambridge, Mass.: Harvard University Press, 1967.

Rupp, Ernest Gordon. *The Righteousness of God: Luther Studies.* London: Hoder & Stoughton, 1953.

————. *Studies in the Making of the English Protestant Tradition.* 1947; rpt. Cambridge: Cambridge University Press, 1966.

————. "Word and Spirit in the First Years of the Reformation." *Archiv für Reformationsgeschichte,* 49 (1958), 13–25.

Sanders, Wilbur. *John Donne's Poetry.* Cambridge: Cambridge University Press, 1971.

Sasse, Hermann. *This Is My Body: Luther's Contention for the Real Presence.* Minneapolis: Augsburg Publishing House, 1959.

Scholem, Gershom G. *Major Trends in Jewish Mysticism.* Rpt. New York: Schocken Books. 1961.

Stachniewski, John. "John Donne: The Despair of the 'Holy Sonnets.' " *ELH,* 48 (1981), 677–705.

Stein, Arnold. *George Herbert's Lyrics.* Baltimore: Johns Hopkins Press, 1968.

————. *John Donne's Lyrics.* Minneapolis: University of Minnesota Press, 1962.

Strier, Richard. "Changing the Object: Herbert and Excess." *George Herbert Journal,* 2 (1978), 24–37.

————. "George Herbert and the World." *JMRS,* 12 (1981), 211–36.

————. "Herbert and Tears." *ELH,* 46 (1979), 221–47.

————. "History, Criticism, and Herbert: A Polemical Note." *PLL,* 17 (1981), 347–52.

————. " 'Humanizing' Herbert." *MP,* 74 (1976), 78–88.

————. "Ironic Humanism in *The Temple.*" In *"Too Rich to Clothe the Sunne": Essays on George Herbert,* ed. Claude J. Summers and Ted-Larry Pebworth, pp. 33–52. Pittsburgh: University of Pittsburgh Press, 1980.

————. " 'To All Angels and Saints': Herbert's Puritan Poem." *MP*, 77 (1979), 132–45.

Summers, Claude J., and Ted-Larry Pebworth, eds. *"Too Rich to Clothe the Sunne": Essays on George Herbert.* Pittsburgh: University of Pittsburgh Press, 1980.

Summers, Joseph. *George Herbert, His Religion and Art.* Cambridge, Mass.: Harvard University Press, 1954.

Taylor, Mark. *The Soul in Paraphrase: George Herbert's Poetics.* The Hague: Mouton, 1974.

Thompson, Elbert N. S. "*The Temple* and *The Christian Year.*" *PMLA*, 54 (1939), 1018–25.

Tuve, Rosemond. *A Reading of George Herbert.* Chicago: University of Chicago Press, 1952.

————. "George Herbert and *Caritas.*" *JWCI*, 22, 303–31; rpt. in *Essays by Rosemond Tuve: Spenser, Herbert, Milton*, ed. Thomas P. Roche, Jr., pp. 167–206. Princeton, N.J.: Princeton University Press, 1970.

————. "Sacred 'Parody' of Love Poetry, and Herbert." In *Essays by Rosemund Tuve: Spenser, Herbert, Milton*, ed. Thomas P. Roche, Jr., pp. 207–51. Princeton, N.J.: Princeton University Press, 1970.

Vendler, Helen. *The Poetry of George Herbert.* Cambridge, Mass.: Harvard University Press, 1975.

Vickers, Brian. "The 'Songs and Sonnets' and the Rhetoric of Hyperbole." In *Johne Donne: Essays in Celebration*, ed. A. J. Smith, pp. 132–74. London: Methuen, 1972.

Wakefield, Gordon Stevens. *Puritan Devotion: Its Place in the Development of Christian Piety.* London: Epworth Press, 1957.

Walker, G. S. M. "The Lord's Supper in the Theology and Practice of Calvin." In *John Calvin*, ed. G. E. Duffield, pp. 131–48. Appleford, Abingdon, Berkshire: Sutton Courtney Press, 1966.

Wallace, Ronald S. *Calvin's Doctrine of the Word and Sacrament.* Edinburgh: Oliver & Boyd, 1953.

Walton, Izaak. "The Life of Mr. George Herbert." In *The Lives of John Donne, Sir Henry Wotton, Richard Hooker, George Herbert, and Robert Sanderson.* Intro. George Saintsbury. London: H. Milford, Oxford University Press, 1927.

Walzer, Michael. *The Revolution of the Saints: A Study in the Origins of Radical Politics.* 1965; rpt. New York: Atheneum, 1969.

Watkins, Owen C. *The Puritan Experience.* New York: Schocken Books, 1972.

Weber, Max. *The Protestant Ethic and the Spirit of Capitalism.* Trans. Talcott Parsons. 1930; rpt. New York: Scribner, 1958.

White, Helen C. *The Metaphysical Poets: A Study in Religious Experience.* 1936; rpt. New York: Collier Books, 1962.

Wicks, Jared. *Man Yearning for Grace: Luther's Early Spiritual Teaching.* Wiesbaden: Steiner, 1969.

Williams, George Huntson. *The Radical Reformation.* Philadelphia: Westminster Press, 1962.

Williamson, George. *The Senecan Amble: A Study in Prose Form From Bacon to Collier.* 1951; rpt. Chicago: University of Chicago Press, 1966.

Winters, Yvor. "The Sixteenth Century Lyric in England: A Critical and Historical Reinterpretation." In *Elizabethan Poetry: Modern Essays in Criticism,* ed. Paul Alpers, pp. 93–125. New York: Oxford University Press, 1967.

Index of Herbert Poems

"Aaron," 54 n. 57, 114, 127–34, 150, 200, 203
"Affliction," (I), 163 n. 52, 226
"Affliction" (III), 137 n. 47
"The Agonie," 40, 42–44, 48, 54, 58, 238
"The Altar," 12, 153, 179, 191–95, 208
"To all Angels and Saints," 104, 211
"Artillerie," 97–104, 188
"Assurance," 105–14, 116, 118, 129, 136–37, 223, 227 n. 24, 238, 242

"The Bag," 22, 94, 135, 171 n. 71
"The Banquet," 78, 135–36
"H. Baptisme" (I), 141
"Bitter-sweet," 138, 165–67
"The British Church," xv, 217
"The Bunch of Grapes," 12, 134, 154–59, 161, 165, 185, 221

"The Call," 227
"Christmas," 154–55
"The Church-floore," 146–50, 179–80
"Church-lock and key," 100, 198 n. 58
"The Church Militant," 4 n. 6, 6, 22 n. 41, 85
"The Church-porch," 225
"Clasping of hands," 104 n. 48, 131
"The Collar," 12 n. 20, 208 n. 87, 219–27, 242, 244
"Coloss. 3. 3," 35 n. 18, 131
"The H. Communion," 31
"Complaining," 8–9, 178, 220
"Confession," 31–32, 34–35, 39, 47
"Conscience," 115–16, 188, 190
"The Crosse," 99, 209, 251

"The Dawning," 83 n. 54
"Death," 123–24, 233 n. 34
"Decay," 21 n. 36, 181, 184
"Deniall," 100, 190–91, 194, 202, 220
"Dialogue," 22, 80–82, 93, 99
"The Discharge," 115–16
"Discipline," 8
"Divinitie," 40, 44–48, 209
"Dotage," 133 n. 38
"Dulnesse," 196

"Easter" (part 1), 58, 122 n. 15, 231 n. 30
"Easter" (part 2), 48 n. 46, 58–61, 64, 172
"Easter-wings," 7, 58
"The Elixir," 206–8, 233
"Employment" (I), 172–73
"Ephes. 4. 30," 9–10
"Even-song," 6

"Faith," 127, 206–7, 233 n. 34
"The Familie," 188–90
"The Flower," 6, 9, 39 n. 30, 62, 89 n. 16, 113, 243–52
"The Forerunners," 196, 200 n. 62, 208–18, 229 (quoted), 248

"Giddinesse," 10–12
"The Glance," 134–43, 160 n. 46, 162, 182, 233
"The Glimpse," 138 n. 48, 227
"Good Friday" (part 1), 54, 58, 60
"Good Friday" (part 2), 55
"Grace," 22, 31, 34, 141

271

"Gratefulnesse," 27–28, 64, 183–87
"Grief," 196

"Heaven," 78, 140, 252
"The Holdfast," 53 n. 54, 65–74, 77–78,
    90 n. 20, 111, 113, 117, 120, 201, 219
    (quoted)
"Home," 5, 196
"Hope," 159, 219, 220
"A true Hymne," 196, 201–5, 208, 210,
    216

"The Jews," 221
"Jordan" (I), 35, 196, 202
"Jordan" (II), 39, 47, 73, 131, 180, 183,
    196–98, 201, 209, 212
"Josephs coat," 137 n. 47, 138
"Judgement," 2–4
"Justice" (I), 21, 35
"Justice" (II), 116–27, 130, 139, 182

"Longing," 169–72, 178, 188, 220, 234–36
"Love" (I), 212
"Love" (II), 212
"Love" (III), 6, 17, 73–83, 94, 117, 120,
    139
"Love unknown," 159–64, 171 (quoted),
    179, 185, 249
Lucus XXIX, 180 n. 20, 182 n. 22

"Man," 23 n. 43
"Mans medley," 165
"Marie Magdalene," 134
"Mattens," 40, 166–68, 172
"The Method," 6, 98, 100, 238
"Miserie," 4–5, 11, 21, 39, 93, 96–97,
    135, 172

"Nature," 223, 242

"Obedience," 25 n. 48, 91–96, 110, 135
"The Odour," 132 n. 35
"An Offering," 208

"Paradise," 165, 185, 251
"A Parodie," 238–44, 246
"The Pearl," 41 n. 32, 87–93, 96, 103,
    110, 252 n. 63
"The Pilgrimage," 219
"The Posie," 239
"Praise" (I), 7

"Praise" (II), 195
"Praise" (III), 168, 172
"Prayer" (I), 187
"Prayer" (II), 6, 47, 73, 183, 187, 197,
    203, 206
"The Priesthood," 8 n. 15, 129, 132, 134
"Providence," 5, 106, 166, 168–70
"The Pulley," 11, 23, 172

"Redemption," 55–58, 68, 73, 98, 159,
    162, 183
"Repentance," 7–9
"The Reprisall," 52–54, 58
"The Rose," 216

"The Sacrifice," 12, 48–49, 105, 153
"The H. Scriptures" (I), 34, 135
"The H. Scriptures" (II), xii n. 1, 151–52,
    157
"The Search," 234–38, 244
"Self-condemnation," 12 n. 21
"Sepulchre," 12–17, 20–21, 27, 48 n. 46,
    58, 65, 83
"Sighs and Grones," 2, 4, 8–9, 27, 32–
    33, 178
"The Sinner," 12, 15
"Sinnes Round," 17, 35–39, 209
"Sion," 179–86, 193, 197, 203
Sonnets from Walton's *Life*, 212–13
"The Starre," 189
"The Storm," 165, 185–89
"Submission," 95–96
"Superliminare," 193 n. 46

"The Temper" (I), 5, 227–34, 243, 247–49
"The Temper" (II), 189, 238, 242, 247
"The Thanksgiving," 49–54, 58, 67, 73,
    195
"Time," 122–24
"The 23d Psalm," 2, 141

"Ungratefulnesse," 17 n. 30, 21 n. 36,
    22–27, 29, 31, 33
"Unkindnesse," 17 n. 30, 18–22, 26, 164

"Vanitie" (I), 40–42, 44, 234
"Vertue," 111 n. 63, 129 n. 28, 208 n. 87

"The Water-course," 85
"The Windows," 128–29, 150, 198 n. 58
"The World," 33–34
"A Wreath," 10 n. 17, 35

General Index

Agape, xviii–xix, 17, 22, 27, 58, 78–81, 95, 113, 134–35, 140, 253
Allen, Don Cameron, 34 n. 17
Ames, William, 85
Andrewes, Lancelot, xv, 201 n. 66, 253
Anfechtung, 107, 109, 112, 136, 167 n. 62, 241
Anglicanism, xv, xvi, 145–47, 217, 254
Aquinas, Thomas, Saint, xviii–xix, 1, 18, 139 n. 53, 169, 170 n. 68
Aratus, 62, 63 n. 5
Aristotle, 18, 20, 30, 81
Arminius, James, 84–85, 141
Art, Herbert's attitude toward, 31–32, 37, 39–40, 52, 175, 180, 190–217
Articles of Religion, Anglican, 16, 21 n. 37, 66, 142 n. 58
Asceticism, xiii–xiv, 116
Asals, Heather, 150
Assurance, 104–16, 133, 141–42, 144–45
Athanasius, Saint, 152
Atkins, Samuel D., 63 n. 5
Auerbach, Erich, 57–58
Augustine, Saint, xviii–xix, 1, 11, 26 n. 50, 57, 127, 152, 175 n. 3, 200 n. 63, 236
Austin, J. L., 92 n. 24

Bacon, Francis, 45 n. 39, 88, 118, 199 n. 61
Bainton, Roland H., 50 n. 48, 108 n. 53, 112, 124 n. 20, 167 n. 62, 179 n. 18
Baker, Herschel C., 214
Bald, R. C., 67 n. 16
Baptism, 133, 141, 160

Barnes, Robert, 125 n. 24
Baxter, Richard, xvi, 87 nn. 11–12, 108, 109 n. 60, 112, 154 n. 36, 166, 174–76, 178 n. 15, 186, 199 n. 60, 205, 253
Beckett, Samuel, 226 n. 20
Bell, Ilona, xvii n. 17, 12 n. 22, 49 n. 47, 50 n. 50
Bellarmine, Robert, Cardinal xix
Bercovitch, Sacvan, 85 n. 6, 154 n. 33
Bernard, Saint, xix
Billing, Einar, xiii n. 7
Blake, Thomas, 87 n. 11
Bloch, Chana, 77 nn. 35–37, 79 n. 45
Bornkamm, Heinrich, xiv n. 11
Bowers, Fredson, 230 n. 28, 231
Bredvold, Louis I., 225 n. 18
Breiner, Lawrence A., 37 n. 28, 208 n. 85
Brilioth, Yngve, xiv n. 11
Brooks, Peter, xiv n. 12
Browne, Sir Thomas, 47 n. 42, 63 n. 7, 130 n. 31
Bruno, Giordano, 236 n. 39
Bulkeley, Peter, 112
Bullinger, Heinrich, 86 n. 10
Bullough, Geoffrey, 93 n. 25
Bunyan, John, xiii, 69 n. 21, 77 n. 37, 108, 115, 125 n. 24, 151 n. 24, 152, 164 n. 54, 178 n. 15, 187, 205, 223 (quoted)
Bush, Sargent, Jr., xiii n. 9, 108 nn. 55 and 57, 135 n. 41

Calvin, John, xii, xiv–xv, 1 n. 2, 2, 4 n. 7, 15, 24 n. 46, 26, 29 n. 1,

35 n. 19, 62–63, 65 n. 10, 70–71, 84,
114 n. 1, 124 n. 19, 130, 144–46, 152,
161 n. 47, 162 n. 50, 164 n. 53,
171 n. 70, 174, 176–78, 180, 197 n. 55,
233 (quoted), 236, 243
Carlyle, Thomas, 126
Cavell, Stanley, xii n. 2, 79
Charles, Amy M., 212 n. 91
Cicero, 57 n. 64, 167, 213
Clark, Ira, 160 n. 45, 161 n. 47, 162 n. 50
Clebsch, William A., xiii
Clements, A. R., 62 n. 3, 97 n. 35
Coleridge, Samuel Taylor, 4 n. 6,
46 n. 41
Collinson, Patrick, xv n. 15
Concupiscentia, xx, 29, 33, 35, 48 n. 45
Coolidge, John S., 7 n. 12, 86 n. 9, 108
nn. 56–57, 114, 182 n. 22
Cope, Jackson I., 154 n. 34
Cotton, John, xv, 71, 73, 97, 104 n. 51,
135, 144, 146
Covenant theology, 85–105, 135
Cranmer, Thomas, xiv
Croll, Morris W., 176 n. 9
Cromwell, Oliver, 142

Dante, 171
Davies, Godfrey, 84 n. 1
Davies, Horton, xvii n. 18, 78 n. 41
Decorum, 57–58, 73, 177, 179, 183, 187–
88
Deguilleville, Guillaume de, 121
Delany, Paul, 175 n. 3, 178 n. 15
Dell, William, xv, 144, 175, 198
Dewsbury, William, 206
Dickens, A. G., xii n. 4, xv n. 14
Dickinson, Emily, 255
Dionysius the Areopagite, 62 n. 4
Donne, John, 11 n. 19, 45, 64, 66–67,
74–75, 83, 100, 103 n. 47, 124, 130,
152, 164 n. 54, 182, 198 n. 58, 210 n.
88, 228, 233 n. 36, 244 n. 52, 246 n.
55, 252 n. 63, 253
Dort, Synod of, 84
Downame, George, 108 n. 56
Downame, John, xv, 16, 29 n. 1,
108 n. 55, 177, 179, 194, 205, 219, 243
Duncan, Joseph E., 208 n. 87

Eckhart, Meister, 63 n. 7
Eliot, T. S., 49, 161 n. 49, 218, 252
Ellrodt, Robert, 63 n. 6
Emerson, Everett H., 86 n. 9
Emerson, Ralph Waldo, 26
Empson, William, 37 n. 25, 49 n. 47, 82,
94 n. 27, 105, 153
Endicott, Annabel M. *See* Patterson, An-
nabel M.

Entrapment of the reader, 10, 34, 89,
90 n. 20, 149, 202
Erasmus, 50
Erdt, Terrence, 174 n. 2
Eucharist, xiv, xvii n. 18, 46 n. 41,
63 n. 6, 78, 163–64, 191, 221, 222,
230 n. 28

Fish, Stanley E., xx, 5 n. 10, 13,
14 n. 24, 16–17, 23 n. 43, 42 n. 34, 45,
53, 61–72, 77 nn. 36–37, 79 n. 45,
82 nn. 50, 52–53, 88–90, 149–50, 156–
58, 175 n. 7, 182 n. 22, 191–94,
196 n. 51, 200 n. 65, 201–4, 206,
210 n. 89, 212 n. 91, 213, 215–16,
221 n. 11, 232, 236 n. 41
Fox, George, 47 n. 41, 150, 154 n. 54,
198
Foxe, John, xiii
Freeman, Rosemary, 163 n. 51
Freer, Coburn, 2 n. 5, 116, 118,
120 n. 12, 121, 125, 127, 248 n. 60

Gallagher, Michael P., 200 n. 62
Gardner, Helen, 67 n. 16
Gelassenheit, 42 n. 34
George, Charles H., xv n. 14
George, Katherine, xv n. 14
Gerrish, B. A., xiii n. 7, xiv n. 13,
30 n. 6, 139 n. 54
Gilman, Ernest B., 163 n. 51
Goodwin, Thomas, 178 n. 15
Grabo, Norman S., xvi n. 17
Grant, Patrick, xvii, 58 n. 68, 146 n. 16
Gray, Hanna H., 213 n. 92
Greville, Fulke, 93
Grotius, Hugo, 87 n. 11
Gunkel, Hermann, 152 n. 28
Gunn, George S., 152 n. 28

Halewood, William, xvii, 16 n. 28, 116
n. 7, 122, 134, 172–73, 175, 207 n. 80
Haller, William, 86 n. 8
Hanson, R. P., 156 n. 40
Harbison, E. Harris, 117
Hardy, Barbara, 252 n. 63
Harman, Barbara Leah, 163 n. 52,
226 n. 21
Hart, Jeffrey, 221 n. 10, 222 n. 13,
223 n. 15
Hartshorne, Charles, 166 n. 59
Herbert, George: for poetry, *see* Index of
Herbert Poems; prose: *The Country
Parson*, 2 n. 4, 11, 17, 35, 44, 55,
91 n. 23, 93, 128, 132, 164 n. 54,
185 n. 26, 187, 192, 198–201, 204, 217,
222, 247–48, 252; Letters, 86; "Notes

on Valdes," 65, 98, 145–46, 176, 250;
"Prayer before Sermon," 4–6, 129
Herbert, William, third earl of Pem-
broke, 239–43
Hermogenes, 199 n. 62
Herrick, Robert, 203, 222
Hill, Christopher, 142 n. 59
Hoffman, Bengt R., 42 n. 34
Holifield, E. Brooks, xvii n. 18
Hollinworth, Richard, 205
Homer, 121
Hooker, Richard, xv, 102, 147, 150,·169,
183
Hooker, Thomas, 86, 102 n. 43,
108 nn. 55, 57, 135, 246 n. 56
Hooper, John, Bishop, 101
Howell, A. C., 176 n. 9
Hubler, Edward, 32 n. 14
Hunt, Clay, 75 n. 33
Hunter, Jeanne Clayton, 63 n. 6
Huntley, Frank Livingstone, xvi n. 17
Hutchinson, Anne, 144
Hutchinson, F. E., 4 n. 6, 23 n. 44, 36,
95, 143 n. 2, 192, 198, 207 n. 81, 230,
236 n. 39, 246 n. 55
Huxley, Aldous, 42 n. 33, 227 n. 22
Hyma, Albert, 50 n. 48

Idolatry, 22–23, 30, 172
Imitatio Christi, 50–52, 54–55, 73
Imputation, 127, 130, 205, 207
Irresistibility of grace, 82–85, 94, 104

Jonas, Hans, 64 n. 8, 230 n. 28
Jones, Rufus M., 146 n. 17
Jonson, Ben, 67 n. 18, 189
Jordan, Richard Douglas, 200 n. 63
Joyce, James, 31 n. 10
Justification by faith, xii–xiv, xvi, xviii,
51, 66–67, 69–73, 116–17, 143–46,
161 n. 47, 164

Kalstone, David, 68 n. 20
Kaufman, U. Milo, xvi, n. 17
Keats, John, 133 n. 38, 215
Keble, John, xvi, 176 n. 8
Keizer, Garret, 181 n. 21, 185 n. 28, 187
Kelley, Maurice, 63 n. 5
Kermode, Frank, xii n. 6
Knieger, Bernard, 95 n. 30
Koppl, Sebastian, 143 n. 2

Lactantius, 167
Laud, William, Archbishop, xv, xvi
Leach, Elsie A., 97 n. 33
Lein, Clayton D., xv n. 15
Levin, Richard, 66 n. 13

Lewalski, Barbara Kiefer, xvi n. 17, xvii–
xviii, 2 n. 5, 57 n. 64, 66 n. 15,
85 n. 4, 151 n. 25, 152 n. 27, 153,
154 nn. 33–34, 155 n. 38, 159,
161 n. 47, 163 n. 51, 175, 190 n. 37,
195 n. 48, 196, 197 n. 56, 204 n. 71,
238 n. 43
Lewis, C. S., xiv n. 11, 47 n. 44,
93 n. 25, 144, 224
Lovejoy, A. O., 168, 169 n. 64,
170 n. 68, 214
Loyola, Ignatius, Saint, xvii, xix, 12, 50
n. 50, 238 n. 43
Lucretius, 63 n. 5
Luther, Martin, xiii–xv, xviii–xix, xxi, 1,
4 n. 7, 16, 19, 21 n. 38, 22 n. 40, 23,
24 n. 45, 25–26, 27 n. 53, 29–31,
33 n. 15, 35–36, 42 n. 34, 44–45, 47,
48 n. 45, 50, 52, 54 n. 58, 57, 62, 65,
67 n. 17, 70–73, 78–79, 81 n. 47, 84,
91 n. 23, 97 n. 34, 99, 107, 109, 111–
12, 114–17, 119, 121, 123–25, 127, 130,
131 n. 33, 133, 139 n. 53, 141, 144,
146, 151–52, 154, 162 n. 50, 165, 167,
171 n. 70, 174, 176–77, 183,
208 nn. 84, 86, 219, 227, 235–36, 241,
249, 254

McCanles, Michael, 52 n. 52, 53 n. 54,
81 n. 48, 82 n. 53, 166 n. 58, 170 n. 68
McDonnell, Killian, xvii n. 18
McGiffert, A. C., 85 n. 5
McGiffert, Michael, 86 n. 9
McGuire, Philip C., 193 n. 45
MacIntyre, Alasdair, 20 n. 34
Maclean, Norman, 176 n. 8
Madsen, William G., xvi n. 17, 154
Mahood, M. M., 173 n. 73
Marcus, Leah Sinanoglou, 196 n. 51
Marlowe, Christopher, 88, 92, 124, 226
Martz, Louis L., xvi–xvii, 12 n. 22,
46 n. 41, 78 n. 39, 188 n. 33, 215
Mazzeo, Joseph A., 57 n. 64
Mede, Joseph, 34 n. 16
Meinhold, Peter, xiv n. 13
Melanchthon, Philip, 139, 207 (quoted)
Miller, Perry, xx, 71, 85–87, 90 n. 18,
95 n. 29, 96 n. 31, 102, 102 nn. 43–44,
103 n. 46, 112, 114, 135, 144 n. 5, 169,
175, 215 n. 97, 254
Milton, John, 10 n. 17, 22 n. 39,
25 n. 48, 45 n. 38, 63 n. 5, 98,
139 n. 52, 150, 179, 183, 196 n. 51,
219 (quoted)
Miner, Earl, 233 n. 36, 245
Mitchell, W. Fraser, 201 n. 66
Møller, Jens G., 86 nn. 9–10, 101 n. 41
Montgomery, Robert L., 158

More, Thomas, Saint, 47 n. 44
Morgan, Edmund S., 143 n. 1
Murrin, Michael, 34 n. 16

Nestrick, William V., 97 n. 35
Newman, John Henry, Cardinal, 218
Nuttall, Geoffrey F., xvi, 47 n. 41,
　144 n. 3, 206 nn. 78–79, 218 n. 2
Nygren, Anders, xviii, 1 n. 1, 17, 18 n.
　31, 26 n. 50, 27, 52 n. 51, 78, 254

Oberman, Heiko A., 1 n. 1, 18 n. 31,
　20 n. 35, 42 n. 34, 90 n. 21
Osiander, Andreas, 63
Otto, Rudolf, 4, 63 n. 7, 65 n. 10, 104,
　166 n. 59, 193
Ozment, Steven E., 42 n. 34

Pagels, Elaine, 230 n. 28
Palmer, George Herbert, 151 n. 24
Partridge, Eric, 89 n. 16
Patterson, Annabel M. (Endicott),
　198 n. 58, 199 n. 62
Paul, Saint, xviii–xix, xxi, 15, 16 n. 28,
　21, 25, 29–30, 35, 62, 65 n. 10, 129,
　132, 139, 145 n. 12, 177, 182, 200
Pennington, Isaac, 178 n. 15
Perkins, William, 85–86, 101, 108 n. 54,
　175, 196, 199 nn. 60, 62, 200 n. 64
Perseverance of the saints, 84, 141–42
Pettit, Norman, 135 n. 41, 144 n. 3
Philia, 18–20
Pinomaa, Lennart, 167 n. 62
Plato, 37, 214
Platonism, 62, 63 n. 7, 196 n. 51, 197,
　214
Poggi, Valentina, 230 n. 27
Popper, Karl, 174 n. 1
Pound, Ezra, 185
Preaching, Herbert's attitude toward,
　128–29, 133, 199–201
Prenter, Regin, 54 n. 58, 146 n. 15
Preston, John, 85–86, 101–2, 103 n. 46,
　112
Preus, James Samuel, 87 n. 17, 151 n.
　25, 159 n. 44
Puritans, xv, xx, 85–86, 143, 150, 156,
　175, 196 n. 51, 223, 254
Puttenham, George, 11 n. 18, 130 n. 31,
　240

Quanbeck, Warren A., 151 n. 26,
　154 n. 37

Rader, Ralph W., 174 n. 1
Radical Reformation, xv–xvi, 143–47,
　174–75, 198–99, 217
Ramism, 215 n. 97

Rasmussen, Carl J., xii n. 9
Ray, Robert, 143 n. 2
Rickey, Mary Ellen, 68 n. 19, 191 n. 40,
　192
Ricks, Christopher, 230 n. 28
Ricoeur, Paul, 193 n. 44
Rogers, John, 135 n. 42, 143 n. 1, 145
Ross, Malcolm Mackenzie, 47 n. 41,
　183 n. 23
Roston, Murray, 153 n. 30
Rudenstine, Neil, 68 n. 20
Rupp, Gordon, xiii n. 9, 26 n. 50,
　30 n. 6, 125 n. 24, 146 n. 15, 167 n. 62
Ryley, George, 17 n. 28

Sales, François de, Saint, xix
Sanders, Wilbur, 64 n. 9, 228 n. 25
Sasse, Hermann, xiv n. 11
Scholem, Gershom G., 64 n. 8
Sedgwick, Obadiah, 90
Seneca, 176 n. 9
Servetus, Michael, 63
Shakespeare, William, 22–23, 82 n. 51,
　135, 161 n. 49, 182, 184, 187, 210, 216,
　219, 224 (quoted), 226, 252
Shepard, Thomas, 145 n. 13
Sibbes, Richard, xv, 35–36, 85–86, 138,
　145, 176, 197 n. 55, 205, 208, 219, 253
Sidney, Sir Philip, 37, 197, 210, 241
Spenser, Edmund, 34 n. 17
Stachniewski, John, 67 n. 16
Stein, Arnold, xx, 5, 26–27, 32, 33 n. 15,
　52 nn. 52–53, 57 n. 64, 59 n. 70, 76–
　77, 78 n. 38, 81 n. 48, 94, 103 n. 47,
　123, 166, 169, 175, 185, 188 n. 33, 191,
　195　nn. 48–49, 196, 197 n. 57,
　199 n. 61, 200, 203, 204 n. 71,
　207 n. 83, 212 n. 91, 214–215, 217,
　225–26, 227 n. 24, 231 n. 29, 232–34,
　247, 249, 251
Strier, Richard, xiv n. 12, xv n. 15,
　xvii n. 17, 5 n. 9, 9 n. 16, 11 n. 18,
　23 n. 43, 35 n. 20, 104 n. 50, 116 n. 5,
　117 n. 9, 122 n. 15, 134 n. 40,
　141 n. 55, 180 n. 19, 211 n. 90,
　225 n. 19, 248 n. 59
Summers, Joseph H., xvi–xvii, 2 n. 4,
　65, 66 n. 15, 78 n. 39, 88 n. 14,
　89 n. 16, 143 n. 2, 146, 149–50,
　153 n. 32, 175, 190 n. 37, 191,
　195 nn. 48–49, 203

Taylor, Edward, 190 n. 37
Taylor, Mark, 190, 204 n. 71
Tertullian, 166
Thompson, Elbert N. S., 176 n. 8
Traherne, Thomas, 196 n. 51

Tuve, Rosemond, xvi–xix, 2, 7, 121, 150, 151 n. 24, 153 n. 33, 156–57, 196–97, 203, 212 n. 91, 230 n. 28, 231, 239 40
Tyndale, William, xiii, xiv n. 11, 11, 47 n. 44, 138 n. 50, 208
Typology, xvi, 152–60, 183

Valdes, Juan de, 145–46
Vaughan, Henry, 41 n. 32, 45, 96 n. 32, 139 n. 51, 203, 229 n. 26, 238 n. 43, 246 n. 56, 253–54
Veeder, William, 124 n. 18
Vendler, Helen, xxi, 8 n. 13, 11 n. 18, 16 n. 28, 21 n. 36, 39 n. 30, 42 n. 34, 44 n. 36, 48 n. 45, 56 n. 61, 81 n. 48, 82 n. 52, 90, 116, 120 n. 12, 126–27, 130, 132–33, 163 n. 51, 171 n. 71, 175, 188 n. 33, 190, 204, 216, 227 n. 22, 232, 233 n. 35, 236 n. 39, 237 n. 42, 245, 247–48, 252 n. 62
Vickers, Brian, 64 n. 9

Walker, G. S. M., xvii n. 18
Wakefield, Gordon Stevens, xv n. 15

Wallace, Ronald S., xvii n. 18, 146 n. 15
Walton, Izaak, xv–xvi, 18 n. 32, 85 n. 6, 130 n. 30, 178, 195, 200 n. 63, 212 n. 91
Watkins, Owen C., 156 n. 39, 223
Walzer, Michael, 173 n. 73
Weber, Max, xiv n. 11
Westminster Confession, 145 n. 12
White, Helen C., 207 n. 83, 222
Wicks, Jared, 42 n. 34
Willard, Samuel, 94 n. 29
Williams, George Huntston, xiv n. 16, 63 n. 7, 146 n. 17
Williams, Roger, 154 n. 36
Williamson, George, 176 n. 9
Wilson, Thomas, 37 n. 28
Winstanley, Gerrard, 154
Winters, Yvor, 241

Yeats, William Butler, xii, 208, 210–12, 216

Zwingli, Ulrich, 86 n. 10